INDONESIAN SOCIETY IN TRANSITION

A STUDY OF SOCIAL CHANGE

by

W. F. Wertheim

Professor of Modern History and Sociology of Southeast Asia
University of Amsterdam

SECOND REVISED EDITION

GREENWOOD PRESS, PUBLISHERS
WESTPORT, CONNECTICUT

Library of Congress Cataloging in Publication Data

Wertheim, Willem Frederik, 1907-
Indonesian society in transition.

Expanded version of a paper originally written as a preparatory paper for the 11th conference of the Institute of Pacific Relations held in Lucknow, Oct. 1950 and issued as its Secretariat paper no. 11.
Reprint of the 2d rev. ed. published in 1959 by W. van Hoeve, The Hague.
1. Indonesia--Social conditions. 2. Social change--Case studies. I. Title.
[HN703.W45 1980] 959.7 80-19660
ISBN 0-313-22578-8 (lib. bdg.)

Reprinted with the permission of N. V. Uitgeverij W. van Hoeve

Reprinted in 1980 by Greenwood Press
A division of Congressional Information Service, Inc.
88 Post Road West, Westport, Connecticut 06881

Printed in the United States of America

10 9 8 7 6 5 4 3 2 1

ANSITION

This
Books

Issued under the auspices of

THE INSTITUTE OF PACIFIC RELATIONS

The Institute of Pacific Relations is an unofficial and non-partisan organization, founded in 1925 to facilitate the scientific study of the peoples of the Pacific area. It is composed of autonomous National Councils in the principal countries having important interests in the Pacific area, together with an International Secretariat. It is governed by a Pacific Council, composed of members appointed by each of the National Councils.

INDONESIA
SCALE OF MILES
0 100 200 300 400 500
120° 125° 130° 135° 140°
5° 0° 5° 10°
PHILIPPINES
PACIFIC OCEAN
N ISL.
Menado
Minahasa
TERNATE
HALMAHEIRA
SULAWESI
(CELEBES)
MOLUCCAS
CERAM
AMBON
BANDA ISL.
BUTON ISL.
Malino
FLORES SEA
FLORES
SUMBA
TIMOR
Port.
IRIAN BARAT
(WESTERN NEW-GUINEA)
STATUS IN DISPUTE
Boven Digul
120° 140°

Author's Preface

Some years ago I arranged with the International Secretariat of the Institute of Pacific Relations to write a social history of Indonesia, paying special attention to the impact of Western civilisation past and present and to the dynamic processes within Indonesian society.

In 1950 the Secretary General of the Institute suggested that I should write a preliminary report on *The Effects of Western Civilization on Indonesian Society*, with special reference to contemporary Indonesian nationalism, which report could later on become a part of the larger volume in preparation, and at the same time, could serve as a preparatory paper for the Eleventh Conference of the Institute of Pacific Relations, held at Lucknow in October 1950. I accepted the proposal and finished my report during the summer of that year. In that report, which was mimeographed and published as Secretariat Paper Nr 11, I paid in particular a good deal of attention to a number of social processes which the literature on the subject had so far tended to neglect. Thus, apart from economic developments (on which an extensive body of literature already exists) I also treated changes in class structure, urbanisation and the modernisation of Islam, subjects which have received far too little attention in the past.

The present book can be considered as an extension of the above report. Two new chapters have been added dealing with subjects not treated in the paper ('The Changing Pattern of Labour Relations' and 'Cultural Dynamics in Indonesia', Chapters IX and X). Moreover, the chapters already published have also been thoroughly revised and supplemented. I was enabled by a certain amount of research undertaken in the archives of the Indonesian Department of the State Institute for War Documentation at Amsterdam to deal in the chapters on 'Shifts in the

Economic System' and 'The Changing Status System' (V and VI) more extensively with developments during the Japanese occupation. Moreover, I thought it advisable to add some preliminary chapters (Chapters I–IV) providing a geographical and historical frame of reference for the chapters dealing with the social history proper. These chapters have no scientific pretensions whatever, but are intended solely to acquaint the reader with the background of the developments described later.

The following chapters (V–XI), dealing more strictly with Indonesian social history are an attempt to describe the social background of Indonesian nationalism, not unlike that which A. R. Desai provided for India.[1]

The processes described are mainly viewed in their social significance. As I am aware of being neither an expert in Islamic religion as such, nor an Orientalist in the traditional sense, I could not claim to give a full account of the history of religion with regard to Indonesia, still less a comprehensive cultural history of that country. But I think that a sociologist might be able to draw the attention of the specialist to a few social implications of these processes.

Most chapters have been divided into four sections. The general pattern, everywhere followed except in the introductory chapter I and the geographical chapter II, is as follows. The first section tries to establish as succinctly as possible the situation in the Eastern society before the advent of Western representatives. In some respects the impact of the West begins quite early, about 1600, in some other respects it makes itself felt about 1800 only. My view of early Indonesian society is based to a large extent on the analyses of J. C. van Leur.[2] The second section deals, somewhat more extensively, with nineteenth century developments. The main stress, however, is laid in this book upon the social

[1] A. R. Desai, *The social background of Indian nationalism*, University of Bombay publications, Sociology series Nr 2, Bombay, 1948.

[2] J. C. van Leur, *Indonesian trade and society. Essays in Asian social and economic history*, Selected studies on Indonesia by Dutch scholars, Vol. I, The Hague/Bandung, 1955.

history of the present century, which is my special field of study. The third paragraph deals, in general, with the period up to the Japanese occupation; sometimes the beginning of the crisis of 1930 is considered a turning point. The fourth section, dealing with the last period, tries to establish from the scattered materials available some of the most important recent trends.

I have sought to emphasise some of the main outlines of the history of Indonesia as I have discerned them. It may well be that others will not be able to perceive the same outlines as I have, but will have observed others which escaped me. Therefore, I have added to each chapter a bibliography in order to enable the reader to check my interpretation.

The reader will be well aware that this interpretation of facts is based upon a definite sociological concept of Asian social processes. This concept is related to my conviction that the present trend among sociologists and cultural anthropologists to visualise the various societies as separate entities, each of them showing its own cultural pattern is too static a view. In my opinion this concept lacks the historical perspective indispensable to a better insight into the real meaning of separate facts. Moreover, this sociological school of Ruth Benedict, Margaret Mead and others considers culture, as far as I can see, too much as a concept apart, without bringing cultural phenomena sufficiently into relation with the technical and economic bases of society.

Only a sociology giving full attention to the genesis of the various human societies and relating their present structure to their economic history and technical development, or, more generally speaking, to human dynamics, would be in a position to increase our understanding of human behaviour. Max Weber owed, to a high degree, his greatness as a sociologist to his mastery of economic history.

Asian societies are, moreover, precisely those where social conditions are intertwined in such a way that it would be impossible, without damaging our total insight, to attack them with specialised scientific disciplines such as economics, social psychology, cultural anthropology or the study of religious systems. Those societies are in a need of a more embracing historical approach shunning any one-sidedness. Anyone tackling social reality in that area in terms of theoretical economics, as they have been refined in the course of time in connection with the realities of the Western capitalist world, will never be able to understand the agrarian base of Eastern society and the phenomena related to it. Anyone attempting to deal with Asian society in terms of theoretical sociology born, too, in the West and adapted mainly to the structure of Western societies, incurs the danger of taking too static a view of conditions in Asia. Anyone using exclusively the tools of cultural anthropology risks overlooking the quick processes of modernisation, in particular in the Asian cities.

Generally speaking, anyone trying to reduce Asian developments to regularities and causal processes registered elsewhere overlooks the novel element, characteristic in each development of human society even when events go largely parallel with processes known from the past.

Only a sociological concept viewing humanity as a dynamic entity which has taken its fate, within certain limits, in its own hands and whose history never completely repeats itself, may help us to a better understanding of present happenings in Asia. Processes from the past are lessons to be studied most seriously. They are not, however, irresistible laws to be accepted passively by humanity. They are no more than regularities applying only within a social pattern, at a given historical period.

Human history is a constant interaction of repetition and novelty, the repetition ever appearing in a new garment and the novelty ever fit for a repetitional scheme.

I sincerely hope, in this way, to have contributed to a better understanding of present difficulties and seeming contradictions in Indonesia. It seems, if one takes a superficial view, that the force of nationalism should have lost much of its vigour, now that political independence has been achieved. This book tries, however, to show that nationalism was, before the Pacific War, an amalgam of various social movements, taking their origin in different strata of society. As the desires underlying nationalism are far from being satisfied, it is clear, that nationalism is still in full swing, directing itself against other aspects of foreign interference and foreign power.

The purpose of this book is also, to demonstrate the way dynamic forces in Indonesia have throughout its history expressed themselves in various, often veiled forms. It would be a mistake for those in power to speculate that it might be possible to avert those forces from their revolutionary course.

Finally, the purpose of this book is to deflect the attention of those interested in the Indonesian scene from externals to essentials. There is far too much concern about such things as the parliamentary system, political parties, leading personalities, elections, as if these were the motive forces in society. This book attempts to pay due attention to basic processes and facts such as competition between social strata, rural discontent, hunger, human bondage, class strife, which are decisive for future developments. It is understandable that the daily worries near at hand are so numerous that many of the new political leaders have insufficient time to reflect upon the basic problems which affect the society as a whole. This book attempts to help them to recover their grasp upon realities. At the same time it tries to give foreign observers a better understanding of why many Indonesians react to foreign influences, such as technical assistance, economic incentives or political advice as they actually do.

The report on *The Effects of Western Civilization on Indonesian Society* published in 1950 has been translated from Dutch into English by Mr. James T. Brockway. Its revision and the new chapters are, however, largely my own work, except for some re-editing by the International Secretariat of the Institute of Pacific Relations, for which I express my deep appreciation. I hope I have not spoilt too much Mr. Brockway's good English and beg indulgence from him and the reader, in view of the difficulties faced by the inhabitant of a small country obliged to express himself in a world language in order to attain a wider audience.

I am further much indebted to my assistants, first Mr. A. van Marle, later on Miss Lily E. Clerkx, Miss Mady A. Thung and, last but not least, Mr. The Siauw Giap for various kinds of invaluable help. In the last stage of preparation, also Messrs. S. B. Martokusumo, L. E. L. Sluimers (who was entrusted with the index) and S. E. Wrazlowsky have afforded a good deal of 'technical assistance', for which I gladly express my thanks. I am also very grateful to the publisher and his staff for the excellent cooperation. A few colleagues, Messrs. C. C. Berg, G. J. Resink and G. H. van der Kolff have been so kind as to read, upon my request, one or two chapters in the original form and to convey me their frank criticism on several points. I was glad to take into account their remarks; the final version remains, however, fully my own responsibility.

Moreover, I have to express my acknowledgements to the librarians of the Royal Institute of the Tropics at Amsterdam and their staff and to the Indonesian Department of the State Institute for War Documentation at Amsterdam for much help afforded in the course of my studies; and to the Institute of Pacific Relations, and especially to its Secretary General Mr. William L. Holland, for the grant to make the completion of this work possible, and for much encouragement and assistance received. I have to express my gratitude to many Indonesians from various social strata for providing me, in the course of many years, with the knowledge and insight needed to achieve a work like this. I am quite aware of the fact, that any treatment of human beings – or of human societies for that matter – as an object may be felt as an infringement upon the human personality. This feeling may be enhanced, if a former colonial society is being analysed by a national from the previous colonial power. I have tried to avoid such sentiments by viewing the Indonesians not as objects, but as dynamic subjects of their own history. My interest in their society is not purely an impersonal, scientific approach as of a surgeon to his patient, still less it is the cumbersome meddlesomeness of the former colonial ruler who cannot forget his 'responsibility' towards his former pupil. My attitude towards the Indonesians is mainly one of sympathetic warm interest in their uniqueness and their specific way of responding to the challenges of the modern era and of solving universal human problems. It is perhaps inevitable that in a sociological study remarks must occur which could be taken for criticisms by individuals, social groups or even by an entire nation. This may especially be the case for a young nation still very sensitive to criticism. The only thing an author can do is to express his hope that no offense shall be taken at such critical remarks and that they be considered as signs of his genuine interest in the actual conditions and in the future of the population or group concerned.

I dedicate this work to her, to whom acknowledgement would be out of place, as my indebtedness to her exceeds any tribute which could be paid.

W. F. Wertheim

Amsterdam, January 1956

Preface to the Second Revised Edition

The revisions in this second edition are of a limited scope. Most of the changes, which affect primarily the sections dealing with the post-war period, have been necessitated either by developments after the conclusion of the first edition, or by publications in recent years. I have also been able to utilise a number of critical appraisals of the original volume, both those published and those brought to my personal attention. It was impossible to include within this volume the results of the field investigations in several areas of Indonesia in which I had the privilege of participating, and the materials I was able to collect, during my year as a visiting professor at the Agricultural Faculty of the University of Indonesia in Bogor, from October 1956 to October 1957.

As such an attempt would have been irreconcilable with the historical character of this work, it seems more appropriate for me to present my findings in a separate volume concerned specifically with present problems and characteristics of Indonesian society. Even so, in so far as my recent investigations have brought to light definite errors of fact or of judgement in the first edition, I have now been able to correct them.

The original 'Postscript', dealing with the period from July till December 1955, has been replaced by a new chapter entitled 'The Latest Phase', which brings the story up to the end of 1958.

Because of their demographic significance, I have included in an appendix the figures on voters registered for the elections held in 1955, figures which to my knowledge have not yet been published elsewhere.

The short bibliographies at the end of each chapter have been brought up to date. Acknowledgements are due to the Amsterdam office of the Indonesian National News Agency *Antara* for the regular supply of their News Bulletins, which formed a useful basis for the survey of recent events to be found in the final chapter; to Messrs. L. E. L. Sluimers and M. P. S. Tjondronegoro for their help in analysing these bulletins and other kinds of cooperation in preparing this second edition; to Madame H. van Weel-Frankenhuis for her tireless assistance in typing the additions to the manuscript and revising the index; and to Messrs. James S. Holmes and A. van Marle for their valuable comments and suggestions.

W. F. W.

Amsterdam, January 1959

Contents

Author's Preface v

Preface to the Second Revised Edition xi

Chapter One *Bhinneka Tunggal Ika* 1
1 Unity and diversity in early Indonesia 1
2 Unity and diversity to-day 8
3 Social change 11

Chapter Two *Geographic Survey* 15
1 The land 15
2 The people 21

Chapter Three *A Cursory Survey of some Social Developments in South and Southeast Asia* 39
1 Ancient South and Southeast Asian society 39
2 Social changes during the nineteenth century 40
3 The rise of an Asian bourgeoisie 44
4 From individualism to collective action 48

Chapter Four *General Outline of Indonesian Political History* 52
1 Early Indonesian states and first contacts with Europeans 52
2 The archipelago during the nineteenth century 58
3 The twentieth century up to the second World War 66
4 Japanese occupation, revolution and after 76

Chapter Five *Shifts in the Economic System* 90
1 The historical background 90
2 Nineteenth century changes 91
3 Shifts in the era of 'Ethical Policy' 96
4 Economic crisis, war and revolution 105

Chapter Six *The Changing Status System* 133
1 The status system in the old native society 133
2 The rise of a new status system based on race 136
3 The decay of the colonial status system in the twentieth century 141

4 War and Revolution. Reversal and continuity 153

CHAPTER SEVEN *Urban Development* 170
1 The old Indonesian cities 170
2 Interchange of East and West 172
3 The modernisation of the 'Indian' towns 175
4 Problems of urban growth 185

CHAPTER EIGHT *Religious Reform* 195
1 Islam in the old Indonesian coastal towns 195
2 Western penetration and the expansion of Islam 198
3 Bourgeois currents in religion 207
4 Conservative and progressive Moslems 217

CHAPTER NINE *The Changing Pattern of Labour Relations* 236
1 Labour in early Indonesia 236
2 Between freedom of contract and forced labour 241
3 Paid labour as a basis of colonial economy (1870–1930) 244
4 Labour adrift 255

CHAPTER TEN *Cultural Dynamics in Indonesia* 280
1 Early Indonesian cultural patterns 280
2 European cultural influences 286
3 Cultural revival 294
4 The struggle for a cultural reintegration 305

CHAPTER ELEVEN *Nationalism and After* 315
1 Early Indonesian forms of association 315
2 The flight from the West 316
3 Indonesian nationalism 318
4 Problems of freedom 327

CHAPTER TWELVE *The Latest Phase* 340

APPENDIX *Registered Eligible Voters for the 1955 Elections* 369

INDEX 380

MAPS

Indonesia *inside front cover*

Peoples and Tribes of Indonesia 26/27

Chapter One

Bhinneka Tunggal Ika

1 *Unity and diversity in early Indonesia*

Bhinneka Tunggal Ika, which means 'unity in diversity', is the official motto of the Indonesian Republic. It expresses a strong desire, not only among political leaders but among broad layers of the population as well, to achieve unity despite the heterogeneous character of the newly built state. This common will presupposes, in its turn, the existence of common cultural characteristics underlying the apparent heterogeneity.

In order better to understand this interplay of unity and diversity we need to go back to a time when a common political will was fairly absent. Such a situation was in evidence during the sixteenth century, at the time when the first European sailors visited the archipelago in search of spices and other Oriental luxuries.

Indonesian geography makes for diversity. The numerous islands, large and small, which are scattered over a sea surface exceeding the total land area of the United States of America, foster a cultural isolation, even though the cultures of the different islands have a common root.

A second cause of diversity may be found in the ethnic field. It is not primarily a diversity in a racial sense. Though other racial elements are discernible among some of the Indonesian tribes, the Malayan element is strongly dominant. Anthropologists sometimes include this Malayan stock, which is akin to the other peoples of Southeast Asia, with the Palaeo-Mongolid sub-race. It is accepted, at present, that these Malayan peoples penetrated the islands by waves from the Asian continent. On the other hand, however, these Malays are generally subdivided again by anthropologists into Early and Late Malays. According to this division the Early Malays are mainly to be found in the interior of the large islands: they are held to include the Bataks on Sumatra, the Dayaks on Borneo and the Torajas on Celebes. Beside the population of Java and Bali, the inhabitants along the coasts of the three big islands are considered as Late Malays.

However, this difference between Early and Late Malays belongs to the field of cultural (rather than physical) anthropology. It was mainly the Late Malayan stock, which underwent the impact of Hindu civilisation. For the rest, this influence was largely restricted to the western part of the archipelago, the Strait of Macassar forming the borderline.

Apart from natural geography and race, however, there were still other factors making for diversity. The impact of human technology has led, during a process of many centuries, to a number of strongly differing kinds of civilisations. Among these types, there are three which deserve special mention.

(*a*) Large parts of Central and East Java had already, for many centuries, been intensively cultivated. Rice cultivation on irrigated fields was known for over thousand years. The density of the population was, in the irrigated plains, very high. Village life was largely based on a closed economy. Though there was some trade and some circulation of copper coins in the markets interconnecting a number of adjacent villages, the peasant used to produce the normal necessities of life within his household.

Contact with distant regions was generally slight. Roads were scarce and usually not fit for rapid transport. The sole link connecting the isolated village communities economically and socially, was the authority of feudal chiefs or provincial governors. These political units, in their turn, were over-arched by imperial rule. The mansions of the chieftains and the palaces (*kratons*) of the princes (*rajas*) were the centres of Javanese civilisation. Numerous artisans and traders, largely of foreign origin, were to be found there. These centres were the cradle of court dances and court literature. They were the places where a leisure class, with a large retinue of parasites, house slaves and body-guards, flocked together to amuse themselves night and day.

These centres were fed from the surpluses provided by the villages. The rural population had to contribute tithes, men liable for forced labour or capable of bearing arms, and beautiful women to please the high and the mighty. They received in return hardly more than the sacral, magic power radiating from the royal dynasty. The prince, surrounded by the feudal or official aristocracy representing him, was significant in the eyes of the rural population more by what he was than by what he accomplished. In times of crop failure or penury the population turned to those with supposed magic powers, who were thought to be in communication with the gods. Among such persons the prince was prominent. Court literature tended to strengthen his magic omnipotence and to safeguard its use against any criticism.

The power of the princes and chiefs over the rural population was, in theory, all but absolute. But hardly a beginning had been made with what is at present understood by administration. Centralised upkeep of roads, the construction of irrigation works, storing of grains, care of general security, all this was princely charity rather than public duty.

(*b*) Along the coasts of Java, Sumatra and Malaya, on the mouths of the broad rivers of Borneo, scattered over the eastern islands, the harbour principalities flourished. They presented a picture quite different from the rural hinterland of Java. These coastal towns stood in close contact with the coasts of Hindustan, Further India, China and Japan. From immemorial times precious linen and silk, chinaware, gold and silver, spices, sandalwood, camphor and all kinds of petty luxuries were traded along the sea-roads. Javanese script was generally known among the Javanese merchants.

The rulers of the harbour principalities were the princes assisted by an aristocracy related to them and by high officials, some of whom were, quite often, foreigners. These rulers were actively engaged in sea-trade, as ship-owners or participants in cargoes, though the actual trade was carried on by pedlars crowding the ships and the ports. Further income of the harbour principalities was derived from customs and harbour dues, from tribute and piracy. The social structure of the early Indonesian towns was, despite a large number of foreign traders, rather stable. Dwellings of the ordinary urban population were poor and primitive, and there was no bourgeois prosperity in evidence. The social distance between the aristocratic rulers and the urban population was hardly less pronounced than that between the rulers of the Javanese inland-states and the rural population.[1]

(*c*) The hinterland of the harbour principalities in Sumatra and Borneo was quite different from the densely populated irrigated areas of Java. The population of those huge islands was very sparse. It had available vast tracts of land and was able to cultivate pepper in addition to food crops. In this respect most of Western Java was, about 1600, still a continuation of the Sumatran jungle. In the neighbourhood of Batavia (the present capital of Jakarta, known as Jakatra in the first Dutch diaries) it was about the end of the seventeenth century still possible to shoot rhinoceri. The Preanger peasant was not yet a sedentary farmer – he moved from one place to another, cleared a stretch of jungle, burned it and planted some rice and pepper. As a rule, the peasantry of these *ladang* (shifting cultivation) areas did not actively participate in the pepper trade, as they had to deliver the crop to their chiefs. It was traded by the chiefs to the *raja* of Bantam, in exchange for linens, chinaware or metals from overseas. In the same way the harbour princes of Acheh and Palembang secured the pepper, cultivated in the Sumatran hinterland.

Though the harbour princes thus succeeded in economically exploiting the population of the *ladang* areas, there was no integration of the rural regions into larger political units, comparable to the larger kingdoms formed in the *sawah* (irrigated field) regions of Java.

[1] Both the 'bureaucratic inland-states' and the harbour principalities of Indonesia have been brilliantly described by J. C. van Leur, *Indonesian trade and society. Essays in Asian social and economic history*, Selected studies on Indonesia by Dutch scholars, Vol. I, The Hague/Bandung, 1955, p. 104 ff.

Though the contrast between the three types of societies may have been, in practice, less pronounced than outlined above,[1] the three main patterns are clearly discernible in the numerous accounts of the Indonesian scene given by the early Western travellers.

On the other hand, the culture of early Indonesia presented a basic similarity in more than one respect. Beneath all outward differences the archipelago showed an unmistakable unity with regard to cultural traits. With respect to customary law (the so-called *adat* law) most peoples in Indonesia present a kindred pattern, whereas from a linguistic point of view all Indonesian languages, except a few of minor importance, equally belong to the same family.

The divergence of social patterns should not be overstressed. The three types of societies sketched above have a very important characteristic in common. For all the apparent differences they were largely based on *tradition*. In the *sawah* and *ladang* areas alike the great majority of the villagers worked for the needs of their households, and the household formed an economic unit. It not only provided for its own food but also took care of its further needs by spinning, weaving, tanning and other forms of home industry. After the tribute, required by the feudal chiefs or princely authorities, was paid, most of the remainder of the harvest was used for home consumption; only a small surplus was taken to the market for sale. Where the marketable surplus was increasing, the rulers were quick to raise the tribute demanded. Thus in many areas the growth of private enterprise was deliberately thwarted.

The social functions within the village were fulfilled according to tradition. A son as a rule followed the trade of his father. In so

1 B. Schrieke mentions in his *Indonesian sociological studies. Selected writings*, Part 1. Selected studies on Indonesia by Dutch scholars, Vol. II, The Hague/Bandung, 1955, p. 233, referring to an article by M. B. Smits, 'that all phases of irrigated rice cultivation are found in Sumatra even at the present day'.

far as there were specialised artisans within the village, their function was assigned them by heredity and tradition. Tradition, too, determined each person's status within the social hierarchy. In communities organised on genealogical lines, mainly to be found in *ladang* areas, the rank one held depended upon the social status of the clan one belonged to, and upon one's traditional position within the clan.

Agriculture was also governed by tradition. Farming techniques in early Indonesia were often very elaborate and ingenious, especially in wet field rice cultivation. But for lack of machinery the productivity per man remained low, and total output could not exceed certain limits. Like the Chinese peasants, the Javanese *sawah* cultivators could justly be called 'farmers of forty centuries.' Their farming practices, already highly specialised in very ancient times, had not changed substantially since.

This traditional way of life was the common characteristic of agrarian communities in early Indonesia, but it also included the princely and urban spheres as well. On the surface, Indonesia's dynastic and religious history seems to bear the imprint of dynamic change, but this picture hardly holds up under thorough investigation. One of the salient features of Indonesian history is that the numerous changes within higher social strata did not appreciably affect the total structure of society. Within a period peasants might suffer more than usual from feudal or military suppression or they might sometimes starve as the result of calamities such as flood, war or crop failure; but their general way of life did not change greatly. The imperial or feudal superstructure remained only a loosely built edifice on a solid base of peasant life. Dynasties might follow upon each other, and each of them might bear its specific cultural mark, but the position of the dynasty with respect to the common people did not appreciably change. Each ruler followed the general pattern by claiming produce and services from the rural population and, on the other hand, by providing certain basic services such as road building, construction and upkeep of irrigation works, storing of food, by giving a certain measure of security and by fulfilling a religious function as intermediary between the deities and the people, in order to stave off calamities.

Moreover, the life of the higher social strata, the nobility and the literati and priestly groups, was also largely tradition-bound. Despite the dramatic changes within this sphere of secular and spiritual leadership, the social groups and their members generally had their economic function and their social status assigned them by age-old tradition. Every new dynasty had to conform to the ancient pattern. As a rule, not even a religious struggle resulting in the overthrow of those in power succeeded in bringing about a basic change in the social structure of society, though minor changes in the system of administration occasionally occurred.

Even the Indonesian coastal towns teeming with numerous traders, many of them Moslems, should not be mistaken for dynamic islands amidst a static Oriental society. The ruling power was generally in the hands of an aristocracy which dominated foreign commerce. The artisans and traders never formed an urban community that could rival the nobility. They catered mainly to the needs of the court, the feudal nobility and a few patricians.[1] For them, also, economic and social function was, as a rule, determined by tradition.

The blend of unity and diversity as outlined in the foregoing pages was typical of a much larger area than early Indonesia. The three patterns of societies, which could be distinguished in the archipelago, were all replicas of a type easily to be found in other parts of Asia. Irrigated rice areas integrated in a large kingdom dependent on tithes and compulsory services remind us of Southern China; shifting cultivation was prevalent in the mountainous areas of Further India, whereas the harbour principalities scattered along the coasts of the islands belong to a type widely spread along the coast of the Asian mainland.[2] The

[1] See, besides van Leur, *op. cit.*, also Maurice Zinkin, *Asia and the West*, London, 1953, p. 9ff., and A. R. Desai, *The social background of Indian nationalism*, Bombay, 1948, p. 6.

[2] See van Leur, *op. cit.*, p. 66 ff.

basic Indonesian culture, including *adat* law and language, is related to that found among the adjacent peoples inhabiting the Philippines, Malaya and Madagascar.[1] Where Hinduism, Buddhism and Islam had spread and got a foothold, these religions had established important cultural contacts and affinities with the Asian mainland.

Nor was the dominance of tradition restricted to the Indonesian scene. Its rule extended, at the time of the first contacts between Western Europe and Southeast Asia, over the whole Asian world and even, to a large extent, over pre-industrial Europe.

Thus, the two concepts of unity and diversity were not only characteristic of the internal situation in the archipelago; they could also serve as a typification of the relationships between early Indonesia and the surrounding Asian world.

2 *Unity and diversity to-day*

For the present situation in the archipelago, however, the symbol 'unity in diversity' is no less appropriate than for early Indonesia.

The basic difference between *sawah* and *ladang* regions has still an all-pervading influence. Irrigated rice field cultivation has spread, from Central Java, to both extremities of the island and even, after some organised migration in the course of the twentieth century, to parts of South Sumatra. The difference between both types of regions has been accentuated by an enormous population increase in Java from the beginning of the nineteenth century, which occurred without a basic change in the pattern of Javanese rural society. Except for a few smaller islands or districts, the Outer Islands are still very sparsely populated, and though, in several areas, extensive rubber cultivation by Indonesian farmers has thoroughly uprooted the age-old pattern, *ladang* cultivation is still at the base of non-Javanese society.

On the other hand, the character of Indonesian towns has

[1] See C. van Vollenhoven, *Het adatrecht van Nederlandsch-Indië* (The *adat* law of the Netherlands Indies), Leiden, 1918–1933, Vol. I, p. 77/78.

greatly changed, and the modern cities bear but little resemblance to the old harbour principalities. The urban centres of to-day are true dynamic islands amidst a preponderantly static rural society and thus add to the intrinsic diversity of modern Indonesia. But it is not only the urban centres where the pulse of modern life is beating. Oilfield and Western plantation areas have also been strongly affected by a dynamic foreign capitalism, which differentiates those areas, even though they are essentially rural, from regions where native farming dominates. In general, the increasing intricacy of economic, social and political structures has brought about a marked differentiation of social patterns, which now range from archaic to ultra-modern.

But as in ancient times, several factors make for unity beneath all appearances of heterogeneity. The Dutch colonial government for many years provided a connecting political tie which has been preserved in the succeeding unitary Indonesian state. External economic factors have a similar unifying impact on Indonesian life. Though vigorous change has affected urban centres and places where Western enterprises were established far more than rural society, it has not left Indonesian village life untouched. World trade and a money economy have made deep inroads in rural life. The great majority of Indonesian peasants have, at present, to earn money in addition to producing for home consumption. All of them are more or less influenced by price changes of agricultural products in the world market. Most of them are deeply involved in credit transactions and constantly in debt.

In the field of culture, unifying factors also operate. Modern education, though remaining at a most elementary level throughout the colonial period, has spread similar patterns of thought over distant areas of the archipelago. The common origin of Indonesian languages has contributed to an endeavour to build an Indonesian national language. The Malay languages, which are most widely used in Sumatra and the adjoining islets, along the Borneo coast and on the Malayan peninsula, supply by far the greatest contribution to this Indonesian language. This fact is not surprising if account is taken of the unifying function which certain branches of the Malay speech performed in the past by their use at the courts of Sumatra and Malaya, in intertribal and international intercourse and lastly in official correspondence.[1]

In addition, the peoples of Indonesia even at present possess a certain degree of unity in religion. Islam is the official creed of the overwhelming majority of Indonesians and Islam has also contributed to a measure of unity in the domain of culture. But it would be as erroneous to overlook the basic patterns of ancestral and mythical beliefs in ancient Indonesia, providing a common background for religious experience – not only in the so-called pagan regions (mostly inhabited by Early Malay peoples in the interior of the great islands), but in the Islamised and Christianised regions as well. Furthermore, Hindu and Buddhist influences have not been restricted to Bali, where these faiths are still consciously professed. In Java especially these influences are still clearly traceable in culture and religious life. The Islamic faith, as it was professed at the courts in the Principalities of Central Java, contained many elements adapted from Hinduism and animism. This syncretistic religion is sometimes even given a special designation: *Agama Djawa*, the Javanese religion.

Finally, the influence of Christianity is not restricted to the peoples ready to accept that faith in its formal sense. Apart from the spread of Protestantism (mainly on Ambon, in the Minahasa region of North Celebes, on Timor and in the Batak region of Sumatra) and of Roman Catholicism (mainly on Flores) some elements from Christianity have penetrated the folk ways of other Indonesian peoples and have even obtained a certain influence on many of those who officially profess the Islamic faith.

It would thus be quite erroneous to believe that what unity existed in Indonesia could be altogether accounted for by Dutch domination, and was doomed to disappear with the end of colonial rule. Spiritual and economic factors were no less influential

[1] See G. W. J. Drewes, *Van Maleis naar Basa Indonesia* (From Malay to Indonesian), Leiden, 1948.

than Netherlands policy, and were to prove more lasting than many Dutchmen expected.

Again, the differences and similarities discernible in modern Indonesia represent social patterns to be found in large parts of present day Asia. The contrast between large rural areas relatively untouched by modern life and urban centres seething with activity is typical of most of South and Southeast Asia. Mechanised mining and the cultivation of commercial crops on Western plantations furnish enclaves amidst a largely static rural life in Vietnam, the Philippines and Malaya no less than in India and Ceylon. Widespread rural indebtedness caused by the introduction of a money economy is to be found throughout this entire region. The impact of education along Western lines affects all the neighbouring Asian countries. And even recent developments in the field of religion may run, as will be argued in Chapter VIII (*Religious Reform*), parallel to a certain extent despite the prevailing differences in denomination.

Last but not least the situation in Indonesia resembles that in most surrounding countries insofar as World War II presaged the end of colonial rule. The fight to overcome internal disruptive tendencies is shared with Indonesia by most South and Southeast Asian countries. Despite many years of Dutch rule Indonesia, though possessing its own distinguishing traits, still exhibits a certain unity with the rest of Southeast Asia.

3 *Social change*

The transformation of Javanese village society is far less striking than social change in urban centres. There is even a widespread belief that Javanese rural life has hardly changed since times immemorial. The diversity between the *sawah* pattern of Java and the *ladang* pattern of the Outer Islands still persists – but is there between the ancient Javanese *desa* and the present village any identity which has outlasted colonial rule?

This question is difficult to answer, as an accurate reconstruction of early Javanese village life is far from easy. Ancient Javanese literature was much more concerned with the life at the royal courts than with the daily life of ordinary people. Nor were the merchants of the Dutch East India Company much interested in Javanese rural life, except insofar as their trade was directly affected by it. Before Raffles wrote his *History of Java* in 1817, knowledge of Javanese society conformed to the pattern characterised by Malthus in the following words: 'The histories of mankind that we possess, are histories only of the higher classes.'[1] The only way early Indonesian village life could be reconstructed is from our piecemeal knowledge in fields such as linguistics, ethnology, customary law, agricultural technology and archaeology, in addition to what scattered historical evidence is available. Any attempt to read back in history from our knowledge of Javanese rural life as it was many centuries later seems, however, rather hazardous. To my knowledge, no attempt to describe early Javanese *desa* life has ever been undertaken. It seems much safer to ascertain what elements in present day rural life are decidedly new.

If a Javanese peasant, who had fallen asleep in 1600, were to awaken to-day, he would find a good deal to gape at. Even before seeing one of the occasional motorcars visiting his *desa* or hearing an airplane high in the skies, he would have a deadly fright at seeing the numerous bicycles traversing the main *desa* road. The outward appearance of many huts might look rather familiar, but the larger brick houses covered with tiled roofs, the *desa* school and the clinic would be novel. So would the medicines or injections administered to the patients. Though the interior of most houses is still extremely sober, the use of the majority of the objects found there would probably be unknown to him. So would the photographs and pictures pricked on the walls of some houses, the empty tins pasted over with coloured brands used for various purposes, and the papers mostly utilised as packing-paper. Neither would clothes have a familiar look, as he used to wear coarse home-made *luriks*, whereas at present most peasants

[1] T. R. Malthus, *First essay on population* (1798). With notes by Jam. Bonar, London, 1926, p. 32.

wear manufactured and printed imitation *batiks* or other cotton prints. The rice fields might remind him of his own times, and even some of the tools, such as the rice-knife (*ani-ani*) and the hoe, might have a familiar look, but the two other main crops, cassava and maize, would be quite unknown to him. Nor would he remember ever having drunk the coffee offered him by his descendants. He would even hardly be able to understand their speech, and their manners towards elders (and perhaps even the topics of their talk) would seriously upset him, especially if they were to discuss their experiences at a nearby town or plantation. The importance of money in village economy would be new to him, but some of the institutions, such as mutual help, *slamatans* (religious feasts), *wayang* (shadow-play) performances and magic practices in connection with birth and death might still remember him of former times.

Almost certainly he would not agree that rural life had remained unchanged throughout three and a half centuries.

Yet social change was comparatively slow in Java, and the changes in rural life were not nearly as radical as in Western Europe. Tradition still plays an extremely important role in Javanese village life, and it seems as though the terms unity and diversity, used above in a geographical sense, might equally be used to characterise the relation between old and new in Java, unity standing for identity and diversity for change. This seems the more appropriate as old and new elements are often to be found side by side, without being blended into a whole. Schrieke has described a similar situation in the rice growing upland areas of Sumatra's Westcoast Residency, where the old and new are found unblended side by side. 'Social requirements are still strongly in evidence side by side with the emerging economic needs, the modern spirit interpenetrates traditional values: we find the old system of mutual help, *tolong menolong*, but also wage labour, the need for personal freedom side by side with the feeling of solidarity, a clinging to inheritance in the matriarchical line while the sacred family property grows less and less and intestate inheritance law is introduced, compensation according to traditional standards side by side with payment according to work accomplished, economic development without elementary education, old-fashioned agrarian conditions combined with advanced mental development.'[1]

Though the Indonesian peasants still belong to the type of 'farmers of forty centuries', there is an enormous distance between Indonesian society as it was at the time of the first journeys by European sailors and as it is at present.

The purpose of this book is to analyse the social change which occurred in various fields during the intervening centuries. But first we need a brief general survey of the land and the people whose social history we are studying.

[1] B. Schrieke, *op. cit.*, p. 130.

Chapter Two

Geographic Survey

1 *The land*

Only ten years ago the term *Indonesia* was all but unknown outside of the country itself. Yet, the term had already been introduced by some scholars in the course of the nineteenth century. During the twentieth century scientists began to use this term more or less systematically and the nationalist movement also adopted it as a slogan. But the official name was, until World War II, *Netherlands India* (in English sometimes the names Netherlands East Indies or Dutch East Indies were used), and under these names the archipelago was also known outside of Indonesia. As a result of the revolution which, at the end of the Japanese occupation, led to the foundation of the Republic of Indonesia, the name suddenly came into the headlines.

The erstwhile Netherlands India was an island empire stretching on either side of the equator from 95° to 141° eastern longitude, covering a surface of nearly two million of square kilometers, about a quarter of the size of the United States.

At the moment, the whole territory forms part of the new Republic of Indonesia, with exception of the western part of New-Guinea which still is in dispute between the Netherlands and Indonesia, as its status was not finally settled at the Round Table Conference of 1949. The actual administration of the territory of Western New-Guinea is still in Dutch hands.

Politically, Indonesia, even after achieving its independence, remained part of a Dutch-Indonesian Union, until it unilaterally abrogated the Union in 1956 after negotiations with the Netherlands had failed.

The islands

The western part of the archipelago is occupied by the big island of *Sumatra*, with the numerous small islands surrounding it. Sumatra is separated from the Malayan peninsula by the Strait of Malacca, an important trade route between the Middle East and the Far East. Throughout the centuries there were narrow commercial and cultural bonds between Sumatra and Malaya. Under the Japanese occupation Sumatra even for a time fell under the jurisdiction of the Military Headquarters in Singapore.

Along the western coast of Sumatra a few parallel chains of mountains, most of them of a volcanic nature, stretch from the northwest to the southeast. On the coast a number of harbours are found, the most important among them being Padang and, on an islet at the northern top of Sumatra, Sabang. Not far from the coast there are a few gold and coal mines.

From the mountains a vast plain, crossed by broad rivers, extends to the eastern coast. Especially in Central and Southern Sumatra the plains run out into impenetrable marshes. By far the greatest part of Sumatra still consists of jungle, which is largely left in its wild state by a sparse population settling along the rivers and assuring itself by some shifting cultivation of a frugal living. Only in this century a part of the woodlands was permanently occupied by the population for the purpose of opening up their rubber plantations. In some regions there is also a rather intensive exploitation of timber.

In this region the big settlements, such as Palembang and Jambi, are situated on the banks of the large rivers, as a rule a good distance up the river. In this flat part of the island at present a number of very important oilfields are to be found.

Farther to the north, adjoining the Strait of Malacca, lies the most extensively cultivated region of Sumatra: here the big Western estates of the Sumatra's Eastcoast Residency extend over huge territories.

The vast rubber plantations operated by Western companies stretch over the southern part of this region. The northern part is the famous tobacco region of Deli, with Medan as the urban centre and Belawan as the shipping port.

The tropical climate of Sumatra is preponderantly humid. There is no sharp distinction between the wet monsoon season and the dry one, as is the case in the southern islands of the archipelago. In great parts of Sumatra conditions for intensive agriculture seem to be less favourable than on Java. Yet there are, scattered over Sumatra, rather small regions near the coasts or plateaus in the highlands, where rice culture on irrigated fields (*sawahs*) is being practised. One of the largest *sawah* regions is now to be found in the extreme south, where a vast territory has been opened up, during the past half century, by Javanese colonists and transformed almost into a second Java.

In many regions, however, the inhabitants did not find the way to intensivation. Vast stretches of *alang* grass, especially to the north, testify to the failure of human attempts to tame nature. In mountainous regions, however, grasslands afford some cattle-breeding as a supplementary source of agrarian income.

Some of the smaller islands off the eastern coast of Sumatra are of interest. Separated from Sumatra by a narrow strait, lies the tin island of *Bangka*, also known, like some regions of Sumatra, for its pepper cultivation. Farther to the east the island of *Billiton* is, equally, a source of tin. Farther to the north, around Singapore, the islets of the *Lingga* and *Riau* archipelagoes are scattered. Some of these small islands, too, are important sources of ores, such as tin and bauxite.

Separated from Sumatra and Malaya by the Sunda Sea, which near Billiton narrows into the Strait of Karimata, the huge island of *Borneo* is situated, which is now called *Kalimantan* by Indonesians. The northern part of the island is under British administration.

Borneo still largely consists of impenetrable jungle. Human life is mainly concentrated along the few extremely broad rivers. The northern part of West Borneo, the basin of the Kapuas river, with Pontianak as a port town, is cultivated somewhat more intensively than the remainder of the Indonesian part of Kalimantan. This region is separated from the remainder by a mountain chain. Yet, the landscape is not very different. Endless woods, in the last decades partly transformed into rubber plantations which, nearer to the coast, alternate with coconut and pepper cultivation, are characteristic of Kalimantan.

The main system of agriculture practised on this island is, as on Sumatra, shifting cultivation. In several places the system has led to an exhaustion of the soil, thus causing soil erosion and giving birth to vast *alang* grass fields. However, in a part of southeastern Borneo, in the region called Hulu Sungei, a more intensive form of rice culture is to be found, the rice being grown on marshy wet fields. This is the region where the greatest number of urban centres is to be found, the town of Banjermasin, situated on the banks of the Barito river, being the seaport of the area.

Diamonds and gold are found in the northwest and south, coal and oil at the eastcoast and on some small islands off that coast. But perhaps the greatest wealth of Kalimantan is still being preserved in the woods. Only for a short time the timber has been exploited somewhat more thoroughly.

The principal island of Indonesia is still *Java* which, together with the adjoining small island of *Madura*, was treated by the Dutch so much as a focus of administration that the remainder of the archipelago was lumped together as the *Outer Islands*. Java is much smaller than Sumatra or Borneo, and it is longitudinally situated almost as an extension of Sumatra, separated from it by the narrow Strait of Sunda. In this strait, on an islet of the same name, lies the famed volcano of Krakatoa, which in 1883 caused the worst eruption recorded by man. Java also includes a continuation of the long chain of volcanoes found on Sumatra. The coastal strip along the Indian Ocean is, just as on Sumatra, rather narrow. The big plains of Java extend to the north, to the quiet Java Sea, which separates Java from Borneo.

The human hand has laid its inprint on the landscape of Java much more than on the greater islands of Sumatra and Borneo.

The jungle has receded in great parts of Java before the cultivator. Rice cultivation on irrigated fields is not only practised in the broad river valleys, rich in silt supplied by the rivers, but also on terraces along the slopes of the volcanoes and on the spacious plateaus of Western Java. In part of the *sawah* territory rice alternates with cane-sugar or tobacco.

However, in non-irrigated areas of Java intensive agriculture is also widely practised. On the eastern part of the island, where the climate is drier than in the west, the population grows great quantities of maize and cassava on dry fields. Maize is also being grown on *sawahs* as a second crop during the dry season. Another example of intensive agriculture is provided by the big rubber estates, and in the mountainous regions by the vast estate areas planted with coffee, tea and cinchona.

In general, the soil of Java is very fertile. There are areas, however, where the soil is limy. Such a region is to be found along the southern coast, and to the northeast of the island along the hilly strip prolongating itself into the smaller island of Madura.

The remaining forest land has become dangerously small. Since the Japanese occupation the afforestation of the mountain slopes has visibly waned as a result of reckless land reclamation. Periodic floods during the wet monsoon threaten to wash away valuable tracts of fertile soil.

On the island of Java the greatest urban centres of Indonesia are to be found. Beside the series of seaport-towns along the north coast, with Jakarta by far the largest, the cities in the valleys of the Solo and the Brantas rivers especially deserve to be mentioned, among them the old inland capital of Surakarta (Solo), and the big seaport of Surabaya.

Mining on Java is of less importance, than in Sumatra and Borneo and the adjoining islets, though the oilfields not far from Java's northeast coast are worth mentioning. Salt pans on Madura are also intensively operated. In the Java Sea there is considerable shipping and fisheries. On land, too, transport and communications are rather developed, a net of highways and railroads spanning Java from west to east. Industry is also of some importance, water-power providing a source of energy.

Still more than the eastern half of Java, where the difference between the dry and the wet season is rather pronounced under the influence of the Australian continental climate, the series of smaller islands to the east of Java, called the *Lesser Sundas* (Indonesian: *Nusa Tenggara*, the Southeastern Islands) feel this influence.

The small populous island of *Bali* shows a *sawah* landscape, rather similar to that in Java. Farther to the east, however, the islands are less intensively cultivated. Shifting cultivation is the dominant agricultural system on many islands, but in addition, cattle-breeding has an important place on several of them. The savannah landscape in great parts of *Sumbawa*, *Sumba* and *Timor* – the eastern half of which is a Portuguese colony – is very suitable for raising cattle and horses. In the coastal plains coconut cultivation is practised on some of the islands.

The Flores Sea lies between the Lesser Sundas and the eastern great island of the archipelago, *Celebes* (now called *Sulawesi* in Indonesian), which is separated from Borneo by the broad Strait of Macassar. This island of Celebes, with its queer starfish shape, is the most mountainous one of the archipelago. Yet, this island has also areas which carry the signs of a thorough interference by human hands, not always to its advantage. Erosion is a very serious problem especially in the Toraja lands of Central Celebes, as a consequence of shifting cultivation practised in a rather imprudent manner.

The most fertile part of the island is the rather level region of the southwestern arm. It is a vast agricultural region, where coconut cultivation plays an important role beside rice cultivation on *sawahs* and *ladangs* (the Indonesian term for shifting cultivation on burnt woodlands) and maize cultivation. The lakes in this region abound in fish, and Macassar is an important urban centre. The fertile volcanic extremity of the northern arm, the so-called Minahasa region, with Menado as its capital, is also an important area of coconut cultivation. On the southeastern arm of Celebes sources of iron and nickel are known to exist, but they have not been very intensively developed. The island of *Buton*, adjoining the southeastern arm, has also some mineral wealth, asphalt being its main product.

The eastern island group of the archipelago, the *Moluccas*, were the original goal of the Europeans sailing to the Indies. They were the Spice Islands from which the Portuguese and Dutch derived most of their wealth. At present these mountainous, woody islands are a rather neglected part of the archipelago. On most of the islands sago provides the main foodstuff, supplemented by some hunting and fishing. The same applies to the coasts of Western *New-Guinea* (called by the Indonesians *Irian*). The interior of New-Guinea is still largely *terra incognita*, a great part of which is overgrown with jungle. Mineral wealth is supposed to be present, but for the time being it is, except for some oilfields to the northwest of the island, still in mainly a stage of exploration.

2 *The people*

The total population of Indonesia is difficult to estimate. The last fairly accurate census was held in 1930. In some remote, sparsely populated areas in the Outer Provinces, however, the administration contented itself with a summary registration.

The total outcome of the census was, broadly speaking, as follows. On the principal island Java with Madura upwards of 40 million of people were living in 1930. In addition, under 20 million were counted, scattered over the other islands. If account is taken of the fact, that the figures for Java are far more reliable than those for the Outer Islands, and that vast areas, especially on New-Guinea and Borneo, were not yet explored, it is perhaps not too rash to assume, that the number of inhabitants of the Outer Islands, including Western New-Guinea, had already at that time attained 20 million.

Little is known with certainty about the details of population changes since 1930. The vital statistics concerning births and deaths published by the Central Bureau of Statistics in Batavia

(Jakarta) before the war, are far from reliable. Where it was possible to introduce a new method of birth registration and to check the figures with a certain amount of precision, the real birth rate proved to exceed the rate registered in the traditional way by some 50 per cent.[1] However mortality, too, was certainly higher than is commonly assumed.[2] My own estimate based, *inter alia*, on the proportion of children to adults at the 1930 census amounts for Java between 1930 and 1940 to a birth rate of 40 or more and a death rate of at least 23 per thousand.[3]

The census, projected for 1940, was not held as a result of war-time difficulties. If one considers that in India the census of 1941 was carried through, despite the war situation in Europe, one may doubt, whether the difficulties were, in reality, insuperable. Because of this unfortunate circumstance there are no reliable population figures available since the census of 1930.

The Japanese took a number of regional censuses during the occupation, which, according to de Meel, show a fair degree of reliability. Only a few of the figures collected by them, however, are still available; most of them seem to have been lost.[4] Nor has any census been held since. Thus, any estimate of the present population of Indonesia amounts to a guess, unless the registration

[1] See E. V. Ch. van Os, 'Het weekkaarten-systeem en het bewijssysteem voor de registratie van geboorten en sterften' (The system of weekly cards and the verification system for the registration of births and deaths), in *De hygiënische organisatie* (The hygienic organisation), Bulletin Nr 66 of the Dienst der Volksgezondheid (National Health Service), Batavia, 1939, January.

[2] The official figures, mostly collected in the traditional way, were published in the *Netherlands Indian report 1941. Statistical abstract for the year 1940*, Batavia, 1941. J. van Gelderen, however, estimated the crude death rate at ± 23 per thousand (see *inter alia* his 'The numerical evolution of population, with particular reference to the population of Java', *Population Congress*, Rome, 1932).

[3] See my article 'The forty-percent test, a useful demographic tool' in *Ekonomi dan Keuangan Indonesia* (Economics and Finance in Indonesia), Vol. VIII, 1955, p. 174 ff.

[4] H. de Meel, 'Demographic dilemma in Indonesia', in *Pacific Affairs*, Vol. XXIV, 1951, p. 270.

of voters in 1954 be considered a satisfactory basis (see *Appendix*, p. 370 ff.).

Considering the scattered indications available, one is authorised to assume a rather rapid, steady increase in population, temporarily slackening during the Japanese occupation. On Java during the later years of the Japanese occupation there were in fact powerful factors, such as an increasing lack of food and the shipment overseas of large numbers of Javanese as forced labourers, which brought about a reversal of the general trend, resulting even in a decrease in absolute numbers. Very little is known about population trends on Java during the revolution and the ensuing military actions of the Dutch. After the official transfer of sovereignty in 1949 the pre-war trend towards a steady and rapid increase resumed. Improved methods of birth and death registration in large parts of Java even point towards a more rapid increase than before the war, as birth rates are still at the same level of forty per thousand and more, whereas death rates on the average seem to have fallen to the twenty per thousand level or even lower, owing to much more widespread and comprehensive hygienic services and a growing health consciousness among the people.[1]

Contrary to de Meel's assumptions[2] natural increase in the Outer Islands would appear to be, if anything, lower than in Java. Though economic conditions are, on the average, better there than in Java, the factors which are most instrumental in reducing mortality rates in post-war Asia, improved hygienic conditions and expanded medical services, are much more in evidence in Java than in the other islands, where poor communications seriously hamper such improvements. Therefore de

[1] An estimate of a natural increase of two per cent or more is being agreed upon by demographic experts; see *e.g.* 'The population of Indonesia. A joint-statement by the Indonesian participants to the United Nations Seminar on Population in Asia and the Far East, held in Bandung from November 21–December 3, 1955', in *Ekonomi dan Keuangan Indonesia* (Economics and Finance in Indonesia), Vol. IX, 1956, p. 92–93.

[2] H. de Meel, *loc. cit.*

Meel's estimate of the total population of the Outer Islands as 30.6 million in 1951 seems exaggerated, and even Keyfitz's more conservative estimate of 28.6 million as a lower limit in 1953[1] was not borne out by the registration of eligible voters in 1954.[2]

On the basis of all materials available it seems safe to estimate the present population of Java at a figure somewhere between 55 and 60 million, and that of the Outer Islands at between 25 and 30 million. This much is practically certain, that the total population of Indonesia will not be very far from 85 million.

With exception of a small percentage the population of Indonesia consists of *Indonesians*. This term is no less novel than the term *Indonesia*. Until recently the inhabitants of the different islands were designated by their regional denominations: Javanese, Sundanese, Achenese, Dayaks, Buginese etc. In Indonesia the term Malays is generally restricted to the coastal population of Eastern Sumatra and of West and East Borneo, and to the inhabitants of the many smaller islands between those two. Sometimes other peoples, such as the Menangkabau of Western Sumatra, the Banjarese of South Borneo and the Batavians of the capital on Java, are included, when the term Malays is used. The collective denomination for all these peoples used by the Dutch colonial regime was: *Inlanders* (natives). Distinguished from them were the minorities of foreign origin: the *Europeans* and the *Foreign Orientals* (Chinese, Arabs and Indians).

Among the Foreign Orientals at the census of 1930 the most important elements were one and a quarter million of Chinese, the majority of whom were of mixed Chinese-Indonesian ancestry, and about seventy thousand of Arabs, many of them also of mixed origin. The number of Europeans, in majority equally of mixed ancestry, amounted in 1930 to almost 250,000.

It can be assumed without doubt, that the number of Chinese has been considerably augmented by natural increase. The number of Europeans, too, had increased until the war by natural

[1] N. Keyfitz, 'The population of Indonesia', in *Ekonomi dan Keuangan Indonesia* (Economics and Finance in Indonesia), Vol. VI, 1953, p. 640 ff.

[2] See *Appendix*, p. 370 ff.

PEOPLES AND TRIBES OF INDONESIA (see map p. 26/27)

I Sumatra and adjacent islands
- 1 Achenese
- 2 Bataks
- 3 Menangkabau
- 4 Coastal Malays
- 5 Others

II Kalimantan (Indonesian Borneo)
- 1 Dayaks
- 2 Coastal Malays, Javanese, Banjarese, Buginese

III Java and Madura
- 1 Javanese
- 2 Sundanese
- 3 Madurese

IV Sulawesi (Celebes) and adjacent islands
- 1 Macassarese and Buginese
- 2 Torajas
- 3 Menadonese, Gorontalese, Sangirese, Talaudians
- 4 Others

V Nusa Tenggara (Lesser Sunda Islands)
- 1 Balinese
- 2 Sasaks
- 3 Timorese
- 4 Florinese
- 5 Others

VI Moluccas
- 1 Ambonese
- 2 Others

VII Western New-Guinea (Western Irian) and adjacent islands
Papuans

Adapted from R. KENNEDY, *The ageless Indies*, New York, 1942, p. 23 ff.

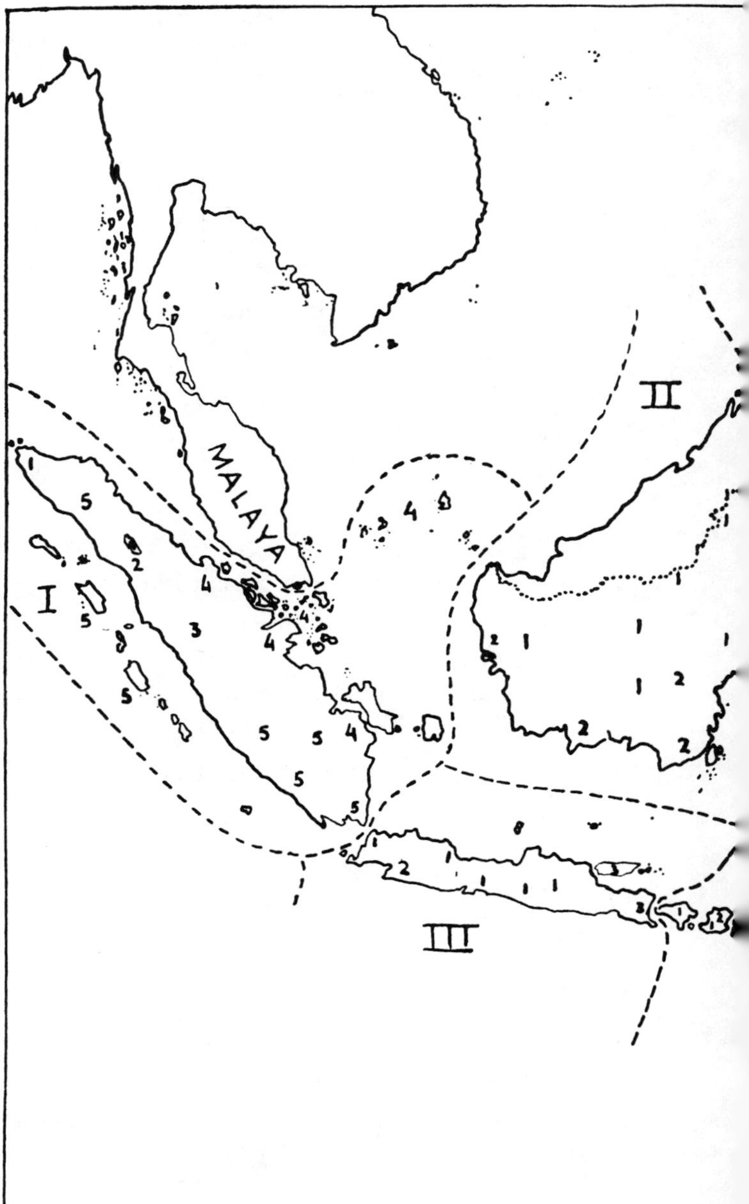

MALAYA
I
II
III

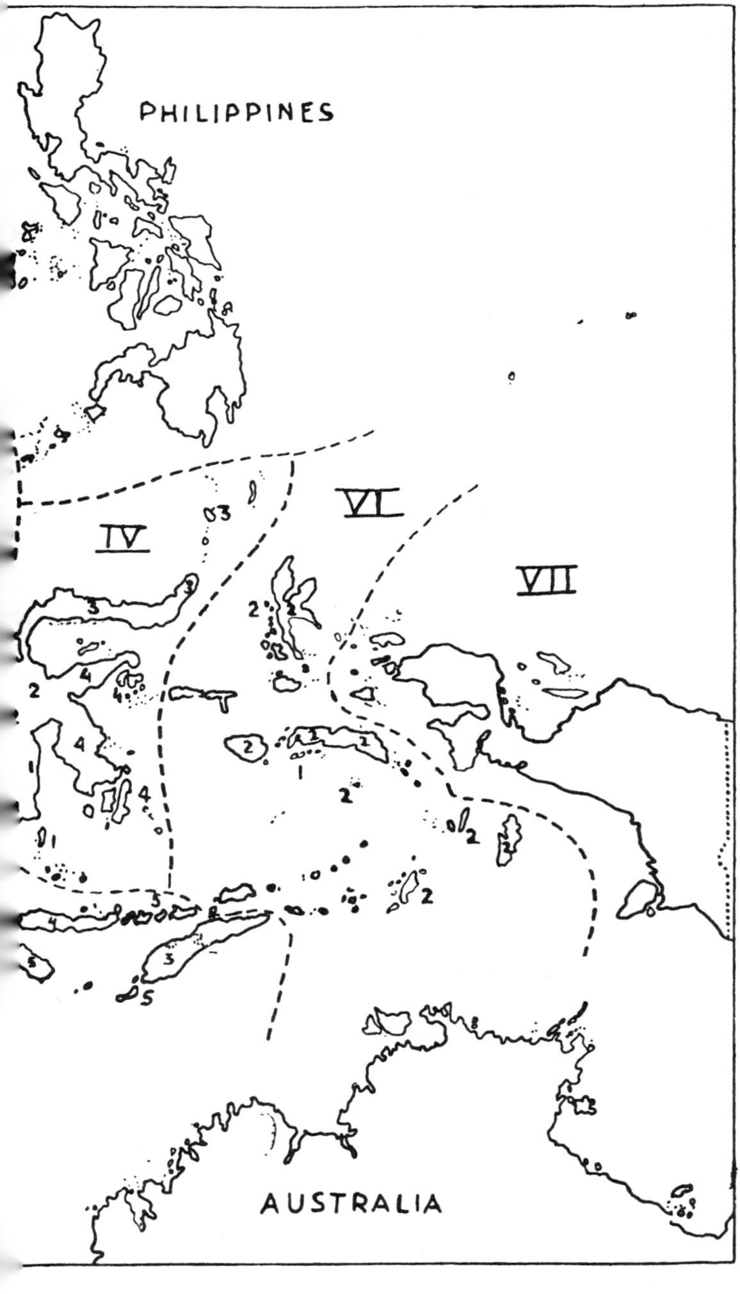
PHILIPPINES
IV
VI
VII
AUSTRALIA

factors, to something like 300,000, despite a vigorous emigration especially among those born in Europe and a diminished immigration during the depression of the thirties.[1]

During the Japanese occupation, however, it was the latter population group which suffered the heaviest losses. On the whole, after 1945, the number of Europeans strongly decreased again, especially by departure of many to Holland. This factor was not compensated by the inflow of many thousands of Dutch conscripts, as their stay was only temporary, the great majority of them leaving again in 1949 and later.

Since the transfer of sovereignty the former division into *Natives*, *Foreign Orientals* and *Europeans* has lost most, but not all of its significance. The Foreign Orientals born in Indonesia have, at that time, automatically acquired Indonesian citizenship and lost the status of Dutch subjects, in so far as they have not repudiated Indonesian nationality expressedly. Those who fall into the former category, forming an overwhelming majority of those who were formerly considered as Chinese and Arabs, are to be reckoned among the Indonesians now. Still, in so far as the Chinese are concerned, the problem of dual nationality (Indonesian and Chinese) is not yet definitely solved. In April 1955, at the time of the Bandung Asian-African Conference, a treaty has been concluded between the Indonesian and the Peking Government, which has still to be ratified. Even if the great majority of Chinese born in Indonesia will, eventually, keep Indonesian citizenship and reject their Chinese nationality, for a considerable time they will be looked upon as groups apart socially. Even their legal position still differs in many respects from that of the Indonesians proper.

Any attempt to estimate the present numbers of the different groups of individuals of Chinese ancestry would seem rather hazardous, though it would seem that no more than fifty per cent of the roughly two million of them are Indonesian nationals.

[1] Cf. A. van Marle, 'De groep der Europeanen in Nederlands-Indië. Iets over ontstaan en groei' (The European group in the Netherlands Indies. Something about origin and growth), in *Indonesië*, Vol. V, 1951/52, p. 105.

On Java there will be approximately a million persons of Chinese ancestry, slightly over 600,000 of which are Indonesian citizens.

Persons of European ancestry are at present Indonesian nationals, insofar as they have made use of their right of option for Indonesian citizenship in 1950 or 1951. Legally and socially they also retain, for the time being, a special position, though the designation 'Europeans' should no longer be applied to them. The overwhelming majority of the former 'Europeans', however, chose to retain their Dutch nationality, which fact eventually, with the rise of political tensions, resulted in their mass exodus to the Netherlands. The number of people of European or mixed ancestry still in Indonesia amounts to some 40,000 Indonesian nationals and perhaps a slightly higher number of European and American nationals.[1]

The islands

A cursory survey of the populations of the separate islands shows the following.

In 1930 Sumatra had a total population of about eight million. The great majority of the inhabitants practise agriculture (generally, as noted above, a shifting cultivation). In addition, however, among many peoples of Sumatra a not inconsiderable number of traders is to be found.

The Islamic faiths strongly dominate on this island. It was the first island of the archipelago Islamised from India. To the north of the island the strictly Moslem Achenese are to be found. This people, having defended its independence against the Dutch

[1] These figures are estimates by Mr. A. van Marle. Those for Chinese on Java were computed primarily on the basis of the Biro Pusat Statistik publication *Penduduk Indonesia* (mimeographed, 1958). The numbers of Chinese aliens and citizens of Chinese descent in other parts of Indonesia were then estimated with the help of 1930 census data. The number of nationals of European descent was arrived at by multiplying the number of options for Indonesian citizenship made in the 1949–1951 period (more than 13,000) by a factor 2½ to 3 to cover wives and children included in such options. Further allowance has been made for increase of the group since 1951. For European aliens, see *Statistical Pocketbook of Indonesia 1957*, p. 14–15.

longest of all, still retains the fame of great martial prowess and a strongly developed sense of freedom. During both military actions in 1947 and 1948 the Dutchmen wisely refrained from an attack on Acheh.

On the west coast of Central Sumatra lives another population which can be counted among the fervent believers of Islam: the Menangkabau. This population is known by its matrilinear family structure and by the relatively independent position of the women, a fact which in former times gave rise to the not quite justified interpretation of the kinship structure in Menangkabau as a matriarchal system.[1]

Many Menangkabau traders and intellectuals have migrated to other parts of the archipelago, because conditions in their homeland, as a consequence of a rigid *adat* family system, were not too conducive to settlement for individuals who had slackened their bonds with tradition. Among the well-known nationalist leaders quite a number came from Menangkabau.

Somewhat oppressed between the Achenese and the Menangkabau in the interior of North Sumatra are the Bataks, who are included within the sub-race of Early Malays. Most Batak peoples are not Islamised or only partially adherents to that creed. Protestantism, however, has found an ample following among several of these tribes, while many are still considered pagan.

Cattle-ownership plays an important part in several Batak tribes. The kinship system is preponderantly patrilinear. Among the Christian Bataks also many have spread all over the archipelago, as a rule fulfilling more or less intellectual functions.

[1] See for better understanding of the position of the Menangkabau women the little known study of V. E. Korn, 'De vrouwelijke mama' in de Minangkabausche familie' (The female mama' – the mother's brother, head of the family – in the Menangkabau family), in *Bijdragen tot de Taal-, Land- en Volkenkunde van Nederlandsch-Indië* (Contributions to the Philology, Geography and Ethnology of the Netherlands Indies), Vol. C, 1941, p. 301 ff. See further G. D. Willinck, *Het rechtsleven der Minangkabausche Maleiers* (The customary law of the Menangkabau Malays), Leiden, 1909; and P. E. de Josselin de Jong, *Minangkabau and Negri Sembilan. Socio-political structure in Indonesia*, Leiden, 1951.

Along the east coast of Sumatra, on the smaller islands of Bangka and Billiton and scattered over the Riau and Lingga archipelagoes the Islamised Malays in the strict sense are to be found. Southern Sumatra, too, is mostly inhabited by peoples related to the Malays, such as the Palembangese and the Lampongers.

The plantation area of Sumatra's Eastcoast Residency is a typical immigrant area. Not only in the town of Medan, but also in the countryside the population has quite a mixed character. The labour force on the estates was in early years largely recruited from China, but later on a majority came from Java. In these regions the Malays proper are often reduced to a vanishing minority. Chinese are equally to be found outside the Western plantations, scattered along the east coast and over the islands round Singapore. They are fishermen and lumbermen in Bengkalis and on the Lingga archipelago, and miners and pepper growers on the tin islands. Before the war the Chinese in this region largely consisted of migrants who returned to their homeland after a stay in Indonesia.

Great numbers of immigrants are equally to be found in the southern part of Sumatra, the Lampong districts. Here are first of all the settlements of Javanese pioneer farmers, but in addition, in this region Western plantations exist employing labourers from Central Java and Bantam (the western part of Java).[1]

A pattern similar to that of Sumatra, marks the population of Indonesian Borneo, assessed at the census of 1930 at some two million, but in reality perhaps considerably higher at that time. Shifting cultivation is the dominant agricultural system again, as it is nearly everywhere in the Outer Islands. In addition, the tribes along the coasts engage in commerce. Again, tribes of the

[1] In the above survey only those peoples are mentioned who belong, by numbers and by the economic role they fulfil, to the chief elements of the present population of Sumatra. Neither this enumeration nor the following descriptions claim to be complete. For those anxious to make a more detailed study of the peoples mentioned and of smaller tribes omitted from this survey a bibliographical list is attached to this chapter. See also the map of peoples with an explanatory table.

Early Malay type are found farther to the interior, generally designated by the collective appellation of 'Dayaks'. The tribes along the coasts are called Malays, those of Southeast Borneo sometimes Banjarese. Most of these coastal tribes and the kindred population of Hulu Sungei, living along the rivers of Southeast Borneo, profess the Islamic creed. It is a custom, indeed, of Dayaks converted to the Moslem faith to call themselves henceforth Malays instead of Dayaks. The Dayaks proper as a rule practise their traditional religious rituals and activities, on account of which they are considered as 'pagans'. Moreover, among the Dayaks Christianity, both Protestantism and Roman Catholicism, has made headway, albeit to a lesser degree than among the Bataks.

In Western Borneo, nearest to Singapore, a great concentration of Chinese is to be found. In this region there are even districts with a pure Chinese population. Differing from those of Sumatra, however, the Chinese of Western Borneo are to a great extent settlers, many of them being engaged in agriculture. They play an especially important role in rubber, coconut and pepper cultivation. In the town of Pontianak, too, a very great portion of the population is Chinese.

The population of the island Java is rather heterogeneous. Most of the inhabitants are agriculturists, but unlike the people in the other islands, they practise either *sawah* cultivation or an intensive cultivation on dry fields (*tegalans*). Many peasants have, moreover, become labourers on the Western plantations. The cities, the rather developed communication system and the rise of industry account for a greater amount of social differentiation than is commonly found on the Outer Islands. However, many functions outside agriculture are mainly performed by individuals of foreign origin. Thus, many crafts and much trade is in the hands of people of Chinese ancestry.

Most of Western Java is inhabited by the so-called Sundanese numbering some eight million in 1930. The Bantamese to the extreme west are more akin to the Javanese proper, as are the inhabitants of Cheribon and surrounding areas. The city of

Jakarta (formerly Batavia) contains a notable medley of peoples, as a consequence of its historical origin as chief headquarters of the Dutch East India Company. Sometimes the Batavians, who speak a Malay dialect of their own, are considered a separate people.

In addition Jakarta, like other big cities of the archipelago, has a considerable percentage of Chinese and a smaller percentage of European residents.

The Javanese proper, the most numerous group of the archipelago amounting to nearly 28 million in 1930 (including the emigrants on Sumatra), are mainly found in Central Java and in most parts of Eastern Java. In some other parts of Eastern Java however, a very high percentage of Madurese is to be found, who emigrated from their unfertile island and either are practising agriculture and cattle-breeding or are engaged in fishery. The total number of Madurese on Java and Madura exceeded in 1930 four million. Many Madurese sail the seas with their praus or work as crew hands on steamships owned by European companies.

The Sundanese and Madurese are generally known as faithful observers of the Islamic faith. It is not by chance that the centre of activities of the *Darul Islam* movement, which creates a good deal of trouble since the past few years and tries to establish an Islamic state by violence, is found in Western Java. The Javanese proper, especially those of the Principalities of Central Java, though in great majority equally professing the Islamic creed, are generally considered less strict in the observance of their religious duties. Yet, the influence of Islamic religion and culture among them is considerable.

East of Java the Balinese, totalling one and a half million in 1930, are found on the island of Bali and also in parts of Lombok. Like the Javanese they are mainly engaged in rice cultivation on *sawahs*. They differ, however, from the Javanese by professing still the Hinduist and Buddhist religions. As a result, temple building is still a living cultural asset here, making Bali a favoured centre for art lovers and foreign tourists. The caste system has also taken root here, albeit in a mitigated form.

The remaining peoples of the Lesser Sunda islands do not need mention in this cursory survey, except insofar as Islam has made headway among the populations of Lombok and Sumbawa, while on the eastern islands Christianity has won a great influence on the population. We have seen already, that on Timor, at least the western, Indonesian, part of it, Protestantism dominates while Flores is a centre of Roman Catholic missionary activity.

The population of Celebes numbering about four million people in 1930, shows an equally great diversity. On the rather densely populated southwestern arm are the Macassarese and Buginese, both thoroughly Islamised. The Buginese have won a great fame all over the archipelago as prau sailors: they are found scattered over the islands.

The Torajas who live in Central Celebes belong to the Early Malay stock. During this century Protestantism has made headway among these 'pagan' tribes, but along the coast Islam is exerting a greater proselyting power.

The densely populated northeastern extremity of Celebes, the Minahasa, is inhabited by the Menadonese, the majority of whom profess the Protestant faiths. This group has for a long time supplied contingents for the Dutch colonial army. Among these Christians who earlier than most Indonesians profited from Western education, a disproportionate number moved away from the Minahasa, where the possibilities for employment and further development were insufficient. Many of them were employed in the lower ranks of administration in Java and, to a lesser degree, in the other islands.

All the above applies also to the Ambonese, the most important population group of the Moluccas. The island of Ambon itself has a considerable group of Moslem inhabitants, as is the case on most islands of the Moluccas. Yet the Moluccas are the region where conversion to Christianity has progressed most of all, ever since the time of the Portuguese in the sixteenth century. The Ambonese were for long years the cherished children of the Dutch colonial regime. Together with the Eurasians (called *Indos* or Indo-

Europeans in Indonesia) they formed a kind of intermediate layer of minor officials. In the army, too, they held a privileged position, possibly to be compared with that of the Karens in Burma. In Ambon itself the intermixture and assimilation with the Europeans had progressed very far, which explains why the Ambonese did not really consider themselves *Inlanders*. The situation, there and in the Minahasa, presented a picture somewhat comparable to that in the Philippines, where religious unity also to a certain degree bridged over racial antagonism.

From the above remarks it can be understood why it was groups of Ambonese who, by proclaiming the so-called Republic of the South Moluccas, after the transfer of sovereignty opposed most strongly the formation of an Indonesian unitary state.

Finally, the aborigines of Western New-Guinea, the Papuans (since the revolution called Irians by the Indonesians), are a population group falling within the Melanesian stock and differing markedly from the inhabitants of the archipelago proper racially, culturally and linguistically. Along the coasts the Islamic faith has a hold here and there under the impact of Indonesians, mostly from the Northern Moluccas. Although, during the last few decades, Protestant and Roman Catholic missionary activities were much in evidence, most of these peoples are still reckoned among the so-called 'pagans'.

Apart from a few cursory comments on general qualities ascribed to some of the Indonesian peoples, I have deliberately refrained in the preceding survey as much as possible from attempts to characterise the various peoples mentioned. Though the current literature on Indonesia abounds in comments upon the character of the peoples described, most of it rests on a completely unscientific basis. Moreover, many of the stereotypes used reflect the prejudices and hidden political wishes of colonial rulers rather than real traits of the peoples concerned. To a large degree these stereotypes, even if clad in a scientific cloak, served as rationalisations for a desire to keep colonial rule intact by ascribing to the Indonesian peoples those traits marking them as unfit to rule themselves.[1] Even the changing characteristics of the Javanese people, as described in Western literature, reflect the changes in the attitudes of the observers rather than real changes in character. At the start of the nineteenth century the Javanese, still engaged in continuous warfare against the Company, was described as warlike and fierce, prone to leave any work on the slightest provocation and to revenge any supposed wrong with fire and murder.[2] About 1900 he had become a member of 'the gentlest people on earth', calm, pliable and meek, an ideal subject for colonial rule. The Encyclopaedia of the Netherlands Indies[3] still reproduced the stereotype adding, however, that Indonesia forms part of awakening Asia and consequently, before long, the description might prove to be no longer true. And indeed, probably present descriptions would, after the experiences of the revolutionary years, once more reflect the changed attitudes of the observers.

But there are still other reasons to distrust such generalisations. Any population is far more complex than might appear at first sight. According to social status or occupation the characteristics may differ appreciably. Farmers tend to show, on the whole, similar traits; but these are functions of the occupation and of the mode of living rather than inherent qualities. More often than not there is a greater similarity between farmers of different peoples than between farmers and traders of the same stock. On the other hand, trade or membership of an aristocratic ruler class are also likely to produce special characteristics due to a different way of life.

Thus, a so-called national character may decompose into group characteristics dependent upon common cultural influences experienced by the group. Any attempt to lump the groups together in one description runs the danger of using group characteristics as a *pars pro toto*. On the other hand, a justifiable group description

1 For a more extensive treatment of the pre-war psychological theories I may refer to my book *Herrijzend Azië* (Resurgent Asia), Arnhem, 1950, p. 73ff., 130ff.

2 As for instance in an official report ascribed to S. C. Nederburgh.

3 *Encyclopaedie van Nederlandsch-Indië* (Encyclopaedia of the Netherlands Indies), The Hague/Leiden, 1917–1939, Vol. II, p. 215, *sub voce* 'Javaan'.

would, largely, amount to a discription of the cultural influences working upon the group in question, such as Margaret Mead for instance attempted to give in her remarkable study *Balinese Character.*[1]

Moreover, it must be remembered that the cultural surroundings of the Indonesian peoples are rapidly changing. If the prewar Javanese of colonial times was already a much more complex type than was generally assumed, an attempt to characterise the typical 'new Indonesian', to be found both in the cities and in the countryside, would be too risky. On the other hand, there are certainly cultural traits which have of old worked upon the Javanese people, as for instance the Javanese ideal of chivalry, which assigned the highest possible value to self-possession.[2] Through the vehicle of the *wayang* play, frequently attended by the Javanese peasants from childhood, this ideal, originated among the aristocracy, has been conveyed to broad masses of Javanese people. It is quite possible, that these and similar cultural influences are still working very effectively upon the youth, even though it is affected by modern Western influences much more intensively than was the pre-war generation. But even so these are not innate traits but peculiarities dependent upon cultural factors. Any such so-called typically Javanese traits, as Javanese delicacy, Javanese courtesy, Javanese modesty or Javanese servility – often mentioned in contrast with a certain rudeness, self-confidence and sense of equality among the populations of the Outer Islands – may prove characteristics closely allied with the traditional social structure, and they might well lose their importance with changes in that structure.

It seems, therefore, as if a really scientific study of popular psychology would amount, for Indonesians as for any other

[1] G. Bateson and M. Mead, *Balinese character. A photographic analysis*, Special publications of the New York Academy of Science, Vol. II, New York, 1942.

[2] See W. F. Stutterheim, *Iets over de cultuurbasis onzer leerlingen* (Remarks about the cultural background of our pupils), Publicatie van het Bureau van den Onderwijsraad (Publication of the Office of the Board for Education), Nr XII, Mededeelingen (Communications) VI, Batavia, 1931, p. 5 ff.

nation, to a study largely of social and cultural influences working upon them.

A short bibliography

J. O. M. Broek, *Economic development of the Netherlands Indies*, New York, 1942.

Census of 1930 in Netherlands India, Batavia, 1933–1936.

J. P. Duyvendak, *Inleiding tot de ethnologie van de Indische archipel* (Introduction to the ethnology of the Indian archipelago), Groningen/Batavia, 1954.

Encyclopaedie van Nederlandsch-Indië (Encyclopaedia of the Netherlands Indies), Second Edition, The Hague/Leiden, 1917–1939.

K. Helbig, *Indonesien. Eine auslandkundliche Übersicht der Malaiischen Inselwelt*, Stuttgart, 1949.

A. D. A. de Kat Angelino, *Colonial policy*, Amsterdam/Chicago, 1931.

R. Kennedy, *The ageless Indies*, New York, 1942.

R. Kennedy, *Selected bibliography of Indonesian peoples*, Yale Anthropological Studies, Vol. IV, New Haven, 1945.

N. Keyfitz and Widjojo Nitisastro, *Soal penduduk dan pembangunan Indonesia* (Population problem and reconstruction in Indonesia), Jakarta, 1955.

H. de Meel, 'Demographic dilemma in Indonesia', in *Pacific Affairs*, Vol. XXIV, 1951, Nr 3.

J. Ormeling, *The Timor problem. A geographical interpretation of an underdeveloped island*, Jakarta/Groningen, 1955.

Kampto Utomo, *Masjarakat transmigran spontan didaerah W. Sekampung (Lampong)* (Spontaneous transmigrant settlements in the W. Sekampung area, Lampongs), Jakarta, 1957.

A. Vandenbosch, *The Dutch East Indies. Its government, problems and politics*, Berkeley, 1942.

C. van Vollenhoven, *Het adatrecht van Nederlandsch-Indië* (The *adat* law of the Netherlands Indies), Leiden, 1918–1933.

Chapter Three

A Cursory Survey of some Social Developments in South and Southeast Asia[1]

1 Ancient South and Southeast Asian society

As we have seen before, Indonesia still has close ties with the Southeast Asian world. It may therefore be useful to give here a brief sketch of social changes throughout the South and Southeast Asian world during the past centuries, as a background for Indonesian developments.

As we have seen in Chapter I, the social structure of ancient Asian society was predominantly static; already a hundred years ago Karl Marx spoke of: 'the unchangeableness of Asiatic societies, an unchangeableness in such striking contrast with the constant dissolution and refounding of Asiatic states, and the never-ceasing changes of dynasty. The structure of the economic elements of society remains untouched by the storm-clouds of the political sky.'[2] And he was still more outspoken with regard to Indian society, when he wrote: 'Indian society has no history at all, that is to say, no history known to us. What we call its history is only the history of conquerors following upon each other and building their empires on the foundation of that obsequious immovable society.'

European influence in the Far East first made itself felt with the Portuguese discoveries. European powers conquered several

[1] This chapter is an adaptation of the author's contribution 'The changing structure of Eastern society' to *Eastern and Western world*, Selected readings with a foreword by S. Hofstra, The Hague/Bandung, 1953.

[2] Karl Marx, *On India*, cited from A. R. Desai, *The social background of Indian nationalism*, University of Bombay Publications, Sociology series Nr 2, Bombay, 1948, p. 6.

strongholds on the coasts and proceeded to dispute the supremacy of the large Asian states. But in so doing they soon adapted themselves to Oriental patterns of ruling; even the pattern of behaviour of the Westerners, after a short stay in the East, lost its bourgeois stamp and adapted itself to the Eastern surroundings. And trade as practised by Europeans also followed the Oriental patterns. The Westerners usually dealt only with the Oriental princes and aristocratic chiefs and they succeeded in obtaining a part of the intra-Asian traffic in fine quality products, the object of Oriental trade for centuries. Only a modest part of these products was shipped to Europe. In general neither Asian agriculture nor Asian industry was affected by Western influence in an appreciable way before the beginning of the nineteenth century.[1]

2 *Social changes during the nineteenth century*

It was only after 1800 that Western impact made itself generally felt in Asia. Then the growth of British industry served to bring about a fundamental change in the relationship between East and West. The expanding textile industry in England was in constant need of a regular supply of raw materials. Conversely, the products of European industry were in search of a market in the East. So the bases of Eastern society were shaken by Western capitalism for the first time in history.

In the economic field the Western impact made itself felt in various ways, according to the political relationship between the Western power and the Eastern society involved. On the whole, however, a broadly similar general development could be observed in the various South and Southeast Asian countries, although there might be a time lag between similar processes in different countries. Indian society was first to suffer from the

[1] See J. C. van Leur, *Indonesian trade and society. Essays in Asian social and economic history*, Selected studies on Indonesia by Dutch scholars, Vol. I, The Hague/Bandung, 1955, p. 5, 283; Maurice Zinkin, *Asia and the West*, London, 1953, p. 42 ff.; G. B. Sansom, *The Western world and Japan. A study of the interaction of European and Asiatic cultures*, New York, 1950, p. 145 ff.

impact of Western capitalism. The protection which the British government provided for British industry in the early years of the nineteenth century amounted to a death blow to the famous traditional Indian textile industry; British colonial power brought a flood of British products into Indian society, and the railways built across India made it possible for Britain 'to deliver the goods.'[1] In the same way, in most parts of Burma home industry also gradually gave way to the import of cotton prints from England.[2]

The introduction of a money economy into South and Southeast Asian countries was the first effect of modern Western capitalism. The farmer was no longer able to base his production almost exclusively on home consumption; he had to look for a supplementary money income. As a result he became involved in production for the world market and dependent on price fluctuations. Some peasants became growers of market crops. Others had to provide for a supplementary money income as labourers on commercial crop plantations. Both developments were equally disruptive of Asian village life. Many traditional institutions were gradually forced to give way. Family property, inalienable before, was transformed in many areas into individual property which could be mortgaged. Such institutions as the money lender, the professional trader, the artisan working for a market, the land tenant and the absentee owner were already discernible in ancient Southern Asia in an embryonic state, but they now made headway in agrarian society and began to cut across the traditional status systems.

Among the ordinary villagers some attained a certain degree of prosperity under the new system and therefore challenged the privileges of the rulers or elite. On the other hand many peasants ran into debt and became more or less 'proletarianised.'[3] These

[1] See A. R. Desai, *op. cit.*, p. 71 ff.; P. K. Gopalakrishnan, *Development of economic ideas in India (1880–1914)*, The Hague, 1954, p. 10 ff.

[2] J. S. Furnivall, *Colonial policy and practice. A comparative study of Burma and Netherlands India*, Cambridge, 1948, p. 100 ff.

[3] See Maurice Zinkin, *op. cit.*, p. 34 ff., on 'bankruptcy'.

people felt resentful: they lost the sense of security which tradition and membership in a collective group had given them. Agrarian society was being atomised and the peasant felt isolated and frustrated by forces which he could not master or even understand. As a result serious uprisings occurred in several areas about the middle of the century. The violent *Wahhabi* peasant revolts culminating in the Indian Mutiny[1] were to a certain extent reactions against the disturbance which Western imports had caused in India's agrarian economy. In their traditional way the uprisings aimed at an overthrow of those in authority who had failed to protect the peasantry from distress. But this time they did not succeed, as a basic change in the structure of society had occurred, and the influence of Western economy could not be eliminated. The Western powers usually chose the policy of backing the Oriental rulers and so propped up the collapsing feudal or feudal-like structures.

The superstructure of South and Southeast Asian society was thus also affected by the impact of capitalism. How it was affected depended on the specific political situation, whether for instance a Southern Asian region was politically under a colonial regime or had only been dragged into some Western power's economic influence. But everywhere the most striking social phenomenon in nineteenth century South and Southeast Asia was the enormous prestige the white race won as a consequence of its political, technological and military domination.

The social change was most manifest in colonial countries, where the whites superimposed themselves on the native status system as a new caste-like upper stratum. A frequent trait of nineteenth century colonialism was the colour line. In most colonial societies the resident white population was 'separated from the native masses by a social barrier that was virtually impassable.'[2] All the relationships, either in the political or in the eco-

[1] See W. C. Smith, *Modern Islam in India. A social analysis*, London, 1946, p. 161 ff.

[2] Raymond Kennedy, 'The colonial crisis and the future', in R. Linton (ed.), *The science of man in the world crisis*, New York, 1945, p. 308.

nomic sphere, were those of superiority and inferiority. In some colonial societies, such as Burma, Cochin-China or the Philippines, not even the middle class of professional traders and artisans was recruited from the native population. This middle class often consisted of Chinese or Indians, who as foreigners had less difficulty in applying themselves to trades considered inferior by members of every level of the native 'feudal' society. This merchant class became an extension of Western capitalism and thus often helped to widen the cleavage between the white ruling class and the native population.

The old native ruling class was generally kept in its superior position over the native population, and the colonial powers made use of the traditional Oriental structure in order to strengthen their hold on the people. Even so the native ruling class was forced to adapt itself to Western governmental practices and to lend its support to Western capitalist forces. The legal authority of this class was given the backing of the colonial power, but at the same time it lost something of its traditional aura. Moreover, the high social prestige of Western ways caused the native ruling class to adopt some of these ways and a small upper layer of Orientals tried to conform to Western standards of living and thinking.

Thus, the nineteenth century could be characterised as a period of breaking up of the traditional economic system. Despite attempts of the Western powers to make as much use as possible of the existing social order, they could not avoid disrupting the Asian village society and eventually reducing the members of the traditional communities to single atoms; nor could they help changing the character of the Oriental ruling class by tying it to Western capitalistic interests. For the first time a dynamic factor had been introduced with sufficient force to revolutionise the total structure of Eastern society. But it was not an intrinsic factor; it was based upon a foreign influence. The peoples of South and Southeast Asia had yet to find an equally dynamic response to this stimulus introduced from without.

3 The rise of an Asian bourgeoisie

Even after closer contact with Western capitalism, the Asian countries for a long time did not follow the pattern of Western society in their development. The main interest of Western capitalist entrepreneurs was in the development of agricultural and mineral production of foodstuffs and raw materials. Transport systems were devised chiefly for an easy flow of the goods wanted by Western industry; the development of industrial equipment lagged far behind. And this was true not only of colonial countries such as India, Indo-China and the Philippines, but of semi-colonial nations such as Siam as well. As a result, the agrarian population had no easy outlet in the cities. The density of agrarian population, especially in the rice growing regions was extreme. As a consequence, an urban proletariat developed much more slowly than in Europe. The formation of a native bourgeoisie was not a quick process, and there were striking differences in its development in the various areas. In India this development had begun some decades before the turn of the century, but in Burma and elsewhere it made itself felt only a few years before World War I. There the division of functions according to 'racial' groups typical of most colonial countries had apparently put a check on the rise of a native bourgeoisie.

Whereas in Western Europe the Third Estate, made up of traders, industrialists and those practising a liberal profession, had been the first exponent of bourgeois culture, the picture in Southern Asia was somewhat different. Expanding commerce did in fact draw an increasing number of Orientals into its orbit; the trading centres and industrial towns expanded to become the home of modern capitalist-minded Oriental businessmen. But they had to fight their way in an environment where Western entrepreneurs had already gained the ascendancy and were still expanding the field of their activities. Besides trade and industry a further individualising factor in the East was modern education. The social texture of modern capitalism, in which government services fulfil an important function and business is carried on largely by big companies, created the need for schooled personnel. Education on Western lines was needed to provide this 'dependent middle class', to be compared to the Western of white collar workers. Furthermore, many Indians and some Filipinos and Annamese also visited Western Europe or the United States and thus became further acquainted with modern cultural life. In some countries it was this group of Westernised Asian employees which formed the core of the rising Asian bourgeoisie.

Both the new businessmen and the new intellectuals came to the fore as bearers of modern ideas and Western individualism. As comparatively well-to-do urban classes they may be labelled 'bourgeoisie', though this does not mean that they considered their own social and economic situation satisfactory. Despite the Western-mindedness of most of them, the prevailing economic situation prevented them from becoming the supporters of Western power and Western interests.

The rising Oriental business class had to compete with the Western enterprises dominating the Asian economic system. Indian businessmen eventually succeeded in starting a number of modern textile factories, but it was difficult for them to hold out against the flow of imported British cotton cloth. The Indian commercial class became aware that it was colonial rule which for a long time prevented it from developing its own full potentialities.

This competitive struggle was only one of many. In some colonial countries such as French Indo-China the educated Orientals dependent on appointments in government services and big private enterprises found their path to the upper stratum of society blocked by a colonial status system in which social prestige hinged upon white ancestry.[1] Western education had given many an Oriental the ability to fill leading posts, which the Western imposed colonial caste-like system then denied him. Here, too, those who stood nearest to Western culture often became the

[1] See *e.g.* P. Mus, *Viet-Nam. Sociologie d'une guerre*, Paris, 1952, p. 152 ff., where he argues that even in French Indo-China the 'colonial axioma': 'que le premier des Annamites eût à passer après le dernier des Français', was not absent.

fiercest adversaries of Western representatives in the East. Western education had the effect of dynamite upon the colonial status system.[1]

There were also other forms of strife between the classes. The Oriental businessmen and Westernised intellectuals both felt that feudal tradition was a bar to their aspirations. Furthermore, on the strength of their wealth or education they challenged the social prestige which tradition had exclusively accorded to the highest nobility and the priestly class or to the official literati. And the political alliance between the native aristocracy and the Western colonial powers made it possible for the Oriental bourgeoisie to identify its struggle against what they often called 'feudalism' with its struggle against foreigners.

It is not surprising, then, that the rising new classes in every South and Southeast Asian country joined forces under the banner of nationalism. The same ideology which in earlier centuries had provided the rising bourgeoisie of Western Europe with weapons to defeat the nobility, now served as a tool against the combined forces of foreign colonial power and native aristocracy. Nationalism, which was basically an idealistic movement, but one not to be fully understood without taking into account its materialistic basis, could enlist the support of all those who were suffering in any way from the existing state of things. Not only were poverty and distress among the peasants increasing; now they too resented conditions which they had endured in earlier times, the more so because they were no longer isolated from other cultures and had become, through the cinema and personal contact with foreigners, more aware of other ways of life. Discontent among the peasantry, which had formerly resulted in outbursts of xenophobia, accompanied by quasi-mystical manifestations and in violent but rather ineffective protests against taxes and compulsory services, could now be channelled into a more effective political movement. Under bourgeois leadership it was transformed from a longing for an imaginary 'paradise lost'

1 R. Kennedy, *op. cit.*, p. 311.

into a dynamic struggle for a better life, a struggle which at the same time had the character of a class struggle against foreign entrepreneurs or (as in the Philippines, Siam, Burma and Cochin-China) against foreign middlemen. The nationalist movement could serve, indeed, against any power which could be branded as foreign. Furthermore it could serve against any force which tended to break up unity by fostering local patriotism, a trend represented for example by the aristocratic rulers of India and Malaya. The bourgeoisie was able to oppose them by laying stress on the common interests of all the people within the territory of the state. In India this nationalist ideology was represented by the Congress Party under Gandhi's leadership during the twenties. In the Philippines the Partido Nacionalista, formed in 1907 and led by Osmeña and Quezon, had a similar character.

The most interesting feature of these movements was that, whereas the bourgeois nationalist leaders had by that time attained a position enabling them to enlist popular support, the imperial and feudal rulers and the religious leaders or literati, on the other hand, were losing their grip on the masses. During the first years of the twentieth century popular movements, directed against the Western powers, still remained under aristocratic or (quasi) religious leadership. The Annamese conspiracy about 1907 was sponsored by circles narrowly allied to the ruling dynasty and to the ancient mandarin class. But in the second decade there was a definite shift in the Southern Asian status systems. Social prestige was no longer vested exclusively in traditional authority. By individual achievement and the acquisition of wealth or education, individuals could challenge the power of the traditional ruling class. In French Indo-China a new 'mandarin' class began to claim the social prerogatives of the old literati.

It might thus seem as though South and Southeast Asia were following the same pattern of development earlier followed by the West. Up to then there had been no remarkable differences, except for a considerable time lag, between developments in Europe and in Asia.

4 From individualism to collective action

Every division of a subject matter is, to a certain degree, arbitrary and may incur the reproach of disfiguring the variegated pattern of reality. Coming events throw their shadow on present happenings, and relics of a bygone past may last for centuries. Therefore, if we say that the fourth phase (in which we are now living) is characterised by a reversal, a trend from individualism toward collective action, this statement should not be misunderstood. Education and private business still account for an individualistic attitude among many Orientals, while nationalism, which had become the leading ideology during the third phase, was already, as we have seen, a source of collective action as well. What needs to be pointed out is, therefore, only a hardly perceptible shift in attitude during recent decades, a shift which could be described as an increasing desire of isolated Asians to seek the support of various groups.

The Asian bourgeoisie arrived on the scene too late to realise to the full its tendencies in the direction of individualism. The Oriental bourgeois came to live in a world where trade and industry were no longer dominated by private businessmen but by ever growing monopolistic concerns. During the twenties it became apparent that the normal ways of competition would not suffice to enable an Oriental middle class to develop its full potentialities. The Oriental bourgeois felt frustrated and many lost their optimistic outlook on society and its future, as is reflected in religious theories of the time.[1] They became aware of something like a ceiling to their endeavours. At the same time they felt threatened by the rise of an Oriental proletariat which they themselves had awakened to class consciousness by their use of nationalist slogans, but which they feared might be a future challenge to the position they themselves had only recently acquired.

The Oriental bourgeoisie retained its competitive attitude, but the members of that class tried to decrease their isolation by

[1] See W. C. Smith, *op. cit.*, p. 81 ff.

looking for support within some kindred group. In a world where the economy, from lack of industrial development, did not expand at a sufficient rate to absorb all aspirants, what had been a competition between individuals now became a competition between groups. Only allegiance to a group could help the individual to attain his social aspirations. Any distinctive trait could serve. In India it was communalism, the religious division of the people into Hindus and Moslems, which served as a shibboleth. In Malaya it was the ethnic distinction between Malays and Chinese. A well-known Dutch scholar, Kraemer, has stated this situation as follows: 'Among the gods of the world there is none that has such a great number of devoted worshippers all over the world as group solidarity in its various avatars. Group solidarity is the Allah of modern world, beating all other gods in popularity, and nationalism is its Prophet.'[1]

Especially during the thirties these groupings under bourgeois leadership organised themselves along party lines in order to enlist popular support: the Indian Congress Party, the Indian Muslim League, and the Nacionalistas of the Philippines had become huge mass-movements making a bid for followers on ethnic or religious appeals. Their primary aim was no longer social reform, but a struggle for supremacy with competing bourgeois groups.

Though these parties originated in revolutionary bourgeois circles, they gradually changed their character. After World War II those movements were even used by the leaders as tools against social revolution. Members of the landed aristocracy joined in as they became aware of the usefulness of the movements as bulwarks against social reform, and added a conservative or even authoritarian and reactionary trend to the parties. Mass support, however, tended to make the parties' official ideologies (and the slogans they proclaimed to the public) more radical. The most important feature of many nationalist movements in South and Southeast Asia at present is that in achieving political

[1] H. Kraemer, *The Christian message in a non-Christian world*, London, 1938 p. 276.

power they seem to have spent much of their revolutionary fervour. After having come to power, they have great difficulties in performing their next task: to accomplish a program of agrarian reform and industrial development. A lack of purposeful effort to revolutionise society is in evidence. Agrarian distress and backwardness prevails in many areas. After having supplanted the former ruling class, the new elite is adopting some of its ways. Their revolutionary momentum is slowing. The disruptive forces along racial or religious group lines are becoming dangerous.

Group solidarity, however, is not restricted to bourgeois circles. The cities, huge and expanding at an increasing rate, harbour a growing poverty stricken proletariat. As the labourers gradually loosen their bonds with agrarian society and their clan relationships, they are developing a class consciousness and building new ties through trade unions. Group solidarity based on family and tradition is more and more being replaced by collective action along rational lines. In some areas this is now beginning to apply to the peasant population as well. The often impoverished peasant has lost his traditional security within the village community or the genealogical group and feels isolated by the effects of modern capitalism. Bankruptcy or severe indebtedness in rural areas has become a characteristic of many South Asian societies. The ever expanding Asian towns often multiply the miseries of agrarian districts. But farmers' unions, cooperatives and political parties are serving as centres where the peasant may look for a new integration which satisfies his needs in modern society. His behaviour within these social groups often exhibits many relics from age old social patterns, as may appear from his attitude towards the leaders. But in general this modern type of group life enables the peasant to play a more active role in the forefront of economic forces instead of passively submitting to them as he has immemorially done.

An interesting feature is the effect which the increasing importance of group formation in the East is having on the scale of social prestige. The trend towards an evaluation of social prestige according to personal achievement is being deflected as a result of the growing influence of group allegiance. Whether one is to be appointed to a certain position depends more and more upon the question whether one belongs to the 'ins' or the 'outs'. Party or group allegiance is becoming one of the most important requirements for social achievement. Who is to be at the top is increasingly determined by a struggle between the largest political parties and other social organisations. Thus a new social pattern is developing, different from the individualistic type of society considered by many Westerners as a model.

It will be our task to examine to what extent Indonesian developments have coincided with the general trends sketched in the foregoing pages.

A short bibliography

W. L. Holland (ed.), *Asian nationalism and the West*, A symposium based on documents and reports of the eleventh conference, Institute of Pacific Relations, New York, 1953.

A. R. Desai, *The social background of Indian nationalism*, University of Bombay Publications, Sociology series Nr 2, Bombay, 1948.

Cora Du Bois, *Social forces in Southeast Asia*, Cambridge (Mass.), 1959.

J. S. Furnivall, *Colonial policy and practice. A comparative study of Burma and Netherlands India*, New York, 1956.

E. H. Jacoby, *Agrarian unrest in Southeast Asia*, New York, 1949.

W. Macmahon Ball, *Nationalism and communism in East Asia*, Melbourne, 1952.

T. Mende, *Southeast Asia between two worlds*, London, 1955.

P. Mus, *Viet-Nam. Sociologie d'une guerre*, Paris, 1952.

J. C. van Leur, *Indonesian trade and society. Essays in Asian social and economic history*, Selected studies on Indonesia by Dutch scholars, Vol. I, The Hague/Bandung, 1955.

G. W. Skinner, *Chinese society in Thailand. An analytical history*, Ithaca, 1957.

G. W. Skinner, *Leadership and power in the Chinese community of Thailand*, Ithaca, 1958.

W. C. Smith, *Modern Islam in India. A social analysis*, London, 1946.

Maurice Zinkin, *Asia and the West*, London, 1953.

Chapter Four

General Outline of Indonesian Political History

1 Early Indonesian states and first contacts with Europeans

Our knowledge of the political history of Indonesia before the advent of the first Western travellers is far from reliable. Attempts to construct a coherent picture of early Indonesian history from bits of archaeological remains and fragmentary descriptions by Chinese and Arab travellers are rather hazardous, owing in particular to the difficulty of correctly identifying the islands and places mentioned.[1] For the fourteenth century the situation is somewhat different, largely because of the first specimen of Indonesian historiography preserved: the panegyric *Nagarakertagama* written by Prapanca, poet laureate at the court of Majapahit (East Java). Until recently it was commonly accepted by Orientalists that the empire of Majapahit had extended its rule, at the pinnacle of its glory, over a large part of the archipelago. A few years ago, however, even this certainty became a point at issue, as a result of new research undertaken by C. C. Berg,[2] which has led him to consider a good deal of the information to be found in old Javanese writings mythical instead of historical. Dr. Berg doubts whether the empire of Majapahit ever achieved supremacy over other islands than Java, Madura and Bali.

[1] An attempt to sketch the early history of Indonesia has been undertaken by G. Coedès, *Les états hindouisés d'Indochine et d'Indonésie*, Paris, 1948, but many of his views are disputed by scholars of high standing.

[2] See *e.g.* his article 'De Sadeng oorlog en de mythe van Groot Majapahit' (The Sadeng war and the myth of Great Majapahit), in *Indonesië*, Vol. V, 1951/52, p. 385 ff.

We are, however, on much firmer ground if we assume, with van Leur,[1] that two types of state structure could be discerned in early Indonesian society: first, the bureaucratic inland-states, mainly found on Java, which were dependent upon services and crop deliveries levied from the peasantry by local chiefs or governors; and, second, the numerous harbour principalities, largely dependent upon overseas trade. A state of either type could temporarily exert a measure of authority over territories of the other kind; but each state structure kept its own characteristics. Since political power over distant territories was confined, at that time, to periodical embassies carrying gifts from the vassal to the suzerain, and the transition from internal to external relations between princely rulers was a gradual one, it is hard to ascertain the real extent of ancient empires. Even if the traditional school of Orientalists was right in assuming that the Majapahit empire extended its power over a much larger area than is admitted by Berg,[2] its inner texture was, no doubt, rather loosely knit.

Portuguese sources enable us, for the first time, to draw a more coherent picture of the political situation in Indonesia in the sixteenth century. It is certain that the Majapahit empire, if it had achieved any political unity during the fourteenth century, had by this time fallen apart.

At the time the Portuguese navigators discovered the route to the long-sought Spice Islands, the archipelago presented anything

[1] J. C. van Leur, *Indonesian trade and society. Essays in Asian social and economic history*, Selected studies on Indonesia by Dutch scholars, Vol. I, The Hague/Bandung, 1955, p. 104 ff.

[2] A strong indication of the correctness of this traditional view may be derived from Chinese sources, cited by Nilakanta Sastri, 'Sri Vijaya', in *Bulletin de l'Ecole Française de l'Extrême Orient*, Vol. XL, 1940, p. 302/303. Tomé Pires also mentions in his *Suma Oriental* (English translation by Armanda Cortesão, titled: The Suma Oriental of Tomé Pires and the book of Francisco Rodrigues, in Works issued by The Hakluyt Society, Second Series Nr XC, London, 1944, Part I, p. 174) a large Hindu state on Java extending its rule a hundred years ago (*sc.* about 1400) over many parts of the archipelago.

but a political unity. In the interior of Java a few Hinduised inland-states were still holding out with difficulty against the harbour principalities along the north coast, which were strongly affected by the impact of Islam. On the other islands, too, the main adversaries of the Portuguese were the harbour princes along the coasts. Only at Malacca and in the Moluccas did the attempts of the Portuguese to acquire a measure of political and military power meet with some success. However, their expansionism, which for the most part had an anti-Moslem character, provoked as a reaction a steady progress of Islamic influence on Sumatra, Java and the Moluccas.[1]

When the Dutch penetrated the archipelago a hundred years later – about 1600 – the situation had greatly changed. The Hinduised states on Java had been forced to submit to the power of the Islamised harbour principalities. As a result the most powerful kingdoms on Java were then under Moslem rule. They were the inland-state of Mataram, under the energetic Prince Sultan Agung, and the harbour principality of Bantam in Western Java. To the north of Sumatra the Moslem kingdom of Acheh kept the Portuguese power at Malacca in check. In the eastern part of the archipelago the Moslem kingdom of Ternate seriously menaced the Portuguese positions in the Moluccas.

Only with the greatest effort did the Dutch trading companies succeed during the first years in establishing a few trading posts. The amalgamation of these companies in 1602 into the United East India Company, which received political and military assistance from the United Republic of the Netherlands, a powerful state in those days, helped the Dutch to hold their own in an exhaustive struggle with Portuguese, Britons, Javanese and the harbour princes of Bantam and Ternate, and even to establish a few centres of political and military power. These centres were the castle of Batavia on the north coast of Java, not far from the strong principality of Bantam, and a fort on Ambon conquered

[1] See J. C. van Leur, *op. cit.*, p. 160, 169. See also B. Schrieke, *Indonesian sociological studies. Selected writings*, Part 1. Selected studies on Indonesia by Dutch scholars, Vol. II, The Hague/Bandung, 1955, p. 39 ff.

from the Portuguese. With the support of these fortifications the Dutch succeeded, in the first decades of the seventeenth century, in maintaining a net of factories in the archipelago. In order to participate in the profitable trade the envoys of the Company had to secure access to the princely courts by the offer of gifts. In the relationship between the Company and the Eastern princes the status of the latter was by far superior.

On Java Sultan Agung of Mataram even aspired to a position of complete domination over the island. But in the siege of Batavia in 1628–1629 his huge army was defeated by Dutch military technique and maritime supremacy. Though the difference between the technical levels of East and West was not very great in those years, their maritime superiority was sufficient to enable the Dutch, like the Portuguese before them, to occupy permanently a few strongholds.[1] Moreover, the conquest of Malacca from the Portuguese in 1640 enabled the Dutch to force into a position of virtual economic dependency the kingdom of Mataram, which in the past had exported large quantities of rice to the peninsula via the ports on the north coast of Java.

This was the start of a steady expansion of Dutch power on Java. The Company's trade system was based on dealing with the Indonesian chiefs, who, using their traditional authority, could force the population to surrender a considerable portion of its produce. Wherever possible the Company claimed a monopolistic position. The state of Mataram joined this system, striving to prevent a free trade in the ports along the north coast and trying to keep a single-seller's position in rice trading with the Company; in this way, however, it unintentionally weakened its own economic strength. In a series of wars during the seventeenth century the Dutch succeeded in gradually reducing the power of the kingdoms of Bantam and Mataram; this result could, however, be obtained only by constantly playing off the Indonesian kingdoms against each other, and with considerable assistance from Indonesian auxiliary forces.

[1] See J. C. van Leur, *op. cit.*, p. 164, 189.

Towards the end of the seventeenth century, the Company using its maritime superiority gradually succeeded in dominating the ports on the north coast of Java. In addition, the Company had won a voice in the constant struggles over the succession to the thrones of Mataram and Bantam.

In the Moluccas also, the Company, by not too gentle means, obtained during the seventeenth century a monopoly of the trade in cloves and nutmeg. This led, however, to reactions in the form of what the Dutch called 'smuggling' by Indonesians, Portuguese, Britons, Danes and others. After the Dutch had broken resistance on Banda and Ternate and had forcibly carried through a system of restricted cultivation of these spices, they were obliged to attack Macassar too, which had become an important centre of Moslem resistance to the economic policy of the Company. Many merchants from the north coast of Java, oppressed by the unliberal rule of Mataram, had evacuated to the harbour principality of Macassar, transforming it into a mighty sea power. But during the second half of the seventeenth century Macassar, too, had to surrender to the Dutch.

On the other two big islands, Sumatra and Borneo, the Dutch position remained, however, extremely precarious. In Northern Sumatra Acheh was still a mighty Moslem state, opposing the projects of the Company with success and even expanding its power over the Menangkabau region in the first half of the seventeenth century, until the Dutch got a foothold in Padang.

On the whole it was an achievement for the Dutch even to be able to keep up a few factories for the pepper trade on these huge islands. After the decline of Macassar, the centre of what the Dutch were pleased to call the 'smuggling trade' became Banjermasin on Borneo. To that place the traders ousted from the north coast of Java now emigrated in large numbers. On Sumatra and Borneo there was not yet any question of Dutch superiority, military or political. Anything like Dutch domination of the archipelago was still a long way off.

During the eighteenth century the picture in the so-called 'outposts', later called the Outer Islands, hardly changed. If anything, the Dutch power on those islands was declining,[1] especially when the British became formidable competitors along the west coast of Sumatra, with Bengkulen as their stronghold. The Dutch Company restricted itself to maintaining factories indispensable for trade and for keeping their monopoly system on Java and in the Moluccas. A number of Indonesian harbour princes made use of Dutch sea power to prop up their authority, while others followed the policy of attacking the Dutch position by fostering piracy.

On Java, however, the Company achieved a consolidation of its power. About 1750 it succeeded in bringing under its control the areas around the great seaports of Semarang and Surabaya. A change had taken place there in the relation between the Company and the Eastern chiefs. The days when Company officials had had to humiliate themselves in order to participate in the Eastern commerce were now long past. At the end of the seventeenth century the Company stood on a level with the other harbour principalities of the Southeast Asia region. It would not be long before the Company replaced the kings of Mataram as a suzerain for great parts of Java. The local nobility, the so-called regents, would henceforth pay tribute to the Governor-General, as they had done towards the *Sunan*[2] of Mataram in earlier times.

The Company's power now extended over the Preanger plateau in Western Java, the regents in this area being also tributary to the Governor-General. In this region the Company fostered the cultivation of coffee, which it had introduced, thus coming into closer contact with the population, though it still largely made use of Indonesian officialdom as an intermediary.

The state of Mataram had been steadily weakened in a series of wars of succession, in which the Company intervened time and again. As a result, in the middle of the century, the kingdom disintegrated into three inland-states, the future 'Principalities' of Surakarta (Solo), Jogjakarta and Mangkunagaran.

[1] See J. C. van Leur, *op. cit.*, p. 274.

[2] *Sunan* or *Susuhunan* is the Javanese title of the king.

At this time the Dutch already completely dominated the north coast of Java. There they used by preference the Chinese whom they had imported in great numbers as labourers throughout the seventeenth century, as intermediaries in their intercourse with the Javanese population. There was even a time when Chinese influence threatened to grow beyond the Company's control. In 1740 the tensions in Batavia led to a notorious massacre in which many Chinese lost their lives. Nevertheless, towards the end of the eighteenth century the influence and power of the Chinese along the north coast of Java was as great as it had been before.[1]

In those years the power of the Dutch was declining, largely as the result of changes in Europe. The Netherlands Republic had not been able to keep pace with the British and French in economic, political and military power, and even in maritime power the Netherlands had lagged far behind England. This was demonstrated by the war of 1780–1781, in which the Dutch fleet was all but decimated. It was not developments in Asia but those in Europe that doomed the Company. But the situation in Asia felt the impact of the shifts of power in Europe. When the Dutch were defeated at sea the Indonesian harbour principalities outside Java seized the opportunity of causing trouble to the Company by fostering piracy at an increasing rate. The time when the Company could pay high profits to the shareholders had long passed. The political structure of the Company no longer met the requirements of an efficient administration. But the final overturn of the Company system came about as a direct consequence of the French Revolution.

2 *The archipelago during the nineteenth century*

In 1795 the United Republic of the Netherlands came to an end. The political structure of the Netherlands underwent great changes, in the course of which the federal constitution was re-

[1] See for example T. S. Raffles, *The history of Java*, London, 1817, Vol. I, p. 224.

placed by a unitary structure. In this process the Dutch increasingly came under French influence, until in 1810 the Netherlands were incorporated within the Napoleonic Empire.

Though the call for liberty, equality and fraternity echoed but faintly in the Indies, the political structure of the Dutch possessions there was strongly influenced by developments in Europe. The 'Batavian Republic' sponsored by the French had in 1799 put an end to the Company's charter, and taken over its possessions.

The core of French power policy was to build in Asia a counterweight against British influence. At the turn of the century the archipelago had become involved in a struggle between Britain and France. The Britons clearly demonstrated their supremacy and took possession of a great portion of the Outer Islands. Among the Indonesian princes and chiefs the British looked, not in vain, for allies in their struggle against the Dutch and French. Napoleon sent his confidant, the Dutch officer Daendels, as Governor-General to the Indies with the task of organising the defence of Java. The few years of Daendels' rule were of great importance for Java's future, because of the steps he took to introduce a modern system of administration. The ruthlessness of his methods procured for him, not without justification, the surname of 'Thundering Marshal'.

In military affairs Daendels' efforts did not meet with success. In 1811 the British, led by the ambitious Thomas Stamford Raffles, succeeded in conquering all Dutch strongholds in the archipelago. The British colonial expansion, largely directed by the rising need for a market felt by a developing young textile industry, had won a victory.

The British interregnum, which lasted from 1811 to 1816, was too short, however, to enable Raffles to carry through his ambitious reform projects. The best-known measure of this able and scholarly administrator was an attempt to leave to the individual peasant the free disposal of the produce of his land, under the obligation of surrendering to the state a proportional part of his rice harvest as a tribute (land tax, called 'land rent'). This attempt to free the landownership of the peasant from its feudal bonds was, however, almost a complete failure. Moreover, Raffles was forced by the stringency of state finances to follow the example set by Daendels in selling large *latifundia* with seigneurial rights to private persons, thus strengthening the feudal system. On the other hand, he continued Daendels' policy of transforming the feudal system of government into a modern Western bureaucratic hierarchy.

After Napoleon's defeat the Netherlands emerged again, as a kingdom including the Southern Netherlands, the present territory of Belgium. Despite strong opposition from Raffles the British decided to restore the colonies in the East to the newly formed kingdom. The Netherlands recovered suzerainty over Java and the Dutch settlements and strongholds in the remainder of the archipelago. The British even withdrew from Sumatra's west coast, after Raffles had attempted in all manner of ways to thwart the Dutch. As compensation they kept the Malay peninsula with the island of Singapore, which Raffles had seized by surprise, as their stronghold. Henceforth the Dutch power in Southeast Asia remained more or less dependent upon the British Empire. Raffles then built Singapore into the emporium of the East. As a port it soon far surpassed Batavia.

Nominally the archipelago had again come under Dutch domination. The re-establishment of Dutch authority was achieved, however, only with great difficulty. The Dutch had suffered a serious loss of prestige with the princes on Java as a result of the French and British interregnums, though both powers had largely made use of the Dutch government apparatus. Moreover, the policy of both Daendels and Raffles, directed towards a restriction of princely authority and an incorporation of the feudal nobility into a hierarchy of officials, which was continued by the Dutch Government after 1816, proved a dangerous one. This policy, based upon modern political views borrowed from Europe, resulted in 1825 in armed resistance on the part of members of the Javanese princely courts, led by the Jogjanese Prince Diponegoro. It took the Dutch five years to bring the Java War to a victorious end. The Principalities of Java were reduced to the position of impotent puppet states with a limited territory. In the course of the five years of war responsible Dutchmen had seriously considered abandoning the island of Java, as the costs of the colony far exceeded its yield.

General Johannes van den Bosch, a confidant of King William I, appointed as Governor-General in 1828, came to the rescue after his arrival on Java in 1830 by introducing a new government system generally designated as the 'culture system'. The core of the system, which was carried into effect over a great part of Java, consisted in creating for the Javanese peasants an obligation to cultivate commercial crops on one-fifth of their land and to deliver the produce to the government. In principle this obligation partially replaced the 'land rent' (land tax) system introduced by Raffles, though in practice the obligations often were cumulated. The regent class was restored by the Dutch to its previous prestige in order to obtain its cooperation with the system. The regents and other native chiefs were rewarded with a share in the yield, and their function became hereditary, which had never been the case under the Javanese hierarchical system.[1] Thus, the traditional authority of the Javanese nobility was henceforth linked with colonial exploitation.

Though the culture system had been introduced by van den Bosch partly as a means of furthering the welfare of the Javanese peasants, it soon degenerated into a complex of oppressive measures serving to assist the Dutch treasury to overcome the losses suffered as a result of the Belgian revolt and secession in 1830. About the middle of the century Java, instead of being an encumbrance, became 'the life-belt on which the Netherlands kept afloat'.

The culture system was introduced at a time when authority over the colony still rested almost completely with the king. After 1848, however, the Dutch bourgeoisie represented in Parliament gained a significant voice in colonial affairs. The bourgeoisie, which had been able to build up considerable capital

[1] B. Schrieke, *op. cit.*, p. 219 ff.

from the profits derived from the culture system, now looked for investment in the colony. The culture system, which reserved almost all economic activities to the state, was considered an impediment to private enterprise. Moreover, in that period the source of profits from the culture system gradually dried up as a consequence of the increasingly oppressive character of the system, which had caused famines in several regions. The conscience of the Dutch people, awakened by the famous novel *Max Havelaar* by Multatuli (Douwes Dekker), reinforced the campaign of the liberals against the abuses of the culture system. The influence exerted by Parliament resulted in the introduction under Minister de Waal, in 1870 and following years, of the so-called agrarian legislation which gradually abolished forced cultivation and created the base for capital investment in private plantations. In this legislation the Javanese peasant was protected to a certain extent against dispossession by the big entrepreneur, for it was part of the liberal policy to offer to him, too, an opportunity for economic development.

In the course of the nineteenth century the Dutch authority over Java had been increasingly consolidated. There were periodic revolts, small or large, especially in Bantam, where the partisans of the expelled Sultan's family were turbulent for a long time, and received assistance from the opposite shore, the Lampong districts of Sumatra, where the Dutch exercised only nominal authority. Yet on the whole Java could be considered as pacified, from the Dutch point of view, after 1830.

In the Outer Islands, however, Dutch power at the time of the recovery of the colonial possessions was restricted to a few settlements at the periphery. Outside Java and the Moluccas there was no question of real authority. On Sumatra and the adjoining smaller islands the Dutch had a few fortified factories, of which the most important were those in Padang on the west coast and in Palembang on the east coast. A Dutch administration in the interior was completely out of question. On Borneo one could mention, with a great amount of optimism, footholds in Pontianak on the west coast and Banjermasin on the southeast coast. In the Celebes the Dutch possessed strongholds in Macassar and Menado and in the Lesser Sundas on the island of Timor (in Kupang), all of them mainly serving to fortify Dutch authority over the Moluccas. That was the extent of Dutch authority.

There was, in fact, no great enthusiasm for territorial expansion among the Dutch during the nineteenth century. Dutch policy aimed for a time at concentrating all energy on Java, which had become, since 1830, the source of high profits. Only under the pressure of events in the field of external policy were the Dutch gradually induced to fortify their positions scattered over the archipelago and to replace a merely nominal authority by a real administration. When this involved military expeditions demanding considerable sums and a significant number of men, they tried to evade the necessity as long as possible. This was even the case when Indonesian harbour princes of their own accord offered the sovereignty to the Dutch, in order to secure their titles against other pretenders, against foreign powers and against the discontent among their own peoples.

In the second quarter of the century the Dutch were forced by British claims to extend their power on Sumatra. The most important Dutch expeditions were dispatched to assist the *adat* chiefs in Menangkabau against the strict Moslem party of *Padris*. Here as elsewhere the Dutch took the side of the feudal nobility and propped up its authority. The result of the prolonged Padri War, which blazed up periodically from 1821 to 1845, was the first expansion deeper into the interior of Sumatra. The Dutch got a foothold in the Padang plateau and there succeeded in carrying through the forced cultivation of coffee. Coffee cultivation also spread to the Minahasa in North Celebes.

Further expansion, however, followed only when the Dutch had realised, after Raja Brooke's exploit in North Borneo, the danger of contenting themselves with only nominal authority. Besides, the proximity of the Lampong region at one side of Java, and of Bali and Lombok at the other, caused some uneasiness about the security of the possession of Java. An important factor in bringing about a change in the Dutch attitude was the discovery or supposition of the presence in several regions of minerals which could be profitably exploited. Coal mines in Central Sumatra, tin mines in Bangka and Billiton, gold mines in West Borneo, coal mines in Southeast Borneo became incentives for a more active colonial policy. In the course of the third quarter of the century Dutch authority over the southern part of Sumatra was strengthened, while the islands along the east coast were also brought more effectively under Dutch sway.

On Borneo the establishment of real power demanded heavier struggles. In the interior of Western Borneo the real power over the mine regions was in the hands of Chinese 'secret societies'. However, the intervention of the Dutch by force, which incidentally had little if any justification, not only put an end to the existence of the societies, but also inflicted a death blow on the mining business in that region. Since that time the Chinese in Western Borneo have applied themselves to agriculture.

In Southeast Borneo the Dutch also had to fight a violent war, known as the 'Banjermasin War'. The struggle resulted in an abolition of the Sultan's authority in Southeast Borneo and in a direct administration of the fertile Hulu Sungei lands farther inland by the Dutch. All such expeditions demonstrated that the Indonesian harbour principalities, when it came to the test, were no longer a match for a Western power. The internal structure of these states proved to weak to meet the requirements of modern times. At critical moments the chiefs could hardly count upon the cooperation of the people, who as a rule were considered by them as no more than objects for exploitation. The Dutch policy towards those potentates was far from consistent. At times they maintained these feudal princes in their authority provided that the Dutch sovereignty was acknowledged. In other cases, however, they simply pushed the native authority aside. And though in that period the Dutch hardly practised a positive welfare policy, the creation of a measure of peace and order, combined with a campaign against the worst abuses of feudal rule, often gained for them the obedience and in some cases even a certain amount of goodwill from the population.

As long as compulsory services, taxes and commercial restrictions did not weigh too heavily the *Pax Neerlandica* meant a significant improvement when compared with the former feudal conditions. Only where the Dutch were tempted to exploit intensively an abundant supply of labour or to encroach drastically upon native land rights, as on the densely populated island of Java, did the colonial regime prove a heavy burden.

To the north of Sumatra the sultanate of Acheh had still held its own, though it had lost much of its ancient glory. In the London Treaty of 1824 the Dutch had promised the British to respect the integrity of that state. Gradually, however, the situation changed, for Acheh became a threat to international shipping through the support of pirates based on its territory. The importance of this argument increased when the shipping route had shifted, after the opening of the Suez Canal, from the Strait of Sunda to the Strait of Malacca. The Dutch about that time introduced an open door policy with respect to their colony, but this implied for them an obligation to protect the trade routes as effectively as possible, which coincided with the interests of the British. Moreover, other powers, among them the United States, had already made preparations for further contacts with the state of Acheh. Under these circumstances the British preferred the Dutch as their neighbours.

The interest of the Dutch and others in North Sumatra was, moreover, enhanced by the prospects for capital investment on a large scale in Deli, where conditions seemed favourable for all kinds of cultivation. In addition, Protestant missions made headway not only in the Minahasa (in North Celebes) but in the Batak country as well, where they paved the way for a deeper penetration of Dutch influence. This missionary activity was used as a supplementary argument for fortifying Dutch authority over the interior of the Batak country.

In 1871 the Netherlands stipulated in the so-called Sumatra Treaty with England a free hand with regard to Acheh. The next year witnessed the start of a military expedition which only twenty-five years later, after an extremely strenuous struggle involving heavy sacrifices of financial resources and human lives, resulted in a final Dutch victory. Only after the Dutch had decided, upon the advice of Snouck Hurgronje, to make a deal with the *adat* chiefs in order to disengage them from the religious leaders, who were to be persecuted unto their remotest hiding places, could Dutch military and technical superiority force a decision.[1]

By achieving Acheh's surrender the Netherlands had more or less secured its colonial possessions at the turn of the century. Until then the resistance that it had met and, in the long run, broken every time, had generally been under the command of feudal chiefs or spiritual leaders. The Dutch regime had not only proved superior in a military and technical sense, but also more progressive in social and economic respects. The Netherlands owed their supremacy to the coincidence of these two factors.

3 The twentieth century up to the second World War

Indonesian developments during the first quarter of the twentieth century were strongly affected by the transformation of most Western countries into industrial states. For Java this impact was less clear, its main effect being a new tendency among the industrialists of Twente (a textile centre in the eastern part of the Netherlands) to advocate a policy of improving the purchasing power of the peasantry on that island. Investigations had proved, indeed, that the liberal economic policy inaugurated in 1870 had not achieved an increase of agrarian welfare to Java. On the contrary, the general complaint at the turn of the century was that conditions were deteriorating. Thus humanitarian considerations combined with industrial interests stimulated the introduction, with the assistance of the Dutch Parliament, of a new economic policy, the so-called 'ethical policy', aimed at positive measures for the enhancement of welfare.

The influence of economic developments in the West was, how-

[1] C. Snouck Hurgronje, *The Achehnese*, Leiden, 1906, Vol. I, p. XVI ff. See also his *Verspreide Geschriften* (Collected Writings), Bonn/Leipzig/Leiden, 1923–1927, Vol. IV, Part 1, p. 371 ff.

ever, much more pronounced on the Outer Islands. The industrial world felt an increasing need for raw materials. Consequently, the colonial and imperial policy of the great powers was largely dictated by their wish to lay hands on the sources of those raw materials. Exploration of mineral deposits all over the world and exploitation of all those which promised profits were the order of the day.

The Netherlands joined the race for raw materials. While throughout the nineteenth century Java, by its vegetable products and its manpower, had been the main source of profits, after 1900 attention increasingly switched to the vast fallow areas in the Outer Islands. Moreover, if these areas were neglected, foreign competitors were certain to appear on the scene. It is understandable, therefore, that about 1900, after the successful conclusion of the Acheh War, the Dutch decided to make use of their military strength, liberated now from other tasks, to round off their colonial possessions. It was General van Heutsz, appointed as a Governor-General after his Acheh victories, who energetically undertook the 'pacification' of the Outer Islands in the first decade of this century.

The numerous principalities, scattered over the archipelago, were forced to sign a 'Short Declaration' in which they acknowledged Dutch suzerainty, renounced any contacts with foreign powers and accepted the validity of a significant part of the Netherlands Indian legislation. Some of the greater principalities signed a longer contract with the Netherlands Indian Government approximately to the same effect. This surrender was the only means by which the feudal chiefs could retain a measure of authority over their territory. The Dutch made use of the traditional aura of the Indonesian aristocracy to keep the population subjected and to acquire from these puppets all the concessions and lands they wanted. If they refused, a more obsequious member of the ruling family was recognised as the native ruler. On the other hand, the Dutch used their suzerainty to modernise the rule in the native states in so far as this coincided with their interests.

Even on the remote island of New-Guinea, where Netherlands authority throughout the nineteenth century had been practically restricted to casual visits of warships, at the turn of the century the first administrative posts were established on the coast of the so-called Bird's Head at the northwestern extremity of the huge island. After Germans and Britons had settled on the eastern part of the island, further neglect would no doubt have meant a loss of all claims to the western half.

The most important raw materials of the Outer Islands were for a long time petroleum, mainly on Sumatra and Borneo, and rubber. The latter product accentuated the importance, from the standpoint of foreign interests, of the Eastcoast of Sumatra Residency, where the tobacco cultivation had already led to intensive exploitation. After the necessary concessions had been obtained from the feudal princes, plantation labour was the chief remaining problem. The local population on Sumatra was too sparse and, in general, too prosperous to be useful for this purpose. While during the nineteenth century the coolies on the tobacco plantations had preponderantly been imported from China, after the turn of the century the proportion of immigrants imported from Java greatly increased. The 'penal sanction' system served to tie the labourers shipped from overseas to the plantations for a number of years.

The 'pacification' of the Outer Islands could not be achieved everywhere by persuasion or by favouring the native chiefs. After the Netherlands Indian Army had been freed from its task on Acheh, military expeditions were used to reinforce the Dutch arguments. Jambi in Central Sumatra, Southeast Borneo, South Celebes, Bali, Lombok and several other areas were subjected by violent means. Acheh, too, remained for a long time a trouble spot.

So far the native resistance against the Dutch had been led by feudal chiefs and princes or, as in the *Padri* War and during the later years of the Acheh War, by religious leaders. After 1900, however, a new phenomenon appeared. In harmony with a general tendency in Asian countries political consciousness began to spread to other social classes as well, a development which resulted in a growing resistance against colonial rule. As in other Asian countries, the Japanese victory against the Russians provided a strong incentive towards this new trend. A few years later, in 1908, the first nationalist association on Java, *Budi Utomo*, was called into being. Although this association emanated from a limited group of Westernised young members of the *pryayi* class (the Javanese nobility), and though its objectives were restricted to the cultural field, its main goal being to foster the creation of schools for Indonesians, this event had great importance as a symptom of a growing national consciousness.

A few years later it became clear that this had only been a beginning, and that a far more extensive and vociferous popular movement was coming into being. Before World War I the first signs appeared foreshadowing the end of Dutch colonial rule. In 1912 the Indo-European E. F. E. Douwes Dekker, a great-nephew of Multatuli, created in cooperation with a few Indonesians the first association truly nationalist in its objectives, the so-called 'Indian Party', which aspired to an independent 'India'. The party was prohibited and the leaders were expelled from the country. About the same time a new movement, the *Sarekat Islam*, was organised, largely as a reaction to the growing consciousness among the Chinese inhabitants of Java who had become activated by the revolution in China. Though originally established by a number of Indonesian merchants *Sarekat Islam* soon acquired the character of a mass movement. As it concentrated, during the first years, on activities in the social and economic field, it succeeded, despite the serious misgivings it evoked among colonial Dutchmen, in gaining a measure of recognition from the government.

During World War I and especially after the Russian Revolution *Sarekat Islam* more and more came under radical influence. In some parts of Sumatra this popular movement even combined with feudal resistance against Western rule, as was demonstrated in 1916 when a serious revolt burst out in Jambi.

Meanwhile in the Netherlands, too, a growing number of people advocated more autonomy for the Indies, though the ultimate power of decision would be retained in The Hague. The factors leading to this demand were rather heterogeneous. It was hard to bring the nineteenth century policy of a 'credit balance', which automatically transferred the surplus from the Indian budget to the Dutch treasury, into harmony with the 'ethical' ideology officially accepted since 1900. Moreover, since the beginning of the Acheh War and since a start had been made in abolishing forced cultivation, no single year had resulted in a 'credit balance'. It was logical, therefore, that in the years preceding World War I the finances of the colony were disengaged from those of the mother country. But the generous idea of the initiator of the 'ethical policy', the liberal lawyer C. Th. van Deventer, of restoring to the Indies the millions poured into the Dutch treasury during the past century as a result of the culture system, did not find acceptance.

A new spur to the economic independence of Indonesia was provided by World War I. As a result of the interruption of communications with the mother country, Indonesia now had to fabricate many products formerly imported from Europe, or to order them from other countries such as the United States and Japan.

In the political field there was also a growing tendency to grant greater autonomy to organs in the colony. With the state activity rapidly increasing, a desire arose for greater decentralisation of power within Indonesia. The situation in which the Governor-General and, consequently, the Minister of Colonies were responsible to the Dutch Parliament for anything happening in the archipelago was no longer tenable. Besides, the private interests which had gained influence in the colony since the abolition of the culture system wanted to have a voice in political affairs, as did the bourgeoisie in the mother country. At first, the citizens striving for representation were mainly the Netherlanders, including the Eurasians, living in the colony, but in later years granting a measure of autonomy was considered as a means of giving the more educated Indonesians some experience in local administration without threatening the overall colonial structure.

Thus in the course of the early decades of this century representative bodies were created, at first only for the smaller territorial units. During World War I, however, the government was compelled by the growing tide of nationalism combined with international political factors to hasten the extension of the representative system to the sphere of the central government. In 1917 the Volksraad was created, and although it was given advisory power only, it exerted from the beginning a remarkable influence on colonial policy. The expectation of far-reaching reforms, evoked by a speech delivered in the Volkraad by the far-sighted, internationally oriented Governor-General van Limburg Stirum under the impact of the tremendous growth of revolutionary forces all over the world, was not fulfilled, however. The post-war conservative cabinets in the Netherlands did not feel inclined to give up any essential part of their control over the colony. Though the term 'Colonies' was left out of the Dutch constitution in 1922, and some political reforms were effectuated, such as granting co-legislative power to the Volksraad, in fact in all important matters, as for instance in the budgetary field, the final decisive power was left in hands of the Dutch Government. And in so far as the decisions were delegated to organs in Indonesia, the key positions were secured by the group of colonial Dutchmen, who could be considered more or less as outposts of Dutch colonial power. Despite the establishment of representative bodies the administration of the native population remained preponderantly in the hands of the indigenous feudal class, the traditional pillars of colonial authority, under the supervision of their Dutch chiefs.

It is, therefore, understandable that the political reforms failed to satisfy the Indonesian political leaders. In the post-war years the popular movement drew inspiration from the Russian Revolution. *Sarekat Islam* came under the strong influence of radical socialists, who were also organised in a group which in 1920 became the Indonesian Communist Party. Trade unionism also made headway in these years, and strikes, both in urban enterprises and in the sugar factories, spread rapidly in the early twenties. But there were also moderate currents, which were apparent within *Sarekat Islam* as well. In 1921 a schism in this organisation led to the expulsion of the leftist elements. In consequence, the organisation lost most of its adherents, mass activity being in those years under strong communist influence.

The government took increasingly rigorous action against the radical wing and against the numerous strikes by adopting new penal provisions and by sending the leaders into exile. Driven into a corner, the communists more and more resorted to illegal action. In November 1926 ill-organised and abortive local insurrections broke out in several places on Java, *e.g.* in the western province of Bantam and in the capital at Batavia, which the government had little difficulty in suppressing. A more extensive revolutionary movement occurred in Menangkabau (west coast of Sumatra) in January 1927, but this also was easily suppressed, though by rather bloody means. The government reacted to these disturbances by exiling over a thousand Indonesians to Boven Digul, a dreaded detention area in Western New-Guinea. For the first time the Netherlands had a use for its colonial power over half of that huge island.

The failure of both the Moslem and the socialist popular movement paved the way, however, for a new current presenting itself as truly nationalist in character. Soon the youthful Ir. (engineer) Sukarno, president of the newly established *Partai Nasional Indonesia* and a formidable orator, became the most popular leader.

According to official pronouncements the Dutch Government was not opposed in principle to the nationalist idea, but it soon appeared that the movement would be allowed only a limited opportunity for expression and action. A distinction was made between loyal nationalism and revolutionary nationalism, and stern action was taken against the latter. In practice all the groups which, following the example set by the Indian Congress Party, had accepted the principle of non-cooperation with the Dutch administration, and whose members consequently refused to hold office in the administration or in representative bodies, were considered disloyal and persecuted. The stringent measures directed especially against these non-cooperative organisations were reinforced under the reactionary Governor-General de Jonge (1931–1936). The nationalist leaders Tjipto Mangunkusumo, Sukarno, Mohammad Hatta and Soetan Sjahrir were successively interned. In this way the government succeeded in silencing the most vehement nationalist opposition for a time. The more moderate leaders, among whom the most prominent were Dr. Sutomo, Thamrin, Ki Hadjar Dewantoro and Haji Agus Salim, could continue their work, though they, too, had to face many impediments. Sutomo, in particular, followed the policy of strengthening the economic position of the Indonesians and furthering their education and technical skill as a condition for achieving political independence.

In the strictly political field nationalist activity was severely hampered during the depression of the early thirties, largely as a result of drastic repressive measures taken by the Netherlands Indian Government. Except for a mutiny on a Dutch man of war in 1933, which was occasioned by economic rather than by political factors, those years were remarkably quiet. In that period the fight for greater independence was directed to other, less dangerous objects. The moderate nationalists increasingly applied themselves to fostering indigenous activity in the economic field. An Indonesian bank was organised, efforts were made to create an Indonesian middle class, all kinds of cooperatives were established, a farmers' union was founded, women's organisations and youth movements prospered. Autonomous cultural activity was also of great importance. There were efforts to build a national language, the *Bahasa Indonesia* (the Indonesian language, a modernised Malay), and to create an Indonesian literature, but the foundation of national schools deserves particular mentioning. In 1932 a strong nationalist movement under Dewantoro's leadership, by threatening to use the weapon of passive resistance, successfully blocked the attempts of de Jonge's administration to establish a preventive supervision over this national education.[1]

For the rest, it would be difficult to find a field where Indonesian aspirations for independence were not in evidence. For example, the hope of the colonial government to secure obedient subjects by promoting Christian missions in a number of regions, proved abortive. Within the churches the young Indonesian Christians, including a number of parsons, increasingly opposed the authority of the older European missionaries, thus adding a new aspect to the Indonesian fight for greater autonomy.[2] All movements among non-Christian groups found a parallel among Christians. Nationalist feelings were no less strong among many Christian groups than among non-Christians, sometimes even stronger, for Christians feared that they might be regarded as pro-Dutch tools of the colonial government.

In some fields, however, aspirations for autonomy were hampered by contrary tendencies. Though the wish for greater independence from the mother country was not restricted to Indonesians, since many local Dutchmen also disapproved of Netherlands interference with local affairs, actual developments were largely in the opposite direction. The improvement of communications, particularly greater use of the telegraph, resulted in more intensive interference by the home government in the daily affairs of the colony. This applied not only to the government policy, inasmuch the Minister of Colonies was now able to supervise the Governor-General more closely than in the past, but to private business as well, for directors located in Europe left but little scope for autonomous activity by their representatives in the East.

During the few years preceding World War II it became increasingly clear that internal conditions in Indonesia would be

[1] See for the thirties J. M. Pluvier, *Overzicht van de ontwikkeling der nationalistische beweging in Indonesië in de jaren 1930 tot 1942* (Outline of the development of the nationalist movement in Indonesia 1930–1942), The Hague/Bandung, 1953.

[2] Cf. A. J. van Zanen, *Voorwaarden voor maatschappelijke ontwikkeling in het centrale Batakland* (Conditions for social development in the central Batak area), Leiden, 1934, p. 71 ff.

strongly affected by external developments. During the depression economic penetration by the Japanese made rapidly headway, and the cheap Japanese imports threatened to disrupt the economic apparatus built up by Westerners. In its attempt to defend Western interests the Netherlands Indian Government to a large extent relinquished its traditional open door policy. By economic legislation and detailed regulation of foreign enterprise in shipping and other fields the government sought to counter Japanese penetration, to the advantage of Dutch and other Western interests, especially those of the British Empire, which still exerted considerable influence on the archipelago via Singapore.

As the preparations for war advanced the nationalist movement split: one branch sympathised with the Japanese and the other regarded fascism and related political ideologies as a greater danger than Dutch colonial rule. This division more or less replaced the former distinction between cooperators and non-cooperators. Both groups were inclined towards collaboration with the colonial government, since non-cooperation had proved ineffective, but the more radical groups, which formerly had been the strongest advocates of non-cooperation, were now the most willing to cooperate with the Western democracies. Both branches, however, combined forces in a campaign for an Indonesian Parliament, chosen directly by the people and endowed with real, decisive powers. This strong unitary front was a new and extremely important phenomenon in the nationalist movement.

A practical occasion for cooperation with the government seemed to present itself when the Germans invaded the Netherlands in May 1940. The nationalists expected that the Netherlands Government would meet their demands to a large extent, in order to increase its strength against Germany. However, the Netherlands Government, which had emigrated to London during the German invasion, shrank from any radical reform, as it had done repeatedly before, for example when it had rejected in 1938 a proposal made by the moderate nationalist Sutardjo, and accepted by the Volksraad, to convene a Round Table Conference. Nor did it adopt the nationalist suggestion that it should arm the

Indonesian people and give Indonesians a voice in the use of the army, since the colonial government feared, not without reason, that the Indonesians, once armed, would turn against its authority.

Thus the Netherlands Indian Government awaited, practically unprepared, the outburst of the Pacific War. The solidarity with the Allied Powers demonstrated immediately after Pearl Harbour by a declaration of war on the Japanese was a noble gesture, but it could be foreseen that the Japanese would not have much difficulty in conquering the archipelago. Though the Dutch Navy fought gallantly, the Japanese operations on land had the appearance of a field exercise, resulting in a serious loss of prestige for the Dutch. In Acheh a revolt had broken out even before the arrival of the Japanese, wiping out Dutch authority.

4 *Japanese occupation, revolution and after*

It would be interesting to draw a comparison between the British occupation of Java in Raffles' time (1811–1816) and the Japanese occupation from 1942 to 1945. When one considers the significance of the impact of Raffles' temporary rule, although he left the Dutch administrative apparatus largely intact, one can imagine the devastating effects of the Japanese typhoon, which wiped out the whole Dutch apparatus and replaced it by a Japanese military administration, assisted by an Indonesian officialdom.

Among many Indonesians there was at first a tendency to greet the Japanese as liberators from colonial domination. It soon appeared, however, that the Japanese did not intend to grant freedom to the Indonesians.[1] The wealth of raw materials in the islands tempted the Japanese to transform Indonesia into a Japanese colony. Not only was the archipelago divided by the *Zaibatsu*, the big Japanese family trusts, into spheres of influence, but the military administration also disrupted the unity of the territory, Java coming within the jurisdiction of the Army Commander in Jakarta, Sumatra first under the Army Commander

[1] See Willard H. Elsbree, *Japan's role in Southeast Asian nationalist movements 1940 to 1945*, Cambridge (Mass.), 1953, p. 22 ff.

in Singapore (Shonan), and later on under separate command, whereas Borneo and the Great East were allotted to the Naval Command. Though each military division was under the centralised authority of Tokyo and the general principles applied in the various territories were largely the same, yet this division stood in the way of the nationalist unitary forces.

In the beginning the national movement was obstructed by the Japanese as far as possible. But their primary aim was to make the population participate in the war effort, consequently, the popular leaders were soon called to prominent posts without, however, being allowed to carry on nationalist propaganda. Several leaders lent themselves to this policy, partly perhaps out of personal ambition, but many of them also, no doubt, with a view to keep and strengthen their grip on the popular movement in order to achieve their national ideals in a not too remote future. For the time being, however, their propaganda had to suit the stereotyped Japanese pattern: a struggle to the death side by side with the Japanese, for a Greater East Asia under Japanese leadership.

As a result of the turning tides of war the Japanese were, however, forced increasingly to meet nationalist aspirations. The advance of the American fleet touched only the periphery of the archipelago, a series of bombings in the eastern part of it (on Ambon and Macassar) being the most noteworthy military operations Indonesia experienced directly. Not until the spring of 1945 were a few important strategic points (the oil centres of Tarakan and Balikpapan along the east coast of Borneo) occupied by Allied units.

The indirect influence of the Japanese defeats was far more lasting. Allied submarines increasingly impeded the Japanese overseas communications and even isolated the separate islands from each other. The Indonesian economy was made more and more subservient to the aims of Japanese warfare, by a ruthless system of forced deliveries of the rice surplus and other crops, leading to a complete disintegration of economic life. Indonesian manpower was also exploited by the Japanese to the utmost, not only for the construction of roads and military works, but also to reinforce their military strength. They did what the Dutch colonial regime had never dared to do: they furnished the Indonesians with arms on a large scale and taught them how to use them. But in order to obtain the cooperation of the Indonesians with their war effort Japan had to grant ever larger concessions in the political field. The Philippines and Burma had already received promises of a future independence. After the tides of war changed these promises were, nominally at least, fulfilled. Developments in Indonesia could not lag too far behind.

Thus in 1944 advisory councils were set up, whose members were Indonesians, but whose power did not even equal that of the pre-war Volksraad and regional or local councils.

Soon, however, the Japanese accelerated the process leading to independence. At first, in their promises of post-war independence they attempted to keep the various territories separated. Java was bound to go through the successive stages at a faster rate than Sumatra; the eastern parts of the archipelago lagged far behind. But shortly before their surrender the Japanese were forced to speed up the process of independence and to grant freedom in the area desired by the Indonesian nationalists: the whole of Indonesia.[1] On the 15th of August 1945, the preparations were already far advanced.

In this way the Japanese occupation in the long run stimulated national consciousness. But the spiritual impact of the occupation went farther. Indonesian thought and sentiment had been deeply influenced by the abrogation and denunciation of what democratic freedoms had existed before the war, by the terror of the Japanese secret police (*Kempeitai*), by the regimentation of the press and of all kinds of associations, by the coercion to which all economic and cultural activities were subjected, and, last but not least, by the militarisation of the youth. Not only were Indonesians affected by an anti-democratic and anti-Western attitude, but

[1] See W. H. Elsbree, *op. cit.*, p. 114 ff.; see also K. A. de Weerd, *The Japanese occupation of the Netherlands Indies.* Prepared Statement International Prosecution Section, Netherlands Division at the International Military Tribunal Far East, 1946. Process Document 2750.

Japanese rule, especially after economic pressure and labour compulsion had claimed an ever heavier toll of Indonesian endurance, met with increasing resistance on the part of the Indonesian population. In the first days of the occupation an underground resistance movement had sprung up, largely under left-wing leadership, and in later years it gained considerable strength. In 1944 the desire for emancipation from Japanese rule had become general, and despite rigorous repression, opposition blazed up openly here and there. Insurrections in the strictly Moslem region of Tasikmalaya (Western Java), and a mutiny of Indonesian military units in Blitar (Eastern Java) are the best known instances.

But the growing discontent with the Japanese did not mean that the Indonesians longed for the return of their old masters. On the contrary, it was their greatest reproach to the Dutch that they had left the Indonesians undefended against the horrors which had overtaken the country.

Since the Japanese surrender Indonesia has attracted considerable international attention. And for the first time Indonesians were taking the lead.

A popular movement in which youthful elements, partly Japanese-trained officers, played a preponderant role, urged Sukarno and Hatta to proclaim on August 17, independently of the Japanese plans and time-table, the Indonesian Republic, of which they were to become the President and Vice-President.[1] As a result of this development an extremely intricate situation arose. The Dutch considered this Republic as a Japanese creation, incompatible with Japanese promises to abstain from any political interference after VJ Day.

Though some of the great powers were, on ideological grounds, not especially anxious to lend their assistance to restoring colonial rule, they had to acknowledge Dutch authority as legal. Thus a

[1] The literature on the birth of the Republic is somewhat contradictory. For example, Moh. Hatta disputes the prominent role claimed by the youth movement in the proclamation of the Republic. See his *Verspreide Geschriften* (Collected Writings), Jakarta/Amsterdam, 1952, p. 330 ff.

parodoxical situation arose, in which the hated Japanese troops remained in control on the instruction of the Allied Command and impeded the Republic's activities as much as possible. The military weakness of the Dutch made them very dependent on their allies for the achievement of their aspirations. On Borneo and in the Great East (including Celebes, the Lesser Sundas, the Moluccas and New-Guinea) they were able to restore their authority to a large degree with the help of Australian troops. But on the islands of Java and Sumatra, which were ultimately under British command, the situation was far more complicated. When arriving on Java, towards the end of September 1945, the Allied Commander, Sir Philip Christison, quite aware of the delicate position of the British, issued a declaration defining the British task as limited to disarmament of the Japanese and liberation of the Allied prisoners of war and internees, his proclamation could be interpreted as an acknowledgement of the *de facto* authority of the Republic.

Meanwhile a revolutionary constellation of forces was developing. At several places Indonesian fighting groups succeeded, sometimes after bloody clashes, in getting possession of Japanese arms. The Republic received moral and even some practical support from abroad, for example from Australian dock workers. When it became clear that British and British Indian troops were preparing for a return of the Dutch, heavy fighting broke out, culminating in the great struggle at Surabaya in October-November 1945, in which the Republican Army vainly tried to wrest the city from the hands of the British forces. Java became the scene of terrorism which claimed many victims on both sides, the worst atrocities occurring in clashes between pro-Republican gangs of Indonesians and pro-Dutch fighting units of Eurasians and Ambonese.

Towards January 1946 the British, assisted by the Dutch, occupied a few large cities, mainly on Java's north coast, while the Republican Government had shifted its seat to Jogjakarta and was attempting to consolidate its authority over the interior of Java.

On Sumatra the idea of freedom also gained ground. The few

places held by Allied troops were but tiny islands in a pro-Republican sea. In several parts of Sumatra, however, the popular movement was not directed primarily against the Dutch, who were still remote, but against the feudal chiefs who had formerly looked for support of their pretensions to the Dutch colonial empire, and later to the Japanese occupying forces. A bloody social revolution broke out in December 1945 and the following months, first in Acheh, then in the plantation area of Sumatra's Eastcoast Residency (where the native rulers had derived great profits from their concessions to the European plantation enterprises), and at last, in a mitigated form, in Menangkabau. As a result, the power of the feudal aristocracy came to an end and many members of the rulers' families lost their lives.[1] Moreover, in the Great East, especially in Southwest Celebes and Bali, a strong pro-Republican movement arose, which the Dutch attempted to suppress without pity, the adventurer Captain Raymond Westerling, nicknamed 'the Turk', playing a very unattractive role.

Meanwhile, within the Republic a moderate wing had risen to power led by the democratic socialist Soetan Sjahrir, who attempted to come to an agreement with the Dutch. A lengthy period of laborious negotiations followed, in which foreign powers played a mediating role. The Dutch Government was now ready, after many months of kicking against the pricks, to bow to facts and to acknowledge the Republic within certain limits. But they wished to restrict the Republic's territory as much as possible. To this end Lieutenant-Governor-General Hubertus van Mook conceived his 'Malino policy', called after a conference held in 1946 in the recreation centre Malino on Celebes, which aimed at creating beside the Republic a number of equivalent states. The state of East Indonesia, with Macassar as its capital, was to become the greatest and most important of these.

[1] See for Acheh: A. J. Piekaar, *Atjeh en de oorlog met Japan* (Acheh and the war against Japan), The Hague/Bandung, 1949, p. 250; for Sumatra's Eastcoast Residency: George McT. Kahin, *Nationalism and revolution in Indonesia*, Ithaca, 1952, p. 179 ff.

In this way the political unity brought about by Dutch authority bade fair to be replaced, at the final stage of colonial rule, by a federal system which was easier for the Dutch to handle. To Indonesian nationalists this policy looked like one of divide and rule, and the Malino states appeared to them to be puppet states, by means of which the Dutch were seeking to maintain part of their power with the support of the feudal classes against whom the popular movement had revolted.

The real fight did not flare up until after the departure of the British towards the end of 1946, when the Dutch had succeeded in building up an army of about 100.000 men and felt confident of imposing their conditions on the Indonesians. Besides the political pressure of the Malino fabric the Republic experienced the economic pressure of the blockade effected by the Dutch Navy. On the other hand, the Republic, which dominated the countryside of Java, applied counter-measures by impeding the transport of foodstuffs to the coastal towns held by the Dutch. The negotiations failed, and on July 21, 1947, the Netherlands began their military attack, labelled 'police action' to prevent international interference.

But the Dutch had misjudged the forces abroad. Though the Dutch Army succeeded in conquering a number of important areas on Java and Sumatra, among them the huge plantation area along Sumatra's east coast and several plantation areas on Java, the Republic was able to reinforce its international position. The Security Council of the United Nations Organization, in which the views of the Asian and Latin-American powers sympathising with the Republic had a considerable influence, acknowledged the Republic as a full-fledged party to the dispute, while the representatives of the Malino states were not admitted to the sessions. The United States acquired an increasing influence over developments through the Committee of Good Offices set up by the Security Council.

Foreign affairs also affected the internal policy of the Republic. The leftist government in power until the end of 1947 was replaced by a more rightist cabinet under Hatta, leaning preponderantly upon the Moslem *Masjumi* party. In the course of 1948 the struggle between these two trends within the Republic led to the so-called communist revolt of Madiun in East Java, which was probably more or less provoked by anti-communist elements.[1] The revolt was a serious threat to the unity of the Republic, but it was all but suppressed by the government towards the end of 1948.

The Dutch attempt to annihilate the Republic in the last days of 1948 by a second military action, notwithstanding the government's defeat of the communists, was a complete fiasco. Though they succeeded without great difficulty, albeit by bloody means, in occupying Jogjakarta and practically all the other towns on Java, and a not insignificant part of Sumatra, this proved to be a pyrrhic victory. The Republican troops, knowing their weakness, avoided any open battle and retired to the mountains from which they were able to harass the Dutch Army and to carry on an exhausting guerrilla war. As the Dutch dominated only the towns, but not the countryside, their communication lines were extremely unsafe. Moreover, large numbers of Indonesian officials, led by the Sultan of Jogjakarta, Hamengku Buwono, who had taken a prominent part in the revolution, refused to cooperate with the Dutch, who thus found it next to impossible to govern the country.

Moreover, the former allies of the Dutch, the rulers of the Malino states, by no means desired the complete annihilation of the Republic and the arrest of its leaders. They, too, felt the pressure of the popular movement; moreover many of them were, in their own way, nationalists. They were afraid lest the Dutch, after having done away with the Republic, would rob them of what real power was left. The existence of the Republic was for them, too, a source of strength.

In the international field, also, the Dutch encountered far more difficulty than they had expected. The Security Council forced them eventually to re-establish the Republic as a political whole,

[1] See G. McT. Kahin, *op. cit.*, p. 272 ff., and in particular p. 288 ff.

to release its leaders and to negotiate with them. Thus the Dutch had no choice but to agree, at the Round Table Conference held in The Hague in 1949, to the formation of the sovereign United States of Indonesia, connected with the Dutch Kingdom by a Union.

But this was not the end. The status of Western New-Guinea remained undecided, the Dutch provisionally retaining *de facto* authority. It is still a bone of contention between the Netherlands and Indonesia, in which Australia supports the Dutch claims, while the United States is also interested on account of strategic considerations.

Many new problems also arose. The federal structure had been accepted under strong pressure from the Dutch. The Republic, with Jogjakarta as its capital, had become only a part of the federation, albeit a very populous and essential part. But there were also ten other states, of which East Indonesia was the most important. When the Dutch troops were successively returned to Holland, some of the Malino states tried to create a small army of their own, consisting of former units of the Dutch East Indian forces.

The federation seemed too much like a Dutch creation and had too many features of Dutch origin to satisfy the victorious Indonesian nationalists. It soon appeared that the political leaders looked upon the federal structure as a temporary arrangement which should disappear as soon as possible. Units of the Republican Army were dispatched to the various islands, where they released the politicians kept in prison and thus acted as pioneers for the abrogation of one state after another in a way which was rather different from the procedure foreseen at the Round Table Conference.

On August 17, 1950, at the fifth anniversary of the Proclamation of the Republic, the unitary state, henceforth called the Republic of Indonesia, became a fact. Its establishment was accompanied, however, by serious clashes, in Western Java and on Celebes. Resistance lasted longest in the Moluccas, where a great number of Ambonese soldiers, the 'Cossacks' of the former colonial regime, were involved. In fact, a 'Republic of the South Moluccas' was set up, which tried to secure international recognition and may have received help from abroad; it was not defeated until 1952, and even in later years local disturbances occurred now and then.

The resistance of the so-called *Darul Islam* movement, which is concentrated in Western Java and some parts of Central Java, is still more serious. It has important ramifications in Acheh, and in South Celebes where local resistance to Javanese troops started as early as 1950. It originated in fighting groups which formerly opposed the Dutch and which are dissatisfied with the Republic in its present form. Though Islam has an important place in the Republic, the followers of *Darul Islam* desire an Islamic state, and claim to have created one in the territory which they control.

Darul Islam is one facet of the problem of security in Indonesia. The young state faces many other problems, five of which appear to be of major political significance.

The first of these is that once national unity is achieved, new centrifugal tendencies manifest themselves. The Dutch-sponsored federal structure was abolished as a remnant of feudalism and colonialism, but the desire for regional autonomy and the resistance to Javanese domination has assumed new forms. The Acheh insurrection of 1953, the disorders in South Celebes, and the much larger rebellious movements of 1956 and following years are partly to be attributed to these centrifugal tendencies. It is a question whether political unity in Indonesia has been established with sufficient solidity.

Another major problem is that the situation in Indonesia cannot be isolated from the cold war. The efforts of successive Indonesian governments to carry on, with a measure of success, an independent policy similar to that of some other Asian countries, India in particular, cannot conceal the fact that Indonesia is situated within the American sphere of influence. But on the other hand there is a strong current of sympathy with the Soviet Union, and still more with New China. This current finds support in SOBSI, the largest trade unions federation. In addition the millions of ill-assimilated Chinese, many of them sympathising with New China, form a serious problem, which was hardly alleviated by the Round Table decision conferring the right to Indonesian citizenship upon most of them.

Conflicts between political parties are also strongly influenced by foreign policy, the *Masjumi* party representing, with some reservations, pro-American trends, while the communists take the opposite stand, and the *Partai Nasional Indonesia* and *Nahdatul Ulama* try to keep the middle of the road.

A third very important problem in Indonesia concerns the concept of democracy. A serious endeavour was made to realise a system of parliamentary democracy, but this, as in other Asian countries attempting a similar system, still functions rather imperfectly. Many of the members of the provisional Parliament were appointed, not elected, and general elections were not held before September 1955. It is questionable whether these elections have solved more problems than they have created. For the time being the Parliament in its present shape and the political parties engaged in a fierce fight diverting from constructive work, are considered by many a hindrance rather than a help to efficient administration, creating a temptation for dictatorial intervention, as foreshadowed in the so-called October 17 affair, an abortive attempt by a military group on October 17, 1952, to dissolve the provisional Parliament.

A further threat to democracy, thus, arises from the fact that the army is not yet well integrated within the Indonesian society – a well-known phenomenon in countries which recently achieved independence. A tendency of officers to mingle in political affairs may, in the future, develop into warlordism. Even though such political action may be intended to check political corruption, it creates great dangers of furthering a military dictatorship.

The fourth outstanding problem is the lack of efficiency still prevailing in many branches of government administration. This is only to be expected in view of the colonial past, which was responsible for a serious lack of higher education for Indonesians, and the large-scale exodus of skilled Europeans caused by the political upheaval, the general distrust prevailing between Indonesians and Europeans, and a feeling of insecurity among the European group. As the number of skilled Indonesians is increasing at a remarkable pace, the phenomenon is, no doubt, temporary. It is important, however, in so far as inefficacy thwarts many well-devised measures and adds, moreover, to the feeling of inferiority that pervades, at the moment, many Indonesian circles.

These feelings of frustration are enhanced by general complaints about increasing corruption in the administration. It is not generally understood that this phenomenon, also, is largely to be attributed to relics of a feudal past leading, at present, to conflicting loyalties between duties towards the government and duties towards one's family; but at the same time it is a modern phenomenon in so far as loyalty to political parties or army friends takes sometimes the place of family ties. The growing awareness of corruption as a social ill is, in itself, a favourable phenomenon. Still, the sudden change in the social position of many Indonesians, with consequent difficulties of readjustment to a new standard of living, and the increasing amount of state intervention in economic affairs, often placing excessive powers in the hands of individual officials, together with the disequilibrium caused by war and revolution, may have led to a temporary increase of corruption. It is not sufficiently understood that the fight against corruption cannot be waged successfully by negative means only, such as severe punishment and strict administrative controls. Corruption is essentially a sign of conflicting loyalties pointing primarily to a lack of positive attachment to the government and its ideals. In so far as corruption shows that the new government, with its enormous task to fulfil in the new Asian world, is not yet sufficiently integrated in society and does not evoke full sympathy, enthusiasm and unfaltering loyalty from subjects and officials, it is a sign of weakness of the present political structure.

A fifth problem is, finally, the prevalent distrust of foreigners and foreign influences. This phenomenon may partly be accounted for by past experiences with colonial rule, partly by a feeling of inferiority accompanied by fear of criticism by foreigners. It has healthy aspects in so far as foreign interests may still seriously hamper the development of Indonesian economy, even if they present themselves under the guise of unselfish aid and technical assistance. But in so far as such a distrust leads, among some officials, to an unreasonable xenophobia, it may dangerously affect Indonesian society by ousting or discouraging foreign experts before their services can be dispensed with.

The Dutch colonial empire has come to an end, and 1956 witnessed the decision taken by Indonesia to dissolve its last remnant: the Netherlands-Indonesian Union. But so far the troubles of the Indonesians have been increased rather than alleviated as a result of political freedom. But the difference is that they need no longer to undergo their hardships passively. For the first time in modern history they can play an active part in the solution of their own problems. Moreover, the Indonesian state has shown already that its existence may exert a favourable influence upon international politics. As a member of the United Nations Organization the Republic has, in cooperation with other Asian countries, played an important role during the past years by mediating between the great powers and by contributing, in this way, to the easing of dangerous tensions. The Asian-African Conference, held in Bandung in April 1955, was a remarkable achievement of the young Indonesian Republic.

A short bibliography

Alexandre von Arx, *L'évolution politique en Indonésie de 1900 à 1942*, Fribourg, 1949.

M. A. Aziz, *Japan's colonialism and Indonesia*, The Hague, 1955.

H. T. Colenbrander, *Koloniale geschiedenis* (Colonial history), The Hague, 1925–1926.

Willard H. Elsbree, *Japan's role in Southeast Asian nationalist movements 1940 to 1945*, Cambridge (Mass.), 1953.

J. S. Furnivall, *Netherlands India. A study of plural economy*, Cambridge/New York, 1944.

H. J. de Graaf, *Geschiedenis van Indonesië* (History of Indonesia), The Hague/Bandung, 1949.

George McT. Kahin, *Nationalism and revolution in Indonesia*, Ithaca, 1952.

E. S. de Klerck, *History of the Netherlands East Indies*, Rotterdam, 1938.

D. M. G. Koch, *Om de vrijheid. De nationalistische beweging in Indonesië* (Towards freedom. The nationalist movement in Indonesia), Jakarta, 1950.

H. J. van Mook, *The stakes of democracy in South East Asia*, London, 1950.

J. Th. Petrus Blumberger, *De nationalistische beweging in Nederlandsch-Indië* (The nationalist movement in the Netherlands Indies), Haarlem, 1931.

J. Th. Petrus Blumberger, *Le communisme aux Indes néerlandaises*, Paris, 1929.

A. J. Piekaar, *Atjeh en de oorlog met Japan* (Acheh and the war against Japan), The Hague/Bandung, 1949.

J. M. Pluvier, *Overzicht van de ontwikkeling der nationalistische beweging in Indonesië in de jaren 1930 tot 1942* (Outline of the development of the nationalist movement in Indonesia 1930–1942), The Hague/Bandung, 1953.

G. J. Resink, 'Onafhankelijke vorsten, rijken en landen in Indonesië tussen 1850 en 1910' (Independent rulers, realms and regions in Indonesia between 1850 and 1910), in *Indonesië*, Vol. IX, 1956, p. 265 ff.

G. J. Resink, 'Veronachtzaamde uitspraken' (Neglected utterings), in *Indonesië*, Vol. VIII, 1955, p. 1 ff.

S. J. Rutgers and A. Huber, *Indonesië*, Amsterdam, 1937.

A. Arthur Schiller, *The formation of federal Indonesia 1945–1949*, The Hague/Bandung, 1955.

C. Smit, *De Indonesische quaestie. De wordingsgeschiedenis der souvereiniteitsoverdracht* (The Indonesian question. The origins and history of the transfer of sovereignty), Leiden, 1952.

F. W. Stapel (ed.), *Geschiedenis van Nederlandsch-Indië* (History of the Netherlands Indies), Amsterdam, 1938–1940.

Verslag van de Commissie tot bestudeering van staatsrechtelijke hervormingen (Report of the Commission for the study of political reforms), New York, 1944.

Bernard H. M. Vlekke (ed.), *Indonesia in 1956. Political and economic aspects*, The Hague, 1957.

Bernard H. M. Vlekke, *Nusantara. A history of the East Indian archipelago*, Cambridge (Mass.), 1945.

K. A. de Weerd, *The Japanese occupation of the Netherlands Indies.* Prepared Statement International Prosecution Section, Netherlands Division at the International Military Tribunal Far East, 1946. Process Document 2750.

A. A. Zorab, *De Japanse bezetting van Indonesië en haar volkenrechtelijke zijde* (The Japanese occupation of Indonesia and its international law aspect), Leiden, 1954.

Chapter Five

SHIFTS IN THE ECONOMIC SYSTEM

1 *The historical background*

When the first contacts with the Western world were made, the islands of the Indonesian archipelago were (as they still are) a predominantly agricultural area. Practically everywhere agriculture was the chief means of subsistence, sometimes supplemented by fishing, hunting and food-gathering. Yet there were, as I have already pointed out in Chapter I, great differences of social structure between various regions. In Central Java rice was grown on irrigated fields, the so-called *sawah* cultivation. There were also extensive areas where the population practised a system of 'shifting cultivation' on woodland areas cleared by burning (*ladang*). An almost closed economy was, however, common to both systems. The peasants produced largely for their own needs. There was a certain amount of exchange of products and of labour within the village, largely on a communal, traditional and non-commercial basis.

External trade was not much encouraged by the chiefs, who generally preferred to tax the farmers' produce to the utmost. In consequence there was no strong incentive for the peasant to increase his production. There was on the whole no question of large surpluses, although the rice surplus in the irrigated areas was usually sufficient to support a governing superstructure of Javanese princes, residing with their retinue in the *kraton* (princely court) towns. Consequently, some of the irrigated areas could be integrated into a bureaucratic state with its headquarters in the interior.[1] The princely government not only possessed a supernat-

[1] J. C. van Leur, *Indonesian trade and society. Essays in Asian social and economic history*, Selected studies on Indonesia by Dutch scholars, Vol. I, The Hague/Bandung, 1955, p. 104 ff.

ural significance for its subjects but also undertook certain responsibilities such as the construction and maintenance of irrigation works and roads, the care of internal security and the building up of stores. In return for this the peasants had to deliver their rice surplus in the form of taxes and to render certain services. Irrigated rice culture made possible great concentrations of population, big enough to explain the construction of the splendid Hindu and Buddhist temples as well as the formation of the great armies levied by the seventeenth century state of Mataram.

The fire-cleared *ladang* areas could support only a sparse population, and seldom produce a food surplus. But these extensive areas made it possible to cultivate marketable crops, such as pepper. The profits usually found their way into the pockets of the chiefs instead of benefiting the agrarian population. The merchants in the harbour principalities at the mouths of the great rivers profited most. These coastal towns were usually enclaves in the agrarian economy. They were links between the different islands of the archipelago and between the archipelago and the Asian mainland. But their social structure was no less traditional than elsewhere. The noble families and rich patricians who ruled there owed their power to their control over the surrounding countryside which was cultivated by their serfs, or sometimes by slaves, and to the levying of tolls and harbour fees, accompanied, at times, by piracy. Foreign traders from other Asian countries, living together in separate wards, nation by nation, in the cities, also usually formed communities on pronouncedly traditional lines. The great majority of these traders were small pedlars. Only a small minority of them achieved a somewhat higher social status and joined the patrician class.[1]

2 *Nineteenth century changes*

Up to about the year 1800 there were no fundamental changes in the pattern of economic structure described above. The Western

[1] Cf. the picture of the old merchant cities of Asia as drawn by J. C. van Leur, *op. cit.*, p. 75 ff.

powers which came into contact with the world of the East adapted themselves as well as possible to the existing pattern. The Dutch traders made the most profitable use they could of the traditional economic system by claiming tribute from the Indonesian chiefs. For the peasant this meant only an extra charge levied by the chiefs on his produce.[1] Only by introducing new crops, such as coffee, during the eighteenth century, did the Company from time to time add new incentives to the peasant economy. In general, however, the Company's influence on Indonesian society was not a progressive one. Where it succeeded in upholding a monopoly system it restricted what little economic freedom had previously existed.

A fundamental change came only when, at the beginning of the nineteenth century, the Westerners appeared on the scene in a new guise, in the role of confident organisers. Daendels, Raffles and van den Bosch[2] represented three stages in the process of an ever deepening penetration into the Indonesian economy by Western government and Western economy. The Javanese *desa* (village community) now felt the disturbing consequences of contact with the West. Raffles' 'land rent' (land tax) system was intended to free the peasant from forced deliveries and, by granting him the net yield of his crop, to spur him to higher production. Though Raffles failed to achieve this objective, his innovations were important in establishing the first contacts between the administration and the *desa* chiefs, which were strongly intensified in later years.[3] This was especially true of van den Bosch's 'culture system', which made it compulsory for the population to cultivate crops for the world market and, insofar as it marked a return to the forced deliveries abolished by Raffles, meant nothing less than

[1] See G. Gonggrijp, *Schets ener economische geschiedenis van Indonesië* (Outline of an economic history of Indonesia), Haarlem, 1957, p. 41 ff.

[2] H. W. Daendels, Governor-General 1808–1811; Thomas S. Raffles, Lt. Governor 1811–1816; J. van den Bosch, Governor-General 1830–1832, Commissioner-General, 1832–1833.

[3] See D. H. Burger, *De ontsluiting van Java's binnenland voor het wereldverkeer* (The opening of the interior of Java to world trade), Wageningen, 1939, p. 245.

an economic revolution. The government's impact on *desa* life exceeded by far the influence exerted by native rulers, who in large areas had left the village economy intact. It was in particular the extension of the culture system to *sawahs*, for the purpose of alternating sugar and rice cultivation, that made deep inroads in the village structure. Insofar as private ownership on *sawahs* had existed, the villagers' rights were weakened and the power of the *desa* chief to dispose of the arable land was increased.

Even as early as the first half of the nineteenth century certain consequences of Western penetration began to be evident. In the economic field the most outstanding results were the increase of population in Java and the introduction of a money economy. Both processes were due initially to Western initiative, the role of the Indonesian population being passive. The increase in population was largely the result of Western administrative measures reducing mortality: the construction of roads, vaccination against the much-dreaded smallpox, greater security, provisions to meet the threat of famines. Nor was any spontaneous action on the part of the Indonesians responsible for the fact that life in the interior of Java became involved in a money economy. This was due largely to the sugar factories, established by foreigners, which employed Indonesian labour and thereby set money circulating, in the form of wages, among the population.

This development accelerated during the following phase of economic policy, the so-called Liberal period from 1870 to 1900. The 'agrarian legislation' of the eighteen-seventies, while seeking, on the one hand, to protect the peasants from dispossession on the part of foreigners, at the same time opened the way for investment of Western capital in private agricultural undertakings on a large scale. It was in this period that the sugar, coffee, tea and cinchona plantations were developed in Java and the tobacco plantations in Deli. Private firms could now lease the irrigated rice fields from the Indonesian owners for the cultivation of sugar cane in rotation with the rice grown by the natives. This process led to a further weakening of the native ownership of land, for it was in the interests of the sugar planters to regard the village areas as one single unit, and the village communities as public corporations, owning the land on a communal basis, so that they were obliged to deal only with the *desa* chiefs, instead of with each landowner individually. The Indonesian peasantry enjoyed incomes in the form of rents paid by the plantation owner and could also earn something more on the plantations as daily wage earners or seasonal workers. Many farmers could find work, too, on the so-called mountain plantations where coffee, tea and cinchona were grown on formerly uncultivated ground let out on long-term leases by the government.

But Western economic penetration was not limited to the cultivation of market crops. The rise of industry in Western Europe caused producers to seek markets in tropical countries for cheap mass-produced goods. British industry began the process and the Dutch followed suit. The import of printed cotton goods from the Dutch industrial area of Twente supplanted the native weaving home industry and drove the Javanese peasant still further along the way towards a money economy.

The expansion of foreign trade created a need for many middlemen's jobs. It was not the Javanese who took advantage of these new economic possibilities, but the Chinese, who had served in former years as a link between the Western authorities and the native population. As a social group in Indonesia, which was bound less than any other by agrarian traditions, these foreigners were the obvious people to fill the 'middle class' positions which were coming into being. The agrarian population on Java was, it is true, becoming more ready to seek part-time occupations outside the *desa* areas than it had formerly been, in order to be able to pay the land tax and to meet the recently fostered demand for imported goods. Indeed, the increasing scarcity of arable land, due to the growth in population, drove many Javanese to seek work on the plantations and even, in later years, outside Java, for example in Deli (in Sumatra) and even in Surinam (Dutch Guiana). The culture system had made the Javanese accustomed to coolie labour under Western supervision. The subsistence economy whereby he had provided for all of his own needs was in a state of progressive dissolution – yet the Javanese persisted to the very last in his desire to maintain his ties to his own land. For the time being the abandonment of agriculture as the chief means of subsistence in favour of commerce as a profession represented too great a conflict with the agrarian tradition.

The result was that the ordinary peasant in Java continued to maintain a predominantly passive attitude towards the incursions of the money economy. He remained a farmer providing for his own needs, sought other income only when he was forced to, and tried to keep to a minimum the periods when he was no longer independent, but employed by a Western-owned undertaking. He preferred to leave profit seeking to the Chinese or the Arabs or even, in some cases, to the Indonesian who had outgrown the old traditional *desa* milieu – such a type, for instance, as the *haji* (the pilgrim returned from Mecca) or the immigrant from Sumatra. But by adopting this passive attitude he made himself the defenceless victim of the middleman and the money lender, both of whom were more calculating and more at home in the price system, and who also possessed some capital.

The population continued to grow in the Liberal period from 1870 to 1900. This increase was largely due to the '*Pax Neerlandica*', which to a certain degree had removed the Malthusian 'positive checks' – famine, plague and internal war – without, however, providing the peasantry with the incentive or the knowledge to reduce fertility.

In this respect also, therefore, the population appears to have reacted to Western penetration only in a passive way. There is little evidence in this period of a conscious effort by the peasantry to improve its standard of living. But this passive reaction to the new cultural influences is to be attributed in the main to the nature of those influences. The investment of capital in big plantations under Western direction did not bring about any fundamental change in the social structure in Java. This form of penetration was based upon the agrarian character of the country and it was essential to preserve the existing structure and the extremely low standard of living which went with it, if the plantation owners wished to benefit from their main source of profit, cheap labour.[1]

It is understandable, therefore, that the people's reaction to encroaching Western influence did not take the form of new dynamic activity but showed itself rather in an extension over an ever-widening area of the traditional pattern of rice cultivation on *sawah* lands, which found its origin in Central Java. For this development Boeke has coined the term 'static expansion'.[2]

3 Shifts in the era of 'Ethical Policy'

Towards the end of the nineteenth century, the Netherlands Government realised that the optimistic hopes of the early Liberal period had not been fulfilled. In particular, the Javanese population had failed to copy the methods of Western enterprise. In Java a state of declining welfare (*mindere welvaart*) prevailed – a fact admitted by Queen Wilhelmina. It was seen that the economic development of the colony could not be left to free individual initiative but that it was the government's duty to protect the population against the unfavourable effects of the economic forces at work. It was realised, too, that the government should make a conscious effort to encourage economic enterprise on the part of the native population.

This new 'ethical policy' enjoyed the approval both of the liberal-minded Dutch industrialists, who hoped for an expansion of their market as a result of increased welfare, and of all those in the Netherlands, socialists and conservatives alike, who had now come to regard the liberal ideology with critical distrust.

From this time onwards the government authorities endeavoured to make a positive contribution to the welfare of the native population by various means: irrigation, education, the promotion of popular credit facilities, and expert agricultural advice.

[1] See for the unfavourable effects of sugar plantations upon the Javanese peasantry G. H. van der Kolff, 'European influence on native agriculture', in B. Schrieke (ed.), *The effect of Western influence on native civilisations in the Malay archipelago*, Batavia, 1929, p. 122 ff.

[2] J. H. Boeke, *Economics and economic policy of dual societies as exemplified by Indonesia*, Haarlem, 1953, p. 174.

But no less important than the whole scheme of government measures was the structural change in the Indonesian economy. It was the age of imperialism. Colonies were no longer desired simply for the production of profitable consumption goods, such as coffee, sugar, tea and tobacco; far more important was the supply of raw materials they offered for Western industry. Consequently, in this period, the attention of investors was turned to the Outer Islands, where Indonesia's mineral wealth, oil, tin, bauxite and coal is largely to be found. The opening up of these territories to investment was preceded by their pacification, which was completed by van Heutsz, Governor-General in the period 1904–1909.

Contact with the world economy developed on different lines on the Outer Islands, however. Western plantations were predominant only in a relatively small area on Sumatra, that is to say, in the Eastcoast Residency, in and around Deli, where first tobacco and later rubber (also an important raw material for modern industry) became the chief objects of investment. Since the Sumatran people never felt much attraction for work in a subordinate capacity on Western estates and were never obliged to seek a subsidiary income, owing to the abundance of land at their disposal,[1] these undertakings had to look abroad for their labour supply, first in China, but later preponderantly in Java.

In the greater part of the Outer Territories the adaptation to modern economy was carried out by the Indonesians themselves. At a time when the Western rubber plantations were still in the experimental stage, Indonesians on Sumatra and Borneo – mostly Malays – were embarking on the cultivation of rubber on their own account on their *ladangs*.[2] The cultivation of coconuts, too, formed an important source of income in large areas. The vast stretches of uncultivated ground provided a considerable proportion of the local population with the opportunity to earn money for the purchase of imported goods, in addition to their usual

[1] See for example J. H. Boeke, *op. cit.*, p. 143.

[2] See R. Broersma, *Handel en bedrijf in Zuid- en Oost-Borneo* (Trade and enterprise in South and East Borneo), The Hague, 1927, p. 121.

occupation of subsistence farming. And even though there, too, nearly everywhere in the Outer Islands, the Indonesian became more or less dependent upon foreign middlemen or upon large Western businesses, the adaptation to Western economy was on the whole more dynamic in character there than on Java or in Deli. By reason of the sparsity of the population, the *ladang* pattern of cultivation offered a better chance of dynamic expansion than did the *sawah* pattern on Java.

It was during the rubber boom of the twenties, in particular when native production of rubber was benefiting from the Stevenson scheme applied in British territories, that many Malays learned how to handle money. For many, assimilation into a money economy meant a certain impoverishment, as land tenure became less stable. Yet it cannot be denied that there was a greater opportunity for gain and a greater degree of differentiation among the population than had formerly been the case.

There were stirrings, too, among the peoples of Java. Little by little Javanese society began to show signs of more differentiation. The modernisation of the Western social superstructure provided new occupations for Indonesians. The expansion of Western businesses and the ever growing functions of government created opportunities of employment for a relatively large number of more or less skilled Indonesian personnel in both administrative and technical positions. Western methods of transport gave rise to a need for mechanics and chauffeurs. The shortage of farm land drove many Javanese into the retail trade, while many others left for the towns in search of work. Some, too, found subordinate positions in the educational and medical branches. In the ranks of the farmers as well, there were several who achieved a measure of prosperity by means of improved techniques and the cultivation of profitable market crops in addition to the main subsistence crops, rice or maize.

But on the whole the economic struggle remained difficult for the Javanese. The way up to the independent middle class was usually barred to him, because foreigners – the Chinese especially – had obtained a firm footing there and succeeded in keeping the advantages in their own hands by means of their connections and by cooperation within their own groups – a cooperation often based on a clan system – and also by reason of their possession of greater capital reserves and superior knowledge of affairs in the outside world. And while a few Javanese managed to rise above the mass, thanks to schooling or technical ability, the numbers of small subsistence farmers, for whom every road seemed barred, increased by leaps and bounds. The population of Java rose from 28 million in 1900 to 41 million in 1930.

Why did the era of 'ethical policy' fail on the whole to fortify the Javanese for the economic struggle? How did it come about that this period, which began with such high hopes, and which included a few crises and several booms, ended in the usual complaints that the general level of welfare had shown little material improvement, if any – or, according to some, had even declined?[1]

To answer these questions we shall need once more to scrutinise the nature of Western influence. There had, indeed, been important changes in the structure of Western business life. The private planter, a pioneer working at his own risk, was no longer the typical exponent of free enterprise. During the succession of crises his place had been taken by the functionary employed by the plantation-owning corporation, a limited liability company. Such a company was, in its turn, often dependent on credits from one of the large 'plantation banks' (*cultuurbanken*).

[1] Cf. W. Huender, *Overzicht van den economischen toestand der inheemsche bevolking van Java en Madoera* (Survey of the economic condition of the indigenous population of Java and Madura), The Hague, 1921; J. W. Meijer Ranneft and W. Huender, *Onderzoek naar den belastingdruk op de Inlandsche bevolking van Java en Madoera* (Enquiry into the burden of taxation on the native population of Java and Madura), Weltevreden, 1926; *Verslag van den economischen toestand der Inlandsche bevolking, 1924* (Report on the economic condition of the native population, 1924), Weltevreden, 1926; J. H. Boeke, 'Het zakelijke en het persoonlijke element in de koloniale welvaartspolitiek' (The material and the personal element in the colonial welfare policy), in *Koloniale Studiën* (Colonial Studies), Vol. XI, Part 1, 1927, p. 157 ff.; J. S. Furnivall, *Colonial policy and practice. A comparative study of Burma and Netherlands India*, New York, 1956, p. 229.

The concentration of power and interest assumed ever larger proportions until, in the twenties, the plantations were all brought under a coordinating superstructure of large syndicates and cartels working in close cooperation with the government authorities. Concentration and the process of cartelisation had made great advances in the import and export trade as well.[1]

The consequences were, on the one hand, that the chances for individuals to develop themselves in the economic sphere were severely reduced, while those who had already found a footing in the middle classes, such as the Chinese middlemen, often became increasingly dependent upon large-scale enterprise. In Indonesia, as in other Asian countries, individual Easterners had to fight their way in business at a time when Western corporations had already secured a more or less monopolistic position. On the other hand, owing to expansion and the concentration of power in the hands of a few, business gained more and more influence over the apparatus of government, so that the government found it ever more difficult to pursue any policy which ran counter to business interests. Then, too, the increasing rapidity of communications – for example, the inauguration of airmail service – made it possible for the directors in the Netherlands to exercise a more intensive control than had previously been the case. In this respect the relationship between the home country and Indonesia became in a certain sense *more* colonial in nature, rather than less.

Furthermore, the growing concentration of power was not restricted to Dutch business. International concerns also began to exert a growing influence on Indonesian affairs. Nominally, ever since the abolition of the 'culture system', the Netherlands had pursued an open door policy in Indonesia. In fact, however, their close connections with the government authorities enabled Dutch interests to outdistance the British who dominated in the middle of the nineteenth century. The monopoly enjoyed by the Royal

[1] See E. de Vries, 'Het economisch leven' (The economic life), in *Verslag van de Commissie tot bestudeering van staatsrechtelijke hervormingen* (Report of the Commission for the study of political reforms), New York, 1944, Vol. I, p. 23 ff.

Packet Navigation Company (*Koninklijke Paketvaart Maatschappij* or K.P.M.), which provided the inter-island shipping services, is a case in point. But during World War I Indonesian trade was chiefly with Asian and American markets, and afterward countries such as the United States and Japan retained their interest in Indonesia. Although the capital invested in Indonesia was still largely Dutch,[1] other powers became intimately concerned in the economic development of the area.

The reason why all these developments failed to bring a rise in welfare is mainly that, up to the crisis in the thirties, there was no significant change in the nature of investment in Indonesia. During the twenties the investments phase was superseded by the 'return phase' of foreign economic development as is evidenced by the enormous export surpluses.

*Netherlands India's Balance of Trade**

In order to remove short-term fluctuations, averages are given for five-year periods from 1876 to 1930, expressed in millions of guilders.

Period	Imports	Exports	Exports surplus
1876–1880 (average)	129	180	51
1881–1885 "	142	189	47
1886–1890 "	130	185	55
1891–1895 "	162	206	44
1896–1900 "	170	227	57
1901–1905 "	197	275	78
1906–1910 "	258	414	156
1911–1915 "	407	643	235
1916–1920 "	685	1339	654
1921–1925 "	817	1417	600
1926–1930 "	994	1501	507

*Adapted from J. H. Boeke, *Economics and economic policy of dual societies as exemplified by Indonesia*, p. 199.

[1] According to reliable estimates (see J. van Gelderen, *The recent development of economic foreign policy in the Netherlands East Indies*, London, 1939, p. 66 ff.) foreign capital invested about 1939 in agriculture, mining and other branches of business was distributed as follows over the different nationalities:

But capital continued to be invested almost exclusively in large-scale agriculture and in mining companies. The economic pattern remained one in which Indonesia supplied agrarian products and raw materials, none of which were processed more than was strictly necessary for their despatch to the manufacturing countries of Europe and America. These countries then attempted to dispose of their surpluses of finished products to such countries as Indonesia. Indonesia therefore retained its predominantly agrarian economic structure. *Sawah* cultivation in Java and *ladang* cultivation in the Outer Islands were both characterised by extremely low productivity of labour. Even the intensified *sawah* culture was carried on by very primitive means. The crop was harvested with a rice-knife (*ani-ani*), the stalks being cut off ear by ear. The entire Javanese economy was based on an abundance of cheap manual labour, which is precisely what made investment in the estates so profitable. The almost complete lack of mechanisation kept the total output – and, at the same time, the general standard of living – low, and a large part of the profits flowed out of the country. There was practically no native capital investment.

The foregoing largely explains why the 'ethical policy' was bound to fail. The government was obliged to take steps to supplement the work of private capital and to mitigate or remove its harmful effects; but it did not endeavour to guide social development as a whole into new channels. The large plantations continued to be regarded as the basis of native prosperity.

According to the 'ethical' program, agricultural productivity

Dutch	British	Franco-Belgian	German	Japanese	American	Swedish	Total
	(In millions of guilders)						
1536	278	112	18	20	53	5	2064
	(In percentage)						
75	13,5	5	1	1	2,5	–	100

The largest amounts of non-Dutch capital were to be found in the rubber industry, mostly in Sumatra, not less than 47 % of the total capital being of British, American and Franco-Belgian origin. Moreover, British and American capital played a very important role in oil extraction.

was to be increased by irrigation and other means. Emigration would relieve the overpopulation in Java. By education and hygiene an endeavour would be made to increase the population's stamina. There was, however, no conscious effort to increase output per head. This would have required large-scale industrialisation. Although, in their original plans, the founders of the 'ethical policy' had paid some attention to the encouragement of industry, during the entire period of 'ethical policy', right up to the days of crisis in 1930, the government never made any serious beginning with industrialisation. Such industry as existed at the end of the previous century was directed mainly at meeting the requirements of the plantations and railways (assembly shops, for instance, making machines for use in the sugar factories). Shortly after the turn of the century and during World War I – owing to the disappearance of imports from Europe – attempts were made to establish industries, but they never met with lasting success. There was enough room for investment in the well-known fields of agriculture and mining and there were no strong incentives for making a break with this tradition. As soon as better times set in again after the end of the war, the government dissolved the Commission on Industrialisation. The powerful estate companies felt little sympathy for industrialisation, fearing that it might cause labour costs to rise and export possibilities to fall off, as a result of diminished imports of manufactured goods. Dutch industry, too, while interested in a rise in the Indonesian standard of living, because this would provide it with a better market for its products, did not wish to see the growth of a competitive industry in Indonesia, which alone could make a rise in the standard of living possible there. Thus the prevailing mood hardly favoured serious efforts on the part of the government to promote industrialisation.

It can, moreover, be said that even the social services resulting from the 'ethical policy' were strongly subject to the influence of the powerful estate companies and other large-scale enterprises. Irrigation measures benefited the sugar concerns as much as the agricultural population. The health service was, in part, closely related to the need of the various enterprises for physically fit labour. The fight against contagious diseases, such as plague and cholera, was a direct gain for Western business. In so far as it exceeded the elementary instruction of the *desa* schools, education mainly provided training for administrative personnel in the service of the government and business. The road system and the experimental stations existed chiefly for the benefit of the plantations.

In saying this, I do not wish to underrate the quality of the work accomplished by the Dutch in a great variety of fields, nor the high-minded intentions of many who lent their cooperation in the 'ethical policy'. But these activities were on a small scale in comparison with the magnitude of the total economic problem in Indonesia; they were even insufficient to cope with the unfavourable effects of economic penetration, to say nothing of achieving any permanent rise in the general level of welfare. To achieve the latter – and to provide a solution to the pressing problem of overpopulation in Java – nothing less than a policy consciously aimed at increasing the productivity of labour could have been effective. Enhancing social welfare is not only a question of the efficiency of the actual work accomplished, but also – and primarily – of the channels into which the process of social development is guided.

We have already seen that in this period the native population's reaction to economic stimuli from the West was no longer merely passive. There were signs of an increasing endeavour on the part of individual Indonesians to improve their economic status. For instance, many endured great sacrifices in order, by means of education, to increase their own and their children's chances of betterment. But in certain social groups there grew up, also, the notion of the importance of mutual cooperation in economic matters. This cooperation revealed itself in diverse forms: in trade unions, in cooperatives, and in political movements, for example, in *Sarekat Islam*. Cooperation and the concentration of power in the purely economic field (trade unions, cooperatives) remained, as regards size and strength, far behind that achieved by Western business. Yet this embryonic cooperation held a promise for the future. In the countryside a movement developed on the sugar plantations which was significant as a sign of dissatisfaction with social conditions. It was not without reason that Erich Jacoby referred to the sugar plantations as 'the classical stage for social unrest.'[1] This attempt at trade union organisation can be regarded as a first rudimentary endeavour on the part of the native world to oppose the growing concentration of power among Western business interests with a similar power concentration of its own.

4 *Economic crisis, war and revolution*

From statistical reports issued by the League of Nations[2] it may be deduced, that the economic crisis lasted longer and weighed more heavily in Indonesia than in most other countries of the world. Western enterprise and the native population both suffered. The catastrophic decline in world agricultural prices brought enormous difficulties both for the Western plantations and for the Indonesian farmer. Innumerable undertakings had to close down or considerably reduce their working acreage, their staffs and their production costs, wages included. In this way many an Indonesian saw his money earnings disappear or shrink to a fraction of their former size.

Dismissed coolies returned by the thousand from Deli to increase the burdens of the Javanese *desas*. Many unemployed left the towns in Java and returned to the countryside they had deserted in better days. And all this happened at a time when the Javanese farmer, like his counterpart on the Outer Islands, was obtaining but a trifle for his crops compared with the price he had been getting in the boom period.

Was it possible, in these circumstances, for the Javanese peasant to retreat to the old methods of a closed economy and subsistence farming on his own lands – now enlarged by the *sawah* fields

1 E. H. Jacoby, *Agrarian unrest in Southeast Asia*, New York, 1948, p. 57.

2 League of Nations, *World economic survey*, Geneva, 1932/33, 1933/34, 1934/35.

Acreage,[1] *production*[2] *and yield*[2] *of sugar estates compared with rents,*[2] *wages*[2] *and other production costs,*[2] *Netherlands Indies, 1927–1936*

Values in millions of guilders

Harvest year	Harvested area on estates (ha)	Production (1000 tons)	Total value *a)*	Rents	Wages *b)*	Compen-sations *c)*	Total costs
1927–28	195,408	2,990	400	22,9	111.3	–	134.2
1928–29	196,754	2,935	350	23,9	105.7	–	129.6
1929–30	198,007	2,971	213	25,0	100.9	–	125.9
1930–31	200,831	2,839	178	25,9	86.2	0.1	112.2
1931–32	166,138	2,611	128	21.7	53.8	0.8	76.3
1932–33	84,343	1,401	64	11.9	22.2	2.7	36.8
1933–34	34.211	644	23.5	6.5	9.9	2.6	19.0
1934–35	27,578	513	19.5	3.5	6.0	2.5	12.0
1935–36	35,572	565	25	3	6,2	1.0	10.2
1936–37*d)*	84,494	1,400	60	6	15.4	–	21.4

a) On account of the slow sales of sugar, the price given is the average price of the following harvest period, so as to make it comparable with the production costs. For example, the Fl. 400,000 entered for 1927–28 actually is the average price in the harvest year 1928–29.

b) Wages and other labour payment.

c) Compensation to landowners for disrupted lease contracts.

d) Figures for the harvest year 1936–37 are rough estimates.

abandoned by the sugar plantations – and thus provide for his own needs? It is true that, for a time, newspapers, official reports and various other publications in the Netherlands fostered the impression that the retreat from a money to a barter economy had met with considerable success. The population of Java was said to have 'adapted itself to the economic crisis in admirable fashion'.

But such a generalisation was false. An investigation in a selected district, made by professor van der Kolff,[3] revealed that where

[1] Adapted from the official *Netherlands Indian Report 1931. Statistical abstract for the year 1930*, The Hague, 1931–1932, table 199, and, for 1930 and the following years, from the official *Netherlands Indian Report 1941. Statistical abstract for the year 1940*, Batavia, 1941, table 197.

[2] J. H. Boeke, *Economics and economic policy of dual societies as exemplified by Indonesia*, p. 247.

[3] Cf. G. H. van der Kolff, *The historical development of the labour relationships in a remote corner of Java as they apply to the cultivation of rice*, Batavia, 1937.

there had been a retreat into a barter economy, it had been accompanied by a serious decline in the level of welfare, as compared with the end of the previous century. The period of 'ethical policy' had brought about a large increase in population which was not accompanied by a comparable increase in the available arable land. External factors, such as greater opportunity for employment on the various plantations, had brought about this growth. It was self-evident that when the opportunity for employment disappeared the swollen population would not be able to feed itself on the produce of an arable acreage which had not increased proportionally. The road back to a subsistence economy, as advocated by Boeke in imitation of Gandhi,[1] did not turn out to be a road towards idealised rural simplicity, but towards misery and pauperism.

This became all the more obvious when the equilibrium between money income and money expenditure was completely destroyed. The unfavourable price relationship resulting from the far greater fall in the price of agricultural exports than in the price of imported manufactured goods was reflected in the individual peasant's budget. His money income in the form of wages or proceeds

Income in money [2]	*Expenditure in money* [2]
Income from the sale of agricultural products declined sharply within a short period. In the *desa* (village) the decline often amounted to more than 70 per cent.	Expenditure on clothes, all kinds of articles for daily use, petroleum, etc. declined less sharply, by only about 50 per cent. The price of salt rose.
Wages declined sharply, often by more than 60 per cent. Employment decreased. Rents paid by plantations declined sharply.	Land taxes declined less rapidly, by about 33 per cent. Excises were not reduced, school fees, railway, tram, and bus fares declined only little and slowly.
The farmer secured money by borrowing from the popular credit banks, *desa* banks, pawnshops or private moneylenders.	The loans had to be repaid. Only in the pawnshop was the client free to decide, whether or not to redeem his pawn.

[1] J. H. Boeke, *The interests of the voiceless Far East*, Leiden, 1948, p. 88/89.
[2] G. Gonggrijp, *op. cit.*, p. 185.

from the sale of market crops declined much more sharply than his expenses. Fixed costs in particular continued to impose a heavy burden on every budget, as is shown by the scheme on p. 107.

The Netherlands Indies, although a large exporting country, maintained the exchange rate of its currency when practically all other countries had devalued theirs. It was not until September 1936 that the Netherlands and the Indies followed suit. The burden not only took the form of payment of interest to the Netherlands on account of the Indies' national debt and on bank credits granted to the plantation undertakings, but was also felt by the small-scale peasant farmer in the form of the land tax and debts. The land taxes fixed for the 10-year period 1927–1937 were not scaled down until 1932–1933, and even then the reduction was relatively much smaller than the fall in the price of agricultural products. Taxation and debts dating from the period during which the money economy had made deep inroads in the village communities were the main obstacles preventing the population's return to a barter economy. In order to be able to pay his land taxes on time – and the village authorities were very eager to obtain prompt payment (sometimes not quite disinterestedly) – the peasant found himself getting ever more deeply into debt. An investigation undertaken on behalf of the People's Credit Bank in 1935 and the years following by two Indonesian experts, with academic training,[1] revealed the very serious proportions rural debt had assumed in many areas in a short period. In numerous districts the harvest had been regularly mortgaged or sold not merely for one year but for several years ahead.

It was no wonder that the peasants had to deny themselves all

[1] See Soenario, *Verschulding en economische toestand op Java's platteland* (Debt and the economic situation in the Javanese rural areas), Batavia, 1939. See also various articles by Soenario and Soekasno in the journal *Volkscredietwezen* (People's credit organisation); and Sumitro Djojohadikusumo, *Het volkscredietwezen in de depressie* (The people's credit organisation during the depression), Haarlem, 1943.

sorts of modest luxuries to which they had grown accustomed in better days. No wonder either that they were obliged to sell a far larger proportion of the rice harvest than hitherto, in order to be able to meet their financial liabilities and to buy, in its place, inferior food for their own and their families' subsistence. The belief entertained for some time by the authorities that the peasants could feed themselves better since they no longer sold what they produced but consumed it themselves was not on the whole borne out by the facts.[1] This theory left out of account the dislocation caused by the money economy. In general the crisis had an unfavourable effect on the people's diet, which even before had failed to meet the most moderate Western standards.

The optimistic picture painted by Sitsen[2] of the economic situation in Java about 1935 was not justified, therefore. The explanation of the draining-off of the native population's gold assets (between 1931 and 1936 158 million guilders' worth of gold left the Netherlands Indies, mainly via government-managed pawnshops) as a sign of increased economic strength and of a tendency to give preference to assets of a more modern type, seems rather euphemistic. And even the large-scale movement of Indonesians into new trading and industrial professions is to be

[1] This impression could be gathered from the so-called Kutawinangun Report: *Geld- en productenhuishouding, volksvoeding en -gezondheid in Koetowinangoen* (Money economy and barter economy, the diet and health of the people in Kutawinangun), Buitenzorg, 1934, p. 135 ff. It was this report which attracted attention to the fact that the Javanese peasant fed himself on 2½ cents a day. Van der Kolff's study, mentioned above, gives evidence among other things of a decline in the standard of nutrition. Boeke, too, declared that the food situation about 1940 was unfavourable. The statistical data provided by the Final Report of the Coolie Budget Commission, *Living conditions of plantation workers and peasants on Java in 1939–1940*, Translation Series, Modern Indonesia Project, Cornell University, Ithaca, 1956, convey a very distressing picture of the food situation in the areas under survey.

[2] Cf. P. H. W. Sitsen, *Industrial development of the Netherlands Indies*, New York, 1942, see the introduction in particular; J. S. Furnivall, *Netherlands India. A study of plural economy*, Cambridge/New York, 1944, Chapter XII, is also, I believe, too optimistic in his opinion concerning the depression period.

interpreted, in the first instance, as a consequence of impoverishment and of the gradual dispossession of large numbers of peasant farmers.

There is just as little justification for ascribing the great demand for the products of the new native industries, after 1935, to the increased purchasing power of the Javanese population. It would be necessary, first of all, to establish the extent to which the demand for clothing and household goods was due to the need to make up in the recovery period for purchases postponed during the years of crisis and the extent to which this demand replaced the earlier demand for imported goods. Further, it would be worth while to investigate what role the increased purchasing power in the Outer Islands played in the demand for these new manufactured goods from Java; for, from 1937 onwards, many Malays had earned significant sums from the native production of rubber, partly owing to the prospect of war and partly as a result of the abolition of the heavy 'special export duty'.[1] There is no doubt that there was an economic recovery, especially after devaluation in 1936, or that native industry, which began to flourish in the thirties, was a symptom of an important dynamic evolution in Javanese society. Neither can it be denied that industry provided a livelihood for many Indonesians, thus creating new purchasing power. But to regard an increased rural purchasing power in Java as the cause of this industrial development is to put things the wrong way round.

There was an element of dynamic adaptation, new to Javanese society, in the way a section of the Indonesian masses reacted to the difficulties of the crisis period. The large number of peasants who sought new opportunities in small-scale Indonesian industries, or in the town factories, in trade or by leaving as colonists for the Lampong, showed that more Indonesians had broken free from the old traditions than ever before, and that the whole social structure had become more fluid. It was not only the landless paupers who sought their chance in industry. Members of the

[1] See for example J. H. Boeke, *Economics and economic policy of dual societies as exemplified by Indonesia*, p. 249.

Indonesian middle class looked for opportunities there, too, as founders and managers of small undertakings and by so doing they created new jobs for the masses. In 1935 and later years, in the Regency of Bandung, many Indonesian traders and landowners invested money in the weaving industry.[1] It was only later, when this industry had demonstrated its vitality, that foreigners, the Chinese included, began to show an interest. And although the danger arose here, too, that the small Indonesian entrepreneurs would become dependent upon foreign middlemen, in this field they managed to retain a high degree of independence and a much larger share of the invested capital than in other middle class occupations, right up to the outbreak of the second World War.[2] In the field of native industry the development of producers' cooperatives showed great vitality.[3]

Yet if the conditions of economic development led to greater social differentiation, the general standard of living of the masses benefited little. For the first time there were signs of a significant development in the direction of native capitalism. But this affected only a relatively small number. Greater social differentiation went hand in hand with impoverishment for many people, particularly in Java, but also, to a lesser degree, in the Outer Islands. This tendency could already be observed during the twenties. S. J. Rutgers[4] calculated from this table that the landless

[1] *De ontwikkeling van de kleine handweefnijverheid in het Madjalaja rayon* (The development of the small handweaving industry in the Majalaya district), Batavia, 1938, p. 15 ff., 63 ff.; W. van Warmelo, 'Ontstaan en groei van de handweefnijverheid in Madjalaja' (Origin and growth of the handweaving industry in Majalaya), in *Koloniale Studiën* (Colonial Studies), Vol. XXIII, 1939, p. 15/16, 18, 20, 22.

[2] P. H. W. Sitsen, *op. cit.*, p. 21; *De ontwikkeling van de kleine handweefindustrie in het Madjalaja rayon*, p. 31 ff., 43 ff.; G. Schwencke, 'De weefindustrie in het regentschap Bandoeng' (The weaving industry in the Bandung Regency), in *Koloniaal Tijdschrift* (Colonial Journal), Vol. XXIII, 1939, p. 161.

[3] P. H. W. Sitsen, *op. cit.*, p. 17 ff.; G. H. C. Hart, *Towards economic democracy in the Netherlands Indies*, New York, 1942, p. 76 ff.

[4] S. J. Rutgers, *Indonesië. Het koloniale systeem in de periode tussen de eerste en de tweede wereldoorlog* (Indonesia. The colonial system during the period between World War I and World War II), Amsterdam, 1947.

Class divisions of native population in Javanese villages [1]

		Percent	Household income per year (in guilders)
A	Officials, native chiefs, teachers of religion	4.0	
B	Permanent workers in European and Chinese enterprises	2.4	370
C	Wealthy farmers	2.5	1090
D	Middle class farmers	19.8	300
E	Poor farmers	27.1	147
F	Share-croppers, having no property of their own	3.4	118
G	Labourers on native holdings	12.4	101
H	Native wholesale merchants and industrialists	0.3	1130
I	Retail dealers, artisans	5.9	248
K	Coolies	19.6	120
	Miscellaneous	2.6	–
		100.0	

peasants and coolies amounted to 37.8 percent of the village population; by adding the poor farmers or semi-proletarians he reached a total of poor people amounting to 65 percent. In the Outer Provinces, judging from a sample survey,[2] also the majority of the population, though a smaller one than in Java (51.26 percent), consisted of proletarians and poor peasants.[3]

The mobilisation of landownership and the increased burden of rural debt created a group of large Indonesian landowners, especially in the Preanger Regencies, the mountainous interior of Western Java.[4] A recent investigation into landownership in a

[1] Adapted from J. W. Meijer Ranneft and W. Huender, *op. cit.*, p. 10.

[2] See table on next page.

[3] S. J. Rutgers, *op. cit.*, p. 118.

[4] N. D. Ploegsma, *Oorspronkelijkheid en economisch aspect van het dorp op Java en Madoera* (Originality and economic aspect of the village on Java and Madura), Leiden, 1936, p. 61; J. W. Meijer Ranneft and W. Huender, *op. cit.*, p. 11, mentioned an increase of the amount of large holdings in West Java and Besuki (East Java).

Class divisions in 7 districts of Sumatra's Westcoast Residency [1]

		percent
A	Officials, native chiefs, teachers of religion	1.91
B	Permanent workers in non-European enterprises	0.30
C	*Wealthy* farmers	
	a. Cultivation of food crops	2.53
	b. Cultivation of commercial crops	0.90
D	*Middle class* farmers	
	a. Cultivation of food crops	25.02
	b. Cultivation of commercial crops	6.87
E	*Poor* farmers	
	a. Cultivation of food crops	17.14
	b. Cultivation of commercial crops	4.35
F	Share-croppers, having no property of their own	
	a. Cultivation of food crops	4.55
	b. Cultivation of commercial crops	0.41
G	Labourers on native holdings	4.70
H	Native wholesale merchants and industrialists	0.50
I	Retail dealers, artisans	11.01
K	Coolies	19.81
		100.00

West Javanese village showed that:

13 percent of all family heads owned 82 percent of the total land area (the average individual held more than one hectare). The remainder was in the hands of 548 owners, with an average holding of 26 ares, while 564 peasants owned no land.

87 percent of all family heads, owning no land, or less than one hectare, constituted a class of labourers and semi-independent farmers.

[1] *Rapport van de Commissie van onderzoek ingesteld bij Gouvernementsbesluit van 13 Februari 1927, no. 1a* (Report of the inquiry committee established by governmental decree of 13-2-1927, Nr 1a), usually referred to as Rapport Sumatra's Westkust (Report on Sumatra's Westcoast), Weltevreden, 1928, Vol. II, p. 20/21. (The first volume of this report, written by B. Schrieke, was inserted in the recently published *Indonesian sociological studies. Selected writings of B. Schrieke,* Part 1. Selected studies on Indonesia by Dutch scholars, Vol. II, The Hague/Bandung, 1955, p. 83 ff., under the title: 'The causes and effects of communism on the west coast of Sumatra'.)

10.5 percent owning 1 to 5 hectares, constituted a middle class of independent farmers.

2.5 percent owning more than 5 hectares, constituted a class of wealthy landowners. This class was based upon the six prominent families in the village, with an average familial property of 55 hectares.[1]

On the other hand there was – as a consequence of this same process – an ever-growing class of landless peasants.[2] In Western Java many peasants, who had been forced to sell their small plot of land, entered the weaving industry as full-time labourers. In the early stages of the development of the new native industries, the workers could earn very reasonable wages, much higher than those paid on the plantations, where employment was actually a side-line for the great majority and not a full-time occupation. Neither were labour conditions in the new weaving industry comparable to those in the older industries, such as the *batik* and native cigarette industries. But after some time the wage level in the new textile industry declined, too, though it remained considerably higher than in the older industries up to the outbreak of the war.[3]

Greater social differentiation and the rise of an Indonesian middle class received outside support as well. This came in the first place from the nationalist party known as *Parindra*, which supported the Indonesian bourgeoisie and the better-off landowners in many ways. In this period, too, the government authorities sought support for colonial rule in the middle classes, whereas they had previously relied exclusively on the feudal nobility, the village chiefs and the Christian groups. Even before the crisis, professor Boeke had advocated the substitution for the large-scale non-differentiating social welfare policy, organised through

[1] H. ten Dam, *Desa Tjibodas*, a report of the Lembaga Penjelidikan Masjarakat Desa dan Usaha Tani (Institute for rural sociological and farm-management research), Bogor, 1951, p. 10 ff.

[2] Cf. H. ten Dam, *op. cit.*, p. 14; N. D. Ploegsma, *op. cit.*, p. 61.

[3] W. van Warmelo, *op. cit.*, p. 5; G. Schwencke, *op. cit.*, p. 159.

the Civil Service – a policy which had failed to achieve the desired results – of one which would select personalities among the more active Indonesians in order to stimulate their activities.[1]

This policy was adopted during the crisis period, when both the agricultural advisory service and the people's credit agencies directed their attention, by preference, to those who had risen above the level of the mass. The public credit facilities were extended even to the urban bourgeoisie, for the latter offered more security than did the majority of farmers. These methods brought with them, of course, the danger that the mass of peasants, instead of receiving a stimulus from the example of more vigorous individuals, would be still further impoverished and become the object of exploitation on the part of the richer farmers and middle class. In Western Java this tendency is very much in evidence, as is indicated by ten Dam's investigation in the desa Tjibodas.[2] The situation is not unlike that during the Liberal period, when a favourable effect on Indonesian small agriculture was expected from the example furnished by the large-scale plantations under Western direction, but the actual result of their introduction was quite the reverse: an impoverishment of the peasantry as a consequence of the economic pressure exerted by the sugar plantations.

In the meantime Western business had also undergone some significant structural changes. The plantations tried, by reducing costs and by rationalisation of working methods, to make their business profitable once more. But in view of conditions in the world market this proved to be possible only by severe restriction of production. And this in turn could be achieved only by cooperation among the producers, if possible on an international scale.

It was, however, difficult to carry out this stringent restriction of production on a voluntary basis. And as there existed no means of compelling those unwilling to cooperate, business turned to the government with a request for direction and control. This

[1] Cf. J. H. Boeke, 'Het zakelijke en het persoonlijke element in de koloniale welvaartspolitiek', *loc. cit.*, p. 191; D. H. Burger, *op. cit.*, p. 234 ff.

[2] H. ten Dam, *op. cit.*, p. 14.

direction was made easier for the government by reason of the existence of the many coordinating superstructures which had already developed in the business world itself, through whose agency it was able to exercise economic control.[1]

Thus we see the government's adoption of a policy of restricting the production of a number of export goods, such as sugar, rubber, tin, coffee and tea, often in accordance with international agreements. The aim was primarily to put Western business back on a profitable basis. The case of rubber restriction, in which, in the most difficult years, the interests of Western estates were accorded very preferential treatment – thus seriously endangering native smallholders[2] – showed the influence of powerful Western firms on the government's policy. The government was also obliged to intervene with measures of regulation in the import field, because of the dumping of Japanese manufactures, chiefly textiles. The Dutch cotton industry in Twente was in danger of losing its entire market in Indonesia. But the partial protection the government accorded to this industry by a system of quotas and limitation on imports tended to raise prices slightly and to restrict the people's opportunity to provide themselves with cheap goods from Japan.[3] The needs of the people, however, eventually forced the authorities to institute more controls in the interests of the population, such as the protection of native industry, a modified policy as regards native rubber production and other native commercial crops, a rice policy aimed at price stabilisation and national self-sufficiency, and intensified resettlement on farms outside Java.

Nevertheless the government's policy continued to be mainly

[1] J. van Gelderen, *op. cit.*, p. 43 ff., 58 ff.

[2] J. H. Boeke, *Economics and economic policy of dual societies as exemplified by Indonesia*, p. 124/125; B. C. C. M. M. van Suchtelen, *Neerlands nieuwe eereschuld aan Indië* (The Netherlands new debt of honour to Indonesia), Hilversum, 1939; P. T. Bauer, *The rubber industry. A study in competition and monopoly*, Cambridge, 1948, p. 117/118.

[3] See R. Saroso Wirodihardjo, *De contingenteeringspolitiek en hare invloed op de Indonesische bevolking* (The quota policy and its influence upon the Indonesian population), Jakarta, 1951.

determined by the interests of the plantation firms, in which vast sums had been invested. The plantation's grip on the Javanese economy was, however, loosened to some extent during the depression years by the abandonment of a number of sugar estates. There was practically no new investment in plantations.

There was, on the other hand, a certain amount of investment in industrial enterprises. The capital came, however, largely from outside the Netherlands. Despite the high cost of electricity, high freight charges and the shortage of skilled labour, the industrial climate in Indonesia proved sufficiently attractive. But it was difficult for Dutch investors to break free from the old tradition of investment in plantations and it was only when it had become quite clear that Twente had permanently lost its textile market in Indonesia that steps were taken, shortly before the war, to build up a textile industry in Java, with the help of Dutch capital. These plans even included the construction of a spinning mill – the first in the archipelago.

World War II and the Japanese occupation were a period of great hardship. Despite the serious decline in many fields, however, the effect of the Japanese occupation on economic life was not all adverse. In some respects the processes just described continued to develop and even to accelerate, the war acting as a catalysing agent.

The first results of the war were heavy capital losses, resulting from destruction carried out by Allied military forces at the approach of the Japanese Army. Attempts by the Japanese to reconstruct some of the destroyed installations met only with partial success. Though the eastern part of the archipelago suffered during the later years of Japanese occupation from heavy Allied bombings, this was not the greatest impediment to the Japanese war economy. Far more serious was the effect of a blockade by the Allied Navy, which increasingly hampered communications with Japan and even inter-island shipping. Exports and imports, already heavily curtailed by the Japanese on their own account, completely ceased. The production of plantations was practically restricted to the need for home consumption. Especially the cultivation of the so-called dessert crops (such as sugar, tobacco, coffee and tea) fell off at a catastrophic rate. Japan attempted to gear Indonesian production to its war needs, and to maintain the plantations only to an extent which was in harmony with the concept of a future economy of a 'Greater East Asia' under the leadership of Japan. In practice this policy meant that extensive areas, formerly part of the plantations, were planted with other crops, such as *ramie* (china-grass) or other fibres, and plants yielding insecticides. Vast areas were also turned over to food cultivation, sometimes for the benefit of the former labour force of the plantations. Many of the factories connected with the plantations were dismantled or rebuilt for the needs of a war industry.

Not only did the Western plantation economy suffer, but native commercial crop production in the Outer Islands almost came to a standstill. The population of these islands, formerly dependent upon the export of rubber, coconuts or pepper and the import of rice, was forced now to resort to food production.

Other elements of Japanese war policy, however, had an extremely unfavourable effect on food production. Free trade, especially in foodstuffs, was severely restricted, for Japanese policy aimed at self-sufficiency in each area and, in Java, even in each residency, perhaps in anticipation of possible guerrilla operations after Allied landings. In deficit areas crop production, particularly of sweet potatoes, was somewhat increased, but this could not compensate for the loss of imported rice.[1] Instead of permitting the surplus areas to sell their surplus to the deficit areas, a harsh system of requisitioning was set up by the Japanese, in order to provide sufficient food for the army and for the urban population working in war industry. It is no wonder that this policy met with

[1] See also 'De economische toestand van Nederlands-Indië tijdens de Japanse bezetting, 1942–1945' (The economic situation of the Netherlands Indies during the Japanese occupation, 1942–1945), in *Statistische en Econometrische Onderzoekingen* (Statistical and Econometric Investigations), New Series, Vol. II, 1947, Nr 4.

passive resistance little short of sabotage, especially in the surplus areas.

Other factors accounting for the serious decline of food production were neglect of irrigation works and of the fight against rats and weeds, partly as a result of the forced labour system, which prevented an essential part of the peasantry from working on their fields; the Japanese policy of slaughtering a great part of the cattle to feed their army; the fact that sea-fishery operations were almost entirely suspended, in consequence of the blockade; and, last but not least, a series of droughts, the most serious of which occurred in 1944.

Another feature of Japanese policy was an increasing rate of coordination and state intervention. A tendency already discernible in Indonesia during the pre-war period was thus continued and reinforced. We have seen, already, some aspects of the Japanese food policy which imposed severe restrictions upon free trade. An important feature of this policy was a distribution system, largely of foodstuffs, requisitioned at low prices from the peasantry. The foodstuffs were distributed at official prices among the urban population, in order to provide officials and workers in vital industries with the essentials of life. The policy thus led to a harsh exploitation of the peasantry in behalf of the most favoured social classes in the cities, consisting of skilled labourers and officials.

Another characteristic of Japan's economic policy was the attempt to concentrate all trading activities in a few big Japanese concerns and in officially recognised unions of traders.[1] Membership in these Japanese-sponsored unions was compulsory and their activities were geared to the Japanese war effort. Many of these organisations had more or less the character of a cooperative society. As the Japanese intended to establish in Western Borneo trading organisations of Indonesians providing for the needs of their own group, the Chinese, who had up to then performed middle class functions on behalf of the Indonesian population, were prevented from continuing these functions except for the

[1] See for instance A. J. Piekaar, *Atjeh en de oorlog met Japan* (Acheh and the war against Japan), The Hague/Bandung, 1949, p. 301.

Chinese population itself. Though this system may have been practised only in Western Borneo, where the Chinese population was very numerous, a general trend toward strengthening Indonesian traders' unions against Chinese competition was in evidence everywhere in Indonesia. Many Chinese traders were ousted from independent trades and crafts and driven either to dependent commercial functions in the service of Japanese monopolistic concerns or to skilled labour on behalf of the military administration. Trade without official licence was not allowed in any part of Indonesia. Those not in possession of a licence were excluded from the distribution system and were liable to be summoned for forced labour, unless they applied themselves to the cultivation of foodstuffs such as sweet potatoes, fruits or vegetables in the neighbourhood of the city.

All these trade regulations required a rigorous system of checks and controls. Naturally many people evaded the regulations and a huge black market made its appearance. A progressive devaluation in the course of the occupation widened the gulf between official prices and those on the free market to the point where, despite harsh punishments in case of detection, black market trade became an extremely profitable business which frustrated many of the Japanese measures.

Though some of the Japanese measures were far from objectionable in theory, their aims were thwarted in practice by the turn of the fortunes of war and by their own consequent harshness. The adverse effect of their agricultural production drive is a case in point, as are their abortive efforts in the field of industrial development. In Java many sugar and tea factories were switched to other purposes, generally in connection with war production; moreover, the population was urged to develop all kinds of small industries. But most of their attemps, and in particular their effort to build up a small-scale spinning industry, connected with the cultivation of cotton, failed, partly owing to an incredible amateurishness in their experiments, and partly as a consequence of the Allied blockade, which prevented indispensable machinery from being imported from Japan.

On the whole, the final result of the Japanese efforts was that what little industry had existed in Java before the war dwindled away during the occupation. This was due to various factors, the most important of which were lack of adequate technical knowledge and the impossibility of importing essential machinery and raw materials. In some parts of the archipelago, however, such as Southern Borneo and Southern Celebes, their policy of industrialisation met with a measure of success.[1] Generally speaking, the attempt to switch part of the agriculture from 'dessert' crops destined for export to fibres, and to integrate the latter cultivation with a home industry, was important as an idea. Their attempt to reinforce the Indonesian middle class against the Chinese was also of great significance.

Despite some well intented measures, however, for the mass of the Indonesian population the Japanese occupation was a period of extreme suffering. The vital statistics, collected by the Japanese, incomplete and unreliable though they may be, indicate a catastrophic development. The increase in population typical for the pre-war period was checked and even reversed in several regions, especially those known as deficit areas with respect to food production. In Java in particular, owing to the forced labour system and to the ensuing increase in deaths and decline in births, the decrease of the population assumed serious proportions.[2]

Trends in Indonesian economy since the revolution are still more difficult to ascertain than those during the Japanese occupation, owing to the complex situation which arose during the course of the struggle for independence.

Throughout the revolutionary years parts of the territory were occupied by Allied or Dutch troops, while others were under

[1] *Economisch Weekblad voor Nederlandsch-Indië* (Economic Weekly for the Netherlands Indies), Vol. XII, 1946, p. 64, 77/78, 106 and passim.

[2] See E. de Vries, 'Geboorte en sterfte onder de Japansche bezetting' (Births and deaths during the Japanese occupation), in *Economisch Weekblad voor Nederlandsch-Indië* (Economic Weekly for the Netherlands Indies), Vol. XII, 1946, p. 43.

Republican administration. The frontier shifted more than once, for example as a result of both Dutch military actions. Moreover, when the Dutch occupied a territory, their actual hold was often restricted to the towns and their immediate environs, the main roads and a few plantations, while considerable parts of the country remained under Republican control or were regularly visited by armed guerrilla bands. Whether an area was controlled by the Dutch or by the Republicans made a good deal of difference. A very important aspect of this difference was the blockade, mainly effectuated by the Dutch Navy, as a result of which the Republican territories were seriously hampered in their communications with the outer world. Exportation of commercial crops was very difficult, and only Acheh and some other not too remote regions were able to carry on some 'smuggling trade' with Singapore. Thus the Republican Government was unable to earn the foreign exchange it needed for its imports. Besides, imports were also practically reduced to zero by the Dutch blockade. The lack of textiles, already serious during the Japanese occupation, became one of the greatest problems of the Republic.

On the other hand, the Republican Government was in a position to withhold indispensable foodstuffs from the cities held by Dutch troops. This counter-blockade was one of the main causes of the first Dutch military action in July 1947, which enabled them to seize control of some of the regions known as rice granaries of Java. After that action the situation was somewhat reversed, and as a result of the Dutch blockade food shortages became more serious, though far from catastrophic, in Republican territory.[1] The situation was aggravated by nearly a million refugees who fled into the shrunken area left to the Republic.[2]

Another important result of the exclusion of a great part of the country from Dutch control was the impossibility for the Netherlands Indian Government of collecting taxes from the rural population in several areas. Whereas during the Japanese occupation

[1] See George McT. Kahin, *Nationalism and revolution in Indonesia*, Ithaca, 1952, p. 261/262.

[2] G. McT. Kahin, *op. cit.*, p. 301/302.

the peasantry was exploited to the utmost in behalf of the urban population, after the Japanese surrender the situation was somewhat reversed.[1] At this time the rural population, even in areas under Dutch control, could impose its conditions on the inhabitants of the cities. Foodstuffs could not be bought for money, if consumer goods were not available. Only by offering textiles and other consumer goods could the government and the traders procure the crops needed.

On the other hand, the Republican Government was, to a large extent, in a position to continue collecting land taxes. Its prestige and control over the rural population was even sufficient to enable it to issue a public loan at the beginning of 1946, of which a high percentage was subscribed. It was part of a monetary reform, intended to supplant the depreciated Japanese currency by a more stable Republican *rupiah*. But even after this revaluation of the *rupiah* land taxes, left at their pre-war nominal value, imposed but a small burden on the peasant population.

This does not mean that the rural population, as a whole, was well off. The profits of high prices for agricultural products accrued largely to those possessing a plot of land.[2] Landless peasants and share-croppers who had to work for others in order to buy their food, were often in a state of penury, especially in the traditional deficit areas. Many young men from the poorer groups joined the Republican Army or guerrilla bands. Fortunately, in some traditional deficit areas of Central Java the process of dispossession of the poorer peasantry and of land accumulation in the hands of few had not yet gone very far.[3] In some areas, however, like Western Java, where there were hardly any restrictions on the sale of land, the concentration of land in the hands of few continued, owing to the increasing indebtedness of the poor peasants

[1] See for Timor: J. D. N. Versluys, 'Maatschappelijke vernieuwing op Timor?' (Social change on Timor?), in *Indonesië*, Vol. III, 1949/50, p. 201 ff.

[2] G. McT. Kahin, *op. cit.*, p. 301/302.

[3] See for example Paul M. Kattenburg, *A Central Javanese village in 1950*, Data paper Nr 2 of the Southeast Asia Program, Cornell University, Ithaca, 1951.

to the wealthy landowners, who had taken over the position of the Chinese as money lenders. Though devaluation during the Japanese occupation had enabled many peasants to pay off their old debts, new indebtedness was arising in many regions.[1]

Sometimes lack of control by the forest service tempted the poorer peasants to clear mountain slopes and to deplete still further the sparse forest resources left intact. The process of deforestation and soil erosion, which had already assumed serious proportions in many parts of Indonesia before the war and which had been hastened by the Japanese, who had used timber as a fuel for the railways, after the revolution took on the character of a catastrophe. For the moment, the peasants could satisfy their need for food. But for the future a tremendous new problem was added, not only from the agronomist's but also from the social point of view, as these settlers were certain to be removed in the long run, with the result that their plight would become still worse than before the reclamation of woodlands.[2]

The impossibility of collecting land taxes caused the Dutch to look for other sources of income. Building up a military apparatus, and the military actions, required large expenditures. Oil and tin, rubber and copra were the chief export products, from which the Netherlands Indian administration derived by far the greatest part of its revenue. But not only was the rehabilitation of the pre-war mines, oil fields and industrial installations subject to great difficulties; it was also hard to get the big plantations going again owing to the prevailing social unrest, the scarcity of labour, and the occupation of vast areas by peasants for food cultivation. An important source of foreign exchange was temporarily provided by the exportation of large stocks found in the country after the Japanese surrender. But in order to keep their administrative system and their military machine going, the Dutch had to bring

1 See G. McT. Kahin, *op. cit.*, p. 326–328; Sumitro Djojohadikusumo, *Persoalan ekonomi di Indonesia* (Economic problems in Indonesia), Jakarta, 1953, p. 151.

2 See H. ten Dam, *op. cit.*, p. 13 ff., describing in a colourful manner the social problems connected with illegal occupations of forest lands.

the plantations into production again. This was a second cause of the first military action. The Republic answered with a scorched earth policy aimed at destruction of all potential sources of foreign exchange for the Dutch. In the end this policy, combined with the social unrest on the plantations, thwarted the Dutch attempts to restore their authority. The expenditure involved in the upkeep of an active military force could not be met by the duties derived from a diminished export volume.

Another source of income was the commercial crops – mainly rubber and copra – cultivated by independent Indonesian farmers in the Outer Islands. Single buyers' organisations under governmental control tried to buy the crops at minimum prices, in order to pocket the difference between these prices and those obtained in foreign trade. But this system also met with difficulties. The farmers were not willing to sell their produce unless they received consumer goods, such as textiles. If the prices paid by the official agencies were not satisfactory, large quantities were sold on the black market and smuggled to Singapore, especially from Borneo. But the greatest drawback was that the puppet states in the Outer Islands began to object to a policy which used the assets earned by their exports for a military and administrative machine mainly stationed on Java.[1]

The impossibility of making both ends meet combined with the untenable military and political situation, finally forced the Dutch to transfer sovereignty at the Round Table Conference.

How far did the achievement of political independence bring about a marked shift in the economic system? It is still too early to assess the full economic implications of the great changes in the political field. It is clear that a new social class, mainly consisting of Indonesian bureaucrats and a few Indonesian traders, has come to power. Many of the new measures, such as the import regulations, are directed at strengthening the Indonesian middle class against European and Chinese businesses. Special state credit facilities for Indonesian traders are easily obtainable.

[1] See G. McT. Kahin, *op. cit.*, p. 358 ff.

Foreign enterprises are subject to many more restrictions than during the colonial period. In general, state intervention in economic affairs has increased. Several of the economic regulations, for example those in the field of labour, are designed to protect the interests of the Indonesian population against foreign entrepreneurs. The distribution system introduced by the Dutch after the war, which distinguished between two classes of consumers and secured in this way a highly privileged position for the whole European and Indo-European class, was immediately abolished.

Yet the break with the past is not as great as it might seem at first sight. Many of the economic regulations were not primarily designed to raise the level of consumption but to stimulate exports. A case in point is the dramatic currency reform of March 1950, when anyone holding paper money had to cut the notes in half, exchange one half for a new note, and buy state bonds with the other half. This reform, combined with new legislation on foreign exchange, amounted to a radical devaluation of the *rupiah*. The practical effect of these measures was to stimulate exports, though only temporarily, to restrict imports, and to provide the treasury with part of the income from the exported goods. The secondary aim of the currency reform, to prevent domestic prices from rising, was not achieved; fluctuations in the price of food became an especially thorny problem. For several years a good deal of state intervention, and regular rice imports, were necessary in order to keep the price of rice within bounds and to fight serious outbreaks of famine.

One of the main reasons why the successive Indonesian governments were forced to follow a policy that emphasised exports was to be found in the economic and financial provisions of the Round Table Conference. The new state began life with a heavy burden of debt to the Netherlands, inherited from the colonial government. The government had to encourage exports in order to pay off its debts. Moreover, the new government had acknowledged the rights and interests of foreign investors. Though there is an increasing tendency to restrict the activities of foreign entrepreneurs and to nationalise vital industries and public utilities, foreign capital still exerts a good deal of power, and uses it in a way which is often detrimental to the Indonesian economy. The threat of losing their assets induces some entrepreneurs to practise an exhausting cultivation and to draw exorbitant profits as long as they can. New capital investments are withheld for fear of heavy governmental restrictions. Besides, the stimulation of exports had only a temporary success, partly due to the Korean War, which raised the market price of some of Indonesia's principal export items, such as oil, tin and rubber. When these prices later declined, the seeming prosperity vanished and the intrinsic weakness of Indonesian economy came to light – a weakness which was never since remedied by all the contradictory economic regulations following upon each other within short intervals.

This weakness is caused by the fact that Indonesia's economic system is still one-sided. Indonesia is still an agrarian country with an extremely low rate of output per man. The total economic structure, though showing many features of a system in full decline, is still unchanged. Government finances are still, as during the colonial period, largely dependent upon the exports of a few mineral and agricultural products. An attempt to build a better balanced economic system would require an intensive effort at industrialisation. Though, in theory, industrial planning plays a certain part in the government's policy, the practical results are, so far, meager in consequence of various factors. As during the colonial period, many vested interests are opposed to an all-out industrialisation program. The obligation accepted by the Republican Government in signing the Torquay treaties, not to raise its import duties above a fixed maximum, made it difficult for Indonesian industries to compete with foreign industries, especially those in Japan. New capital investment from abroad is slow in coming, and most of it is not being directed primarily to industrial projects but to enterprises in the traditional fields of raw materials extraction. Only by a strict policy of discouraging investment in enterprises working only for export and of encouraging investment in industries and other projects essential to a well-balanced economy could the general trend be reversed. The powerful position of foreign concerns has, for the time being, prevented such a departure from the traditional line.

The new Republican Government has thus inherited many of the weaknesses of colonial rule. The new ruling class is, moreover, a mainly urban class, like the white rulers whom it replaced, and is taking on many of the luxurious habits of the former ruling class. Government restrictions on imports of luxuries are difficult to put into effect as many higher officials are easily tempted to indulge in these habits. Distribution no longer discriminates on racial lines, as it did in Dutch controlled areas after the war. But there is a tendency to give petty officials and labourers in vital industries a privileged position in times of rice scarcety, as happened during the Japanese occupation. The interests of the new ruling class are often in opposition to those of the agrarian society, the poor peasantry in particular. The social unrest still prevailing in many areas is caused by widespread rural discontent springing from an unconscious feeling that the interests of the peasantry are being subordinated to those of the urban bourgeoisie. In particular, the attempt of the plantations on Sumatra's Eastcoast to reclaim, with government aid, the fields occupied by small farmers, has given rise to a good deal of trouble.

An attempt to replace the pre-war land tax system by a progressive income tax intended to shift a greater part of the burden to the larger landed properties, has proved difficult to realise in practice.[1] Tax collecting from agrarian areas has met with great difficulties owing to the revolutionary situation in past years and the social unrest still prevailing in some areas.[2] The peasants are paying, on the average, amounts of devaluated *rupiahs* equalling

[1] Rich landowners often try to evade progression. The main difficulty lies in the fact that land registration is confined within the *desa* boundaries. Owners of landed property which is dispersed over various *desas* are often, as a consequence of this lack of centralised administration, classified in a lower category of the progressive tax system than would correspond to the total area of their property.

[2] Douglas S. Paauw, 'The tax burden and economic development in Indonesia', in *Ekonomi dan Keuangan Indonesia* (Economics and Finance in Indonesia), Vol. VII 1954, p. 584.

the amount of guilders they paid before the war. As a consequence the government remains largely dependent upon indirect taxation, which, though luxury imports are much more heavily taxed than essentials, still in general tends to shift a disproportionate share of the burden back unto the shoulders of the poor.

Another difficulty inherited by the Republican Government is the discrepancy between the amount of foreign exchange earned by the Outer Islands and the share they receive of state finances and state activities. The movement for regional autonomy can be largely accounted for by the way the resources of the Outer Islands have been exploited for the benefit of an urban bourgeoisie concentrated mainly in Java.

The general picture of Indonesia seems to be one of a stationary economy. There is a tendency among representatives of foreign interests, and even among some Indonesian authorities, to emphasise the wrong things in discussing the Indonesian economy. It is highly questionable whether the economic problems generally considered as crucial are really of decisive importance.

According to many foreigners the economic health of Indonesia depends upon the strength of foreign enterprise (plantations and mining). The restrictions on foreign enterprise are considered dangerous to the Indonesian economy. It is true that these enterprises provide the greatest part of the exports and that they contribute largely to the state revenue. But high exports should not be an aim in themselves. Exports are valuable for the Indonesian economy as a whole only if the earnings are spent on imports indispensable for economic development, such as industrial machinery, raw materials, or essentials of life which cannot be produced at home. The efforts of the successive cabinets to discourage imports of luxuries and to encourage imports of industrial equipment are still far from effective. Neither is foreign capital investment desirable *per se*. If it is restricted to raw materials extraction, it may hamper industrial development and, consequently, be detrimental to economic health. Providing employment and spending 'money' among the population are by no means boons in themselves, as is proved by past experience in all colonial countries. Creating paid jobs is far from identical with creating wealth. More farmers were impoverished than enriched by the pre-war plantation economy. Whether an enterprise really creates wealth depends upon its character, and upon the extent to which its production is geared to a general plan for economic development. Economic health cannot be measured merely in monetary or budgetary terms, nor in terms of a trade balance. It depends upon realities such as material output and the prospects for an increased production of the necessities and amenities of life.

Neither is the approach of Indonesian authorities to economic problems free from illusions. There are still too many officials who cherish the hope that by supplanting foreign by national firms they are building up 'an Indonesian economy'. Though increasing the Indonesian share in economic activities and profits is, no doubt, of great importance, it would be vain to expect an improvement in economic conditions if the authorities limit themselves to enabling Indonesian nationals to reap what profits there are in the present economy. The core of the problem is not in the field of distribution, but in that of production. It would be illusory to attempt to give Indonesian nationals a greater share in the national wealth if production is at the same time being discouraged. Increasing the material wealth of the country through higher productivity is the only way to create a 'national economy'. The main potential wealth of Indonesia is found in its untapped labour reserves, since partial unemployment of farmers and agricultural labourers is a general phenomenon in Indonesia. Only by organising a full utilisation of these labour reserves for the construction of public works and for an increase of both agricultural and industrial production can a real contribution to economic development be made.

However, dynamic tendencies are already discernible. The Javanese peasantry begins to stir. From several areas there are reports about a growing consciousness and activity in the fields of food production and hygiene. The tremendous growth of the cooperative movement is also a case in point, though many of the cooperatives still function far from satisfactorily. The activities of the trade unions, demanding a fairer share in the profits of all kinds of enterprise, and the support these unions are receiving from many official services, are signs of a newly awakening social conscience. Nevertheless, within the existing economic system the claims of the labourers for higher wages and shorter working days may have dangerous implications. They may deter capital investors from further activities. The core of the problem in the underdeveloped areas is the low rate of output per man. This problem cannot be solved by discouraging capital investment or by granting labourers a fairer share in the profits.

What is needed is a well-planned, full-fledged program of industrial development, accompanied by strict control of foreign capital activities, in addition to a well-devised rural development, to redress the existing one-sidedness. At the end of this book some broader attention will be given to the many problems accompanying this radical change in the economic system.

A short bibliography

G. C. Allen and A. G. Donnithorne, *Western enterprise in Indonesia and Malaya*, London, 1957.

J. H. Boeke, *Economics and economic policy of dual societies as exemplified by Indonesia*, Haarlem, 1953.

J. H. Boeke, *The interests of the voiceless Far East*, Leiden, 1948.

D. H. Burger, *De ontsluiting van Java's binnenland voor het wereldverkeer* (The opening of the interior of Java to world trade), Wageningen, 1939.

D. H. Burger, *Vergelijking van den economischen toestand der districten Tajoe en Djakenan* (*Regentschap Pati, Afdeeling Rembang*), (Comparison of the economic situation of the districts Taju and Jakenan, Pati Regency, Rembang Department), Weltevreden, 1930.

D. H. Burger, 'Structuurveranderingen in de Javaanse samenleving' (Structural changes in Javanese society), in *Indonesië*, Vol. II and III, 1948/49 and 1949/50.

D. H. Burger, *Structural changes in Javanese society. The village sphere;* and *Structural changes in Javanese society. The supra-village sphere,* translations of parts of the foregoing, Translation Series, Modern Indonesia Project, Cornell University, Ithaca, 1957 and 1956.

'De economische toestand van Nederlands-Indië tijdens de Japanse bezetting, 1942–1945' (The economic situation of the Netherlands Indies during the Japanese occupation, 1942–1945), in *Statistische en Econometrische Onderzoekingen* (Statistical and Econometric Investigations), New Series, Vol. II, 1947, Nr 4.

Th. A. Fruin, *Het economische aspect van het Indonesische vraagstuk* (The economic aspect of the Indonesian problem), Amsterdam, 1947.

J. S. Furnivall, *Colonial policy and practice. A comparative study of Burma and Netherlands India*, Cambridge, 1948.

Garis-garis besar rentjana pembangunan lima tahun, 1956–1960 (Outline of Five-Years' Development Plan, 1956–1960), Jakarta, 1956.

Geld- en productenhuishouding, volksvoeding en -gezondheid in Koetowinangoen (Money economy and barter economy, the diet and health of the people in Kutawinangun), Buitenzorg, 1934.

J. van Gelderen, *Voorlezingen over tropisch-koloniale staathuishoudkunde* (Lectures on political economy in the colonial tropics), Haarlem, 1927.

J. van Gelderen, *The recent development of economic foreign policy in the Netherlands East Indies*, London, 1939.

G. Gonggrijp, *Schets ener economische geschiedenis van Indonesië* (Outline of an economic history of Indonesia), Haarlem, 1957.

B. Higgins, *Indonesia's economic stabilization and development*, New York, 1957.

G. H. van der Kolff, *The historical development of the labour relationships in a remote corner of Java as they apply to the cultivation of rice*, Batavia, 1937.

G. Kuperus, 'The relation between density of population and utilization of soil in Java', in *Comptes rendus du Congres International de Géographie*, 1938.

C. B. van der Leeden, *Het aspect van landbouwkolonisatie in het bevolkingsprobleem van Java* (The aspect of rural resettlement in the population problem of Java), The Hague, 1952.

Oei Tjong Bo, *Niederländisch-Indien. Eine Wirtschaftsstudie*, Zürich, 1948.

S. J. Rutgers, *Indonesië. Het koloniale systeem in de periode tussen de eerste en de tweede wereldoorlog* (Indonesia. The colonial system during the period between World War I and World War II), Amsterdam, 1947.

R. Saroso Wirodihardjo, *De contingenteeringspolitiek en hare invloed op de Indonesische bevolking* (The quota policy and its influence upon the Indonesian population), Jakarta, 1951.

P. H. W. Sitsen, *Industrial development of the Netherlands Indies*, New York, 1942.

Soenario, *Verschulding en economische toestand op Java's platteland* (Debt and the economic situation in the Javanese rural areas), Batavia, 1939.

R. M. Sumitro Djojohadikusumo, *Ekonomi pembangunan* (Economics of reconstruction), Jakarta, 1955.

R. M. Sumitro Djojohadikusumo, *Het volkscredietwezen in de depressie* (The people's credit organisation during the depression), Haarlem, 1943.

Verslag van de Commissie tot bestudeering van staatsrechtelijke hervormingen (Report of the Commission for the study of political reforms), New York, 1944.

Chapter Six

The Changing Status System

1 The status system in the old native society

It is not possible to speak of a single original Indonesian status system. There are sharp divergencies according to whether the community is organised predominantly on a genealogical or a territorial basis. The former type is mostly associated with *ladang* cultivation, while the latter is found chiefly among peoples practising agriculture on irrigated rice fields. The structure is dependent in large measure, too, on the extent to which village communities are overshadowed by a feudal or princely superstructure.

Within the Javanese *desa*, a person's social standing was connected particularly with his relationship to the land. The fully qualified member of the village, the 'nuclear villager', was a man who owned farm land as well as his own compound and house. His position often stemmed from an ancestor who was one of the founders of the *desa*, a genealogical element within the territorial structure. The man who owned a compound and a house, but no farm land, fell into the second rank. One who possessed only a house in another man's compound was classed in still a lower category. In the lowest category of all we find those who merely shared another man's dwelling.[1] In communities organised on more genealogical lines social prestige was determined by other factors, such as the clan to which one belonged and the rank held inside the clan by virtue of one's family relationships.

As a rule the position of the chief in the small communities, both territorial and genealogical, was not one of authoritarian com-

[1] B. ter Haar, *Adat law in Indonesia*, New York, 1948, p. 71 ff.

mand but rather one of *primus inter pares*.[1] A certain measure of democracy is inherent to the primitive Indonesian social structure. Important decisions are not made by a single leader with discretionary powers but by a council of elders or a meeting of the nuclear villagers.

Above the village communities were the principalities, bound together by princely authority. A great social gulf divided the noble families from the common man, both in the inland-states and in the coastal principalities. There was also a slave class, usually small in numbers, on which the ordinary freeman could, in his turn, look down. Slavery was, in general, the result of war, debt, or an offense against the *adat* (customary law). In the agricultural areas the nobility represented only a small percentage of the population, far removed socially from the great mass of the peasants. The nobility lived on the labour of the peasants and the slaves. The status system was maintained by a rather strict endogamy which made it, in particular, a mortal sin for a noblewoman to marry a commoner or, worse still, a slave. The nobility left all heavy manual labour to the ordinary freeman and the slaves, limiting its activities to those forms of occupation in keeping with its status (hunting, jousting, war and the more delicate handicrafts). Different modes of social intercourse and manners of speech symbolised the great distinction between the classes. Where Hinduism prevailed, social stratification even assumed the character of a caste system. There was also a high degree of differentiation inside the ranks of the nobility, depending upon the purity of one's line of descent.[2]

Social subdivision was far advanced in the harbour principalities

[1] Alb. C. Kruyt, 'The influence of Western civilisation on the inhabitants of Poso (Central Celebes)', in B. Schrieke (ed.), *The effect of Western influence on native civilisations in the Malay archipelago*, Batavia, 1929, p. 1 ff.; F. H. van Naerssen, *Culture contacts and social conflicts in Indonesia*, New York, 1947, p. 6.

[2] Cf., for example, H. J. Friedericy, 'De standen bij de Boegineezen en Makassaren' (Social classes among the Buginese and the people of Macassar), in *Bijdragen tot de Taal-, Land- en Volkenkunde van Nederlandsch-Indië* (Contributions to the Philology, Geography, and Ethnology of the Netherlands Indies), Vol. XC, 1933, p. 447 ff.

also. There was a wide gulf between the ruling noble families, closely associated with a numerically small class of rich patricians of predominantly foreign origin, and the broad mass of town dwellers, composed of pedlars, artisans and slaves. The small traders grouped in the foreign wards of the coastal towns seldom showed the traits associated with the free bourgeoisie in the commercial cities of Western Europe. There were few traces to be found of an urban democracy. Both the towns and the areas surrounding them were as a rule completely dominated by the ruling noble families.[1]

Naturally there were many factors which cut across this system of social strata. In the countryside particularly, elders often enjoyed a traditional authority over the young. The social and economic functions of the women differed from those of the men; on the whole their status was inferior. Notwithstanding local differences their social position was, however, favourable as compared with the rights of women in many other Asian countries. In agriculture, where women fulfilled an important economic function, their position was by no means subordinate.

Unusual abilities, ascribed to magical powers, also conferred on their possessor a special social status. In the countryside, for example, the medicine man and the smith were usually regarded as being endowed with magical powers. In the towns, too, certain professions gave special status, which often passed from father to son along with the profession itself. Qualifications, mostly of an intellectual character, such as the art of writing or knowledge of the religious scriptures, lent distinction and often brought partial exemption from manual labour. Greater proximity to princely circles and work closely related to the care of the prince's person could also provide enhanced status. On the other hand, remoteness from the centres of princely authority was sometimes associated with greater freedom and independence.[2]

[1] J. C. van Leur, *Indonesian trade and society. Essays in Asian social and economic history*, Selected studies on Indonesia by Dutch scholars, Vol. I, The Hague/Bandung, 1955, p. 66, 92, 137 ff., 204 ff.

[2] F. H. van Naerssen, *op. cit.*, p. 8.

Religion, of course, affected social prestige. Despite a large degree of tolerance and hospitality in most harbour principalities with regard to merchants of different religions, those who held the same creed as the ruler were generally more trusted and more favoured than the others. Thus, the scale of preference varied greatly according to the creed prevalent in an Indonesian state.

These subordinate strands in the web do not, however, substantially blur the primary pattern of the old Indonesian status system.

2 *The rise of a new status system based on race*

As early as the seventeenth and eighteenth centuries a status system had grown up in the enclaves controlled by the East India Company, which differed substantially from the old Indonesian pattern. In Batavia the Dutch employees of the Company formed the uppermost social layer; below them came the free citizens, among whom the Christians (Dutch, mestizos, and enfranchised Christian slaves, in that order) occupied the most privileged positions; after these came the Chinese; and the Indonesian population, a large number of them slaves, formed the lowest layer.[1] Although this structure seemed opposed to that in the majority of Indonesian harbour principalities, there were also certain resemblances, for in Batavia, too, foreign traders and artisans lived together in separate wards under their own chieftains, while those who shared the religion of the rulers, or at least did not profess the Islamic religion – which the rulers of Batavia regarded as a hostile faith – enjoyed a privileged position and a certain measure of confidence.

This status system in Batavia formed the starting point for the colonial society of nineteenth century Java. When colonial dominion spread over the entire island, penetrating, during the culture system period, even into the rural areas, it was inevitable that the old Indonesian prestige scale should be replaced by a new one.

[1] F. de Haan, *Oud Batavia* (Old Batavia), Bandung, 1935, p. 349 ff.

As in the British colonial empire, it was no longer the religion of the settlers that provided the criterion for social prestige, but race. The extension of the white man's power over the coloured races in the nineteenth century was accompanied everywhere by a marked rise in the social standing of the whites and high social regard for all outward characteristics, such as language, dress, and skin colour, which symbolised white race. Thus in a large part of the world the colour line became the cornerstone of the colonial social structure. In the nineteenth century Java, too, came under the spell of the colour line. But since in every colonial area the social pattern showed certain distinctive characteristics,[1] we must examine more closely the particular forms this pattern assumed in Java.

About 1850 the colonial stratification based on race had assumed a fixed form in Java, which was reflected in the laws. The Europeans formed the ruling stratum, resembling a caste. In contrast with the situation in the British colonies, people of mixed blood belonged to this upper stratum if they descended from a white man in the male line and were either legitimate or recognised by the father.

Over against this upper layer stood the Indonesians, referred to as the '*Inlanders*' (natives) and representing the subject stratum. The gulf between the two layers was practically unbridgeable. Apart from one or two exceptional cases, transfer from the lower to the upper stratum was impossible. Discrimination was made on a racial basis in almost all departments of justice and social life. Only the '*Inlanders*' were subject to compulsory service for public works and forced labour on the government plantations. Discrimination was found everywhere in the fields of government and justice, eligibility for official positions and teaching. The native mother of a natural child of a European father had no rights of guardianship after the death of the latter. Her permission

1 See R. Kennedy, 'The colonial crisis and the future', in R. Linton (ed.), *The science of man in the world crisis*, New York, 1945, p. 308, 320 ff.

was not required before the child married.[1] A person's position depended not on what he was himself but on the population group to which he belonged. Punitive measures were framed to ensure that the colour line should not be overstepped – it was forbidden to dress otherwise than in the manner customary in one's own population group.[2] The colonial rulers even succeeded in large measure in forcing the Indonesians themselves to accept the system of values based on race. The members of the colonial ruling class were from their birth, or from the moment of their disembarkation on the shores of the Indies, conditioned to this pattern of behaviour and imbued with all the stereotypes connected with it.

There were many kinds of differentiation within each 'caste'. Thus for a long time Dutch officials enjoyed high social prestige. On the other hand the 'colonials', the Dutch professional soldiers, although part of the ruling stratum, had relatively low social standing. After private capital was admitted into Java, private individuals gradually increased not only in number but also in social prestige, while on the plantations the planters gained a patriarchal power and a social esteem which often equalled that of the Indonesian *pryayis* – members of the Javanese nobility.[3]

[1] See articles 40 and 354 of the Civil Code of 1848:
Art. 40. Illegitimate children, legally acknowledged by the father, are not allowed to marry, when under age, without the consent of their father. In default of the father the consent of the mother is required.
If the mother belongs to the native population or to those legally assimilated with natives, the consent of the Court of Justice has to be secured; in that case the provisions of the preceding article are applicable.
Art. 354. In default of the father, or in case the latter is not able to exercise the guardianship, the Court of Justice also provides for the guardianship of illegitimate children who are legally acknowledged by Europeans or by persons assimilated with Europeans, and whose mothers belong to the native or assimilated population.

[2] See for example art. 2 Nr 6 of the Penal Police Ordinance in *Staatsblad* (State Journal), 1872, Nr 111. See also Gouw Giok Siong, *Segi-segi hukum peraturan perkawinan tjampuran* (Legal aspects of the regulation on mixed marriages), Jakarta, 1958, Ch. I.

[3] See D. H. Burger, *Structural changes in Javanese society. The supra-village sphere*, Translation Series, Modern Indonesia Project, Cornell University, Ithaca, 1956, p. 21.

More important still was the fact that though half-castes were counted in the European group, their social position within the group was determined by a prestige scale closely related to the colonial value system: a scale based on the colour of their skin and other characteristics reflecting the degree of relationship to the white race. The darker the skin, the more 'Indian' the speech, clothing and manners, the lower the social standing. Although the colour line was drawn along the division between '*Inlander*' and 'half-caste', there was no question of equality between white man and half-blood. The entire social life was so imbued by colour-consciousness – though certainly less so than in India – that many Indo-Europeans (then usually known as '*Sinjos*'; later, besides the term 'Indo-Europeans', the term '*Indos*' came into use) were kept fully occupied by the effort to demonstrate as close a relationship as possible with the white race and to dissociate themselves as far as possible from the '*Inlanders*'. Like corresponding groups in the other colonies, they were typical marginal men.

Just as in the days of the Company, many of these *Indos* filled clerical posts. For the Dutch, they represented a loyal and trustworthy group, even though they sometimes had every reason to complain of the treatment they experienced at the hands of the white men. And as they were able, from 1850 onwards, to profit increasingly from Dutch schooling, by degrees they began to regard themselves as the bearers *par excellence* of Dutch culture.

Among the '*Inlanders*' a great part of the original status system was preserved. The Javanese nobility was brought into the framework of the Western government apparatus. After a short period in which an unsuccessful effort was made to introduce more democratic ideas into Javanese society, this nobility was reinstalled in its former authority during the period of the culture system, partly as a result of lessons learned in the Java War of 1825–1830. Its position was even reinforced insofar as the function of the regent was declared hereditary.[1] Colonial stratification based on

[1] See B. Schrieke, *Indonesian sociological studies. Selected writings*, Part 1. Selected studies on Indonesia by Dutch scholars, Vol. II, The Hague/Bandung, 1955, p. 188.

race was merely superimposed on the original Indonesian class system.

All the same, the colonial regime did bring about structural changes in Javanese society. Slavery was abolished – although for some time afterwards Indonesians continued to look down on the descendants of slaves. The culture system had marked effects on the internal structure of the Javanese *desa*. Compulsory labour on government plantations often imposed so severe a burden that the members of the village were compelled to share the burden equally and to break through the dividing line separating 'nuclear villagers' from those of second rank. Sugar cultivation, either under the culture system or after the introduction of private plantations, also had an equalising effect on native land ownership, through the fiction of communal ownership, whereby it was assumed that the land belonged to the *desa* as a whole, the individual peasant having merely a right of use. This assumption had definite advantages from the point of view of the government and the plantation owners, since for purposes of supervision and irrigation it was much easier to deal with compact blocks of land than with tiny holdings. On the other hand, the status of the village chief was raised above that which he had enjoyed under the customary law (*adat*). From being a *primus inter pares* he became an authority, and at the same time a tool of the central government.[1]

Another point deserves attention. In contrast to the Western prestige system, a scale of values was preserved which to a certain extent embodied a protest against the colonial system: a prestige scale based on religion. According to this scale, the Islamic scribe, the *haji* (pilgrim returned from Mecca) and the Arab *Sayyid* (descendant of the Prophet) were men of high standing, whereas white men were merely '*kafirs*', that is, unbelievers.

Finally, mention should be made of a third social stratum besides

[1] See for example Alb. C. Kruyt in B. Schrieke (ed.), *The effect of Western influence on native civilisations in the Malay archipelago*, p. 4 ff.; D. H. Burger, *De ontsluiting van Java's binnenland voor het wereldverkeer* (The opening of the interior of Java to world trade), Wageningen, 1939, p. 128 ff.

the *Europeans* and the *Inlanders*, namely the *Foreign Orientals*, composed of the Chinese and the Arabs; they occupied an intermediate position between the Europeans and the Indonesians. In Java they formed in the main a middle class of independent merchants and artisans. In their function of professional traders, the Chinese were held in little esteem by the Indonesian nobility and peasant class. But in the colonial estimation they were, within certain limits, very useful and usually fairly loyal intermediaries between the white man and the Indonesian population, with greater affinity to the former than the native people.

The above sketch typifies the general situation in Java up to the end of the nineteenth century. The Surakarta (Solo) and Jogjakarta Principalities, too, where an Indonesian princely authority was recognised–though more in name than in fact–came more and more under the influence of the new colonial values, although the resistance put up by the original Indonesian class system was naturally more marked here, as was the social and economic differentiation within the native community.[1] The relatively simple, static pattern of ancient Indonesia was replaced by a new pattern on colonial principles, one which was also fairly stable and simple in nature.

3 *The decay of the colonial status system in the twentieth century*

About 1900 the Netherlands succeeded in establishing its dominion over the whole archipelago. The colonial stratification according to race, prevalent in Java, was thus spread to the Outer Islands. Simultaneously, however, there were dynamic developments in the twentieth century which cut across this rigid pattern and increased social mobility.

In the Outer Islands it was mainly money that made a breach in the old native status system. It was primarily the Indonesian city traders who revolted against tradition and the power of the clan. In many parts of the Outer Islands the indigenous popula-

[1] See the interesting analysis by H. J. van Mook, 'Kuta Gede', in *The Indonesian town. Studies in urban sociology*, Selected studies on Indonesia by Dutch scholars, Vol. IV, The Hague/Bandung, 1958, p. 275 ff.

tion's dislike of professional trading was less marked than in Java, so that the status system based on ethnic groups, which left trade to the Foreign Oriental, did not exert anything like the same influence on the social pattern as it did in Java. The cultivation of market crops in the country areas also created a certain economic individualism which revolted against traditional bonds and against the authority of the *adat* chiefs. The material prosperity achieved by many a farmer and trader caused them to strive after a social prestige which would equal that enjoyed by the *adat* chiefs and to demand for themselves a *ius connubii* (right to marriage) within the chieftain class.[1]

The agrarian unrest which began to make itself evident in the Outer Islands in the twenties (as in the communist rising of January 1927 in Menangkabau) was not simply the effect of the impoverishment of some of the farmers as a result of the mobilisation of landed property, but was due also to opposition on the part of the newly-rich farmers to the traditional social structure.[2] Moreover, in so far as the interests of native planters came into conflict with those of the Western entrepreneurs – which happened in the case of rubber cultivation in the crisis years – this agrarian resistance took on a nationalist tint as well, a tendency strengthened by the fact that the government usually acted as a protector, not only of the traditional authority of the chiefs, but also of the Western plantations. In certain areas, such as the Hulu Sungei (Southeast Borneo), where the feudal *adat* rule had been pushed aside at the time of the 'pacification', as hostile to the Dutch, individualism made further advances and, apart from religious criteria, which had great social significance in this area especially, material welfare represented the chief criterion in

[1] Cf., for example, B. Schrieke, *Indonesian sociological studies. Selected writings*, Part 1, p. 138 ff. In the unpublished part of his Sumatra's Westcoast Report Schrieke describes how the rising 'middle class' challenged the traditional privileges of the aristocracy, in matters of precedence at festivities and of marriage. In 1925 the first marriages between 'middle class' men and girls from the nobility were concluded in Silungkang.

[2] See B. Schrieke, *op. cit.*, p. 131.

determining social prestige – more so than in the '*adat* areas'.[1]

Education, too, had a dynamic influence in the Outer Islands, although less than in Java.[2] There was little employment in the *ladang* and rubber districts for intellectuals or near-intellectuals. The towns, too, were much smaller than in Java. Thus the majority of those with a more Western type of education flocked to Java during and after their study. Hence they formed less of a social problem in the Outer Islands than in Java. The significance of education as a dynamic influence is, therefore, better studied on the latter island.

From 1900 onwards there was increasing professional differentiation to be observed in Java also. The expansion of a money economy and increased contact with the West gave rise to numerous new jobs, *e.g.*, for mechanics, chauffeurs, engine drivers and overseers. A new group emerged, rising to some extent above the mass of the population owing to technical ability. More Indonesians applied themselves to trade than formerly, first as retailers, later as middlemen. The impression conveyed by Kahin[3] that the Indonesian commercial class did not increase in numbers and was, up to World War II, steadily being eliminated by Chinese competition, seems to me debatable, even for Java and for the pre-depression period. It is not confirmed by what statistical material is available. According to the *Onderzoek naar de mindere welvaart der Inlandsche bevolking op Java en Madoera*[4] in 1905 there were 385,472 independent traders without supplementary income from agriculture, or 560,390 independent traders including those in possession of a farm. A rather restricted number of Indonesians in the service of other tradesmen might be added,

[1] See J. Mallinckrodt, *Het adatrecht van Borneo* (The *adat* law of Borneo), Leiden, 1928, Vol. II, p. 154 ff., 181.

[2] See Schrieke's contribution in B. Schrieke (ed.), *The effect of Western influence on native civilisations in the Malay archipelago*, p. 241 ff.

[3] George McT. Kahin, *Nationalism and revolution in Indonesia*, Ithaca, 1952, p. 27 ff.

[4] *Onderzoek naar de mindere welvaart der Inlandsche bevolking op Java en Madoera* (Investigation into the diminished welfare of the native population of Java and Madura), Batavia, 1905–1914, Vol. VIa, Appendix I.

but it is difficult to assess their number correctly, as they are included in the 1905 investigation within a larger number of people working in trade, industry and transport combined. In the 1930 census of Netherlands India[1] there were 908,940 'Natives' who mentioned trade as their chief occupation. Since peasants, male or female, who supplemented their income with trading activities often gave the latter as their chief occupation,[2] it seems fair to compare the 1930 figure with the higher figure of 1905. As the 1930 data include people working for others, the category is broader than the independent traders listed in 1905. But the 1930 Census conveys the impression that Indonesians working in the trade for others were still rather few, as the great majority of those occupied in trade were engaged in retailing food and tobacco, which points towards petty independent trade. Moreover, it is commonly known, that Chinese shopkeepers mostly employed Chinese personnel, which excludes the possibility that a very large number of Indonesians were working for Chinese. The comparison between the group of traders in 1905 and in 1930 shows, besides a considerable absolute progress, that an increased percentage of the total population of Java and Madura was occupied in trading in 1930. For in 1905 1.87% of the total population (thirty million) were traders as against 2.27% of the total population (forty million) in 1930.[3] A different picture might emerge if those employed by others were deducted. But an actual decrease in the percentage engaged in trade, as assumed by Kahin, has still to be demonstrated.

Later developments during the depression of the thirties also suggest, that even before 1930 an incipient native middle class was beginning to emerge, breaking through the old traditional

[1] *Census of 1930 in Netherlands India*, Batavia, 1933–1936, Vol. VIII, p. 126, table 19.

[2] *Census of 1930 in Netherlands India*, Vol. VIII, p. 56.

[3] A modest increase, especially between 1913 and 1920, is also indicated by the *Verslag van den economischen toestand der inlandsche bevolking, 1924* (Report on the economic condition of the native population, 1924), Weltevreden, 1926, Vol. I, p. 177 ff.

order of society and exerting an individualistic influence. The plantations, too, jerked the peasant out of his old environment and brought him into contact with the Western world, in which process growing acquaintance with the Western way of life and movie shows on pay-day played an important part.

In Java, however, the influence of these factors is completely overshadowed by the way in which education changed the traditional structure of society. Its effect was felt even in the simplest forms of teaching in the *desa*. However elementary the teaching of the three R's might be, the fact that the children had to recognise the authority of the teacher, besides that of their parents, had its effect on the traditional scale of social prestige, and in particular on the authority of the elders; for the teacher's authority was exerted in a field in which the parents were quite ignorant, even as compared with their younger children. The effect was even more strongly marked when the child's education enabled him to find employment outside the confines of Indonesian agriculture which brought with it social prestige and material prosperity far beyond anything he could have achieved at home.

Quite apart from the nature of the instruction given – and as a rule it came into sharp conflict with the traditional native conceptions – the mere fact of its existence made a breach in the agrarian structure. However much the schools might try to adapt their instruction to the agrarian scene, even those who received a predominantly agricultural or technical training were readily inclined to seek work in the towns, where they could achieve greater social prestige.[1] This was because in the Indonesian community a social premium was attached to more or less intellectual work, and as few people could both read and write, those who possessed these skills could command relatively high incomes. The clerk was held in higher esteem than the skilled farmer, and could even perhaps achieve a higher standard of living.[2]

[1] See for example J. S. Furnivall, *Colonial policy and practice. A comparative study of Burma and Netherlands India*, Cambridge, 1948, p. 381.

[2] J. van Gelderen, *Voorlezingen over tropisch-koloniale staathuishoudkunde* (Lectures on political economy in the colonial tropics), Haarlem, 1927, p. 68.

Thus education created a new class of intellectuals and near-intellectuals who occupied a special position in society. In a certain sense this had an individualising effect, as the money economy also had in the Outer Islands. The social prestige and the comparative material prosperity attached to an 'intellectual' position were so attractive that many simple people endured the greatest sacrifices in order to afford their children the advantages of a reasonably good education.[1] The individual's effort to rise in the social scale did not express itself, in this society, in a struggle for profit from trade or from an independent profession, but in a struggle to obtain an official appointment by means of diplomas.[2] And since a knowledge of Dutch in particular was a passport to jobs barred to the many, knowledge of the language became involved in the assessment of social prestige.

Traditional bonds played a role in the effort to scrape together enough money to enable a child to study, for several members of the family contributed to finance his schooling, while the whole family tried to profit by it, not only through the successful candidate's enhanced social prestige, but also by his enlarged income. Notwithstanding this, the chase after diplomas had a strongly individualising effect.

Thus education created a whole class of Indonesians with a certain amount of Western education, and the existence of this class had as dynamic an effect on the status system of Java as rubber cultivation had on that of the Outer Islands.

First, the presence of this class affected the social value system within the Indonesian society in the narrow sense of the word. Whereas in the past people had looked up only to the traditional chiefs and religious leaders, they now began to rank the authority

[1] See C. Hooykaas, 'Voldoet de A.M.S. nog?' (Does the A.M.S. still satisfy?), in *Koloniale Studiën* (Colonial Studies), Vol. XXIV, 1940, p. 24; Takdir Alisjahbana, 'De botsing van Oost en West' (The clash between East and West), in *Sticusa Jaarboek* (Yearbook of the Foundation for Cultural Cooperation between the Netherlands, Indonesia, Surinam and the Netherlands Antilles), 1950, p. 58.

[2] D. H. Burger, *Structural changes in Javanese society. The supra-village sphere*, p. 21.

of the new spiritual leaders, the intellectuals, above that of the regents and the *kyahis* (Moslem religious teachers). It was the Western trained school teacher who first and foremost personified this new prestige. But it was modern corporate life which first made it clear how deeply the traditional structure had been affected. The enormous growth of *Sarekat Islam* at about the time of World War I demonstrated that the masses no longer submitted to traditional authority but were prepared to follow the leadership of union chiefs originating from the intellectual group.[1]

Just as the *nouveaux riches* in Menangkabau and elsewhere in the Outer Islands had demanded the *ius connubii* with the *adat* chiefs, so the most prosperous of the new intellectuals in Java, many of them of Sumatran origin, demanded entry into the circles of the higher Javanese nobility.[2] Together with the old ruling aristocracy, these intellectuals were to form a class of 'new *pryayis*' which would become the uppermost layer in Indonesian society.[3]

But it was not only in the traditional Javanese social order that the existence of a class of Indonesian intellectuals and near-intellectuals made a breach. It also broke through the nineteenth century colonial stratification based on race. Western education gave the Indonesians a chance to fill posts which had previously been reserved for the European 'caste'. In this manner the foundations of the colonial status system gradually collapsed. Here, as elsewhere, education acted like dynamite on the colonial caste system.[4]

The great tension in Indonesia in the years before World War

[1] See P. A. A. Djajadiningrat, *Herinneringen van Pangeran Aria Achmad Djajadiningrat* (Memoirs of Pangeran Aria Achmad Djajadiningrat), Amsterdam/Batavia, 1936, p. 284 ff.

[2] D. H. Burger, *Structural changes in Javanese society. The supra-village sphere*, p. 21.

[3] I. J. Brugmans and Soenario, 'Enkele gegevens van sociale aard' (Some data of social order), in *Verslag van de Commissie tot bestudeering van staatsrechtelijke hervormingen* (Report of the Commission for the study of political reforms), New York, 1944, Vol. I, p. 72.

[4] Cf. R. Kennedy, *op. cit.*, p. 311: 'Education would be dynamite for the rigid caste systems of colonies'.

II was associated to a significant degree with the order in which various groups came into contact with education. Expansion of the apparatus of government and of Western business during the second half of the nineteenth century had brought a need for personnel trained in administration and conversant with the Dutch language. The obvious remedy was to draw, in the first instance, on those groups who had already had some contact with Dutch culture. Thus the Indo-Europeans were the first to profit from the opportunities provided for education. Among the Indonesians, the children of chiefs and the Ambonese and Menadonese Christians were the first to gain access on a larger scale to the increased facilities for education.

It was only after 1900 that education was opened to a larger number of Indonesians. The demand for trained personnel continued to increase. Indonesians were being appointed to functions which had previously been the privilege of Europeans. Probably not only for reasons of justice but also in order to prevent lower paid Indonesian personnel from ousting the Europeans, equal pay for equal work for Indonesians and Europeans alike was adopted as a principle after 1913.[1] However, for appointments demanding higher education which for the most part could, for the time being, be filled only by Indo-Europeans, special scales of salary were fixed, adjusted to the Indo-Europeans' higher standard of living; whereas the highest appointments, which were largely filled by personnel brought into the country from abroad, were accorded salaries relatively much higher than the others, in order to attract staff to the tropics. In this way the privileged position of the European upper stratum was preserved for as long as possible. But the progress in education brought jobs of increasing importance within the reach of Indonesians, with the result that the extra remuneration attached to the higher appointments tended gradually to disappear and the number of typically 'European' posts declined considerably. Especially during the

[1] See *Javasche Courant* (Java Journal), 12-8-1913, Nr 67; Paul W. van der Veur, 'The Eurasians of Indonesia: castaways of colonialism', in *Pacific Affairs*, Vol. XXVII, 1954, p. 125.

depression of the thirties 'Indianisation' of the administrative service made headway at a remarkable pace.[1]

Percentage of administrative personnel according to population group in 1938 compared with 1928[2]

	1938			1928		
	Europeans	Indonesians	Foreign Orientals	Europeans	Indonesians	Foreign Orientals
Technical staff . . .	77.14	20.12	2.74	84.77	14.38	0.85
Administrative techn. staff	55.81	41.98	2.21	77.06	22.28	0.66
Financial staff	67.08	30.46	2.46	80.45	18.8	0.75
Administrative staff .	65.18	32.16	2.66	93.66	5.1	1.24
Controlling staff . . .	83.97	15.68	0.35	92.46	7.33	0.21

Percentage of government personnel in different ranks according to population group in 1938[3]

Population group	Lower personnel	Lower medium personnel	Higher medium personnel	Higher personnel
Europeans	0.6	33.3	57.6	92.2
Indonesians	98.9	60.6	38.0	6.4
Indonesians assimilated to Europeans	0.2	3.4	2.0	0.5
Foreign Orientals	0.3	2.7	2.3	0.8
Total	100	100	100	100

Education on the Western model, with Dutch as the medium of instruction, had produced a cultural affinity between large groups of Indonesians and Europeans who had grown up in Indonesia. Did this bring them closer together socially, too? On the contrary, as the barriers of race became weaker, the tension grew. Despite

[1] See the articles on Indianisation in *Koloniale Studiën* (Colonial Studies), Vol. XVI, 1932, Part 1: J. H. Boeke, 'Indianisation', p. 243 ff.; D. M. G. Koch, 'De vakbeweging en de Indianiseering' (The trade union movement and the Indianisation), p. 348 ff.

[2] Adapted from I. J. Brugmans and Soenario, *op. cit.*, Vol. I, p. 56.

[3] Adapted from I. J. Brugmans and Soenario, *ibidem.*

the growth of an Indonesian middle class of officials, clerks and traders, the differentiation of incomes still largely coincided with the division according to race, with the average earnings of Europeans at the top, those of the Chinese in between and those of Indonesians at the bottom. Indonesians who had enjoyed some education no longer accepted the colonial stratification according to race as a matter of course. Legal and social discrimination decreased, but what still remained rankled all the more. Social demarcation lines were beginning to become fluid. Hence many groups of people sprang up who were no longer content with their social status, while others sensed a threat to their own comparatively favourable position. Economic and social competition developed between adjacent groups, which became all the keener the closer they approached each other culturally.

Intensified competition in a society in which, owing to the dominant economic system, there were more applicants than vacancies, caused the members of the bourgeoisie to join forces to achieve group solidarity. And what could be more natural in a society whose cornerstone was the colour line, than that such a fusion should be sought along the existing racial divisions?

Thus, around 1920, the Indo-Europeans joined together in the Indo-European Union (*Indo-Europeesch Verbond*) to protect themselves against the rising class of Westernised Indonesians. Their main object was to maintain the social privileges they had already gained for themselves. They fostered an artificial feeling of superiority towards the *Inlanders* and strove to create a still greater distance between the latter and themselves, while emphasising their own European character. What, in the nineteenth century, had been largely the reflection of a social reality now became segregation maintained by artificial means. It was fear that caused them to entrench themselves behind the racial barriers more solidly than ever before.

On the other hand, a tendency to greater unity appeared also among the Indonesians. This was accompanied by a heightened national consciousness and a diminished respect for the Dutch language as a social factor, as well as for appointments in the

Dutch government service and for assimilation into Dutch circles. The use of the *Bahasa Indonesia*, a modernised form of Malay, and the wearing of the *kopiah*, a black fez, became symbolic of national consciousness. The true nationalist was a non-cooperator; he no longer aspired to a job in the government service. Indonesian women with self-respect cared less and less for employment as housekeeper-concubines in the service of unmarried European men. Eventually, after 1930, even marriage with a European, apparently, had less attraction for an Indonesian woman than before.[1] Thus a new scale of values gradually projected itself across the old colonial scale. Together with education, this new scale of values affected the position of women and the young. In the capacity of Westernised intellectuals and fellow-fighters in the nationalist struggle, the womenfolk and the young could often win for themselves a social prestige which conflicted with traditional Indonesian ideas. In this sense, too, Western education, from which many young girls also profited, had a revolutionising influence on Indonesian society.

In the years of crisis the competitive struggle became more intense. The Indo-Europeans had to follow courses of still higher education in order to keep up to the European level. They competed at this level with the whites who came to Indonesia from abroad in much smaller numbers from 1930 onwards. On the other hand, a growing number of Indo-Europeans failed to keep up the struggle and fell away, entering the *kampong*, the poor native quarter of the city. Unemployment in the crisis years reduced many *Indos* to a condition of material distress.

A similar process could be seen in the world of trade. The Chinese no longer retained the monopoly in this field. A growing body of

[1] A. van Marle, 'De groep der Europeanen in Nederlands Indië. Iets over ontstaan en groei' (The European group in the Netherlands Indies. Something about origin and growth), in *Indonesië*, Vol. V, 1951/52, p. 507. Gouw Giok Siong, *op. cit.*, p. 21, ascribes the decrease of mixed marriages between Indonesian women and European men during the depression to economic factors. However, marriages with Chinese women showed, at the same time, an increasing tendency!

Indonesian traders, some of them organised on cooperative lines, began to threaten their position from below. As Cator put it: 'In East-Java and in the Preanger Regencies there is... an undeniable decrease of the Chinese share in trade', and (for the Preanger Regencies and Palembang): 'Native intermediate traders begin to oust the Chinese.'[1] In the field of industrial enterprise the trend was still more pronounced. According to Sitsen's booklet, written in wartime, during the last ten years, contrary to the trends some decades earlier, 'in Djokjakarta and Solo the Chinese *batik* producers were almost all pushed out by the Indonesian contractors, as in Pekalongan also.'[2] For the rest, it should be remembered that in many regions of the Outer Islands native trade had always competed successfully with Chinese enterprise. In some regions, such as Menangkabau and Hulu Sungei,[3] the latter have hardly been able to get a foothold. Kahin's arguments to the effect that the Chinese were ousting the Indonesians from trade until World War II[4] cannot, therefore, be regarded as conclusive.

Moreover, in the crisis period the Chinese middlemen got into still greater difficulty, owing to the attempts by Japanese importers to eliminate the Chinese intermediate trade. They, too, were obliged either to organise themselves into larger concerns to withstand Indonesian competition from below, or to seek employment in industry or government service – occupations in which they had shown little interest in the past.[5] Chinese intellec-

[1] W. J. Cator, *The economic position of the Chinese in the Netherlands Indies*, Oxford, 1936, p. 74 ff.

[2] P. H. W. Sitsen, *Industrial development of the Netherlands Indies*, New York, 1942, p. 21 ff.

[3] See M. Joustra, *Minangkabau. Overzicht van land, geschiedenis en volk* (Menangkabau. Survey of country, history and people), Leiden, 1921, p. 83; R. Broersma, *Handel en bedrijf in Zuid- en Oost-Borneo* (Commerce and industry in South and East Borneo), The Hague, 1927, p. 119.

[4] G. McT. Kahin, *op. cit.*, p. 27 ff.

[5] See Liem Twan Djie, *De distribueerende tusschenhandel der Chineezen op Java* (The distributive intermediate trade of the Chinese in Java), The Hague, 1947, p. 66 ff. See also the tables reproduced on p. 149 above, showing a remarkable increase of the Foreign Orientals in government service.

tuals began to compete with *Indos* and Indonesians for the higher posts in the administration. On the other hand many Chinese declined into the ranks of the proletariat, which was no longer limited to the *Singkehs*, the Chinese brought in from overseas. The Chinese, too, sought salvation in a greater degree of solidarity. In their case, too, this increased segregation from the Indonesians was artificial, in view of the increasing cultural similarity between the two groups. This was reflected in the fact that the Indonesian Chinese had usually forgotten the Chinese language, the more prosperous of them using Dutch, the less well-to-do an Indonesian language, either a local one or Chinese Malay.

Thus, even before the war, the special position occupied by the Europeans and Chinese, like that of the feudal nobility, had become considerably less stable. There was a strong tendency in the direction of a new status system based on individual prosperity and individual intellectual abilities; but this development was still largely held in check by the remnants of both the feudal and the colonial structure.

4 War and revolution. Reversal and continuity

At first, war and the Japanese occupation seemed to bring about a complete reversal of all values. A white skin and the use of the Dutch language, which had so long been the outward signs of superiority, became symbols of the pariah. Many Indo-Europeans who had previously been ashamed of their half-Indonesian origin, a number of whom had even tried to conceal their ancestry, now left no stone unturned to obtain a declaration that they were *peranakans*, that is to say, children of the Indonesian homeland. Officially the Indonesians, who had for so long provided the lowest stratum, now ranked higher than the Indo-Europeans and the Indonesian Chinese.[1]

The social scale seemed to be turned upside down. Even the

[1] See for instance K. A. de Weerd, *The Japanese occupation of the Netherlands Indies*. Prepared Statement International Prosecution Section, Netherlands Division of the International Military Tribunal Far East, 1946. Process Document 2750.

beo (*Gracula javanensis*), the talking bird in the Batavia Zoo, conformed to the new pattern; he had unlearned the Dutch call: '*Dag Mevrouw*' (good afternoon, Madam) and now amused the children by greeting the lady guests in Indonesian. On top of the ladder the Japanese had settled themselves firmly. Though the Japanese soldiers had at first tried to win the Indonesians by a fraternising attitude which contrasted favourably with the European's haughtiness, their colonial pattern soon proved to be no less caste-like than that of the Dutch. In fact it was more so: whereas the Dutch had long ago accepted situations in which an Indonesian could be a superior of a European, this was, during the first years of Japanese occupation, impossible according to Japanese standards.[1] Indonesians might hold positions much higher than those held under Dutch rule. But a son of the gods could never be an inferior of any Indonesian.

Neither was the reversal for the other groups nearly as complete as it might seem. The intellectual and near-intellectual Indonesians, it is true, had become by the end of the Japanese occupation a privileged group, as the Japanese found it expedient to win them over. To them were assigned prominent posts in the administration that were formerly held by Europeans, either *totok* (of pure descent) or *Indo*. While pre-war educational facilities for Europeans had far exceeded those available for Indonesians, the latter, during the occupation, were given preference for what education remained intact. The children of those Indo-European women who had managed to keep outside the camps, and of Indonesian Chinese, were admitted in limited number only to the Japanese-sponsored schools,[2] though in later years private Chinese schools were tolerated under certain conditions. Moreover, a number of Indonesians from this educated class were given military training, which opened new social opportunities for them as army officers.

[1] See S. M. Gandasubrata, *An account of the Japanese occupation of Banjumas residency, Java, March 1942 to August 1945*, Data paper Nr 10 of the Southeast Asia Program, Cornell University, Ithaca, 1953, p. 8.

[2] See for example K. A. de Weerd, *op. cit.*, p. 41.

Japanese economic policy also favoured the Indonesian trader class against the Chinese. Chinese traders were often excluded from catering for Indonesian consumers' needs, which, for instance in West Borneo, became a monopoly of Indonesian traders.

Still, the privileged position of Indonesians did not extend to the whole population. In the long run, the mass of the people were, under Japanese rule, worse off than ever. At first Japanese policy seemed more or less democratic in so far as special prerogatives of the aristocratic group were abolished and the salaries of higher officials were considerably lowered.[1] In later years Japanese propaganda, directed at achieving active support for the war effort from all segments of the population, fostered a spirit of enhanced self-respect among the masses. Yet the practical effect of Japanese rule was such that the common man felt humiliated as never before. For many years he had not experienced an exploitation, a lack of concern for his life and for his basic needs, or a cruelty comparable to those connected with the 'co-prosperity sphere of Greater East Asia.' For the slightest offence he stood a good chance of getting a beating, an essential part, under the Japanese feudal tradition, of the education of the common man.[2]

In comparing the position of Indo-Europeans and of Chinese with that of Indonesians, certain distinctions must therefore be made. Indonesian intellectuals and other middle class groups were a privileged group. But in comparison with the mass of Indonesians, especially the peasantry, many of the Chinese, and even Indo-Europeans who were able to escape internment, still had resources which were denied to the great majority of Indonesians. Chinese who were ousted from legal trade could engage in illegal trade, or find positions in the administration or with Japanese concerns, owing to the advantage of their material or educational background. As long as Indo-Europeans could keep out of the internment camps, many of them could live for a while

[1] See S. M. Gandasubrata, *op. cit.*, p. 6.

[2] Nor were Indonesians of the higher classes safe from corporal maltreatment. In the early years of the occupation there was a student strike at the medical college in Jakarta as a protest against Japanese educational methods.

on the sale of their furnishings or personal belongings, or engage in illegal trade. Or they might get intermediate jobs in the Japanese administration if they were willing to swear allegiance to the Japanese authorities.

In assessing the impact of the Japanese occupation upon the status system, one must consider not only the shifts in the relative position of racial groups, but also the changes within the Indonesian community. Generally speaking, the intellectual and near-intellectual groups were becoming a new privileged class holding positions comparable to those formerly occupied by the pre-war upper classes. The social distance between this group and the masses tended to increase. On the other hand, trends during the occupation enabled this new middle class to compete with greater success with the aristocracy.

To the very last, the native aristocracy was the main support of Dutch rule. Japanese policy was somewhat different, however. Though most of the Indonesian Civil Service (regents and district officers) and *adat* chiefs were kept in office, or even reinstalled where they had fled before mob violence during the chaos after the Dutch defeat,[1] the main principle of Japanese policy was to keep a balance of power. They never relied exclusively upon the native aristocracy. In contrast with Dutch policy, which had always been rather suspicious of any political activity among Indonesians, the Japanese from the outset attempted to foster political activity, under their own control, of course, and directed at support for their war effort. To this end they needed the prominent nationalist leaders, some of whom had been exiled by the Dutch. By building up political organisations they created a counter-weight, mostly recruited from the intellectuals, against the feudal class. Religious leaders,[2] especially the simple-minded

[1] See A. J. Piekaar, *Atjeh in de oorlog met Japan* (Acheh in the war against Japan), The Hague/Bandung, 1949, p. 193 ff.

[2] See for instance Harry J. Benda, *The Crescent and the Rising Sun. Indonesian Islam under the Japanese occupation of Java 1942–1945*, The Hague/Bandung, 1958, p. 132 ff.; C. A. O. van Nieuwenhuijze, *Aspects of Islam in post-colonial Indonesia. Five essays*, The Hague/Bandung, 1958, p. 127 ff.

ulamas from the countryside, were also accorded a heightened prestige in order to enlist their active support for the Japanese war effort.

But it was above all the economic policy of the Japanese which, in the long run, brought about a gradual shift in the balance at the expense of the aristocracy. From the beginning the Indonesian intellectual and near-intellectual class enhanced their prestige by occupying prominent posts in the administration formerly reserved for Europeans. During the occupation Japanese-sponsored organisations increasingly came to dominate economic life and to exercise powers formerly wielded by the Civil Service. Consequently, a group of intellectuals and near-intellectuals, mostly rather youthful, were able to get a firm footing in the basic fields of crop collection and food distribution. The regents and other officers in the Civil Service, on the contrary, saw themselves gradually deprived of an essential part of their traditional power.[1] This process partially coincided with the tendency in Japanese policy, as described by Gandasubrata,[2] to lower the position of higher officials – who, though belonging to the intellectual group, were largely recruited from the *pryayi* class, which was the only one able to afford higher education – and to favour middle class groups such as teachers and policemen. Thus the distance between those of the highest rank and the urban middle class of near-intellectuals tended to shrink.

On the whole, during the Japanese occupation all authority based upon tradition was gradually undermined. Japanese interference with village life infringed in many respects upon the traditional static order and loosened the bonds of social life. It was not only propaganda which elicited new dynamic forces; police activities of newly-built organisations, involving over a

[1] For Acheh, this process has been described by A. J. Piekaar, *op. cit.*, p. 288 ff. Though the social processes in Acheh are somewhat at variance with those in other areas on account of the outstanding role played by religious leaders, probably most of the total picture holds good for other regions as well. See for Java Harry J. Benda, *op. cit.*, p. 155.

[2] S. M. Gandasubrata, *op. cit.*, p. 6.

million Indonesians, many of them youngsters, and requisitioning of labour on a huge scale, which withdrew large numbers of young men from their birth-place, were still more effective in uprooting the authority of elders and traditional chiefs. Young men, some of whom received military or quasi-military training and most of whom were affected by Japanese propaganda, felt more confident than before in opposing the old traditions. This self-confidence and this protest against authority increased when, towards the end of the war, the young people took the lead in anti-Japanese underground activities, while the authorities and the elders still largely abided by Japanese rule.[1]

Japanese education, the adoption of Japanese manners and Japanese-sponsored political and organisational activities also contributed to a greater freedom of expression and a heightened self-confidence among young women, especially in the cities.

Another phenomenon to be noted is a shift away from the individualistic tendencies of the recent decades to a larger degree of integration within all kinds of organisations. No longer was social prestige largely derived from traditional authority or personal performance and achievement. To a certain degree one's social standing would henceforth depend on one's position within an organisation and on the organisation's status in the society. These groups, including army units and underground organisations as well, became stepping stones for social advance. A man's social status became, to a certain degree, a function of the collective groups to which he belonged.

The shifts in the status system which the revolution brought about were still more spasmodic. For a while, it was hardly possible to assess the total effect. In the areas occupied by Allied troops a partial restoration of colonial relationships occurred for a short period. There was a strained attempt on the part of the Indo-Europeans and groups of Indonesian Christians, closely associated with them socially, to retain some part of their old

[1] See for example the human conflict portrayed in the novel *Perburuan* (Fugitive) by the young talented author Pramoedya Ananta Toer, Jakarta, 1950.

prerogatives. Especially the former Netherlands Indian Army, the K.N.I.L., was the instrument by means of which the *Indos*, and some of the Ambonese and Menadonese tried to hold on to a fraction of their social advantage.

At the same time the feudal nobility, especially in the Outer Islands, attempted to regain the authority which it had lost, to a certain degree, during the occupation. Though a number of aristocratic leaders joined the banner of revolution, either from genuine nationalist convictions or because they expected the Republic to be on the winning side,[1] there were also many who, sooner or later, adhered to Dutch rule hoping for a recovery of their authority with the backing of Dutch military force. After a few abortive attempts to win over the class of Westernised intellectuals, the prominent Dutch officials van Mook and van der Plas were compelled, since they wanted to reassert a measure of Dutch rule, to fall back upon the traditional line of propping up the feudal nobility. Though formally the so-called Malino policy implied a number of democratic elements, such as the creation of regional and local councils, in fact the power of aristocratic rulers was often reinforced rather than diminished.[2]

In the areas controlled by the Republic the situation was quite different. Except for a very limited number of *Indos* whose pledge of loyalty toward the Republic was accepted, all Europeans, even those who had kept out of the camps during the war, were interned. After hard sufferings most of them were eventually released and transported to areas under Dutch control. In several places in the interior of Java, such as Jogjakarta, practically no Indo-Europeans were left. Their places in the governmental system were taken by Indonesians who had received Western education. The pre-war stratification according to race, already seriously undermined during Japanese rule, suffered a death blow.

The position of the Indonesian aristocracy within the Republic was more ambiguous. Some feudal rulers, such as the young

[1] G. McT. Kahin, *op. cit.*, p. 352, 356.

[2] G. McT. Kahin, *op. cit.*, p. 365 ff. See also R. Kennedy, *Field Notes on Indonesia. South Celebes 1949–50*, New Haven, 1953.

Sultan of Jogjakarta, Hamengku Buwono IX, were among the foremost leaders of the Republican movement. There were also many regents who wholeheartedly joined the Republican cause. In so far as the aristocracy was far-sighted enough to perceive the trend of the times and to resign part of its prerogatives it suffered only a slight loss of status during the revolutionary years. Democratisation of the government went farther than in the areas under Dutch rule; but the regents and *wedonos* (district officers) still retained a good deal of power, and, in many instances, members of the aristocracy succeeded in amalgamating with the new upper class of intellectuals.

Some areas, where the feudal rulers were, rightly or wrongly, considered by the population as potential deserters to the Dutch side, present a very different picture. This was especially true in Sumatra's Eastcoast Residency, where the native rulers had greatly profited before the war from the Western plantation economy, and were now suspected by the Republicans of conspiring with the Dutch in order to restore Dutch rule. In the first months of 1946 the sanguinary 'Sumatra Social Revolution' occurred,[1] which resulted in a brutal massacre of many of the local aristocratic leaders and their families. In some other parts of Sumatra similar developments occurred, of which those in Acheh are especially notable. Here it was the traditional struggle for power between the petty feudal chiefs and the religious leaders which accounted for the dramatic events after the Japanese capitulation. The balance of power that the Japanese had managed to achieve by keeping both groups in check could not last. From December 1945 until February 1946 there was an outburst of insurrections led by the *ulamas* (Moslem religious leaders), during which several families of petty aristocratic rulers (*uleëbalangs*) were murdered to the last male descendant, and hundreds of others were interned as 'enemies of the Republic'.[2]

An intermediate situation between these extremes was to be found in the Principality of Surakarta, where the *Sunan* was

[1] G. McT. Kahin, *op. cit.*, p. 179 ff.

[2] A. J. Piekaar, *op. cit.*, p. 250.

stripped of his governmental powers but left in possession of his *kraton* (palace) and his spiritual functions.[1]

Another group with an ambiguous position was the Chinese in the Republican territory. Though some of them were able to take over a considerable portion of the large scale commerce formerly carried on by big Western enterprises, many others, especially those living in the *desas*, became victims of social unrest. They were the greatest sufferers from military friction, as they were regarded by the Indonesians as potential Dutch agents, and there were many casualties among them. A large number, however, at the approach of Dutch troops, fled from the country to the cities, thus leaving the trade and the money-lending business to well-to-do Indonesians.[2]

The substantial shifts brought about in territories under Republican control could not be confined to these areas. The result of the attempts of Europeans and feudal leaders to restore the prewar stratification was quite the reverse of what was hoped for. The shifts in the status system described above assumed a dynamic character and became a decisive force in the political struggle.

The Indonesian intellectual class now proved strong enough finally to overturn the colonial stratification according to race. This was due in large part to the important function they fulfilled in the machinery of society. Increasing economic regulation, particularly since the depression years, had made both the administrative and the economic system dependent upon the cooperation of the 'new middle class,' consisting of officials, employees and technicians in the service of government or business. By corporate action, on an economic or political basis, by strikes and non-cooperation, this class could disable the whole economic life of the country. Economic life in the Eastern world is dominated not by independent businessmen but by large monopolistic enterprises and the state, which are dependent on the cooperation of the new middle class. The power of this class showed itself after

[1] G. McT. Kahin, *op. cit.*, p. 186.

[2] See also G. McT. Kahin, *op. cit.*, p. 327 ff. for the transfer of the money-lending business to Indonesians.

the Dutch military occupation of Jogjakarta at the end of 1948. By refusing to cooperate with the Dutch, the Sultan, supported by practically the entire personnel of the Sultanate, made it impossible for the Dutch to administer the area.

In present-day Indonesia the social supremacy of the upper layer of the new class of Western-educated Indonesians seems, for the time being, to be practically unimpaired. The Indo-Europeans as a group have suffered an especially serious loss of status. *Totok* (foreign-born) Europeans, and Americans for that matter, still have many opportunities in commerce and industry, especially if they are specialists of a type not available in the Indonesian labour market. But Indo-Europeans are in a much worse plight. Most of them must rely on employment in administrative jobs, where, since the transfer of sovereignty, they have to compete with Indonesians without any privilege springing from a colonial system or a linguistic advantage; in fact they are handicapped by ignorance of the Indonesian language. Those Indo-Europeans remaining in Indonesia, most of them belonging to the minority who after the transfer of sovereignty opted for Indonesian citizenship, are still facing difficulties. Their position is not free from discrimination. Those who have retained their Dutch nationality have in great majority, in the course of those years, left Indonesia and sought refuge in Holland, where their assimilation has proved far from easy. Because of the steady deterioration of the relations between the Netherlands and Indonesia the situation of those Dutch nationals who stayed has become increasingly difficult. As a group the *Indos*, of either Indonesian or Dutch nationality, have no future. They will be able to compete with the members of the Indonesian upper group only on a basis of individual merit.

However liberal the legal protection which racial minorities may enjoy in the future, the actual position of such groups in Indonesian society must depend ultimately on the extent to which individuals succeed in becoming assimilated into the new ruling class. Any form of segregation from the Indonesians on a racial, or so-called national or cultural, basis will no longer safeguard their position as minority groups. Eventually it will turn them into groups of pariahs.

The situation of the Chinese in Indonesia seems at the moment less unfavourable, and not only because of the proximity of a powerful China. Their position in trade appears, for the time being, to be largely unimpaired. But there are tendencies which bear resemblance to pre-war developments affecting the Indo-European group, and which may foreshadow a similar fate. Before the war, in the field of government administration, the Indo-Europeans were pressed from below by Indonesian competition and were obliged to set their educational standards ever higher in order to keep abreast. During the years of revolution the Chinese were squeezed out of the small-scale trade in the villages.[1] In international commerce they are still making headway, but only a comparatively small number of Chinese can profit by the new situation. Though the great majority of those Chinese born in Indonesia, at the transfer of sovereignty, automatically acquired Indonesian citizenship, their final status will have to be decided by a treaty between the Indonesian and the Chinese Government.[2] There is still a good deal of discrimination and social tension, and a strong feeling of envy on the part of the Indonesians. Probably there are large numbers of Chinese, living in the cities in a state of poverty, but they attract scant notice. If the Chinese continue to hold together as a group, under conditions making for economic competition on group basis, they are in great danger of becoming, eventually, a pariah group. But even if they will succeed better than the Indo-Europeans in assimilating themselves with the Indonesians, in the long run they will be unable to maintain their privileged position.

It is thus certain that social stratification in the new Indonesia

[1] G. McT. Kahin, *op. cit.*, p. 327 ff. Part of them, however, seem to have returned to the countryside after the conditions had become normal again.

[2] At the Bandung Asian-African Conference (April 1955) such a treaty has been concluded, but several points concerning their status have still to be elucidated.

will no longer be on a racial basis. Racial criteria will fall ever farther into the background. This applies to European descent in particular. The prophecy uttered by Ross[1] in 1920, that 'before the end of this century probably every vestige of European eminent-domain in Asia will have vanished,' now seems well on the way to fulfilment.

But racial stratification was not the only kind to be swept away by the revolution. We have seen that federalism, as embodied in the so-called Malino policy, was a levee thrown up to protect the aristocratic order of society. After the final defeat of colonialism, however, it appeared that in several regions, without the prop of the Dutch Army, the aristocracy was not able to hold its own. The federal structure crumbled before the dynamic onslaught of the new ruling class. The revolution was not directed against colonialism only; it resulted to a large extent in a defeat of the nobility as well. The feudal aristocracy lost a great deal of the aura surrounding it. In many regions it could hold on to some vestige of its authority only by throwing itself wholeheartedly into the nationalist struggle.

Apparently, then, Japanese occupation and national revolution have speeded up the pre-war trend towards an increasing individualism, and towards a pattern of social status based on personal achievement. Moreover, the years of insecurity have forced many members of the *pryayi* class to engage in trade, which they had earlier scorned.[2] The rising Indonesian business class, though still very restricted in numbers, thus enjoys an enhanced social prestige. No longer are race and birth important criteria in determining social standing. During the revolutionary years, the traditional authority of the elders was seriously impaired, while young revolutionary fighters, the *pemudas*, were winning a social esteem for themselves. The youth movement, which had taken the lead in underground activities during the Japanese occupation, added much of its strength and fighting spirit to the revolutionary

[1] E. A. Ross, *Principles of sociology*, New York, 1920, p. 543.

[2] D. H. Burger, *Structural changes in Javanese society. The supra-village sphere*, p. 22.

cause. Women achieved a measure of social equality and recognition during the nationalist struggle, as fighting partners of the men.

Yet the reversal of values was not nearly so complete as it might seem at first sight. After the achievement of the primary aim of the revolution, national sovereignty, much of the revolutionary impulse has gone by the board, and the breach with the past appears to be smaller than was expected. The elders resumed a large part of their authority. Women, no longer needed as partners in the struggle, began to see themselves also relegated to the background once more. What has been preserved of the old aristocratic order has been integrated into the new social order.[1]

In considering the present situation and the prospects for the near future, it should be borne in mind that the large majority of Indonesians are still peasants. Like the feudal nobility and the religious leaders in the past, the new elite of intellectuals and near-intellectuals and the rising merchant class are, for the time being, only a thin upper crust on Indonesian society. The intellectual class is primarily an urban elite deriving its supremacy from the fact that the focus of modern Indonesian administration is centred in the towns. But the present ruling class is hardly able to exercise command over the agrarian masses, and it may be expected that the peasantry will, before long, become a decisive factor in the balance of social power.

It is doubtful, therefore, whether the tendencies pointing to an increasing individualism will last. Individualism has appeared, in Asia, too late on the scene to achieve its full maturity. New criteria of social prestige will soon emerge within Indonesian society. The social prestige enjoyed by the intellectual and near-intellectual class, which, with a section of the feudal nobility, forms at the moment the social upper crust, will not long go unchallenged. Social prestige is increasingly being determined by criteria connected with the struggle between collective groups. In a sense, this was already true in the pre-war period of nation-

[1] In Acheh the *uleëbalang* class was reinstated to part of its former authority, which was one of the causes of the Daud Beureuh revolt (1953).

alist struggle. New norms of value emerged, the main criterion being valour in the nationalist cause. During the Japanese occupation and more especially during the revolution this process was reinforced. Anyone taken to be a '*kaki tangan Nica*' – a tool of the Dutch – was disqualified from the outset. Since the sovereignty transfer, a distinction was drawn between *co*'s and *non-co*'s – those who cooperated with the Dutch and those who remained loyal to the Republic. After the so-called October 17 affair – an abortive *coup d'état* on October 17, 1952, to push the appointed Parliament aside until the elections, for which the P.S.I. (Indonesian Socialist Party) is widely considered responsible[1] – sympathy, real or alleged, for the P.S.I. was used as a criterion for social disqualification. After the formation of the first government led by Ali Sastroamidjojo in 1953 allegiance to *Masjumi* was said to have been a cause for discrimination. On the other hand, if the *Masjumi* should ever gain the ascendancy, there will no doubt be discrimination against those with communist leanings. Thus the prestige of the members of the new ruling class is being determined more and more by the extent to which their attitude accords with prevailing political ideals.

The development towards greater individualism in the first phase of the present century is thus being overtaken by a new movement with greater emphasis on collective action. The old traditional agrarian communities are losing their influence, but new leaders are coming to the fore by way of newly-formed collective bodies such as peasant unions and – for plantation labour – trade unions. Their social prestige is often still of a traditional kind, based on the 'charismatic' tie between leader and group, *i.e.* on a belief in his well-nigh supernatural capacities.[2] But their power and social influence will ultimately depend upon the cohesion and the social significance of the collective body they

[1] Herbert Feith, 'Toward elections in Indonesia', in *Pacific Affairs*, Vol. XXVII, 1954, p. 243.

[2] The term 'charismatic' was introduced into modern sociology by Max Weber. See the edition of H. H. Gerth and C. Wright Mills, *From Max Weber. Essays in sociology*, London, 1947, p. 295.

represent, that is to say, of the political movement or trade union concerned.

Other layers of society are also beginning to challenge the supremacy of the new ruling class. For example, the new middle class of near-intellectuals is sometimes distrustful of the more Westernised upper layer, in whose hands the leadership of the Republic at present lies. Military recruitment from the mass of the population has also brought forward new personalities, who owed their authority over their men to their courage and their talent for leadership. '*Pelopors*' (pioneers) found followers; '*bapakism*' or blind obedience to a 'father', a leader, made its appearance in the army. Independent action taken by combat groups was often scarcely distinguishable from the activities of bandits, which increased during this period of unrest. From early days '*rampokkers*' (robber bands) had been the terror of the villagers. The disorder created by war and revolution brought a serious increase in the number of robber bands, while difficulties arising in the demobilisation of the army made it easy for many a military leader and his adherents to terrorise part of the countryside in similar manner. But there were other military leaders who succeeded in winning respect and followers in the guerrilla war by fighting in the interest of the population.

At the moment many military leaders, by the following they have been able to collect, seriously threaten the power of the intellectual class. Sometimes, they combine forces with religious leaders, who are trying to preserve their traditional grip upon the agrarian population. Other combat groups seem to be siding with the peasant and trade union movement. In a way, this process is also an example of the collectivist tendency.

Consequently it is probable that the most powerful collective movements will eventually cause a split in the ruling class and bind the new elite to the political, social and military organisations which succeed in getting the ascendancy.

Thus we can see that the tendency towards a status system based on individual prosperity and ability is, before having achieved its realisation, being outdistanced by a new trend, represented by the collective organisations which are playing an increasingly important role in social evolution, and at the same time forcing the individual more and more into the background.

A short bibliography

D. H. Burger, 'Structuurveranderingen in de Javaanse samenleving' (Structural changes in Javanese society), in *Indonesië*, Vol. II and III, 1948/49 and 1949/50.

D. H. Burger, *Structural changes in Javanese society. The village sphere;* and *Structural changes in Javanese society. The supra-village sphere*, Translations of parts of the foregoing, Translation Series, Modern Indonesia Project, Cornell University, Ithaca, 1957 and 1956.

Cora Du Bois, *Social forces in Southeast Asia*, Cambridge (Mass.), 1959.

H. Th. Chabot, *Verwantschap, stand en sexe in Zuid-Celebes* (Kinship, status and sex in South Celebes), Groningen/Jakarta, 1950.

H. J. Friedericy, 'De standen bij de Boegineezen en Makassaren' (Social classes among the Buginese and the people of Macassar), in *Bijdragen tot de Taal-, Land- en Volkenkunde van Nederlandsch-Indië* (Contributions to the Philology, Geography, and Ethnology of the Netherlands Indies), Vol. 90, 1933.

S. M. Gandasubrata, *An account of the Japanese occupation of Banjumas Residency, Java, March 1942 to August 1945*, Data paper Nr 10 of the Southeast Asia Program, Cornell University, Ithaca, 1953.

F. de Haan, *Oud Batavia* (Old Batavia), Bandung, 1935.

Paul M. Kattenburg, *A central Javanese village in 1950*, Data paper Nr 2 of the Southeast Asia Program, Cornell University, Ithaca, 1951.

R. Kennedy, 'The colonial crisis and the future', in R. Linton (ed.), *The science of man in the world crisis*, New York, 1945.

R. Kennedy, *Field studies on Indonesia. South Celebes 1949–50*, New Haven, 1953.

Justus M. van der Kroef, *Indonesian social evolution. Some psychological considerations*, Amsterdam, 1958.

Liem Twan Djie, *De distribueerende tusschenhandel der Chineezen op Java* (The distributive intermediate trade of the Chinese in Java), The Hague, 1947.

Ong Eng Die, *Chineezen in Nederlandsch-Indië. Sociografie van een Indonesische bevolkingsgroep* (Chinese in the Netherlands Indies. Social survey of an Indonesian population group), Assen, 1943.

Leslie H. Palmier, 'Occupational distribution of parents of pupils in certain Indonesian educational institutions', in *Indonesië*, Vol. X, 1957, p. 320 ff. and 349 ff.

B. Schrieke, *Indonesian sociological studies. Selected writings*, Part 1. Selected studies on Indonesia by Dutch authors, Vol. II, The Hague/Bandung, 1955.

B. Schrieke (ed.), *The effect of Western influence on native civilisations in the Malay archipelago*, Batavia, 1929.

Hurustiati Subandrio, *Javanese peasant life. Villages in East Java*, unpublished thesis for the London School of Economics and Political Science, 1951.

Verslag van de commissie tot bestudeering van staatsrechtelijke hervormingen (Report of the commission for the study of political reforms), New York, 1944.

Paul W. van der Veur, 'The Eurasians of Indonesia: castaways of colonialism', in *Pacific Affairs*, Vol. XXVII, 1954, p. 124 ff.

W. F. Wertheim, *Het rassenprobleem. De ondergang van een mythe* (The race problem. The decline of a myth), The Hague, 1949.

W. F. Wertheim, *Herrijzend Azië* (Resurgent Asia), Arnhem, 1950

Chapter Seven

Urban Development

1 *The old Indonesian cities*

The old Indonesian cities were to be found in the interior as well as on the coast of Java and the other great islands and near the mouths of the large rivers. But however divergent in character and situation these might be, all of them shared one thing in common: they were all situated in the neighbourhood of the centres of princely government which offered them security. In the case of the cities of the interior, it is at once obvious that they have grown up around an existing *kraton* (princely court), that their function was to provide the *kraton* with all kinds of goods and services, while they also enjoyed their share of the splendour emanating from the royal courts and what crumbs remained from the life of luxury lived there. The old Indonesian cities of the interior were the administrative centres from which the *raja* ruled his surrounding territories.

But the colonies of foreigners on the coast also had no independent existence. They, too, looked for their security to the protection of the princely authority. The atmosphere within the coastal towns was more cosmopolitan than in the inland cities. Foreign traders and artisans represented a large proportion of the inhabitants. They were greatly influenced by numerous contacts with abroad. But this did not imply that the atmosphere in these cities was bourgeois. The town-dwellers did not form an organic whole. The traders and artisans were grouped in wards according to their national origin each under its own chieftain. They were probably also organised into gilds. Authority was vested exclusively, however, in the harbour prince, with his army and administrative apparatus. The inhabitants developed no common will which could find its realisation in civic autonomy and oppose the power of the princely government. A predominantly feudal and traditional atmosphere ruled in these coastal towns as well as in the cities of the interior. The small peddling traders, living segregated in foreign wards, did not presume to call the city their own, nor designate themselves as its citizens.[1]

The foregoing also determines the outward aspect of the old Indonesian cities. They have not sprung up and developed spontaneously out of the communal will of the tradesmen and artisans. Their site, design and size were dependent on the will of the prince. A favourable situation, economic or strategic, on a road junction or in the neighbourhood of a natural harbour, could influence his decision in the first instance. But the plan of the town was laid down according to tradition by higher authority. This original city plan is easily recognisable in the lay-out of the old *kraton* towns on Java, the *alun-alun* (a large public square) in the centre with the most important buildings arranged about it in the traditional manner, according to the four winds. The main roads cross each other at right-angles.

The coastal cities were also built according to a fixed pattern. The nobles quarter, following as far as possible the old Javanese pattern, dominated the whole. This district was as a rule separated off from the merchant city itself. The heads of the foreign wards were subordinate to the harbour prince.[2]

[1] This picture of the old Indonesian cities is largely inspired by J. C. van Leur, *Indonesian trade and society. Essays in Asian social and economic history*, Selected studies on Indonesia by Dutch scholars, Vol. I, The Hague/Bandung, 1955, p. 75 ff., 137 ff., 194 ff.

[2] Cf. for example Herbert Lehmann's contribution 'Das Antlitz der Stadt in Niederländisch Indien', in *Länderkundliche Forschung. Festschrift Norbert Krebs*, Stuttgart, 1936. For a description of old Bantam at the time of the first arrival of the Dutch, see in particular J. C. van Leur, *op. cit.*, p. 137 ff.; G. P. Rouffaer and J. W. IJzerman, *De eerste schipvaart der Nederlanders naar Oost-Indië onder Cornelis de Houtman 1595–1597* (The first sailing of the Dutch to the East Indies under Cornelis de Houtman 1595–1597), Werken uitgegeven door de Linschoten Vereniging (Works published by the Lin-

The general aspect of the old Indonesian cities was static rather than dynamic.

2 Interchange of East and West

The attempt of the Dutch to build a faithful copy of the old Dutch towns, in the shape of Batavia, on the north coast of Java is all but unique in the world. Jan Pieterszoon Coen, the founder of Batavia, wanted to people the town with respectable Dutch citizens as well and to transport to Indonesia the bourgeois character and culture of Holland. The manner in which Batavia – in spite of all these efforts – rapidly developed into a typically Eastern city provides an extremely instructive example of acculturation. The East India Company's monopoly system made the existence of a free Dutch bourgeoisie, as visualised by Coen, impossible. The fact that the centre of government was the Governor-General's castle and not the town-hall, where the sheriff and aldermen had their seat, was not without symbolic significance. The administration was not democratic (as in towns in Holland) but autocratic. The servants of the Company retained the appellation of merchant or merchant-in-chief but their way of living approached ever closer to that of the Eastern nobles. Even the way of living of the clerical class, the *Mixtiezen* (Mestizos) and *Mardijkers* (Christian descendants of former slaves, mostly imported from the coast of India), was predominantly Eastern for all their Christian belief. Here, too, as in Indonesian harbour princedoms, the various nationalities lived in separate wards under their own chiefs. In this manner each national group was able to preserve some of its own way of life in its own ward. The compact building style of the Chinese tended to approach that of the Hollanders. A considerable section of the population were slaves. The Company's Batavia had become an Eastern harbour principality by the eighteenth century. What remainders of Holland were left – the canals and the stuffy tightly-packed,

schoten Society), The Hague, Vols. VII, 1915; XXV, 1925 and XXXII, 1929.

many-storied houses – did not diffuse a bourgeois atmosphere but rather one of pestilence and death.[1]

Daendels, the 'Thundering Marshal', was accordingly justified, viewing the consequences of this development, in leaving the lower town in order to take up his residence in the healthier, more spacious resort of Weltevreden. Here the Dutch applied new building methods. The stuffy Dutch canal-houses were replaced by country villas, roomy, airy and cool, surrounded by extensive gardens. Their style found its inspiration in certain measure in the Javanese *pryayi* mansions. The houses of the less well-to-do Indo-European officials followed the same pattern, though they were smaller and less luxurious. The lay-out of the town was also influenced to some extent by the old Indonesian cities. A wide square formed the centre and the broad main streets traversed each other at right-angles leaving plenty of room for a conveniently arranged network of secondary roads. Hidden behind trees and bushes were the town *kampongs* where the Indonesians lived. These could be found sprinkled all over the city but especially in river bends. The poorer Indonesians occupied the deserted lower town too, particularly those entering the city for seasonal work. A large number of the Chinese population remained there as well.

Thus, like so many other 'Indian' towns in the nineteenth century, Weltevreden took on a typically rural air. There were no traces left of the closed-in bourgeois style of Dutch urban architecture in this spacious and open manner of building. This new architectural style was accompanied by a fundamental change in the mode of living. The prevailing atmosphere in the Indonesian towns of the nineteenth century was neither European nor Indonesian. It was known as '*Indisch*' (Indian). Just as the term '*Indisch*' was used for Europeans of mixed blood, it was employed in like manner for all cultural phenomena which were composed of mixed European and Indonesian elements. People spoke of '*Indian*' villas, '*Indian*' rice dishes, '*Indian*' hospitality. And as this

[1] A very lively account of the Company's Batavia is to be found in F. de Haan, *Oud Batavia* (Old Batavia), Bandung, 1935.

new mode of living was adopted in particular by the class that set the fashion in those days, the Europeans who had become strongly 'Indianised' by long residence in the tropics and by marriage with an Indo-European wife, or concubinage with an Indonesian woman, this nineteenth century urban culture can rightly be called a mestizo culture.

This culture was a reflection of social relations in the 'Indian' towns. The leading group consisted chiefly of high officials. Their incomes were large enough to permit them to live in the big country villas in luxurious fashion. Their mode of living had much in common with that of the feudal nobility of Indonesia. In contrast to bourgeois Holland, where the tendency was towards a thrifty frugality and simplicity which concealed a certain prosperity, the mode of living in the 'Indian' towns aimed at maintaining colonial prestige in a society predominantly feudal. There was no attempt to create the intimate atmosphere of the cosy Dutch parlour. Instead, Indian social life was a life of balls and receptions. Luxury was not to be found in the confines of interior rooms but in open galleries. No particular attention was paid to furnishing and decorating. When one was transferred, returned home on leave, or retired, the furniture was auctioned off. The relation of the 'gentry' to the troops of servants (slavery was gradually declining) was more or less patriarchal. The rural character of the towns and the close ties uniting them to the countryside contributed to creating a seignorial manner of living. Horse-riding and hunting, both typical recreations for a feudal class, were highly popular.

On the other hand, this European upper layer still maintained some contact with the culture of Western Europe. European cultural influences continued to flood Indonesia as a result of periodical leaves, the education of children in Europe and the regular arrival of fresh European personnel. The latest novelties from Holland – or better still, from Paris – were always very much in vogue. But these influences were as a rule only superficial. In a society which offered no breeding ground for bourgeois individualism, Western cultural elements were obliged to adapt themselves to the colonial atmosphere. For this upper social layer, being European did not mean that they were bound to European culture – however much they coquetted with it. It meant that they belonged to a higher caste.[1]

This 'Indian' mode of living did not remain limited to the European inhabitants of the large villas. The minor '*Indo*' (Eurasian) official also tried to copy it as far as his modest means allowed. For him, too, the maintenance of his prestige as a European meant an obligation to give a certain show of luxury and this easily got him into debt with the Chinese and Arab middleman. This life of external display, as contrasted to the bourgeois intimacy of life in Holland, also found its reflection in the furnishing of houses: gardens and galleries full of luxuriant plants, easy chairs, rocking chairs. The interior furnishing was, however, simple to the point of shabbiness. The Javanese *pryayis* also began increasingly to adopt the mode of living of the rich Europeans. They too were imbued by the mestizo culture. It was the princely courts which retained their typically Javanese stamp the longest.

If one looks for traces of a bourgeois culture in nineteenth century Indonesia, one should rather think of the Chinese and Arab middle class. Their position was, however, too much that of foreigners to make their imprint on urban life. It was government officials, representing the mestizo culture, not the merchant class, who led the fashion.

3 The modernisation of the 'Indian' towns[2]

The system of free enterprise, adopted as a general principle of economy since 1870, was also of great significance in the field of

[1] The mode of living of the Europeans in the middle of the previous century is described in A. W. P. Weitzel, *Batavia in 1858, of schetsen en beelden uit de hoofdstad van Neerlandsch-Indië* (Batavia in 1858, or sketches and pictures from the capital of the Netherlands Indies), Gorichem, 1860, p. 111 ff. For a somewhat later period an excellent analysis has been given bij R. Nieuwenhuijs, 'Over de Europese samenleving van 'tempo doeloe', 1870–1900' (About the European society of former times, 1870–1900), in *De fakkel* (The torch), Vol. I, 1940/41, p. 773 ff.

[2] Much useful information was obtained for this section from the brilliant

urban development and not only in the sense that increasing trade and, in later years, a rising industry brought about a rapid increase in the urban population, but also that unbridled individual initiative showed itself clearly in the large-scale extension of the towns. Their aspect became ever more dynamic, yet the progress of individual initiative was disorderly and disturbed the harmonious traditional pattern of former days.

The towns developed along the highroads – especially those leading to other towns, a ribbon-development showing a very great variety in the style of the houses. The well-off wanted to profit both by living out of town and by having their houses favourably situated on a main road. Soon one found Chinese *tokos* and native *warongs* (small shops) mixed up with them. At road crossings in particular one began to see the Chinese shops springing up. In this way a number of 'Indian' towns, already large in area in proportion to the number of inhabitants – due to wide-spaced rural building – often became extended in an incredible manner. It was only much later that the space between the mainroads was built up. Thus these towns often have the form of a star and shade off almost imperceptibly (via the semi-rural *kampong* building on the edges) into the surrounding countryside.

This ribbon-development not only produces a very untidy picture but also creates great problems. The stretched-out shape of the towns conflicts with the intensified contact between their inhabitants, which is the essence of urban development, and causes every social service to be disproportionately expensive. The growth of high-speed traffic presents difficulties. The main traffic arteries also have to serve for local traffic. *Tokos* right on the edge of the road and clustered around crossings present obstacles to the road-widening demanded by modern traffic. Then too, urban expansion was often haphazard so that there was no systematic connection with the network of main roads.

official report on town planning in the Indies, which was chiefly the work of the late Ir. (engineer) Thomas Karsten, now incorporated in *The Indonesian town. Studies in urban sociology*, Selected studies on Indonesia by Dutch scholars, Vol. IV, The Hague/Bandung, 1958, p. 3 ff.

The chaotic picture presented by these new agglomerations in the last decades of the nineteenth century and at the beginning of the twentieth, was still further aggravated by the lack of efficient 'zoning' (a systematic earmarking of certain areas for special purposes). From early times the business quarters had been more or less segregated from the residential districts. But the construction of railways and tramways and the erection of small factories proceeded more or less arbitrarily, with no regard for a town plan and despite the inconvenience for the inhabitants and the dangers of fire. There were no separate residential districts for factory workers. The situation of public buildings, offices, hospitals, cinemas, was also often illogical and inefficient. The laws governing urban land were endlessly complicated and confused. Old legal remnants of the feudal *latifundia* (the so-called private estates) occurred right in the middle of towns. Speculation in land assumed large proportions. The lack of regulations governing the height of buildings made it possible for ground rents to be forced up so high as a result of the construction of high buildings that further building became unprofitable. The economically weaker became the victims of the private exploitation of land. The dynamic character of urban life was achieved at the expense of the least dynamic group, the great mass of Indonesian citizens.

It was not only the outward appearance of the 'Indian' town as a whole that continued to retain a more or less rural character. Indeed the mainly agrarian character of Java and the standard of living in the countryside influenced the nature of the towns since the abundant supply of cheap labour enabled the wealthy to live in semi-feudal fashion for some considerable period. The Indonesian urban population, too, continued for a long time to preserve a preponderantly rural mode of living. The city *kampongs*, hidden behind banana trees and palms, retained a rural aspect. The manner of construction and habit of life also remained predominantly rural.

This presented one of the greatest difficulties facing urbanisation in Indonesia. The semi-rural way of life followed by the great mass of the Indonesian city dwellers was not suited to the many sophistications which go to make up the life of a town. Primitive methods of sanitation, which in the open country did not necessarily represent any danger to health, gave rise to serious abuse in the much more densely built-up urban areas. The traditional attitude to life, suitable enough to a rural environment, made the inhabitants of the city *kampongs* the helpless victims of the more active among the population. The former, who did not participate wholeheartedly in the life of the town and who disposed of neither the discipline nor the organisation required to put concrete desires and demands before the local authorities, profited only slightly from the advantages urban life has to offer. In the struggle for living space which went on within the city boundaries they were gradually driven out. *Kampongs* had to make room for the building of railways and tramways as well as for new European residential districts; their inhabitants repaired to the backyards of the European houses and had to make do with what room there was in the remaining *kampongs*. Land belonging to Indonesians in the areas surrounding the towns was bought up for ridiculously low prices to provide living space for Europeans and the original inhabitants had to live in hovels paying a rent far too high for their incomes.

Thus we see that individual initiative in the towns had a dynamic effect but also brought poverty and dislocation with it. We see the same thing as an accompanying factor in the growth of European towns, but in the case of Indonesia the disparity between rich and poor was further accentuated by the colonial structure of society.

What is remarkable, however, is that the subsequent substitution of the system of private initiative by a certain measure of planning and control effected no fundamental change in this state of affairs. The government recognised the necessity of imposing limits to individual initiative in this matter of town building, before it did so in the economic and social fields. In so artificial an environment offering so mcuh scope for conflict, social evolution could not be left to take its own course. Soon after the institution of urban councils at the beginning of the present century, these bodies included in the scope of their activities many of the problems related to urban expansion.

But the urban authorities did not pay equal attention to the interests of the various groups among the inhabitants. Europeans – the majority of them Indo-Europeans – were preponderant over the other groups on the town councils of the larger towns. The towns were treated as 'Western enclaves' and this was justified inasmuch as they formed centres where the general atmosphere was more dynamic than elsewhere and where Western cultural influences were most potent. But it was unwarranted insofar as this definition was taken to mean that European interests should predominate in the towns and that only Europeans were capable of governing a town in the Western spirit. Although the overwhelming majority of Europeans and a very large section of the Foreign Orientals lived in the towns, the former represented, with one exception, a good deal less than 10 percent and the latter as a rule not much more than 10 percent of the total urban population. The description van Mook gives of the development of the entirely Indonesian town of Kuta Gede[1] showed that there, where there were no Europeans or Chinese to give the lead in the Western sense, the Indonesians proved themselves to be capable of urban development on their own part, which paralleled development in the colonial towns.

If, accordingly, European predominance was maintained in the town governments – to the extent that it was not until 1938 and 1940 that Indonesian mayors were appointed in two of the smaller towns, and then only after much resistance – this was due to the desire to preserve European influence as far as possible in this particular sphere, where so many European interests were involved. The argument that the 'Western spirit' was the monopoly of 'Europeans' was, therefore, more or less a rationalisation of the desire to maintain the colonial stratification on racial lines in the towns.

This makes it clear why the town councils concerned themselves – often unconsciously – with the interests of the European groups in the first place, the groups, that is, to which they were

[1] H. J. van Mook, 'Kuta Gede', in *The Indonesian town*, p. 275 ff.

most closely linked. It is typical, for instance, that one finds no footpaths in the 'Indian' towns, for the group who administered the towns did not walk themselves – they drove.

Housing, in particular, showed how unequally the interest of town councils was divided among the various groups of the population. The new residential districts inhabited by the rich and moderately rich Europeans were very beautiful. Houses with gardens were very much smaller than they had been in the middle of the nineteenth century and reminded one more of English bungalows; but they were extraordinarily comfortable. The ground was obtained by the local authority by purchase of the Indonesians' rights for very small sums and the prices then charged to buyers were so low that it was possible to build in the extremely luxurious open bungalow style quite close to the heart of the town. As a rule these new villa districts were built according to a harmonious plan and were models of what town planning could achieve. A typical colonial feature was that their beautiful appearance was obtained, in part, by clearing away all Indonesian elements, which were regarded as disharmonious.

The housing of the comparatively well-off middle class, consisting chiefly of (Indo-)Europeans, was also reasonably good; but provision for the lower middle class was decidedly bad, especially in the large towns. For the Indonesian middle class there was, as a rule, no adequate housing. Sometimes they had to make do with tumble-down old houses, or with a house in one of the 'better' *kampongs*, where there were no metalled roads, no road lighting, and where one had to put up with bad drainage and sewerage. In other places there were newly-built houses for the lower middle class, better situated, but, all the same, generally much too small and much too expensive for their size. Sometimes, indeed, the lower middle class of Indonesians, or poor Europeans, had to live in one of the people's *kampongs* where their whole environment was in conflict with the rules of hygiene they had learned. The Chinese lower middle class, too, lived either in Chinese districts, which were unduly overcrowded and offered only very limited opportunity for extension, or in *kampongs*.

In many cities the housing of the Indonesian poor was abominably bad. Increasing concentration of building in the city *kampongs* together with primitive, semi-rural lay-out and construction created an extremely serious state of affairs in several places. As a result one sometimes came across whole plots of hovels in these city *kampongs*; often there was a great danger of fire, very serious inadequacy in the sanitation, insufficient supply of drinking water, lack of recreation grounds, far too little light and air and all the discomforts of periodic floods. Even more serious overcrowding was caused not only by an increase in urban population uncompensated for by extra living accommodation but also because the Indonesians were repeatedly driven out of their original residential areas. Even the systematic improvement of the *kampongs*, which was undertaken in later years, did not bring about a fundamental change in the situation. The improvement consisted largely in road-metalling and better sewerage. It was expected that landlords would respond by improving their houses themselves. But this rarely happened: landlords pocketed an increased rent and left the houses in their original condition. Thus the *kampong* improvement did not always benefit the inhabitants, who were often forced by increased rents to leave for the already overcrowded more distant *kampongs*, which had not undergone improvement. It was often the case that members of the lower middle class, who were unable to find housing accommodation elsewhere, moved into the improved *kampongs*. And then again, it was not long before these *kampongs* were suffering anew from overpopulation due to further building, or, when this was forbidden, owing to overcrowding in what houses there already were.

Thus, while the authorities were trying to remove evils in one place, others were springing up elsewhere. This was largely to be attributed to the fact that the authorities were not properly acquainted with the social and economic situation inside the people's *kampongs* and were also often insufficiently interested in the people's needs. It was not the Indonesians alone who were half-hearted in this matter of town life. The governing group of

Europeans also had an intuitive aversion to the urbanisation of Indonesians, feeling that it introduced an alien and unsympathetic element into the Indonesian scene. This caused even experts on Indonesian society to take too one-sided an interest in the idyllic, rustic Java of tradition and to avoid seeing the unsightly reality of the city *kampongs*. This lack of interest was mirrored in the external appearance of the *kampongs*: it was very seldom that one saw there a decent recreation ground or a pleasing public building, such as a school, place of worship, or social hall. The general situation cannot be shown better than by the following figures: in Bandung, where 12 percent of the population consisted of Europeans (the highest percentage in all Indonesia), 10 percent of Chinese, and 77 percent of Indonesians, 52 percent of the residential space was reserved for Europeans, 8 percent for the Chinese, and only 40 percent for the Indonesians.[1]

Colonialism was accordingly reflected not only in the segregation and great difference in character of the residential areas occupied by the various groups of the urban population, but also in their struggle for living space, which was revealed, amongst other things, in the external aspect of the towns. Untidiness and disorder remained even after the advent of town planning. There was really no single group which was interested in the town for its own sake and which could assume responsibility for promoting a sense of local patriotism and a civic consciousness. The great majority of the Europeans felt their stay in an Indonesian town to be temporary only. Even the Indo-European civil servants were liable to be transferred more than once in their life time. Among the Indonesians themselves, an organised, collective will was still insufficiently developed and insufficiently concerned with urban questions.

The social picture outlined above, borrowed largely from the official Town Planning Report, mentioned in note 2, page 175/6, is more or less mirrored in the field of culture. The disintegration of modern town life leads to cultural disintegration. There was no

[1] Cf. H. Lehmann, *op. cit.*, p. 121.

longer any question of one predominant mode of living. That of the European upper class no longer tended to be modelled on feudal lines. It had come closer to resembling the style of living of a prosperous bourgeoisie. The patriarchal 'Indian' houses with their great parks had been replaced by villas on the European model – closed-in and with only relatively small gardens. The large retinue of servants with their families, over which well-to-do Europeans had exercised a patriarchal authority, yielded place to a staff of four or five, mostly living outside the house – a staff which was, however, still large according to Western standards. European wives coming in large numbers brought with them something of the Dutch bourgeois atmosphere; yet the colonial sphere in which they moved and their especial social position still exercised an obvious influence on the mental attitude of the European upper layer. Their mode of living was livelier, more businesslike and more dynamic than formerly. The business quarters in the large towns were also reminiscent in their appearance of European cities.

Traces of this businesslike and dynamic spirit were to be found among the new middle class, the Indo-Europeans and the Indonesian intellectuals and near-intellectuals as well. Yet it cannot be said that the mode of living of Europeans coming from the West represented the leading style of culture generally emulated. The way of life of this middle class, composed chiefly of officials, still retained many characteristics of the nineteenth century mestizo culture. The fact that these groups had taken up residence in the old Indian houses abandoned by the '*totoks*' (immigrant Europeans) was not without a symbolic significance.

But these groups, too, were exposed in large measure to the influence of bourgeois society. Education – with its individualising effect – accentuated the sense of isolation in the modern towns. Urban life exercised the same individualising and uprooting influence on other groups too, such as the Chinese and Indonesian middle class businessmen, and on the various groups of workers.

The disintegration of urban culture was not retarded when isolated individuals began to join more and more together in order to keep pace with their rivals in the economic and social struggle. It was often similar cultural influences, such as Western education and the manifold contacts of urban life affecting the various groups of different racial origin, which made it possible for them to compete with each other. On the other hand these groups tended to become more exclusive, owing to increased social tension, and to lay undue stress on what cultural diversity still existed, in order to accentuate the peculiarity of the own group. Though Indo-Europeans, Indonesian Chinese and modern urban Indonesians were all of them equally imbued with the mestizo culture, they saw themselves as bearers *par excellence* of European, Chinese and Indonesian cultural values. Paradoxically, however, the dwindling cultural differences tended to widen again, insofar as the various groups were also the supporters of divergent ideologies. Thus, communal strife worked towards still further disintegration. Just as town planning had not been able to remove the untidiness from the urban scene owing to the caste-like structure of colonial society, so group solidarity could not put an end to the disintegration of urban culture. But group conflict could introduce a new dynamic element into social life. The mutual association of Westernised Indonesians was in itself a source of new cultural elements for Indonesia. Although this group was not a homogeneous whole – for the lesser officials were, culturally, fairly far removed from the more Westernised upper layer as well as from the small Islamic merchants – yet there was a certain common element in their reaction to the West. On the one hand these urbanised Indonesians had broken free to a great extent from the traditional court culture,[1] on the other hand, their social resistance to the colonial caste-like structure was sometimes reflected in a cultural resistance to the mode of living of the colonial Dutchmen, and sometimes, too, in resistance to the intermediary of the Dutch in the adoption of foreign cultural elements. While Europeans, the Indo-Europeans included, in Indonesia were culturally often strongly orientated towards Holland, among

[1] Cf. Th. Pigeaud, *Javaanse volksvertoningen* (Javanese folk performances), Batavia, 1938, p. 34.

a number of Westernised Indonesians there developed a tendency to turn direct to cultural sources in the outside world.[1] Their interest was often concerned with other things than that of the Europeans: for instance, they often displayed an especial interest in cultural movements expressing social discontent. Among this group the need arose to bridge over regional divergencies and to associate together with their group comrades in all parts of the archipelago in one single political and cultural movement. And just as this new Indonesian class was predominantly urban in character, this new Indonesian culture was to be a typically urban culture.

The new cultural forces awakened by this movement found striking expression in the effort to shape a new general Indonesian language, called *Bahasa Indonesia*. As towns had been in the past the centres from which those in power had governed Indonesia, so now they were the centres where new ideas and new cultural forms came into being and from where they spread out over the countryside. However small a percentage of Indonesians may have lived in the towns, these towns were the most dynamic element in Indonesian society and thus assumed a very great influence on the social and political events throughout the archipelago.

4 Problems of urban growth

The 1920 census showed that 6.63 percent of the population of Java lived in 'towns'. According to the 1930 census 8.7 percent lived in 102 places 'having more or less the appearance of towns', while in those places regarded as 'towns' for the purposes of the 1920 census 7.63 percent of the population was then found to be living. Of these, 3.75 percent, that is almost the half, lived in towns of more than 100,000 inhabitants. Thus the urban population was growing faster than the total population of Java. Some facts are also known about the rate of growth of various types

[1] Cf. *e.g.* Soetan Sjahrir, *Out of exile*, New York, 1949, p. 151. See also the novel *Buiten het gareel* (Out of harness) by Soewarsih Djojopoespito, Utrecht, 1946, pp. 169/170.

of town. In particular, the population in the largest towns, with more than 100,000 inhabitants, increased rapidly: the total number of inhabitants doubled in a period of 10 to 20 years. The smaller the town, the slower in general the rate of growth; it often happened that in towns of under 25,000 inhabitants the number of inhabitants dropped.[1]

category	Inhabitants	Number of towns	Number of inhabitants as percentage of Java and Madura		Increese or decrease
			1920	1930	
A	more than 100,000	6	2.83	3.75	0.92
B	50,000–100,000	6	0.71	0.91	0.20
C	25,000– 50,000	14	1.03	1.12	0.09
D	10,000– 25,000	43	1.88	1.70	0.18
E	under 10,000	8	0.18	0.15	0.03
		77	6.63	7.63	

(adapted from *The Indonesian Town*, p. 6)

This development in the size of towns continued after 1930 – very probably at a considerably increased pace. It is not possible to give precise figures because there has been no census since that of 1930. But if one bears in mind that, according to present estimates, Jakarta has now at least one and a half million inhabitants – and perhaps far more than two million, if account is taken of all the territorial increases of the municipality of Jakarta during the last decades – as compared with the 1930 figure of 533,000 (for Jakarta with the suburb of Meester Cornelis, at present called Jatinegara) and that Surabaya has about one million (342,000 in 1930), one can form an impression of the rapidity with which urbanisation is proceeding.

The town fulfils an ever more important function in Indonesian society. In the Indonesia of former times the towns had been the centres from where the surrounding countryside was administered

[1] See *The Indonesian Town*, p. 6 ff.

– and very often roughly administered. To what extent the towns had something concrete – perhaps iron agricultural tools – to offer in exchange for the stream of goods – and often services – which the peasant population had to provide has yet to be adequately investigated.[1] But from the nineteenth century onwards the towns became ever more integral parts of Indonesian society. The intensified activity of the government, the increase in trade – and in industry, too, in later years – brought about an ever greater exchange of goods and services between town and countryside. Large concentrations of purchasing consumers were no longer to be found in the neighbourhood of the princely courts (Solo and Jogjakarta) alone: they existed also in places where there were many offices and schools, or those which attracted retired people living on pensions, such as Bandung and Malang. The expansion of the civil administration and the increase in trade offered opportunities of employment to a growing number of Indonesians coming in from the countryside. In the crisis years a remarkable number of these disappeared from the towns but it seems, considering the rapid increase of the number of inhabitants of a city like Batavia during the late thirties, that shortly afterwards the influx began anew, stimulated not only by expanding industry but also by the miserable conditions in the country areas. Large numbers of landless farmers flocked to the towns in the hope of finding work. The population of Java began to become more mobile. During and after the war other factors, too, exerted a similar influence: attempts of the Japanese to force part of the urban population back to the country met with partial success only; many young men were torn away from their rural environment by the recruitment of labour forces and soldiers which

[1] Boeke's theory that there was in early Asian society only a unilateral flow of goods from the country to the towns (*The interests of the voiceless Far East*, Leiden, 1948, p. 6) seems an unwarranted generalisation. Mencius mentions already the use of iron ploughshares by the Chinese peasant, who exchanged grain for iron. See Mencius, III a, 4 (1–7), cited by J. J. L. Duyvendak, *Wegen en gestalten der Chineesche geschiedenis* (Roads and figures from the Chinese history). The Hague, 1935, p. 54.

was often on a compulsory basis; and when their term of service had expired, there were many who were no longer inclined to return to their place of birth. The guerrilla struggle had often the same effect. Groups of all kinds, moreover, sought security in the towns in periods of disturbance and never returned home. The number of Chinese who permanently left the countryside was especially high with the result that the number of Chinese now living in the towns has considerably increased.

The government did not discern this accelerated process of urbanisation in time, and so was unable to control it. It became particularly obvious in the crisis years that the development was getting out of its command.

We are acquainted with the slum problem in Europe, too, with the unbridled growth of towns and the rise of industry in the nineteenth century. The towns were far unhealthier than the countryside. Exactly the opposite was the case later on, however, with the development of modern hygiene, since sanitation could be applied on a wider scale in the towns where concentration was simpler. The death-rate in Dutch towns is lower than in the country.

It seemed for some time that this process would be repeated in the Indonesian towns. Mortality figures and especially those for infant mortality showed the same decline as in Europe – though in Indonesia it came about a few decades later! Brand has demonstrated this demographic development for the town of Bandung.[1]

There were significant differences as compared with Europe. In the first place, owing to the more rural environment and the tropical climate, a number of the extreme forms of slum conditions could not arise so easily here. But it was an especial characteristic of colonial society that stages of development far removed from one another in time could be found existing side by side here. It was not the same as in nineteenth century Europe, where rich and poor alike suffered from the lack of sanitary arrangements.

1 See W. Brand, 'Differential mortality in the town of Bandung', in *The Indonesian town*, p. 227 ff.

In Indonesia one found the typical colonial picture of one small section of the population living in hygienic conditions, which could easily bear comparison with the most favourable conditions prevailing in Europe, while the great mass of the population lived in the most primitive of conditions. This distinct difference was reflected in the death-rate. There was a very obvious connection between prosperity on the one side and good health and expectation of life on the other. The average death-rate and the infant death-rate were, for Europeans, generally only slightly higher

Mortality according to age group and ethnic group in Batavia (1935–1937) as a percentage of total mortality.

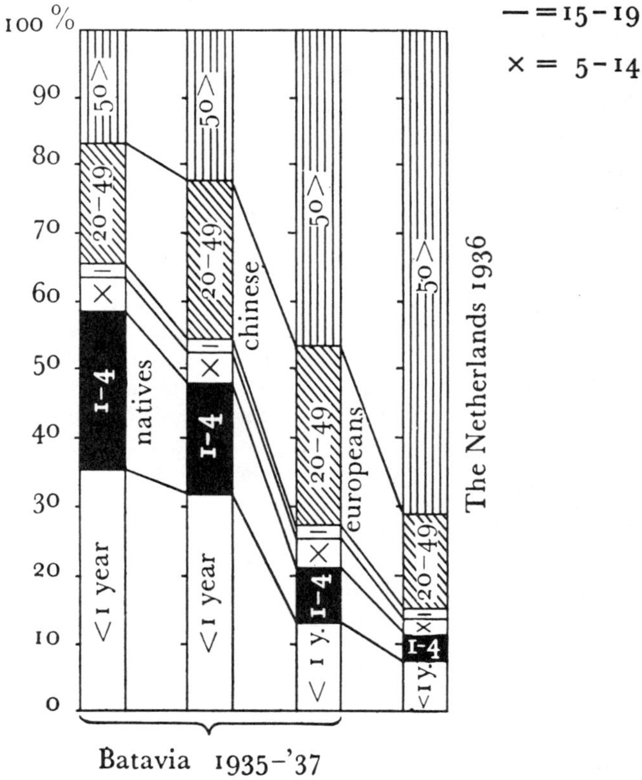

than in the towns of Europe; for the class enjoying the highest standard of living they were even more favourable. For the intermediate group of Chinese they were considerably less favourable, while for the Indonesians the figures were very high indeed.[1]

And even inside the *kampongs* there was a correlation between housing conditions and the death-rate. The figures for those living in the '*pondoks*' (large primitive barracks where one family usually lived in a single room) were less favourable than for those who had a detached, single dwelling to themselves. Health conditions were better, too, in the *kampongs* in proportion as money incomes were higher.[2] Since the investigations carried out by de Haas no doubt remains that, in the case of Batavia, the very high death-rate was first and foremost a result of undernourishment and overcrowding.[3]

But at the same time the investigations of the last mentioned raise doubts about the general validity of the parallel with the demographic development in European towns as drawn by Brand. There are, it is true, signs that more understanding of the rules of hygiene gradually developed among the population, naturally stimulated by the example before their eyes of the conditions existing among the Europeans. Government and private activity

[1] J. H. de Haas, 'Sterfte naar leeftijdsgroepen in Batavia in het bijzonder op den kinderleeftijd', in *Geneeskundig Tijdschrift voor Nederlandsch-Indië* (Netherlands Indian Medical Journal), Vol. LXXIX, 1939, p. 707 ff., see in particular p. 712. The same article 'Mortality according to age groups, especially amongst children', in *Indian Journal of Pediatrics*, Vol. VI, 1939, p. 231 ff. The graph on p. 187 is adapted from de Haas' study.

[2] Cf. J. W. Tesch, *The hygiene study ward centre at Batavia. Planning and preliminary results (1937–1941)*, The Hague, 1948. See also the official report of an investigation of 'The living conditions of municipally employed coolies in Batavia in 1937', in *The Indonesian town*, p. 87 ff.

[3] Liem Tjay Tie and J. H. de Haas, 'Over de zuigelingensterfte in eenige onderdistricten van het Regentschap Tasikmalaja (West-Java) in 1935, 1936 en 1937' (Concerning infant mortality in a number of sub-districts of the Tasikmalaya Regency, Western Java, in 1935, 1936 and 1937), in *Geneeskundig Tijdschrift voor Nederlandsch-Indië* (Netherlands Indian Medical Journal), Vol. LXXIX, 1939, p. 5024–5027 (correct paging: 2324–2327). See also other publications by the second author in the same journal.

in the field of hygiene was also gradually extending. But in contrast to this favourable tendency one less favourable was manifesting itself. Compared with the conditions in the three large coastal towns of Java, the most unfavourable state of affairs in Bandung where Brand carried out his investigations was, in the words of an Indonesian engineer, 'paradisaic'. And although there are indications that between the years 1910 and 1920 the death-rate among Indonesians in Batavia were considerably higher than in the thirties, even in the latter period it still proved to be terribly high: about 25 per thousand was the average for the total Indonesian population and about 25 percent for children under one year. It is moreover highly questionable whether there was a further decline in the death-rate during the thirties.[1] The rapid and insufficiently controlled growth of the urban population might well have reversed the favourable trend, or at least have neutralised it. As long as the immense difficulties of undernourishment and overcrowding have not been brought under control, the most disturbing problems of urbanisation continue to exist in their direst form.

Since then, war, Japanese occupation and revolution have aggravated the situation in an alarming degree. A demographic

[1] In his article 'Sterfte te Batavia 1929–1931' (Mortality in Batavia 1929–1931), in *Geneeskundig Tijdschrift voor Nederlandsch-Indië* (Netherlands Indian Medical Journal), Vol. LXXX, 1940, p. 1477, W. Brand writes: 'The general mortality among the natives in Batavia was between 25 and 26 per thousand in 1930. De Haas estimated the figure for 1934 at 30 per thousand and for 1935/1936 at 29 per thousand, but his figures are too high since he assumed too low a figure for the native population of the city'. 'Among the natives in Batavia the death expectation for infants below 1 year of age was about 30 percent, whereas de Haas also assumed an infant mortality in 1934 and in 1935/1936 of about 30 percent. It would appear, therefore, that in spite of the crisis infant mortality among the natives has not increased since 1930, although the figures remain extremely high.' As both Brand and de Haas have probably underrated the birth-rate in pre-war Batavia, an estimate of infant mortality at 25 percent seems more plausible. See W. F. Wertheim, 'The forty percent test. A useful demographic tool', in *Ekonomi dan Keuangan Indonesia* (Economics and Finance in Indonesia), Vol. VIII, 1955, p. 170.

investigation undertaken in post-war Macassar revealed a state of affairs even worse than that in Jakarta (Batavia) at the time of de Haas' investigation.[1] And though the situation has, no doubt, improved during the past ten years, one has only to remember the tens of thousands of homeless met with a few years ago in the large towns and the way crime flourished there at that time to know that urbanisation is still one of Indonesia's most serious problems.

However, these observations need not end with the gloomiest of pictures. It seems that the urban population of Indonesia is gradually assuming a more progressive attitude towards city problems. The national revolution has also set free new forces in this field, individual as well as collective forces. Collective action in the large hospital in Jakarta in August 1948, when from top to bottom the entire staff laid down tools as a protest to the occupation of the hospital by Dutch authorities, was a clear indication of this new sense of unity. And now, at last, the trade unions as well are showing signs of vitality in Indonesia. The many strikes, however troublesome and dislocating in their effect, show a stronger tendency on the part of the inhabitants of the *kampongs* to act collectively in their own interests. Collective protests against increased electricity rates some time ago give also proof of a newly-awakened dynamism in the urban *kampongs*. If the new ruling class should show signs of the aloofness characteristic of the former colonial topclass, it will be pressed hard by the various urban groups set into motion by the Japanese occupation and the ensuing revolution. However, there are signs of a growing sense of social responsibility among Indonesian officials; while inefficiency and corruption are widely discussed in the foreign press, the admirable initiatives of many unassuming workers receive scant attention. The revolution has created the conditions for the gradual development of a sense of unity which is brought to bear on the town as a whole.

[1] R. Soemitro, 'Zuigelingensterfte te Makassar' (Infant mortality in Macassar), in *Medisch Maandblad* (Medical Monthly), Vol. III, 1950; see in particular p. 81 ff.

Furthermore, it is not inconceivable that the problem which the towns present is only a concentrated form of the population problem of the whole of Java. A new census might quite possibly show that the rural population has increased, relatively, far less than the total population. This could partly be attributed to war and revolution. But it could also be due to reasons of structure. Is it not possible that Java's overpopulation problem is in process of transferring itself at least in part from the countryside to the town?

This would have one advantage: the population problem is, in principle, more capable of solution in the cities than in the countryside. There is in fact only one conceivable solution to the problem of the urban population: speedy and energetic industrialisation. Only by rapidly increasing the urban population's production can work and food be found for everyone. But to achieve this aim it will at the same time be necessary for town-planning, which in the past was too closely related to the colonial structure, to become far more comprehensive in scope and more harmonious in its general concepts. It will need, too, to be based on an ideology which does not regard the town as an agglomeration of individuals but as a collective, living entity.

A short bibliography

W. Brand, 'Sterfte te Batavia 1929–1931' (Mortality in Batavia 1929–1931), in *Geneeskundig Tijdschrift voor Nederlandsch-Indië* (Netherlands Indian Medical Journal), Vol. LXXX, 1940, p. 1470 ff.

Census of 1930 in Netherlands India, Batavia, 1933–1936.

E. A. Gutkind, *Revolution of environment*, London, 1946.

F. de Haan, *Oud Batavia* (Old Batavia), Bandung, 1935.

J. H. de Haas, 'Zuigelingensterfte in Batavia, II. Bewerking der gegevens over 1935 en 1936', in *Geneeskundig Tijdschrift voor Nederlandsch-Indië*, Vol. LXXVIII, 1938, p. 1467 ff. The same article 'Infant mortality in Batavia', in *Indian Journal of Pediatrics*, Vol. VI, 1939, p. 12 ff.

J. H. de Haas, 'Sterfte naar leeftijdsgroepen in Batavia in het bijzonder op den kinderleeftijd', in *Geneeskundig Tijdschrift voor Nederlandsch-Indië*, Vol. LXXIX, 1939, p. 707 ff. The same article 'Mortality according to age groups, especially amongst children', in *Indian Journal of Pediatrics*, Vol. VI, 1939, p. 231 ff.

H. J. Heeren (ed.), 'The urbanisation of Djakarta', in *Ekonomi dan Keuangan Indonesia* (Economics and Finance in Indonesia), Vol. VIII, 1955, p. 696 ff.

Karl Helbig, *Batavia. Eine tropische Stadtlandschaftskunde im Rahmen der Insel Java*, Hamburg, 1931.

The Indonesian town. Studies in urban sociology, Selected studies on Indonesia by Dutch scholars, Vol. IV, The Hague/Bandung, 1958.

Herbert Lehmann, 'Das Antlitz der Stadt in Niederländisch Indien', in *Länderkundliche Forschung. Festschrift Norbert Krebs*, Stuttgart, 1936.

J. C. van Leur, *Indonesian trade and society. Essays in Asian social and economic history*, Selected studies on Indonesia by Dutch scholars, Vol. I, The Hague/Bandung, 1955.

Liem Tjay Tie, *Tentang angka kematian baji dikota Semarang dalam tahun 1952 dan 1953* (On infant mortality rates among Indonesians in the town of Semarang in 1952 and 1953), Jogjakarta, 1954.

J. H. A. Logemann, 'The characteristics of urban centres in the East', in *Eastern and Western world. Selected readings*, The Hague/Bandung, 1953.

R. Nieuwenhuijs, 'Over de Europese samenleving van 'tempo doeloe' 1870–1900' (About the European society of former times 1870–1900), in *De fakkel* (The torch), Vol. I, 1940/41, p. 773 ff.

Penjelidikan biaja hidup di Djakarta (Investigation of the cost of living in Jakarta), in *Ekonomi dan Keuangan Indonesia* (Economics and Finance in Indonesia), Vol. X, 1957, p. 738 ff.

C. Thomas Nix, *Bijdrage tot de vormleer van de stedebouw, in het bijzonder voor Indonesië* (Contribution to the morphology of townbuilding, in particular for Indonesia), Heemstede, 1949.

Soemitro, 'Zuigelingensterfte te Makassar' (Infant mortality in Macassar), in *Medisch Maandblad* (Medical Monthly), Vol. III, 1950, p. 81 ff.

J. W. Tesch, *The hygiene study ward centre at Batavia. Planning and preliminary results (1937–1941)*, The Hague, 1948.

A. W. P. Weitzel, *Batavia in 1858, of schetsen en beelden uit de hoofdstad van Neerlandsch-Indië* (Batavia in 1858, or sketches and pictures from the capital of the Netherlands Indies), Gorichem, 1860.

Chapter Eight

Religious Reform

1 *Islam in the old Indonesian coastal towns*

The Islamic faith invaded the archipelago via the trade routes. It was first introduced there by merchants coming from India and appeared in the form it had assumed on the Asian mainland. It was an Islam which had become adapted in the course of centuries to the social structure of the South Asian merchant cities, a secularised Islam, which served as a support to the existing social structure with all its inequalities and also to the powerful and successful in this world with all their human frailties. The pious man was, as in the tale of Sindbad, recompensed with wealth. All he needed to do to keep Allah's favour, was to spend part of it on the poor. The prince, reasonably observant as regards his religious devotions, the victorious general, the prosperous merchant, all of them enjoyed the backing of Islamic law and of the officially recognised scribes who had entered the service of the princely authority as judges or advisers. The provisions of the law concerning impediments to marriage confirmed social inequality and reflected the class structure of the Asian merchant cities: at the top we find the nobility, the *Sayyids* or *Sharifs*, who could prove their kinship with the Prophet; below them, the scribes and lawyers; and next, the merchants and the artisans – with a great deal of internal differentiation – and lowest of all, the unfree. The observance of the Islamic faith was on traditional lines: the accent was laid on the observance of the prescribed ritual and on external behaviour in accordance with the most elementary religious duties. One submitted to the authority of Islamic law just as one submitted to the traditional feudal structure of society. The city merchant was not a free and independent citizen, who thought as an individual and stood in a personal relationship to his God. The man who felt the need of a more personal religious experience was obliged to turn to mysticism. But the individual had little independence in this field either. Here, too, he had to submit to the power and authority of the religious teachers.

All the same, beneath this secularised upper-current in the world of Islam, an under-current can always be distinguished which puts greater emphasis on human equality, the value of the individual and the spiritual side of life. It was not in vain that the Prophet had introduced many Christian and Jewish elements into his religion – especially in the Meccan period – and it was also significant that in the period when Damascus was the centre of the Arab Empire many elements from ancient civilisation and Roman law had invaded Islam. In the East Islam fulfilled a civilising function similar to that of Christianity in the West. In the Koran, too, great importance was attributed to the concepts of brotherly love, forbearance, mercy, reasonableness, humility and honesty. Islam contributed in large measure to the humanising of numerous Asian customs. The idea of human equality did not lead to the abolition of slavery but, as was the case with Christianity too, to better treatment of slaves and an adoption – even by the free – of the symbolic attitude of slaves, *i.e.*, the sitting posture (instead of reclining) which embodied a recognition of the fundamental equality between free man and slave. The rich Sindbad invited the poor Hindbad to sit down by his side at his meal; in his outward behaviour he had to remain humble.

An individualising trait is to be found in the adoption of the principles of Roman law concerning the protection of private property and in the rejection of the idea of an intermediary between the individual and God as well as in the denial of any autonomous community other than the all-embracing Islamic community, known as the *Ummat Islam*. The anti-materialistic, or spiritualising, feature is discoverable in a counter-current – usually weaker than that which regards wealth as a sign of Allah's favour, but one which is still clearly noticeable, which rejects excessive luxury, preaches frugality and simplicity and sometimes even glorifies poverty.

The foremost exponents of the more spiritual side of Islam were the religious teachers, who in every Islamic state were the principal, if not the only, opponents of the secular governments; who refused to become tools of princely authority; who kept up a sustained criticism of all the doings of the prince and his royal household; who were regarded by the secular authorities as 'troublesome', and yet were tolerated by princes and the rich on account of the prestige they enjoyed with the urban dwellers, traders and craftsmen, and by reason of the aura of sanctity which often surrounded them. It can pay the powerful to offer a holy man hospitality and surround him with tokens of respect.

This was the traditional Islam which the merchants brought with them from Gujerat and other parts of India[1] – and to which many Indonesian city dwellers were converted. For the time being it affected only the ordinary townsmen. For a long time the situation in many coastal places remained as Ruy de Brito, Governor of Malacca, says, referring to Brunei: '*ho rey he cafere: os mercadores sam mouros.*'[2]

What attraction had Islam for the ordinary small-scale city tradesmen and artisans in the small Indonesian harbour principalities? Not as was formerly believed by providing a new '*Wirt-*

[1] In an article in the *Journal of the Malayan Branch of the Royal Asiatic Society*, Vol. XXIV, 1951, p. 28, G. E. Marrison argues that the first Islamic influences in Northern Sumatra did not stem from Gujerat, but from Southern India. This theory receives some support from Tomé Pires, *Suma Oriental* (English translation by Armando Cortesão, titled 'The Suma Oriental of Tomé Pires and the book of Francisco Rodrigues', in Works issued by the Hakluyt Society, Second Series Nr XC, Part 1, London, 1944), which points to ancient relations between Pasei and the Benghal coast (Vol. I, p. 88, p. 143).

[2] 'The king is an unbeliever: the merchants are Mohammedans' – from a letter dated January 6th 1514 addressed to King Manoel of Portugal. See B. J. O. Schrieke, *Het boek van Bonang* (The book of Bonang), Utrecht, 1916, p. 37/38.

schaftsgeist' which foreign Islamic traders were said to have brought with them.[1] The technique of international trade was and remained traditional: petty Islamic traders from the Asian mainland introduced no new economic element into the archipelago. The attraction of Islam for the traders living under Hindu princely rule was rather to be discovered in the world of ideas: Islam gave the small man a sense of his individual worth as a member of the Islamic community.[2] According to Hindu ideology he was merely a creature of lower order than the members of the higher castes. Under Islam he could, as it were, feel himself their equal or, even, in his quality as a Moslem, the superior of such of them as were not Moslems themselves, even though he still occupied a subordinate position in the social structure.

In this sense Islam can be regarded as the fermenting agent for the revolutionary process which has taken place in the twentieth century.

2 Western penetration and the expansion of Islam

In the sphere of religion Western penetration of the archipelago had clear consequences far earlier than it had in the spheres of economics and the social structure. One can, indeed, sustain the paradox that the expansion of Islam in the Indonesian archipelago was due to the Westerners.

It was mainly the arrival of the Portuguese which induced a large number of Indonesian princes to embrace the Islamic faith as a political move to counter Christian penetration.[3] It has been

[1] Cf. for example B. Schrieke, *Indonesian sociological studies. Selected writings*, Part 1. Selected studies on Indonesia by Dutch scholars, Vol. II, The Hague/Bandung, 1955, p. 28; contested by J. C. van Leur, *Indonesian trade and society. Essays in Asian social and economic history*, Selected studies on Indonesia by Dutch scholars, Vol. I, The Hague/Bandung, 1955, p. 116, 364 ff.

[2] Cf., for example, C. Snouck Hurgronje, *Verspreide geschriften* (Collected writings), Bonn/Leipzig/Leiden, 1923–1927, Vol. IV, Part 2, p. 242.

[3] This hypothesis has been derived from B. Schrieke, *Indonesian sociological studies. Ruler and realm in early Java. Selected writings*, Part 2. Selected studies on Indonesia by Dutch scholars, Vol. III, The Hague/Bandung, 1957, p.232 ff.; see also J. C. van Leur, *op. cit.*, p. 111 ff., 169. A confirmation of this theory

pointed out by Schrieke, that the Islamic scribes and religious teachers, who were already living in the coastal towns and were sometimes foreign in origin, played an important part in the conversion of the princes. The tradition, according to which the holy men or *walis* contributed largely to the spread of Islam in Indonesia, is certainly not wrong on this point. The conversion, for holy men and princes alike, was made all the easier by reason of the fact that the Islam as practised in Indonesia could in its early stages associate itself closely with the religious traditions of the Hindu period, for the form in which it was introduced had already been largely adapted to the mystical religious atmosphere of India.

One does, however, need to ask what precisely political considerations induced the princes to accept Islam under the influence of Portuguese penetration. Did they hope thereby, in the first place, to recruit a reliable army from the ranks of the city dwellers? Or was the prime motive the possibility of joining forces with the powerful Mogul or other Islamic princes? Probably both considerations played their part. Even though the armies of that time were largely slave armies, a trustworthy core could often be of importance.[1] It may be, however, that the whole urban atmosphere exerted more influence than definite rational considerations. We have already seen that the urban population (especially in the harbour towns) was in most cases predominantly Moslem. In times of disturbance this could provide a special spur urging the prince to follow suit. The religious teachers could exert great influence on the citizens of the towns. By refusing to recognise the prince, they could seriously impair his position in the struggle with the Portuguese, with rulers of neighbouring

may be derived from Tomé Pires, *op. cit.*, Vol. II, p. 241–243 (about the attempts of *mullahs* to convert the king of Malaya) and p. 245 (dealing with a parallel development in Java's north coast).

[1] Cf., for example, the fight between the Moslem harbour principality of Demak and the inland-state of Pajang, in which the slave armies fled the scene of battle, but the 'real Demakkers', probably Islamites, continued to offer fierce resistance; H. J. de Graaf, *Geschiedenis van Indonesië* (History of Indonesia), The Hague/Bandung, 1949, p. 102.

kingdoms on the coast, or inland, or with pretenders to the throne. On the other hand, by recognising him as the 'Islamic Prince', by investing him as it were, the holy men could reinforce his position considerably. And the greater the number of Indonesian kingdoms converted to Islam, the greater the incentive not to lag behind.

And once the harbour prince had embraced the Islamic faith it was in his own interest to encourage the country population to follow suit. Here, too, the religious teachers played an important role. Certain villages exempt from taxation were allocated to them by the prince for the purpose of founding schools. By means of these schools the internal missionary work which, according to the rules of Islam, should always follow on formal conversion, was able to proceed. The religious schools were often former Hindu or Buddhist cloisters. In this manner Islam was able to spread out also over the countryside, exerting its civilising influence as the monasteries in Northwestern Europe had done earlier.

In a few places, however, Portuguese and Spanish policy did not foster Islam but Christianity. This was notably the case in those islands of the Moluccas, where they themselves for a time held sway. In contrast with the spread of Islam, however, it was not primarily native traders who were converted to the new religion. Insofar as Christian missionary activity met with success, it was largely through the intermediary of native *rajas* (chiefs), who expected from the Europeans military help against their Moslem enemies. Where a *raja* fostered Christianity, missionary activity among the villagers could meet with a measure of success. The mode of living of the converts remained, however, largely the same. After the Dutch East India Company had ousted the Portuguese, the Catholic converts were forced to adopt Protestantism. Missionary activity was at its lowest under the Company's rule, the directors being more interested in commerce than in spiritual values. The influence of Protestantism on daily life was not very deep either. The individualising tendencies of Calvinism did not find a fertile soil under a Company inimical to any sign of free initiative. The only Dutch missionary activity of social importance was the founding of schools; but these were no less traditional than the Moslem Koran schools, the main teaching consisting of the recitation of holy texts in an incomprehensible language. Nor was conversion to Protestantism always a matter of personal conviction. The system introduced by Coen of distributing a pound of rice to any child actually attending a Christian school, called into existence the category of 'rice Christians', people embracing the new religion for reasons of profit. A Company regulation of 1635 promising a fixed sum to any convert was another instance of a deliberate appeal to extra-religious motives.[1] Moreover, conversion could pave the way for a rise in social status in the territories under the Company's rule. In Batavia, for example, Christians enjoyed a privileged status, as many of them had received enough education to enable them to fill clerical posts. But there was no equality of status among Christians – not even in the churches, where the parish had to rise when the members of Council entered.[2] In practice Christianity, like Islam, sanctioned social inequality.

For two centuries, during which the Dutch East India Company extended its rule over large parts of the archipelago, the political situation in Indonesia was dominated by a three-cornered relationship between the three most powerful groups: the Indonesian royal families, the Dutch rulers and the Moslem religious teachers. On the one hand, the centuries following the first expedition under Vasco da Gama were characterised by the struggle between the Cross and the Crescent. This struggle sometimes took the open form of warfare or the half-concealed form of 'piracy' and 'smuggling' on the part of Indonesian princes to the detriment of the East India Company. But the struggle

[1] See C. W. Th. Baron van Boetzelaer van Asperen en Dubbeldam, *De Protestantsche kerk in Nederlandsch-Indië. Haar ontwikkeling van 1620–1939* (The Protestant church in the Netherlands Indies. Its development from 1620 till 1939), The Hague, 1947, p. 152.

[2] C. W. Th. Baron van Boetzelaer van Asperen en Dubbeldam, *op. cit.*, p. 89/90.

occurred far more frequently in the political sphere in the form of pressure exerted by the Dutch on the Indonesian royal families to force them to keep control over fanatical Moslem elements within their kingdoms.

These extremist Moslem elements were usually headed by the religious teachers, who were (as was generally the case throughout Islam) the principal opponents of the secularised Islamic governments. The conversion of the archipelago to Islam, which led to pilgrimages to Mecca, strengthened the link with Arabia, and brought numbers of Arabian divines to the Islamic centres in Indonesia. Under their influence, the sober under-current of believers who stood somewhat opposed to the secular government with all its pomp, and were ever ready to brand court *etiquette* as superstition and heresy, gained in power. They were the Company's fiercest enemies. Conversely, there were some Indonesian princes who had been formally converted to Islam but feared the influence and the criticism of the severe religious teachers and still continued to live in the Hindu-animistic tradition.

A well-known instance of this internal strife was the massacre, organised by the *Sunan* of Mataram Amangkurat I among the so-called 'popes', and the later Dutch attack, inspired by the Mataram Prince, on the 'Prince Priest' of Giri (the so-called 'Mohammedan Pope').

It was always the policy of the Dutch to support these Indonesian princes against others who took the Faith seriously and who were prepared to tolerate the much-feared 'popes' in their territories. If possible, when any conflict arose concerning succession they always supported the party whose attitude to Islam was more superficial and formal.

A new factor came into play, however, in the nineteenth century. In various areas of Indonesia the agricultural population also became converted to Islam.[1] This considerably strengthened the position of the *kyahis* (religious teachers) since they could now reckon on a strong following. This showed itself on several occasions.

[1] See William Marsden, F.R.S., *The history of Sumatra*, London, 1784, p. 278, 282.

Time and again the Dutch authorities came into conflict with the Indonesian princes. By uniting with the religious teachers and hoisting the Islamic flag these princes could now unleash a general popular rising. This revealed itself in the Java War between the Dutch and Prince Diponegoro of Jogjakarta, from 1825 to 1830, in the Banjermasin War from 1859 onwards and the Acheh War in the last quarter of the nineteenth century. Moreover, war conditions proved to reinforce both the prestige and the power of the extremists among the religious teachers, who were prone to use the weapon of proclaiming a Holy War.

For this reason, it was the policy of the Dutch government to ally itself even more closely than before with the secular royal houses of Indonesia and with the *adat* chiefs and to respect their authority over the population.

This policy was pursued in the war waged during the eighteen thirties against the stern, sober, *Padris* of Central Sumatra. It was applied too in the last phase of the Acheh War, upon the advice of Snouck Hurgronje. The culture system under van den Bosch could also be considered as a return to the policy of cooperation with the feudal chiefs of Java after the lessons of the Java War.

Yet it was as dangerous for the Indonesian princes and chiefs to oppose Islam as for the Dutch, and this was why repeated attempts were made by the latter on the basis of past experience, to seek a *modus vivendi* with Islam. This *modus vivendi* resembled that in other Islamic areas: a number of scribes were found ready to unite in some measure with the secular authority and lend it their support. The Dutch left the practice of the Islamic faith free, no longer impeded pilgrimages and in turn received from the scribes a pronouncement to the effect that the Moslems, if unable to found an Islamic state themselves, should submit to the authority of a non-Islamic government. The government confined itself to taking action against expressions of so-called 'fanaticism' and to disapproval of too strict an observance of religious duties on the part of Indonesian government officials.[1]

[1] C. Snouck Hurgronje, *op. cit.*, Vol. IV, Part 1, 1924, p. 195 ff.

In the meantime Islam had been exerting a certain psychological and social influence on the population. It is true that such scholars as Snouck Hurgronje and van Vollenhoven have convincingly demonstrated that only a small part of the Islamic law had been adopted as an obligatory code governing social behaviour in Indonesia as it had been in other countries as well. People behaved according to the *adat*, or customary law, projecting their behaviour on to the Islamic faith and believing that by behaving in this way, they were acting in accordance with the Faith.

But in other respects the Faith certainly exerted an influence in social life. It gave to large numbers of Indonesians, including the simple peasants, a feeling of individual worth and a sense of solidarity. In Indonesia Islam tried, as it had in ancient Arabia, to bridge regional and tribal particularisms by means of a single Islamic unity. It threatened the position of the *adat* chiefs most of all. Their local patriotism was exposed to the criticism of the sternest Moslems who saw in the Faith a strong unifying force – a kind of pre-nationalism. Religious instruction – which was in a measure uniform throughout the Islamic world – and the pilgrimage to Mecca also made for unity.

Moreover, the customary laws kept in force by the *adat* chiefs were in danger of being condemned by strict Moslems as superstitious and heretical. The comparatively luxurious life led by some of these chiefs was exposed to criticism by the more 'puritanical' section. In particular the Arabian influence – later with something of a *Wahhabite* strain in it – stimulated resistance by unsophisticated peasants to the wordly rulers in the towns. Forms of family property rights preserved by the *adat* chiefs were also contested by strict Moslems, especially by the many city merchants among them, who wanted to see the more individualistic Islamic law of inheritance adopted.

Thus the Islamic faith had in many respects a revolutionising and modernising effect on Indonesian society.

Dutch authority strove to limit these influences, to support, where possible, the rule of *adat* chiefs and to stimulate local patriotic feeling. In some places, mostly regions where the Dutch colonial administration had not yet penetrated (as in the Batak areas), Dutch Christian missionary propaganda met with some success. As with Portuguese and Spanish missionary activities in the eastern part of the archipelago during the sixteenth century and with the Roman Catholic mission on Flores and in some other smaller areas in this century, modern Protestant mission made special headway in regions where the *adat* chiefs could be won over to the new religion. By maintaining the aristocratic order of society, the missionaries could assure themselves of the influence of those leaders on a large part of the agrarian population.[1] 'Fishing with the net' proved, in quantitative terms, more efficient than 'fishing with the hook', as it was called. Where missionaries, inspired by Protestant individualism, chose the latter approach, which was more personal and far more penetrating, the religion spread to very limited groups only. The best propagandists proved to be Indonesian Christians. It were Christians from Ambon who contributed most to the conversion of the Minahasa region.

Where 'the net' was used, however, the spiritual and social influence of Christianity was more limited. The most effective contribution of Christianity to social change was to be found in education. Missionary schools became centres of popular enlightenment. As they affected mainly the young generation, they became forceful agents in undermining ancient traditions. In agriculture missionaries also repeatedly fostered revolutionary innovations. But most of the social changes were wrought unwittingly by a constant fight against 'pagan' practices, which proved to be far more essential elements in the social fabric than most missionaries suspected.

There were, however, many factors restricting the influence of Christianity on social life. A colonial society did not provide the most suitable soil for missionary activities. Among the European

[1] A. J. van Zanen, *Voorwaarden voor maatschappelijke ontwikkeling in het centrale Batakland* (Conditions for social development in the central Batak area), Leiden, 1934, p. 95 ff.

part of the population, Christianity had adapted itself fully to the social structure in existence. The 'Indian Church' supported the stratification according to race and thus counteracted the endeavours of the Protestant missions to win over large portions of the Indonesian population. Christianity had come to mean the religion of the dominating race. There were, indeed, not a few Indonesians for whom Christianity was a means to attain equality with the Europeans. They assumed the dress and manners of Europeans and attempted to act as equals of the Dutch. But for most Indonesians the prestige scale worked the other way. In those places where the Dutch had already set up their government, the missions were as a rule unable to secure any footing.[1] When they were forced to submit formally to Dutch authority, the Indonesians did not wish to surrender their spirit as well by becoming converted to Christianity. On the Outer Islands Dutch rule was, moreover, usually represented by an Indonesian administrator who was practically always a Moslem. The prestige he enjoyed encouraged a large section of the population to become converted to the Islamic faith,[2] especially because, by so doing, the Indonesians felt they could preserve something of their independence against the Dutch. This was a field in which the Indonesian could reject the Dutch claim to authority and maintain a certain independence which satisfied his self-respect. Here again we find the paradox that the Dutch government unintentionally aided the spread of Islam.

It is, moreover, striking that Christian propaganda could succeed only among 'pagans'. Among Moslems conversion to Christianity was a rare exception. In practice, therefore, missionary activities were mainly confined to those remote regions, mostly in the interior of the great islands, which were not yet affected by Islam. There opposition to the Moslem traders colonies, inhabiting the coastal areas, could provide a fertile soil. But in predominantly Moslem areas the missions were wise to abstain.

[1] See N. Adriani, *Verzamelde geschriften* (Collected writings), Haarlem, 1932, Vol. I, p. 166 ff.; also A. J. van Zanen, *op. cit.*, p. 90 ff.

[2] C. Snouck Hurgronje, *op. cit.*, Vol. IV, Part 2, p. 242/243.

It is thus understandable, that the government, in order to avoid friction, excluded missionaries from typical Moslem areas. For many Indonesians, Islam had become the symbol of resistance to the colonial caste system, as previously it had been the symbol of resistance to the Hindu caste system. But the Islamic community was no longer confined to the urban population. The vast majority of Indonesians found in Islam a unifying force and a refuge.

3 Bourgeois currents in religion[1]

'Every new period in the history of civilization obliges a religious community to undertake a general revision of the contents of its treasury,' wrote Snouck Hurgronje.[2] Islam in Indonesia did not escape this process of renewal.

At the beginning of the present century the upper stratum of Indonesian society came into closer touch with the civilisation of Western Europe. Its ways of thought and feeling were strongly influenced by contacts with individual Westerners, by education, familiarity with European literature and European travel. Cultural elements derived from European bourgeois civilisation, such as Western individualism, rationalism, naturalism, bourgeois

[1] The author is much indebted to the fruitful ideas developed by Wilfred Cantwell Smith in his book *Modern Islam in India. A social analysis*, London, 1946, which was used for this and the following section. The development in Indonesia proved to have a number of interesting analogies with that in India.
Cf. especially the ethical teachings of the *Muhammadyah* Society to be found in R. L. Archer, 'Muhammadan Mysticism in Sumatra', in *Journal of the Malayan Branch of the Royal Asiatic Society*, Vol. XV, Part 2, 1937, p. 112 ff. Cf. also Kenneth P. Landon, *Southeast Asia. Crossroad of religions*, Chicago, 1948, p. 189 ff.

[2] C. Snouck Hurgronje, *Mohammedanism. Lectures on its origin, its religious and political growth and its present state*, New York/London, 1916, p. 138. See further B. Schrieke, 'Bijdrage tot de bibliografie van de huidige godsdienstige bewegingen ter Sumatra's Westkust' (Contribution to the bibliography of the contemporary religious movements on the Westcoast of Sumatra), in *Tijdschrift voor Indische Taal-, Land- en Volkenkunde* (Journal for Indian Philology, Geography and Ethnology), Vol. LIX, 1919–1921, p. 281.

morals, obtained a hold on the Indonesian nobility, especially the younger ranks.

This process of acculturation took place largely outside the boundaries of Islam. In particular the nobility of Central Java, though Moslem in name, had always maintained its attitude of reserve towards the stricter forms of the Faith. In *kraton* (court) circles in Solo and Jogjakarta 'Javanism' prevailed: it was a syncretic religion in which Hindu and pre-Hindu elements still played an important part. In Central Java the stricter forms of the Islamic faith were found among the city traders; the nobility were inclined to deprecate this strict conformity to the Islamic law. Bousquet describes how an aristocrat from Central Java reacted to his question, whether he approved of the plans for founding a Moslem University, in the same aloof and puzzled way as if a French aristocrat had been asked whether he approved of the foundation of a Marx-Lenin Institute.[1] Apart from a general tendency among aristocrats to observe religious duties less rigorously than petty traders do, it was also Dutch policy which had helped those elements inclined to reject Islam in its stricter form, to rise to the top.

It is thus understandable that modern ideas influenced the younger generation of Javanese *pryayis* without their feeling any inner need to confront these ideas with Islam as a religion. The letters of Raden Adjeng Kartini,[2] the highly cultured daughter of a regent, a young woman of modern ideas who died at an early age and who is in some ways regarded as a precursor of the nationalist movement, exhibit a spirit of free-thinking liberalism similar to that of free-thinking Christians; she shows tolerance also in religious matters and believes that her religious and moral principles can be found in every faith. Nevertheless she calls herself a Mohammedan and traces her modern liberal opinions regarding religion back to her own faith just as the Moslem

[1] G. H. Bousquet, 'Introduction à l'étude de l'Islam indonésien', in *Revue des études Islamiques*, 1938, p. 259.

[2] Raden Adjeng Kartini, born 1879, died 1904. Her letters were published in English in *Letters of a Javanese Princess*, London, 1921.

peasant projected his *adat* on to the Islamic faith. She writes that she did not find it possible to examine the principles of the Islamic faith more deeply, however, since the scribes reserve the Holy Scriptures to themselves and deny the layman access to it.

The utterances of other Westernised Indonesians of the early years of this century are even more negative regarding Islam.[1] Time and again one finds expressions of opinion in that period which completely reject the Faith, seeing the Islam of tradition either as a brake on all progress, or as a corruption of the great Hindu-Javanese culture of former times. The first nationalist society on Java, the *Budi Utomo*, a movement of younger Indonesians of Western education, adopted a more or less indifferent attitude towards religion.

When Western ideas and bourgeois culture began to stir the Indonesian middle class as well, this comparative indifference could not continue. Islam was a valuable asset to many Indonesian traders or teachers. They witnessed its decline in public esteem and saw it losing its recruiting power owing to the tendency of those who became acquainted with Western ideas to regard it as a backward religion, without real value for the modern age. There was a strong tendency among the young, especially, to turn away from Islam and to regard its customs, at best, as traditional folklore. The Christianity proved to have an attraction for certain young people among the educated class; others among the younger intellectuals turned to theosophy which was, in a way, related to Hinduism. Still others were completely indifferent to religion.

Thus it was realised that if Islam was to retain its hold on the people, it would have to rehabilitate itself. In Indonesia its adaptation to the modern world found its expression first and

[1] Cf., for example, *Onderzoek naar de mindere welvaart der Inlandsche bevolking op Java en Madoera* (Investigation into the diminished welfare of the native population of Java and Madura), Batavia, 1905–1914, Vol. IXe: 'Inlandsche stemmen over de laksheid van den Inlander' (Native voices concerning the Native's indolence).

foremost in the *Muhammadyah* movement, the aim of which was to purify the Faith of traditional admixtures and formalism, both of which had caused it to be stigmatised as backward. It was chiefly inspired by the Egyptian reform movement led by Muhammed Abduh, who had tried to bring the Faith into harmony with modern rational thought. As the Christian Reformation had preached 'back to the Bible', so Muhammed Abduh and his disciples preached 'back to the Koran and the true Islamic faith.' In both instances it was a matter of loosening the grip which tradition had on the Faith and creating the freedom necessary for a return to the source of religion, in search of values better fitted to the modern age.

In Indonesia, the *Muhammadyah* sought likewise to create a more modern and more personal kind of religious experience. Subjection to the authority of tradition and the lawgivers was no longer the ideal of religion; the individual had the right to scrutinise and criticise the tradition in the light of the true sources of Islam. The purely formalist manner of religious observance caused Islam to lose its hold on the spirit. The Friday sermon in Arabic was never understood. The mumbling of the Koran in Arabic, which children had been obliged to learn at the Koran schools in former years, as a sort of incantation, was too far removed from the requirements of modern living as was also the religious teaching of the '*pesantrens*' (the institutes of higher religious learning). The *Muhammadyah* no longer sought to approach the human mind by imposing authority and invoking tradition, but rather by appealing to reason. It took up the fight against all kinds of practices – for example in the field of marriage and funeral rites – which were regarded as harmful superstitions. The Friday sermon was henceforth given in the regional tongue and its contents were sensibly adapted to the needs of daily life. Religious teachers of modern education tried, by lecturing in small discussion groups, to bring the Islamic faith and its ethical philosophy closer to believers, both men and women. The movement cooperated in the foundation of schools where the same subjects were taught as in the government schools according to the same rational methods of the West, and where religious teaching was included as a separate subject. It was active in other social fields, too, helping in the establishment of hospitals, libraries, homes for the blind and others of the needy, organising a scout movement, concerning itself with girls' education. In short, the movement entered those fields in which the Christian missionaries had been working for some time. Indeed the desire to compete with the Christian mission and keep a place reserved for the Islamic faith in the hearts of believers (the young in particular) played a great role in this process of renewal. And in this way there developed a certain outer resemblance between Islamic and Christian activities.

The similarity went further. The attitude of modern Moslems to life resembled that of many modern Christians. Mohammed was no longer worshipped as a worker of miracles, but as a human being. His miracles, such as the Ascension, were often interpreted as symbolic.[1] Love of the Prophet from whom one sought consolation in one's difficulties was a typical feature of modern Mohammedanism. The descriptions of his character often show a striking resemblance to the description of Christ: it was even suggested by missionaries in India, where similar developments were discernible, that the figure of Mohammed had been painted 'in colours drawn from a Christian paint box.'[2]

The reformed ethical teaching also showed a similarity with modern Christianity. Islam was no longer fatalistic, turning aside

[1] G. F. Pijper, *Fragmenta Islamica. Studiën over het Islamisme in Nederlandsch-Indië* (Fragmenta Islamica. Studies about Islamism in the Netherlands Indies), Leiden, 1934, p. 148/149.

[2] 'The Jesus of History replaced, in liberal circles, the Christ, and the qualities ascribed to him are so similar to those now ascribed to Muhammed, that Christian missionaries are wont to say that the modern character of the latter has been painted 'in colours drawn from a Christian paintbox' (W. C. Smith, *op. cit.*, p. 67). My colleague from Leiden, C. C. Berg, who was so kind as to read this chapter critically, draws my attention to the possibility that other Islamic schools of thought, such as the *Shiah* and the *Ahmadyah* movement, also had an influence on the development described in the text.

from the things of every day life.[1] Asceticism (abstinence) which had survived as an under-current in the Faith, was rejected. Modern Islam believes in progress and in science as the means of achieving it. From the individual is now required an inner purity of heart in relations with others, modesty, tolerance of his fellows, conscientious service and industry. The *Muhammadyah* believes in the possibility of shaping human character by practice and of improving behaviour.

Kenneth P. Landon therefore writes with justice that 'there will be more difference between conservative and liberal Moslems or between conservative and liberal Christians than between liberal Moslems and liberal Christians.'[2] But he is incorrect when he attributes this similarity to the simple adoption by Moslems of the Christian ethic and the Christian ecclesiastical customs for their own use. The new attitude to life is neither typically Christian nor typically Moslem. It is the attitude of the urban trader of the first years of the present century. In this ethical philosophy and faith one can trace that typical bourgeois individualism and rationalism, which regards mankind not as a totality but as a collection of individuals. Just as the city dweller resists the authority of the feudal nobility and the feudal tradition, so, too, he resists the authority of the recognised scribes and the religious tradition. He lives in a world which offers opportunities to the energetic, conscientious individual: he is full of confidence. He sees no sin in acquiring earthly possessions: he can become a virtuous Moslem by devoting himself diligently and honestly to his business. He has duties, not to mankind as a whole, but to his individual fellow creatures. The Prophet, too, is a fellow creature to whom he turns for comfort if he feels lonely and isolated in his urban environment.

The modern Moslem projects this attitude to life on to his faith as nineteenth century bourgeois Christians grafted it on to theirs. The virtues he ascribes to the Prophet are all those he can think of – the typically bourgeois virtues. They are no more typically

[1] Cf. K. P. Landon, *op. cit.*, p. 191, and R. L. Archer, *loc. cit.*

[2] K. P. Landon, *op. cit.*, p. 192.

Moslem than they were ever typically Christian. The modern age needed a new Islam and a new Prophet just as every new era has created a new Christendom and a new Christ.

The main reason why the average middle class Indonesian did not go over to Christianity but remained Moslem was that he felt strong traditional emotional ties with Islam such as most Europeans feel with Christendom. Moreover, in a colonial country there was all the more need to distinguish oneself from the foreign overlords. What this Indonesian really needed was to be able to call himself a Moslem without having to feel ashamed of his faith in the presence of Westerners – to profess a faith which harmonised with the modern age and his own aspirations as a man of his time.

Modern Islam became a religion which made few positive claims on the conduct of its adherents,[1] but rather afforded them the gratification which belonged to a life of reasonable prosperity and permitted them to go through life with an attitude of tolerance and pleasurable satisfaction with their own progressive ambitions.

Besides the *Muhammadyah* movement, the *Ahmadyah* movement, imported from India, was also rather influential as a bearer of liberal enlightened ideas. Though its following was not nearly as large as that of *Muhammadyah*, the Lahore branch of it in particular had a qualitative advantage in that it had a good deal of influence among the younger intellectuals.[2]

The people's movement '*Sarekat Islam*' which had rapidly blossomed forth during World War I also displayed many bourgeois traits. The movement had been originated by Indonesian traders as a counter-balance to the strong Chinese middle class. During the first years the middle class background of the movement was noticeable, not only in its activities, but in its ideology as well. The movement laid stress on the virtues of honesty and sobriety.

[1] K. P. Landon, *op. cit.*, p. 192.

[2] See for a description of the *Ahmadyah* movement G. F. Pijper, 'De Ahmadyah in Indonesië' (The Ahmadyah in Indonesia), in *Bingkisan Budi* (The mental gift. Collection of articles presented to Dr. P. S. van Ronkel), Leiden, 1950, p. 247.

But the most typical bourgeois trait was the stress it laid upon industry. In a government report[1] an interesting parallel was drawn between modern trends in Islam and the Reformation of the sixteenth century, notably the Calvinist trends, which embodied the new ethics of the rising middle class in Western Europe.

Whereas labour, according to traditional popular attitudes (as during the Middle Ages in the West), was considered a necessary evil at best, at the first *Sarekat Islam* Congress in 1916 the improvidence and negligence of the Indonesians were strongly criticised.[2] At the second Congress in 1917 it was stated that religion commands people to exert themselves in allowed professions, such as agriculture, handicrafts, trade etc. and strictly forbids laziness, idleness, resignation to poverty and living from the charity of others. 'Religion prescribes all the people to acquire knowledge and to practise the sciences.'[3]

The eighteenth century *Wahhabi* movement, which had embodied a protest of the agrarian communities against the modern luxuries of town life, and had also preached a way back to the primary sources of Faith and to simplicity, had some traits in common with Lutheranism. Both religious movements, *Wahhabism* and Lutheranism, were, on the whole, regressive,[4] though showing a few traits already of an incipient bourgeois mentality such as Luther's approval of the conscientious discharge of the ordinary duties of daily life. But it is an interesting parallel that both movements also paved the way for a progressive bourgeois religion, originating in town life and accepting wholeheartedly its spiritual implications. The return to the Bible and the return

[1] *Mededeelingen omtrent onderwerpen van algemeen belang* (Informations about subjects of general interest), Weltevreden, 1920, p. 6 ff. The pertinent section, which gives an evidence of a thorough acquaintance with Max Weber's theories on sociology of religion, is to be attributed to the able sociologist D. M. G. Koch.

[2] *Sarekat-Islam Congres* (1st National Congress), 1916, p. 29 ff., 69 ff.

[3] *Sarekat-Islam Congres* (2nd National Congress), 1917, p. 43, 120.

[4] See R. H. Tawney, *Religion and the rise of capitalism*, Pelican Books edition, Harmondsworth, 1938, p. 95 ff.

to the Koran proved to be temporary retreats to the sources of religion to find new interpretations, better adapted to the demands of modern life than the traditional ones. Just as Luther became a precursor of Calvinism, the *Wahhabi* sect paved the way for the so-called *new-Wahhabi* movements of Muhammed Abduh and *Muhammadyah*, which were also reflected at the *Sarekat Islam* Congresses.

Though in the *Sarekat Islam* propaganda much was made of the 'interests of the people', there are many signs that the union was really mainly concerned about the interests of the rising middle class, the 'Third Estate'. The demands made in connection with education were more in accordance with the interests of this middle class than with those of the poor *tanis* (peasants) and coolies.[1] It is understandable, therefore, that *Sarekat Islam* soon set about opposing the privileges of the feudal nobility and the power of the native officials, as well as the colonial caste system and the large Western entrepreneurs. It did this by appealing to the broad mass of Indonesian Moslems. But the enormous support the movement obtained in no time convincingly shows the extent to which the mass of Moslem peasants regarded the Faith as a unifying force. It became thus obvious that Islam had assumed the role of a pre-nationalism.

At the same time it became clear that now that the peasant mass had begun to stir, it would continue to do so and would no longer seek protection from Western influence by a flight into the past, and by rejecting all that was new (as had been the case with the Samin movement[2] at the close of the nineteenth century). The Indonesians were now striving to combat the West with its own weapons. Organised political action provided a means to this end, and it was, also, a means which showed that the two powerful classes of former times – the *pryayis* and *kyahis* – were losing their authority over the masses.[3] From now a new type of leader,

[1] *Mededeelingen omtrent onderwerpen van algemeen belang*, 1920, p. 11.

[2] This movement is discussed in Chapter XI on *Nationalism and After*.

[3] Cf. *Herinneringen van Pangeran Aria Achmad Djajadiningrat* (Memoirs of P.A. A. Djajadiningrat), Amsterdam/Batavia, 1936, p. 285 ff.

mainly urban intellectuals, would succeed in making use of the Islamic and nationalist impetus. The *kyahis* could only retain their influence by joining the movement.

Even Christianity, formerly used by the colonial power as a means to win support among parts of the population, became a weapon which could be directed against the rulers as well. The protest against aristocratic rule and traditional authority also arose among Christianised populations. For the central Batak country this process has been vividly described by van Zanen in his dissertation.[1] The missionaries in this territory (mainly Germans of the Rhenish Mission) were rather authoritarian and paternalistic in outlook. They had found the Batak country an agrarian society and wanted to keep this society free from the materialist tendencies of which they disapproved in Western society, and to imbue the Christian Bataks with higher spiritual values. But the Bataks themselves, especially the younger people, gave a quite different interpretation to their new religion. They were also affected by the awakening of Asia and by the revolutionary developments in Europe during the first decades of this century. The education they had enjoyed at missionary schools could not fail to evoke individualistic tendencies, which made themselves felt in economic life and social attitudes as well. Despite the continuous warnings of the missionaries they were increasingly being affected by a capitalist spirit which made them apply themselves to commercial crop cultivation and trade. Batak dynamics found their expression in a call for '*hamadjuon*' (progress), which became little less than a magic formula. People craved for higher education, material wealth and higher social prestige, to emulate the Europeans. The young Christian Bataks, too, established a union (the *Hatopan Kristen Batak*) which had, in the eyes of missionaries, rather revolutionary leanings. Since the missionaries tried to block such wayward activities, the young Bataks clashed against the authority of the white missionaries and against the aristocratic order of society. They did not like being told by

[1] A. J. van Zanen, *op. cit.*, p. 65 ff.

European missionaries, which Western cultural elements were fit for consumption in Indonesia and which were not. Rationalism proved to appeal to the younger Indonesian Christians more than the thin infusion of Western culture, which the European missionaries wanted to spoonfeed them.

Thus, Christianisation proved quite inadequate to stem the rising tide of nationalism. Within Christian communities, the clash between modernism and traditionalism presented itself in a specific shape, which was but a variety of the general pattern.

Thus it seemed as if the bourgeois developments of former centuries in Western Europe were to repeat themselves in Indonesia. But there was a tremendous difference, springing from a divergent combination of time factors. Whereas the Third Estate in Western Europe had ample time to consolidate its position before a Fourth Estate raised its claims, in Asia the latter closely follows the former. In Indonesia, especially in the Islamic field, the enormous following the *Sarekat Islam* had been able to raise was soon to prove a threat and not simply a support to the bourgeois Moslems. The small man's aspirations went much further than those of the urban traders, who had founded the *Sarekat Islam* in the beginning.

4 *Conservative and progressive Moslems*

The first signs that the rising middle class of Indonesian traders would be caught in a cross-fire were already apparent during World War I. On the one hand one could witness a swing to the left on the part of the masses, who, influenced by the Russian Revolution, proved susceptible to fanatical socialist slogans. On the other hand, a concentration of Western businesses was to be observed in the form of ever larger firms and syndicates, a process which greatly reduced the chances of the independent middle class Indonesian to make good in life on his own account.

Modern Islam began to change in character under the influence of this situation. It gradually lost its lively optimism and was forced on to the defensive. A certain rigidity was the outcome. A mature bourgeois Islam arrived too late on the scene to be what Protestantism had been for centuries: the bearer of new ideas and a fructifying influence on civilisation. No sooner had a bourgeois Islam come into existence than the conditions permitting it to exert a regenerating influence on society disappeared. It soon lost its *élan* and became conservative.

There was great tension within the *Sarekat Islam* especially. A radical wing in the movement under strong communist domination wanted to take up the fight against capitalism. Opposed to this wing were elements, under the leadership of R.U.S. Tjokroaminoto and Agus Salim, which rather represented ideologies prevailing among middle class Moslems. They wanted to combat only 'sinful' capitalism – in other words, the colonial capitalism which exploited Indonesia for the benefit of foreign countries. This group did not wish to see any obstacles put in the way of the formation of a class of Indonesian capitalists. After the left wing had been defeated in 1921, the leftist elements split off from the organisation.

Moslem reformists outside the political movement (those of *Muhammadyah*) were also put on the defensive. Bourgeois Islam took its stand on the individualist point of view. The trader ought to be permitted to carry on his business undisturbed. The ethics of the *Muhammadyah* were purely individualist, concerned exclusively with conduct towards one's individual fellowman. No especial demands were made on the Moslem's general social behaviour. He was urged to lead a sober life and to perform pious works with the wealth he had won for himself. But the movement did not concern itself with the manner in which this wealth was earned. The bourgeois economic structure as such was never subjected to criticism. Protection of private property and the economic system based upon it was one of the cornerstones of bourgeois Islam.

Thus the bourgeois Moslems stood opposed to the more radical socialist movements. But this resistance was based on the contention that Islam already comprised everything to be wished for in the way of democracy and socialism.[1] Remnants from the pre-capitalistic period (such as the prohibition of interest on loans, the distribution of property among a testator's children and the annual levy for the benefit of the dispossessed) were brought forward as evidence of socialism and as an argument that the Islamic economic system could never lead to such abuses as Western capitalism had brought. As for democracy in Islam, this was said to lie in the spiritual disposition of the Moslem and in his recognition of the fundamental equality of all human beings as symbolised, among other things, at the great feast of Mecca in the common dress adopted by rich and poor alike. This trend of thought is clearly perceptible in the following quotations.[2]

'We must never forget, that all substance is unequal by its nature. We cannot possibly eliminate or destroy this inequality and diversity from the world of substance, however we may strive for it, to say nothing of other objects of creation. We cannot make two human beings look alike, feel alike, think alike or act alike. It is useless, therefore, to strive for accomplishing equality or unity by staying the course of diversity. Actually the impulse for unity, equality and brotherhood does not belong to the world of substance.

It is an intense spiritual desire, though it strives after satisfaction in a material environment. The *Koranic* program of action starts, therefore, with spiritual training, with disciplining and ennobling the human mind.'

'This is accomplished by spiritual means, equal to the task of socialising the human emotions in an adequate manner. Among those means are the following: jointly reciting the prayers five times a day, in a mosque or in the open air, without any distinction

[1] See, for example, H. Bouman, *Enige beschouwingen over de ontwikkeling van het Indonesische nationalisme op Sumatra's Westkust* (Some observations regarding the development of Indonesian nationalism on the Westcoast of Sumatra), Groningen/Jakarta, 1949, p. 54/55.

[2] From the brochure of the former regent of Bandung, Al-Hadj R. A. A. Wiranata Koesoemah, *Islamietische democratie in theorie en practijk* (Islamic democracy in theory and practice), Bandung, 1949, p. 29 ff.

being made between high and low, between poor and rich. Then, fasting once a year during thirty days, causing the rich to a certain degree in their home to experience the lot of the poor and the needy. Further, the *zakat* or the annual levy for the benefit of the dispossessed and, finally, the annual gathering of Moslems of all nationalities, all races, all colours and all countries over the whole world in Mecca, where not only the Islamic principle of equality and brotherhood is being strictly observed, but where it is also required from all believers, without an exception, from the richest to the poorest, from the King to the lowest subject, to stand on a foot of absolute economic equality. It is a duty of all at that occasion to wipe out even the last vestige of difference, *i.e.* clothing. Thus clad in two seamless white garments only, they assemble around the Holy House, the Ka'ba, and call, going round it, as from one mouth: 'Labbaika-llāhumma, labbaika!' ('Here I am, oh Lord, wholly at your service!')'.

Thus this bourgeois Islam does not aspire to change the social structure. It is quite content with democracy on one day of the year which may serve to excuse the extremes of inequality existing on all the other 344 days of the Islamic year.

From all this it may be understood why not only the *Sarekat Islam* but also the *Muhammadyah* gradually became more conservative. At the time of the communist insurrections of 1926 and 1927 the *Muhammadyah* movement proved, on the whole, completely loyal to the Netherlands Indian Government. Moreover, in the purely Javanese town of Kuta Gede, where there were neither Europeans nor Chinese, and where accordingly the class contrasts within Indonesian society could develop normally, the division between the supporters of the *Muhammadyah* and of communism coincided almost perfectly with the division between established merchants and the poorer artisans.[1]

But the increasing rigidity of bourgeois Islam had another side

[1] Cf. the article by H. J. van Mook on Kuta Gede in *The Indonesian town. Studies in urban sociology*, Selected studies on Indonesia by Dutch scholars, Vol. IV, The Hague/Bandung, 1958, p. 288, 312/313.

to it. Diminished opportunity for the middle class individuals caused the weaker people to combine on a basis of group solidarity far more than formerly. And as group solidarity on a racial basis (as we have already seen) began to play an ever more important role in Indonesia, so, too, Moslem solidarity became a weapon in the economic and social competitive struggle between members of the urban bourgeoisie. If, in India, this Moslem group solidarity tended to take the form of 'communalism', of a struggle against the Hindus, in Indonesia it directed its attention to opposing not only the Christians and Chinese but those indifferent to religion as well.

This caused bourgeois Islam to change in character. It was now no longer a question of demonstrating that Islam, too, had a part to play in the modern world, and had room for all kinds of up-to-date ideas. Its task now was to prove that the Islamic faith was superior to all other ideologies and was the real source of all that is good in the world. There was a heightened sensitivity to anything that could be interpreted as an 'insult to Islam' or, worse still, 'an insult to the Prophet.'[1] There was increasing solidarity with the Islamic world beyond Indonesia and sharp reaction to any 'attack on Islam' from whichever quarter it came in the world. Just as it was asserted that Islam was pre-eminently socialist and democratic, so the Faith was now also regarded as the source of everything good and noble in the world, the source of knowledge, of progress, of the emancipation of women, of tolerance. Bourgeois Islam became less tolerant than in the early days of the *Muhammadyah* movement – but woe to him who dared to say so!

In short, as Wilfred Cantwell Smith writes, bourgeois Islam was less concerned at this stage with the salvation of man than with the salvation of a religion.

If one bears all this in mind, further developments within the realm of the Indonesian Islamic faith become comprehensible. By opposing the more radical socialist trends about the year 1922, *Sarekat Islam* lost a great part of its huge following. In accordance

[1] H. Bouman, *op. cit.*, p. 46.

with the principle of group solidarity the movement then attempted to follow the lines of the international Pan-Islamic movement, which was socially rather conservative. But this idea, too, met with an inadequate response from the masses, especially after the abolition of the Caliphate. On the other hand, the communist postulates proved to have insufficient attraction for the broad mass of the Indonesian peasants. After having attacked Islam, as it had every other religion, the *Partai Komunis Indonesia* altered its tactics about the year 1925 and tried to demonstrate a similarity between communist doctrines and passages from the Koran. By appealing to their anti-colonial susceptibilities, it also succeeded in winning over a number of the old-style religious teachers, in Menangkabau and Bantam, to the revolutionary movement.[1]

But in this period neither Islamic nor socialist thought proved to be strong enough in the hearts of the people to serve as the basis of a popular movement. Islam had completed its work as a pre-nationalist ideology. For the time being the nationalist idea was to become the unifying concept, as was shown by the rise of Sukarno's *Partai Nasional Indonesia* after the failure of the communist insurrection. *Sarekat Islam*, too, was to find itself obliged to pay its toll to the nationalist idea. In 1929, it said farewell once and for all to the Pan-Islamic idea and changed its name to *Partai Sarekat Islam Indonesia.*

In the meantime modern Islam gradually, almost imperceptibly, changed in character. When the independent trader lost his

[1] See *Rapport van de Commissie van onderzoek, ingesteld bij Gouvernementsbesluit van 13 Februari 1927, no 1a,* (Report of the inquiry committee established by governmental decree of 13-2-1927, Nr 1a, known as Report on Sumatra's Westcoast), Weltevreden, 1928, Vol. III, p. 38 ff.
See also *Verslag van de Commissie voor het onderzoek naar de oorzaken van de zich in de maand November 1926 in verscheidene gedeelten van de Residentie Bantam voorgedaan hebbende ongeregeldheden, ingesteld bij het Gouvernementsbesluit van 26 January 1927, No 1x* (Report of the committee for the inquiry into the causes of the disorders which occurred in November 1926 in different parts of the Bantam Residency, established by governmental decree of January 26th, 1927, Nr 1x), w.p., p. 18.

economic significance, the individualist trend in the Islamic reform movement fell into the background. The Moslem in the towns regarded himself less as an individual and more as a member of a group.

An important section of the modern urbanised Moslems felt especially that they were members of a threatened group – threatened by social developments. For many people of conservative conviction in social matters, Islam gradually became a bulwark against leftist tendencies. Conservative Islamic movements laid increasing stress on mass support rather than on personal observance of the Faith. For some period of time the old-style orthodox scribes, seeing their support and their social prestige dwindling, treated the modernists as heretics. In 1926, they founded in East Java an association called *Nahdatul Ulama*, which at first bitterly opposed *Muhammadyah* and other reformist movements. But the opposition between the two trends gradually began to fade. The orthodox adopted some of the practices of the *Muhammadyah*: they, too, discovered that they could obtain a greater hold on believers by having the Friday sermon delivered in the regional tongue and by engaging in popular education; while those modernists who considered Islam a barrier against social radicalism saw themselves compelled, in their turn, to regard the Islamic tradition as the principal factor making for unity. Their social conservatism also made them fear too radical trends in religion. For example, the modern movements ultimately failed to fight for a real change in the status of women. Prins has demonstrated how little change Islamic reform had achieved, before the war, in Islamic law as applied in Indonesia.[1]

Nevertheless the *Muhammadyah* did take on massive proportions with the passage of time, losing at the same time some of its individualistic traits.[2] But its mass support did not originate from

[1] J. Prins, *Adat en Islamietische plichtenleer in Indonesië* (*Adat* and Islamic law in Indonesia), The Hague/Bandung, 1954, p. 152.

[2] Cf. C.A.O. van Nieuwenhuijze, *Mens en vrijheid in Indonesië* (Man and freedom in Indonesia), Bandung, 1949, p. 65; see also the same writer in the periodical *Wending* (Turning point), Vol. IV, 1949, p. 143 ff.

the pauperised peasantry, as had been the case with *Sarekat Islam* in its incipient stage, but from the urban and rural middle class. Its appeal to a huge following forced it, on the other hand, to water its reformist wine.

One could in fact pretend that reformism has gradually developed into a particular kind of orthodoxy of a more puritanic character than the traditional orthodoxy of the old-style *kyahis*.

The countryside, in particular in East and Central Java, did not provide a fertile breeding ground for modernism. In that unsophisticated world Islam as practised by the common peasantry remained largely traditional. There was a clear distinction between, on the one hand, those considered pious Moslems, who followed meticulously the prescripts of Islam as they knew them and (probably because of the white garments they preferred to wear while praying[1]) were called the *putihan*, the 'white ones', and on the other the mass of the Javanese who were less strict in the observance of the duties prescribed by religion and were called *abangan*, the 'red ones'. This distinction has been elaborated by Clifford Geertz[2] as one between the so-called *santris* (literally the students of Islam, but in Geertz' terminology evidently including all those following their religious duties to the letter) and the *abangan*, who were nominally Moslems, but whose way of life was largely dominated by Javanese pre-Islamic traditions. Although the term *putihan* would seem to be more appropriate, I shall follow Geertz' terminology, which has been adopted by scholars such as Benda and Feith.

Though the *santri* group included both the small traders in the Javanese provincial towns and the well-to-do *hajis* and their dependants in the villages, their way of life could hardly be called bourgeois. There was certainly a clear contrast between their individualistic thriftiness and the more community-centred spirit of the *abangan* villagers, who were inclined to call the

[1] I owe this suggestion to Professor G. F. Pijper.

[2] C. Geertz, 'Religious belief and economic behavior in a Central Javanese town. Some preliminary considerations', in *Economic development and cultural change*, Vol. IV, 1956, p. 134 ff.

economical *santri* stingy. But since the *santris*' economic activity was less directed towards capital formation than towards hoarding in order to make the pilgrimage to Mecca, their outlook on life remained largely a traditional one. Accordingly, their strict observance of Islamic prescripts was of an orthodoxy in which Arab influences were mixed with old Javanese traditions, and was much less affected by modernist influences than was the case with their counterpart in larger towns.

It would, however, be erroneous to conclude from this distinction between the *santri* and the *abangan* groups that the influence of orthodox, traditional Islam was restricted to small groups of villagers. Though the *abangan* in general left the strict observance of religious duties to the *putihan*, and even sometimes tended to censure or mock certain aspects of the *santri* way of life, they also needed their assistance at such occasions as births, circumcisions, marriages, or deaths and at the frequent *slamatans* given to avert misfortune. The *abangan* also considered themselves true Moslems, and in most cases held the pious members of their village society in reverence. Benda, then, is right in pointing to the often under-estimated influence of rural Islam at the grass-roots level.[1]

After the turn of the century, gradually, the position of the *kyahis* in the countryside of Java began to undergo changes. In an era of expanding popular education, the traditionalist *kyahis* were likely to lose a good deal of the aura and prestige formerly attributed to their wisdom and knowledge of the holy scriptures. On the other hand, Islam had a deepening influence on the ordinary people of Java, if only because of its function as a pre-nationalism and as a rallying point against foreign dominion, as was evidenced by the huge following *Sarekat Islam* was able to secure within a few years after its inception. Here was a chance for the *ulamas* and *kyahis* to regain and even increase their former glory. According to Benda, at the village level *Sarekat Islam* rested primarily on the traditional leadership of the *kyahi* and *ulama*.[2]

[1] Harry J. Benda, *The Crescent and the Rising Sun. Indonesian Islam under the Japanese occupation 1942–1945*, The Hague/Bandung, 1958, p. 13 ff.

[2] *Op. cit.*, p. 42.

But in contrast to the progressive bourgeois trends prevailing among the urban *Sarekat Islam* leadership, in Benda's view the rural following of the party flocked to its banners rather to give expression to their pent-up revolt *against* changing times. Disaffection centred around the *kyahis* as exponents of traditional rural life, and was directed against Western influences and against the *pryayi* officials as the exponents of Westernisation.

This anti-Western attitude of many *kyahis* even led some of them to lend support to leftist ideologies and to place their traditional authority at the disposal of the communist movements, for example during the insurrections in 1926–1927. Koranic texts proved sufficiently malleable to yield egalitarian and revolutionary quotations useful to communist propaganda.

In the long run, however, the *santris* would have to catch up with those who had enjoyed modern education after the Western model if they wished to retain some of their traditional prestige. The Japanese were well aware of the potential force which their influence upon rural society, combined with their fundamentally anti-Western attitude, still could provide. They attempted to make use of this group to strengthen their grip upon the agrarian population, by calling them to the cities for short indoctrination courses and by imbuing them with Japanese propaganda. As a result *santri* leaders lost to a certain extent their character as an isolated backward group, and regained a more dynamic attitude towards life, though Japanese propaganda as such was wasted on them as being contrary to the Faith. The upshot of Japanese occupation was that religious leadership, concentrated within the *Masjumi* organisation founded in 1944 as a Japanese-sponsored merger of orthodox and reformist trends, came to occupy a position of much more importance than under Dutch rule in the pre-war period.[1]

Since the advent of the revolution, an increasing competition has arisen between religious and lay elements for the spiritual leadership of Indonesia. A large part of recent developments

[1] H. J. Benda, *op. cit.*, Part II (The Japanese occupation).

must be seen in the light of that struggle for ascendancy. During the years of revolution religious leaders aspired to a position of prominence within the new Republic. But it was primarily left-wing intellectual leaders who came to the forefront, since they were much better trained for the intricacies of politics and modern administration. Despite its huge mass support, the *Masjumi*, reconstituted in 1945 as a political party, had a disadvantage from the very beginning in comparison to the socialists and secularised nationalists, many of whom came from *pryayi* families and consequently had profited from better educational opportunities. Again, because of the pre-war activities of *Muhammadyah* in the educational field, the modernists had a distinct advantage over the traditionalist orthodox in providing appointees for political leadership.

Since the revolution the religious leaders have been building up an apparatus in order to enable their younger adherents to catch up with those subject to secularised influences. The Ministry of Religious Affairs has become the main instrument for this policy. It is active in establishing religious schools, often called *madrasahs*, which are better adapted to the requirements of modern society than the old-fashioned Koranic schools.[1] Much attention is being given to the training of religious teachers more conversant with contemporary society and Western scholarship than the traditional type of *ulama* or *kyahi*. The competition between government schools sponsored by the Ministry of Education and religious schools founded with subsidies of the Ministry of Religious Affairs is beginning to develop into a counterpart of the historic struggle in the Netherlands known as the 'parochial school issue'.

In the political field the Islamic struggle for ascendancy is finding expression in the propagation of the idea of an Islamic State. Fervent adherents of Islam conceived the new Indonesian state for which they fought in the revolution as one ruled by true Moslems in accordance with Islamic principles. But the Indo-

[1] See M. Hutasoit, *Compulsory education in Indonesia*, Unesco, Paris, 1954, p. 74 ff.

nesian Republic was born in August 1945 under a different sign, that of the *Pantja Sila*, the five principles, as formulated by President Sukarno.[1] Though the first principle lends the *Pantja Sila* a religious flavour, it does not mention one definite religion as a dominating one, but gives expression to the idea of fundamental equality of all religions. President Sukarno was well aware that to the Christian and other non-Moslem groups, mainly to be found in the eastern part of the archipelago, the idea of an Islamic state would hardly be acceptable.

Still, the fight between the two ideologies, the *Pantja Sila* upon which the Republic in its present form has been founded and the idea of an Islamic State – whatever that may mean – as propagated by *Masjumi* and other Islamic parties, is still going on. In the constitutional domain, the battle is being fought in the Constituent Assembly as a dispute regarding the basis of the future constitution. But besides this struggle on paper, a real fight is going on in large parts of Indonesia on the same basic issue: groups of fervent Moslems are fighting the Republic in its present form in the name of the *Darul Islam*, which they claim to have founded in 1949 in Western Java, after the Republic had started negotiations with the Dutch. Behind this struggle led by traditionalist religious teachers one may detect a protest against both the incursions of a money economy and the growing influence of an urban class of modern intellectuals and near-intellectuals. The traditional leaders of village society are embittered at a process which is gradually robbing them of their authority. They are able to gather a following of poor peasants who feel their age-old way of life endangered by processes they cannot understand, and who are increasingly resentful of what they feel to be an exploitation by the urban ruling class, which is mostly of *pryayi* origin.

It is natural that a movement has risen which preaches a return to the rural simplicity of yore and the preservation of traditional social values, in the same way peasants opposed modern trends

[1] They are: 1 Belief in one God, 2 Respect for human values, 3 Democracy, 4 Social justice, 5 Nationalism.

about the turn of the century.[1] It is a new phenomenon, however, that this longing for a Paradise Lost is embodied in a fictitious 'State of Islam' (*Darul Islam*) as opposed to the present Republic, which is held to be governed by a class of urban unbelievers.

It is questionable, however, in how far the *Darul Islam* still retains its original rustic aspect as outlined by van Nieuwenhuijze.[2] In the course of the years the movement has become involved in international politics, and there are indications that it may have received appreciable material help from abroad. As a strongly anti-communist movement the *Darul Islam* was liable to receive, in the present world situation, more and more a cold-war aspect blurring its original simplicity.

But even apart from the Islamic State issue, Indonesian politics are becoming increasingly dominated by tensions between religious and non-religious elements. In both national and international affairs, a sharp conflict between *Masjumi* and the communists has been an outstanding feature of Indonesian politics ever since the proclamation of the Republic in 1945. During the first years, the *Sajap Kiri* (Left Wing), in which socialists and communists co-operated, had a strong influence within the successive cabinets. After *Masjumi* had obtained powerful representation in a cabinet led by Hatta in 1948, the Madiun communist revolt led to a number of atrocities, in particular between adherents of *Masjumi* and communists. Since the transfer of sovereignty the two parties have consistently occupied opposite positions, the communists siding with the Soviet bloc and the *Masjumi* rather sympathising with the Western coalition, whereas the other two major parties, P.N.I. and *Nahdatul Ulama* have more or less kept the middle of the road as exponents of a policy of active neutrality. *Masjumi's* refusal to cooperate with the com-

[1] Regarding the Samin movement of circa 1900 – which was not, as a matter of fact, based on Islamic religious principles – see Chapter XI on *Nationalism and After*.

[2] C. A. O. van Nieuwenhuijze, *Aspects of Islam in post-colonial Indonesia. Five essays*, The Hague/Bandung, 1958, p. 176 ff.

munists has been the main hindrance to a realisation of President Sukarno's concept of a guided democracy.

In the rural sphere of East and Central Java the contrast between the *santri* and *abangan* or *pryayi* groups is increasingly dominating political life as well. As was pointed out above, the distinction between those ways of life existed even before the war. But developments since the revolution have caused a process of polarisation in which the different ways of life have crystallised into opposing group attachments. The manifold organisations springing up in the countryside of Java tend to follow the same distinctive pattern, in accordance with the growing tendency towards group solidarity within Indonesian society. Political parties proselytising on the village level had to adjust themselves to this fundamental division, *Nahdatul Ulama* and *Masjumi* finding their adherents mainly in the *santri* group, and P.N.I. and P.K.I. having to look for their following mainly among *pryayi* and *abangan* groups.[1] If there is a process of de-Islamisation going on in the urban and rural society of Java[2] there would on the other hand seem to be a deepening Islamic consciousness among those who take their religious duties to heart.

Undoubtedly this polarisation process, reinforced by the political party system, has been disruptive for the village community in large parts of Java.[3]

The foregoing analysis would seem to indicate that Islam is generally to be found, in present-day Indonesia, on the conservative side of the political scale. In the rural environment the *kyahis* and *ulamas* often represent the elements opposing progressive trends from the towns. Both in the national and international

[1] Herbert Feith, *The Indonesian election of 1955*, Modern Indonesia Project, Cornell University, Ithaca, 1957, p. 31 ff.

[2] As an indication in that direction I might mention a *desa* in Central Java named Keputihan – which points to a past as a religious centre – where at present the P.K.I. appeared to be dominant, and where hardly any traces of a *putihan* element were left.

[3] See for example C. Geertz, 'Ritual and social change. A Javanese example', in *The American Anthropologist*, Vol. LIX, 1957, p. 32 ff.

setting *Masjumi* is consistently to be found at odds with the communists, whereas foreign capital quite often looks for its advocates among the prominent members of the former party.

Even so, an unqualified designation of present-day Islam in Indonesia as 'conservative' would not do. Religious movements are not as simple as that. If one branch of Islam, based upon individualistic trends of previous decades, tends to become conservative in outlook and eventually to join forces with more traditional and even reactionary currents, it is not surprising that present-day radical tendencies are also struggling to find expression within Islam. This applies more especially for the Islamised non-Javanese regions of Indonesia, where the *santri-abangan* antithesis of Central Java and the Western part of East Java is lacking. In those areas, such as Western Java, Madura, most of Sumatra, coastal Borneo and South Celebes, where the whole population is accustomed to rather strict observance of Islamic prescripts, both ideas opposed to social change and those embodying some kind of social protest may assume an Islamic flavour.[1]

Though Moslem political leaders may use religion as a bulwark against social change, as the rank and file have been affected by radical trends of thought they are unlikely to let popular wishes go unheeded for long. Perhaps again the time has come for Indonesian Moslems to re-examine the contents of their ideological treasury. Though the shape of things to come is not yet clearly discernible, there are many signs that social radicalism may invade organisations representing Islamic thought. In many Moslem organisations, beside a more or less conservative wing which sometimes forms the upper-current, one discovers a more radical wing as an under-current. Thus in Menangkabau pronounced leftist elements have always existed in the modernist ranks. In the early thirties they even joined to form a separate party, the *Permi* (*Persatoean Moeslimin Indonesia*). The search for mass support by the main Islamic parties has also brought a

[1] See Herbert Feith's interesting analysis of the elections for parliament in *op. cit.*, p. 33 ff., 77 ff.

radical tendency as a matter of course – and not only in the form of slogans: in certain measure the party adherents have determined the policy of the leaders.

Whereas the city traders joined forces for the sake of group solidarity, the Islamic masses were strongly motivated by the class struggle with non-Islamic capitalist groups. The proclaimed policies of P.S.I.I. (*Partai Sarekat Islam Indonesia*) were fairly radical during the early thirties, and the *Masjumi* is also obliged to fly the socialist banner in order to retain its following.

Since the Indonesian middle class differs from its counterpart in earlier Western Europe in that it consists largely of government workers and employees of big enterprises who are not too much interested in the protection of private property, the political outlook of many members of the class tends to radicalism, especially as high costs of living are creating widespread discontent among the lower salaried of them.

In this connection certain orthodox religious leaders might also be mentioned. Just as there were some such leaders who lent their support during the communist insurrections in 1926–1927, in present-day Indonesia their generally anti-Western outlook may induce some of them again to side with leftist elements against the new urban bourgeoisie and against foreign capital. Perhaps this factor may help to explain the paradox that Islamic parties like *Nahdatul Ulama* and *Perti* (a rather important party which finds its adherents mainly in Menangkabau and Acheh, and in some respects not unlike *Nahdatul Ulama*), which are essentially orthodox in outlook, are less opposed to cooperation with leftist groups in national politics than the urban-centred and more sophisticated *Masjumi*. There is even a possibility that some religious teachers, who as a rule do not hail from the wealthy landowners, may take the lead in movements of poor peasants for land-redistribution, directed against the urban bourgeoisie.

1 For the Samin movement of circa 1900 – which was not, as a matter of fact, based on Islamic religious principles – see Chapter XI on *Nationalism and After*.

Thus, it is not certain that the struggle between Left and Right in Indonesia will be fought exclusively between a conservatism embodied in Islam and a radicalism embodied in an irreligious communism or socialism. As the claim for land distribution, which springs from a desire to own a piece of ground of one's own, is quite reconcilable with Islamic teachings, it may well be that in some parts of Indonesia the struggle between Left and Right in Indonesia will assume the form of a struggle between Islam and... Islam!

But whereas bourgeois Moslems tend increasingly to advance Islam as a badge distinguishing them from all other middle class groups, among the poorer classes the Faith will probably gradually lose its distinctive character and Moslem peasants and workers are likely, in their struggle, to become ever more aware of the ties binding them to those members of their own class broken away from Islam or belonging to other religious denominations.

A short bibliography

N. Adriani, *Verzamelde geschriften* (Collected writings), Haarlem, 1932.

R. L. Archer, 'Muhammadan mysticism in Sumatra', in *Journal of the Malayan Branch of the Royal Asiatic Society*, Vol. XV, Part 2, 1937, p. 1 ff.

C. H. Becker, *Islam Studien. Vom Werden und Wesen der Islamischen Welt*, Leipzig, 1924-1932.

Harry J. Benda, *The Crescent and the Rising Sun. Indonesian Islam under the Japanese occupation of Java 1942–1945*, The Hague/Bandung, 1958.

C. W. Th. Baron van Boetzelaer van Asperen en Dubbeldam, *De Protestantsche kerk in Nederlandsch-Indië. Haar ontwikkeling van 1620–1939* (The Protestant church in the Netherlands Indies. Its development from 1620 till 1939), The Hague, 1947.

H. Bouman, *Enige beschouwingen over de ontwikkeling van het Indonesisch nationalisme op Sumatra's Westkust* (Some observations regarding the development of Indonesian nationalism on the Westcoast of Sumatra), Groningen/ Jakarta, 1949.

G. H. Bousquet, *La politique musulmane et coloniale des Pays-Bas*, Paris, 1939.

G. H. Bousquet, 'Introduction à l'étude de l'Islam indonésien', in *Revue des études Islamiques*, 1938, p. 135 ff.

G. H. Bousquet and J. Schacht (eds.), *Selected works of C. Snouck Hurgronje edited in English and French*, Leiden, 1957.

P. A. A. Djajadiningrat, *Herinneringen van* – (Memoirs of P. A. A. Djajadiningrat), Amsterdam/Batavia, 1936.

G. W. J. Drewes, 'Indonesia. Mysticism and activism', in G. E. von Grunebaum (ed.), *Unity and variety in Muslim civilization*, Chicago, 1955, p. 284 ff.

H. Th. Fischer, *Zending en volksleven in Nederlandsch-Indië* (Mission and folk life in the Netherlands Indies), Zwolle, 1932.

H. A. R. Gibb (ed.), *Whither Islam? A survey of modern Moslem movements in the Moslem world*, London, 1932.

E. Gobée and C. Adriaanse (eds.), *Ambtelijke adviezen van C. Snouck Hurgronje 1889–1936* (Official recommendations by C. Snouck Hurgronje 1889–1936), Vol. I, The Hague, 1957.

Raden Adjeng Kartini, *Letters of a Javanese Princess*, London, 1921.

H. Kraemer, *Agama Islam* (Islamic religion), revised by C. A. O. van Nieuwenhuijze, Jakarta, 1952.

H. Kraemer, *From missionfield to independent church. Report on a decisive decade: the growth of indigenous churches in Indonesia*, The Hague, 1958.

J. H. Kramers, 'L'Islam et la démocratie', in *Orientalia Neerlandica. A volume of Oriental studies*, Leiden, 1948.

Kenneth P. Landon, *Southeast Asia. Crossroad of religions*, Chicago, 1948.

J. C. van Leur, *Indonesian trade and society. Essays in Asian social and economic history*, Selected studies on Indonesia by Dutch scholars, Vol. I, The Hague/Bandung, 1955.

Reuben Levy, *The social structure of Islam*, Cambridge, 1957.

Mededeelingen omtrent onderwerpen van algemeen belang (Informations about subjects of general interest), Weltevreden, 1920.

M. Natsir, *Capita selecta*, Bandung/The Hague, 1954.

C. A. O. van Nieuwenhuijze, *Aspects of Islam in post-colonial Indonesia. Five essays*, The Hague/Bandung, 1958.

C. A. O. van Nieuwenhuijze, *Mens en vrijheid in Indonesië* (Man and freedom in Indonesia), Bandung, 1949.

J. Prins, *Adat en Islamietische plichtenleer in Indonesië* (*Adat* and Islamic law in Indonesia), The Hague/Bandung, 1954.

G. F. Pijper, *Fragmenta Islamica. Studiën over het Islamisme in Nederlandsch-Indië* (Fragmenta Islamica. Studies about Islamism in the Netherlands Indies), Leiden, 1934.

A. Salim, *Djedjak langkah Hadji A. Salim. Pilihan karangan, utjapan dan pendapat beliau dari dulu sampai sekarang* (The path of Haji A. Salim. Selections from his writings, speeches and opinions from early times until the present), Jakarta, 1954.

B. Schrieke, *Indonesian sociological studies. Selected writings*, Part 1. Selected studies on Indonesia by Dutch scholars, Vol. II, The Hague/Bandung, 1955.

B. Schrieke, *Indonesian sociological studies. Ruler and realm in early Java. Selected writings*, Part 2. Selected studies on Indonesia by Dutch scholars, Vol. III, The Hague/Bandung, 1957.

B. Schrieke, 'Bijdrage tot de bibliografie van de huidige godsdienstige bewegingen ter Sumatra's Westkust' (Contribution to the bibliography of the contemporary religious movements on the Westcoast of Sumatra), in *Tijdschrift voor Indische Taal-, Land- en Volkenkunde* (Journal for Indian Philology, Geography and Ethnology), Vol. LIX, 1919–1921, p. 249 ff.

Wilfred C. Smith, *Modern Islam in India. A social analysis*, London, 1946.

Wilfred C. Smith, *Islam in modern history*, Princeton, 1957.

C. Snouck Hurgronje, *Verspreide geschriften* (Collected writings), Bonn/Leipzig/Leiden, 1923–1927.

Al-Hadj R. A. A. Wiranata Koesoemah, *Islamietische democratie in theorie en praktijk* (Islamic democracy in theory and practice), Bandung, 1949.

A. J. van Zanen, *Voorwaarden voor maatschappelijke ontwikkeling in het centrale Batakland* (Conditions for social development in the central Batak area), Leiden, 1934.

Chapter Nine

The Changing Pattern of Labour Relations

1 Labour in early Indonesia

Paid labour as a means of subsistence, that typical institution of the modern age according a man freedom, yet forcing him to hire himself in the service of others, does not fit in at all with the pattern of early Indonesian social relationships. Labour was either a contribution to a collectivity in which one participated, or a service performed by the orders of a traditional authority.

Activities falling within the former category were, in the first place, those in the field of agriculture, performed on a cooperative basis by all members of the family fit for work. In addition, they performed, in conformity with the traditional division of labour, work in behalf of the peasant household, including home industry for the needs of the family. The work of a restricted number of village artisans was also performed in behalf of the collectivity on the basis of exchange of their products against the food which the peasantry provided for their maintenance.

The relations which gave rise to services for the authorities were more varied. Slavery existed in ancient Indonesian society, though not on a large scale. In agrarian society, in general, only those of standing held slaves, largely for household services. This slavery might originate from debts, from trespasses against the *adat* (custom), from captivity in war or from piracy. It seems that the treatment of these house slaves was, in general, rather humane. The power of the master was restrained by tradition. Compared with the common people a slave in the service of a prominent master might even enjoy some social prestige.

More important from an economic point of view was the bondage of the peasantry in relation to princes and landlords. The obligation to perform services and pay tribute could weigh heavily. An instance is provided by the descriptions of the way Sultan Agung of Mataram levied in the course of several successive years, during the dry monsoon after the rice had been harvested, huge armies of tens (perhaps even hundreds) of thousands for his conquests.[1] From early times large numbers of peasants liable to service had been mobilised for the building of famous temples, roads and irrigation works.

There were also voluntary labour relations, as free men offered themselves as 'followers' to a chief in exchange for protection and maintenance. This form of 'vassalage' has been described in particular for the society of South Celebes.[2]

In early Indonesian cities the pattern of labour relationships was different in that slavery fulfilled perhaps a more important economic function. The number of slaves serving at the *kraton* could be considerable. Many of them were specialised in a craft. In his account of a mission to Mataram Rijcklof van Goens describes how some thousands of female

[1] B. Schrieke, *Indonesian sociological studies. Selected writings*, Part 1. Selected studies on Indonesia by Dutch scholars, Vol. II, The Hague/Bandung, 1955, p. 250, nt. 132. Interesting details are provided in 'Verbaal, gehouden door Dr. de Haan, als afgezant van den Gouverneur-Generael Jan Pietersz. Coen, namens de Ver. Oost Indische Comp. aan den Panembahan van Mataram, in 1622' (Record held by Dr. de Haan, as a delegate from the Governor-General Jan Pietersz. Coen, in the name of the United East India Company to the *Panembahan* of Mataram, in 1622), in J. K. J. de Jonge (ed.), *De opkomst van het Nederlandsch gezag over Java* (The rise of the Dutch power over Java), Amsterdam/The Hague, Vol. I, 1869–1888, p. 298, 316. See also the report of de Haan's second mission to Mataram (1623) in the same series, Vol. II, p. 32 ff.; the report of J. Vos' mission (1624) in Vol. II, p. 53, and the reports on p. 140/141, 143, 160.

[2] P. J. Kooreman, 'De feitelijke toestand in het gouvernementsgebied van Celebes en Onderhoorigheden' (The actual situation in the governmental districts of Celebes and dependencies), in *Indische Gids* (Indian Guide), 1883, p. 375 ff.; H. Th. Chabot, *Verwantschap, stand en sexe in Zuid-Celebes* (Kinship, status and sex in South Celebes), Groningen/Jakarta, 1950, p. 102 ff.

workers were employed at the *kraton* in the *batik* industry and other crafts.[1] To a certain extent, therefore, these *kraton* trades have the character of large-scale industries carried on with slave labour.

It is also probable that estates of the gentry in the neighbourhood of cities were cultivated by serfs.[2] Repeatedly mention is made of slave armies, used by the princes ruling over coastal towns, while the inland-state of Mataram seems to have used armies levied from the peasantry.

The larger expansion of slavery in the cities, especially those situated at the coast, may perhaps be accounted for partly by slave trade and piracy. Some scholars have suggested a connection between the expansion of slavery and the spread of Islam,[3]

[1] Ryckloff Volkertsz. van Goens, 'Reisbeschrijving van Samarangh naar Mataram' (Description of a journey from Semarang to Mataram), in *Bijdragen tot de Taal-, Land- en Volkenkunde van Nederlandsch-Indië* (Contributions to the Philology, Geography and Ethnology of the Netherlands Indies), 1856, Vol. IV, p. 342 ff.; G. P. Rouffaer and H. H. Juynboll, *De batikkunst in Nederlandsch-Indië en haar geschiedenis* (The art of *batik* in the Netherlands Indies and its history), Utrecht, 1914, text, p. 177, 414/415.

[2] When de Haan, on his mission to Mataram in 1622, passed by Pekalongan, in the neighbourhood of which those cultivating rice and coconuts were all serfs of the prince, he learnt that those living at the other side of the mountains, deeper inland, were free men paying yearly tribute to the Sultan of Mataram (J. K. J. de Jonge (ed.), *op. cit.*, Vol. I, p. 292). According to de Haan they were exempted from military service in contrast with the serfs liable to be called for service without pay. It seems, however, that this 'freedom' was a special privilege afforded to the population of a certain region, as this exemption from military service does not apply at all, as we have already seen, to the empire of Mataram as a whole. It seems, thus, an erroneous notion of de Haan's to use liability to military service as a criterion for slavery. The real difference was probably between harbour princes making use of slave armies and the princes of inland-states not in the possession of a standing army (see B. Schrieke, *op. cit.*, p. 81).

[3] See S. J. Rutgers and A. Huber, *Indonesië*, Amsterdam, 1937, p. 44 ff.; van Leur takes a quite different position pointing out that the social conditions in the Islamic coastal towns, such as in evidence in Bantam about 1600, represent an age-old pattern, which has nothing to do with Islam. According to the latter author the introduction of Islam had no influence whatever upon the system of international trade, nor upon social and political

but any clear relationship between both phenomena is hard to prove. Nor could the expansion of slavery during the period of the Dutch East India Company be attributed to the spread of Christianity. At best one may suggest as a primary cause increased navigation and commercial shipping and the resulting intensivation of maritime struggles between warfaring powers and creeds.

During the first few years after the foundation of Batavia (1619) a secondary cause was provided by the Company's need to populate the city with large numbers of workers, partly for the construction of fortifications. For this purpose many people were captured at sea or along the shores of the Asian continent; later on most slaves were imported from the Outer Islands of Indonesia.

Apart from the slaves, every Indonesian city had a category of independent artisans working on their own account for the needs of the *kraton* or, in later years, for the Company. Slaves were also often allowed to keep part of the money earned by their trade or craft and some could thus become fairly prosperous.

It is true that slavery considerably expanded during the Company's rule. In later years perhaps more than half of the population of Batavia consisted of slaves. House servants were, at any rate, all slaves, male or female, mostly supplied from Bali, Timor or other parts of the archipelago. The treatment of those slaves could not be compared, as a rule, with the brutalities which the African plantation slaves suffered in the American colonies. Yet, under the influence of more enlightened ideas breaking through in Europe during the eighteenth century, serious criticism was raised against the way many European and Mestizo women treated their house slaves. This found literary expression in Dirk van Hogendorp's stage play '*Kras-poekol of de slavernij*' (Hit hard or slavery).[1]

organisation. See J. C. van Leur, *Indonesian trade and society. Essays in Asian social and economic history*, Selected studies on Indonesia by Dutch scholars, Vol. I, The Hague/Bandung, 1955, p. 113 ff.

[1] See *inter alia* John Bastin, 'The rivalry between Dirk van Hogendorp and S. C. Nederburgh', in *Indonesië*, Vol. VII, 1953/54, p. 80 ff., describing a performance of this play in The Hague.

Slavery in Indonesia remained largely an urban phenomenon. Apart from the institution of serfdom in the neighbourhood of towns, as mentioned above, plantation slaves were never to be found in large numbers, except in regions such as the Banda islands where the agrarian native population had been decimated or driven out by Jan Pieterszoon Coen, and the nutmeg estates leased out by the Company to the so-called '*perkeniers*' (park proprietors) had to be cultivated by imported slaves. In several parts of the territory under the Company's rule, notably in Java, the abundance of native agricultural workers made it preferable to use the existing feudal institutions for the exploitation of tropical products. The Company made contracts with the regents and princes for the delivery of the crops desired. The regents had to see that the crops were delivered by the agrarian population on the basis of the traditional obligations of servitude. In large part, the deliveries of the regents to the Company replaced the former deliveries to their suzerain, the *Sunan* of Mataram. Yet the interference of the Company led, in the long run, to an increased burden upon the peasantry, partly due to the introduction of new crops such as coffee which the population was forced to cultivate.

This does not mean that the work had always to be performed without pay. The Company intended to pay the peasants for the work performed but in practice most of the pay went into the pockets of the regents or of those private persons, mostly Chinese, who 'farmed' whole villages from the regents, thus acquiring a right to exact duties and services.

The system of selling or granting private estates (*particuliere landerijen*) applied by the Company, contributed to the spread of servitude, as the lands were transferred along with the native cultivators. On these estates, too, as on the apanages granted by Indonesian princes to members of their family or to high officials, a kind of serfdom developed.

2 *Between freedom of contract and forced labour*

During the nineteenth century enlightened ideas from Europe began to influence the East. Forced deliveries demanded by the regents' intermediaries were increasingly criticised, the more so as the system of forced labour was ineffective and the yields often proved disappointing. Some suggested, after the example of British India, allowing the Javanese peasant the fruits of his labour and replacing forced deliveries by a tax. It was expected that he would then have a personal incentive to raise his production and market the surplus.

Raffles got the opportunity, during the interval of British rule, to introduce this practice under the name of the 'land rent' (land tax) system. It thus seemed as if the policy of free labour had triumphed.

Moreover, outside the field of agrarian labour there was also a trend towards greater freedom. House slaves were no longer a paying proposition. The owner bore the risk if a slave died. In view of the increased supply of voluntary labour it proved much more profitable to recruit workers in the free market. About 1830 the ownership of house slaves had in practice been reduced to a special privilege of some well-off families, the ladies taking a pride in dressing up their female slaves. The decision of the enlightened regent of Sumenep (in the island of Madura) to free his fifty slaves during Raffles' rule proves, that modern ideas were not confined to the Europeans living in Indonesia. According to the regent's explanation, he had kept his slaves only to wait upon the Dutchmen when they visited his palace, but when the Dutch were deprived of their power he was free to do as he liked! He had been ashamed, seeing the slave markets in Batavia and Semarang, where human beings were exhibited and examined as if they were cattle.[1]

[1] W. R. van Hoëvell, *Reis over Java, Madura en Bali in het midden van 1847* (Journey through Java, Madura and Bali in the middle of 1847), Amsterdam, 1849–1854, Vol. II, p. 58.

When about 1860 slavery was officially abolished, this was, as far as Javanese society was concerned, rather a confirmation of an already accomplished fact than a revolutionary development. In several Indonesian principalities of the Outer Islands, however, it was to take many more years before practice accorded with law.

The nineteenth century also witnessed the first breaches in the prevailing system according to which unskilled labour in the urban sphere had to be performed under compulsion. During the eighteenth century the work of dredging the harbour of Batavia had been executed as compulsory service by '*modder-javanen*' (mud-Javanese) supplied by the Sultan of Cheribon, but in 1849 the first experiment with paid coolie labour was made by government on the harbour and defence works of Surabaya, and its success induced the government to order all government buildings to be constructed with paid labour.[1] The voluntary workers proved to be more efficient and industrious.

Nevertheless, the nineteenth century was no period of uninterrupted development toward greater freedom of labour. The intensive exploitation of the colonial possessions led to an increased demand for labour, which could most readily be met by using the available Javanese farmers for unpaid compulsory services under the traditional feudal system. Practice paid little heed to enlightened theories.

It started with the rule of Daendels, 'the Thundering Marshal', who, though he came to the Indies to make a clean sweep of the antiquated remains of the Company's administrative system and to end compulsory services, was forced by the needs of the time to introduce more coercion in Java than it had ever experienced. His construction for military purposes of the east-west Trunk Road across Java by forced labour on an unprecedented scale still lives in the memory of the Javanese as an episode of horrors. And the need for funds to build a defence system seduced Daen-

[1] J. S. Furnivall, *Netherlands India. A study in plural economy*, Cambridge/New York, 1944, p. 184.

dels into granting private estates (based on the servitude of the native cultivators) far more than ever before.

Despite his liberal theories Raffles also followed Daendels' example by granting new estates (with their native inhabitants) to private persons. Moreover, in the Preanger Regencies the obligation of regents to deliver agricultural products was kept in force, together with their feudal authority over the peasantry.

But the element of coercion inherent in all those regulations was minor in comparison with the compulsion introduced by van den Bosch's culture system in 1830. This measure had been preceded by vehement discussion on whether private entrepreneurs, if granted waste land for exploitation instead of private estates already cultivated, could obtain sufficient workers on a voluntary basis. As there was little confidence in this possibility, van den Bosch cut the Gordian knot. Since he rather doubted the advantages enjoyed by labourers under a system of private entreprise, he preferred compulsory labour provided that it was controlled not by individuals (as was the case with private estates) but by a modern state. Thus, the culture system came into being, which compelled the peasantry of vast areas on Java, and in a few regions of the Outer Islands as well, to cultivate, besides the usual food crops, commercial crops for export.

The work had to be performed without pay, as in theory it replaced the obligation to pay 'land rent'. Other activities such as work performed at private sugar factories and the transport by carts from the fields to the factories, were paid for. Thereby, the culture system also helped to spread the institution of paid labour more widely in the agrarian society.

Possibly van den Bosch's intentions were good, but they were no more likely to be accomplished than those of Raffles. In practice the over-riding Dutch interest was in maximising production.

For this purpose the feudal aristocracy was a convenient instrument. In this period the regents and other native officials were in reality little more than 'plantation overseers'[1] using their tradi-

[1] B. Schrieke, *op. cit.*, p. 190.

tional authority to enforce a maximum performance from the population and rewarded with percentages of the yield.

About 1850 the abuses appeared so serious that efficiency suffered. Protests from humanitarian circles gained strength, in particular after publication of Multatuli's *cri de coeur*, the novel *Max Havelaar*, which met a wide response in Holland.

But opposition to the culture system also came from the liberals who opposed state exploitation on principle. As a result, the 'agrarian laws' of the seventies prepared the way for a gradual elimination of forced cultivation.

3 *Paid labour as a basis of colonial economy* (*1870–1930*)

It was easier to proclaim by law that the Indonesian should be free to work for pay, than to enforce this principle. Even more than disposal of land, control of human labour was the basis of colonial economy. 'If there was at times a greed for land bordering on the irrational, there always was an insatiable greed for man power', says Bruno Lasker.[1] Multatuli had already warned, that the introduction of a system of 'free labour' would mean anything but an improvement for the Javanese peasant. In practice, according to his admonitions free labour would amount to a 'subjection of the Javanese to oppression by the first machinator at hand, in complicity with the chiefs'.[2] The difference between the conservative advocates of the culture system and the liberal supporters of free labour was seen by Multatuli as follows:

'The liberals want to draw from the Indies as much as possible, and the conservatives want to draw as much as possible from the Indies'! What Multatuli was striving after was not an abolition of the culture system as such, but a fight against its abuses only.

New forms of bondage arose, indeed, from the abolition of the bondage connected with the culture system. The new servitudes

[1] Bruno Lasker, *Human bondage in Southeast Asia*, Chapel Hill, 1950, p. 210.

[2] Multatuli (E. Douwes Dekker), *Nog eens: vrije arbeid in Nederlandsch-Indië* (Again: free labour in the Netherlands Indies), Delft, 1870, p. 103.

may be partly explained as after-effects or remnants from the past, but to a large extent they are undoubtedly due to new capitalistic forms replacing traditional 'human bondage' by a wage slavery sometimes still harder to endure.

There were, indeed, still many stubborn relics of the ancient forms of forced labour. Among them, the remnants of slavery and debt bondage still prevailing, especially in the Outer Islands, were certainly not the most important. The economic significance of those phenomena was slight.

More important was the preservation of compulsory services in various forms. True, forced cultivation connected with the culture system was gradually abolished and the so-called *pantjen* services (consisting of obligatory house work and garden work in behalf of the feudal chiefs) were legally prohibited and, against a strong opposition, combated in practice. But work on roads, bridges and aqueducts was still for many years performed by government agencies making use of compulsory services.

At last in 1917 these compulsory public services were abolished in Java, where plenty of labour was available, and were replaced by a head tax. However, the *desa* services, such as the upkeep of roads and small-scale irrigation works, remained and weighed heavy upon the peasantry. Moreover, compulsory services were kept in force on the private estates, which still occupied vast areas mainly in the neighbourhood of Batavia. Though it was decided in 1912 in principle that the government should end these feudal survivals by repurchasing the estates, and a modest beginning had been made with this, there were still by 1941 many estates in private hands with feudal rights such as the capacity to appoint officials and police, to levy taxes in kind and demand unpaid services for the construction and upkeep of roads and bridges.

Similar feudal practices still existed in the Principalities of Central Java. Though the apanages granted by the princes to members of their families or to public functionaries (with the right to require services from the native inhabitants) had been abolished by the 'reorganisation' of about 1920, there were still vast tracts of land leased in former times by the prince or one of his retainers to Western plantations for the cultivation of coffee or sugar, with the accessory feudal right to use the labour of the resident population. Even after the 'reorganisation' the lessees were temporarily allowed to employ involuntary labour, in accordance with the so-called 'conversion' regulations still in force at the start of World War II.

On the sparsely populated Outer Islands about 1930 the situation was still such as to allow the government to summon over two million men for an average work period of over twenty days a year on public works, such as roads, bridges and aqueducts. Less than a third of those liable for service could commute their obligation.

Remnants of traditional bondage were also present in the sphere of private agriculture for export, though the principle of free contract had replaced forced cultivation. The regulations might say that, except for the special conditions prevailing in the Principalities of Central Java mentioned above, it was henceforth forbidden to grant a private person tracts of land together with rights over the resident population. In theory, one might decide that in the future labour should be available only on the basis of individual free contracts, but in practice it was not so easy to break through an age-old attitude of peasant servitude towards his chiefs. During the rapid expansion of commercial crop cultivation on private plantations, with the cultivation of sugar leading the way, the planters attempted to profit, within the bounds of the new legislation, as much as possible from the influence of native chiefs. Just as sugar plantations invoked the intermediary of *desa* chiefs and higher officials to acquire *sawah* lands, their intermediary could serve to provide the plantations with cheap labour as well. Granting the village chiefs a commission for every worker was, from the plantation's point of view, a paying proposition. It was hard for a simple peasant to understand that, when his ever respected chiefs mediated in behalf of the plantation, he was yet free to say no. He had acquired, not merely from early times but during the culture system as well, a habit of obeying without question. It was difficult for him to conceive that those whites, who seemed to be on excellent terms with the chiefs, were not heirs to the government's authority.

Moreover, the plantation owners, by building imposing mansions and living in high style, gave the peasant the impression that they wielded as great authority as the Javanese regents. The planters also had other methods of tying the peasantry down to the plantation. Once the peasant had been induced, through the *desa* chief, to lease his *sawah* to the plantation, he soon spent the rental paid in advance and thus had to depend for his livelihood on supplementary income until his next rice harvest. Such income was obtainable by working at the plantation during the working season. A system of advance payments contributed towards the peasant's feeling of being tied down, thus creating conditions comparable with ancient debt bondage.

In this way new obligations (presupposing again the traditional peasant mentality and authoritarian relations rooted in the old *adat*) replaced the traditional compulsory services.

Traditional relations were reflected in working conditions as well. The relation of the planter to the workers was still paternalistic. In practice his authority was often all but absolute. Sometimes it was coupled with a warm human interest in the fate of his subordinates, but the system permitted abuse of power and tyranny as well.

The worker had only very primitive defences: running away from the plantation, theft of sugar cane, or (in extreme cases) burning the cane fields or an attempt on the life of *mandur* (foreman) or supervisor. After 1900 the number of cane field fires increased at a terrific rate, bearing witness to numerous grievances among the peasantry which felt themselves deprived of their land or their water rights, and among the labourers who had to acquiesce in an unaccustomed discipline and working speed.

In the long run labour relations underwent certain changes. The concentration of enterprises under a centralised management led to a type of management which gradually became less paternalistic and more modern and matter-of-fact. The administrator was becoming an employee bound by strict written regulations, and to a large extent lost his freedom of action. The relation between entrepreneur and labourers was also becoming more impersonal and more in harmony with modern trends. The government began to fight abuses springing from the cooperation between the plantations and the native chiefs. The element of traditional authority gradually disappeared from labour relations. With the steady increase of Java's population the peasantry was increasingly driven to plantation work by purely economic motives. Many plantations no longer needed the intermediary of chiefs or an intricate system of money advances to get the personnel wanted. There were now more businesslike expedients available to tie the labourers to the plantation. Plantation *kampongs* were constructed for the regular workmen who no longer worked at the plantation for supplementary income but were definitely separated from their farms. In areas where a dearth of labour prevailed measures were taken to attract workers.

However, the change in the status of labour did not imply, on the whole, an improvement in working conditions. The general tendency was one of declining real wages. This phenomenon was related to the structure of most large estates. Their profitableness was based upon cheap, hardly mechanised labour which was plentiful on Java with its rapidly increasing population. The composition of the plantation's personnel varied according to the crops cultivated. But the general picture was such that the managerial personnel were almost all recruited from the European group (including Indo-Europeans). Among the Indonesian workers hardly any skilled labourers were to be found, except for a few administrative employees. There was, however, a restricted group of labourers who had acquired by their practical experience within the plantation enterprise a certain craftmanship. This group of so-called *tukangs*, who could be classed as trained rather than as skilled personnel, was, in general, comparatively well-paid. The same applied to the *mandurs*, the foremen occupying a position of confidence with the enterprise. Besides, there was a group of full-time workers, in most cases rather restricted in numbers, whose livelihood was more or less assured.[1]

But in areas where much of the labour was performed by seasonal workers, for whom work at the plantation was merely a half-time occupation in addition to their own farming, the pay was mostly very poor, especially if labour supply was plentiful. Most members of this group had to content themselves with wages of a few cents a day, even for rather strenuous labour. As replacements were abundant, the social services for this category of part-time workers were negligible. Moreover, a great portion of this seasonal work was performed by women, including the strenuous work at the centrifuges in the sugar factories. During the working-season this work had mostly to be performed night and day in shifts. The working day often amounted to twelve hours, and this working might often be at night for a whole week.

The mechanisation of parts of the working process was not necessarily a boon for the population, in particular when it occurred in densely populated areas. The replacement, on the sugar plantations of Central and Eastern Java, of cart transport by motor-lorries deprived many Javanese of a means of subsistence.

However, the increasingly businesslike relations on the plantations were matched by a corresponding attitude on the part of the labourers. The most important symptom of this change was the rise of a trade union movement towards the end of World War I. Especially in the post-war period several strikes occurred, which forced the plantations to raise the wages. Yet, the trade union movement suffered from many weaknesses. Solidarity between the workers was still largely of a traditional character, rooted as it was in the agrarian community. This could be an advantage when, in case of strikes, they received a passive support from the peasantry of which they formed part in the shape

[1] The best analysis of labour conditions on Java plantations is to be found in the publications of P. Levert, more in particular in his thesis *Inheemsche arbeid in de Java suikerindustrie* (Native labour in the Java sugar industry), Wageningen, 1934.

of food and shelter. On the other hand, it was precisely this possibility of returning to the *desa* which undermined the will to fight to a finish for better labour conditions.

Besides, it should be noted that the employers exerted themselves to break the force of the trade union movement, and even succeeded in acquiring some support from the government. For example, a Dactyloscopical Bureau was founded which enabled employers to fingerprint all labourers considered troublesome with the intention of excluding them from employment with any enterprise[1].

It follows that on the densely populated island of Java the replacement of paternalistic conditions by a cold impersonal atmosphere did not yet mean an unqualified improvement for the workers.

As for the sparsely populated Outer Islands, the conditions on Sumatra's Eastcoast Residency, where a vast expansion of the plantation economy had occurred since the final quarter of the nineteenth century, are of the greatest interest. In this region the foremost problem was labour supply. The way this problem was solved is very instructive for a better understanding of problems of bondage and freedom. At first the labourers needed for the tobacco plantations were imported mainly from China. In later years, when other crops such as rubber competed with tobacco, the labourers came predominantly from overpopulated Java. Recruitment gave rise to serious abuses. By means of misleading promises and money advances, recruiting agents tried to induce young men and women to undertake the long journey.

Another problem was how to keep the labourers. To this end, at a time when forced cultivation had to yield, in Java, to a system of free contract, a regulation was introduced for the Outer Islands which again deprived the labourer of his freedom. According to this system the recruited worker was to engage himself by contract for a period of some years. A 'penal sanction' was in

[1] See B. Lasker, *op. cit.*, p. 229.

force, according to which the labourer violating his contract was liable to punishment. A labourer running away from his plantation could be arrested by the police and, after undergoing a prison sentence, be forced to fulfil his contract to the end. The plantation also had various other means to induce the labourer, at the end of his term, not to return to his homeland. By encouraging gambling on pay-day, saving on the part of the workers was hampered. The *mandur* saw to it that the labourer, when his contract expired, was so deep in debt that he had no choice but to sign a new contract.

At the start of this century a pamphlet, van den Brand's *De millioenen uit Deli* (The millions from Deli) aroused much alarm in Holland by its disclosure of conditions which in practice often verged on slavery. Van den Brand mentioned many instances of ill-treatment of coolies by European supervisors against whom they were defenceless, except for recourse to violence, which accordingly occurred quite frequently. Announcements from Medan papers advertising runaway coolies were reproduced in van den Brand's pamphlet and strongly reminded readers of Harriet Beecher Stowe's *Uncle Tom's Cabin.*

The general indignation aroused in Holland by the pamphlet and stimulated by the numerous attacks on plantation supervisors brought about a stricter control by the government. A Labour Inspectorate was established and recruitment in Java was also subjected to strict regulation. In other respects, too, labour relations gradually changed.

During the pioneering era of Deli the life of the European planters had been a hard one amidst a hostile environment. In order to make a stand they had created a community held together by coercion, in which a strict observance of authority and a strenuous fight (sometimes verging on the ludicrous) for prestige of the white people had decisive influence on the living conditions of the Asian coolie population as well. Any symbol of whiteness was invested with an aura of distinction and made an object of reverence, as is evidenced by the ritual required when a coolie passed a white man or even a plantation office.

It was preponderantly a male society, in which the few women were the object of a fierce competition, the white supervisors (for whom marriage had been prohibited for a long time) having the first choice, whilst among the Asians the foremen and the old hands came first. A normal family life was practically out of question, the prevailing sexual relationship being an unstable concubinage. The rather easy-going paternalistic atmosphere mostly to be found in agrarian Java was wanting in this region. In this frontier society the important thing was to get a maximum of work out of the coolies. Among the white supervisors there was keen competition for a rapid advancement and for high bonuses which enabled the successful to return as soon as possible to Holland as rich men.

The Asian workers, notably the Javanese, had broken loose from the social ties of their home country. Against the Western enterprises they were isolated, weak and powerless individuals. The plantation managements used several methods to prevent the labourers from developing a new solidarity. Foremen were played off against the common coolies, Javanese against Chinese, the indigenous Bataks and Malays against both groups. The penal sanction made strikes impossible and thus impeded the development of a trade union movement.

In the long run, however, the Deli community lost some of its frontier characteristics and its resemblance (to quote the words of a Javanese regent who visited Deli) to an out-door prison. An increasing number of female workers gradually led to a more normal family life. Several Javanese succeeded in settling down on plots of land of their own, a process encouraged by some plantations. As a consequence, besides the contract coolies recruited from overseas a new category of free workers came into the market. Several concerns began to resort, not only under pressure from the Labour Inspectorate but for commercial reasons as well, to social services rather than to coercion and legal sanctions as a means of attaching the labourers to the plantation, as a healthy workers' population was to the interest of the plantations themselves, and decent food and hospitals paid their way. Moreover, the fantastic profits easily earned during the post-war rubber boom tended to weaken the rigorous discipline of an earlier period.

The well-known novels by Madelon Székely-Lulofs and Ladislao Székely, mostly written about 1930, bear witness to the fact, however, that Deli, 'the country of unlimited possibilities', had certainly not turned suddenly into a paradise on earth for the Asian workers.[1] And if such literature be considered too unreliable a source of information for social realities, there is plenty of corroborative evidence in other documents, as for instance a booklet by the civil officer Middendorp on the penal sanction,[2] or the demographic data provided by Straub[3] on the high level of child mortality among the coolie families in Sumatra's Eastcoast Residency. Finally, the best evidence of the arbitrary actions of those in power and the hidden discontent among the coolies under the penal sanction system is furnished by the continuing frequent attempts on the life of white supervisors and the still larger number of attacks on the Asian foremen.

Within the indigenous agrarian sphere the paternalistic attitudes based on tradition retained their influence much longer. Ten Dam described in his Tjibodas report[4] how landless peasants living on the premises of their employer were tied to him body and soul. The 'boarder', who is generally a share-cropper, has to perform a good deal of unpaid work and often is in debt to his master. His actual situation is decidedly one of bondage. Yet, even in this agrarian sphere changes were occurring in the direction of more businesslike attitudes, as is indicated by van der Kolff's research in a few districts near the southcoast of Java, one

1 Madelon Székely-Lulofs, *Coolie*, New York, 1936; L. Székely, *Tropic fever. The adventures of a planter in Sumatra*, New York, 1937.

2 W. Middendorp, *De poenale sanctie*, Haarlem, 1924.

3 M. Straub, *Kindersterfte ter Oostkust van Sumatra* (Infant mortality on Sumatra's Eastcoast), Amsterdam, 1928.

4 H. ten Dam, *Desa Tjibodas*, a report of the Lembaga Penjelidikan Masjarakat Desa dan Usaha Tani (Institute for rural sociological and farm-management research), Bogor, 1951, p. 13/14.

of the major changes during the twenties being a gradual replacement of payment in kind by money wages.[1]

Quantitatively the labour problem in mining, industry and transport was of small importance compared with that on plantations and in native farming. However, labour relations outside the agrarian sphere had made far greater strides away from traditionalism. The modern environment of mining, transport and industry inevitably affected the attitudes of workers as well. It was among the personnel of the railways that the trade union movement started. In the early twenties numerous strikes occurred, mainly in the urban industrial centres. However, even in the industrial sphere the development from a traditional bondage towards a measure of freedom was only a gradual process.

In the smaller manufacturing enterprises under Asian management (of Indonesians, Arabs, Chinese or Indo-Europeans), such as the *batik* and the *kretek* (native cigarette) industry, relations were still rather paternalistic. Sometimes, when employer and worker were ethnically related, there was an easy-going mentality. But in an economic sense, exploitation under paternalistic conditions was usually worse. Behind the appearance of more humane relations, labour conditions often prevailed which demanded from the workers a practically unlimited amount of work for a minimum reward.[2] The same was usually also true of servants employed in Asian households.

On the other hand, in larger industries under European management, and also in households of European new-comers, a more

[1] G. H. van der Kolff, *The historical development of the labour relationships in a remote corner of Java as they apply to the cultivation of rice*, Batavia, 1937, p. 22 ff. See also Soejitno Mangoenkoesoemo, 'Nji Pohatji Sanghjang Srie in de desa Tjaringin nabij halte Masing' (Nji Pohatji Sanghjang Srie, the Javanese Rice Goddess, in the Tjaringin desa near Masing station), in *Koloniaal Tijdschrift* (Colonial Journal), Vol. XXX, 1941, p. 495 ff.

[2] See the interesting *Batikrapport. Rapport betreffende eene gehouden enquête naar de arbeidstoestanden in de batikkerijen op Java en Madoera* (Batik report. Report on an inquiry into the labour relations in the *batik* enterprises in Java and Madura) by P. de Kat Angelino, Weltevreden, 1930–1931.

businesslike atmosphere prevailed, often coupled with higher real wages. The Western way of dealing with Indonesian personnel vacillated between artificial attempts to imitate the authoritarian ways of the Indonesian *pryayi* class rooted in tradition and accepted by the people without dispute, and more democratic European convictions. In practice, the behaviour of Europeans often reflected a mixture of humanity and a struggle for prestige born from an inner insecurity.

Though material conditions in the European sphere were, usually, somewhat better than under Asian management, wages remained extremely low, working days very long, social services practically non-existent and the employers' powers excessive.

As long as there was plenty of labour available among the poverty-stricken agrarian population of Java, and education and mechanisation remained at a low level, neither the best governmental measures nor democratic and humanitarian ideas could alter the essential bondage of the workers. Multatuli was right in his warnings against the system of 'free labour'. The freedom acquired was formal rather than real. To quote Lasker: 'Workers who have to accept such wages are not really free men'.[1] And again: 'Colonialism, even under the most favorable circumstances, condemns the masses to live in poverty.'[2]

4 Labour adrift

The 'favourable circumstances' did not last beyond 1930. The economic depression weakened Indonesia's economic and social position to such a degree that most of the progress achieved during the previous period seemed to have been lost.

Still, social developments in colonial areas are rarely consistent. One thinks of the Chinese fable about the peasant, whose horse had run away. His neighbours came to express their compassion, but the peasant retorted: 'How do you know it is a misfortune?'

[1] B. Lasker, *op. cit.*, p. 228.

[2] B. Lasker, *op. cit.*, p. 227.

A few days later the horse returned, accompanied by a herd of wild horses. The neighbours came to congratulate him with his good luck, but they were met with the question: 'How do you know it is good luck?' When the next day his son, trying to tame one of the wild horses, fell and broke his leg, the peasant was still not willing to consider it bad luck. And indeed, within a short time it appeared that his son had been saved by this accident from recruitment into the army, and it was not easy in ancient China to think of a greater piece of luck.

In the same way the misfortunes which the depression brought for the coolies of Sumatra's Eastcoast Residency were accompanied by a piece of good luck. The keener competition on the tobacco market led to the adoption in the United States of a legal provision (a typical American blend of humanitarian principles and commercial self-interest) prohibiting imports of tobacco harvested under conditions of indentured labour. Whereas a few years earlier high Dutch authorities had retorted to Middendorp's denunciations, that abolition of the penal sanction system was still economically unwarrantable, the government's position now radically changed. There was now a surplus of labour. Javanese were dismissed by the ten thousands and sent back to Java. A decision was taken to abolish the penal sanction in stages. Shortly before the end of 1941 the labour contracts under penal sanction appeared to have decreased at such a rate that there could be no more objections to immediate abolition of this form of bondage.

The end of compulsory services in the Outer Islands (listed by Middendorp with the penal sanction under the heading 'Two backward labour systems for natives in the Netherlands East Indies'[1]) also came much nearer at the outbreak of World War II. The government now found it possible to obtain the labour force required for the construction and upkeep of roads, bridges and

[1] W. Middendorp, *Twee achterlijke arbeidssystemen voor inboorlingen in Nederlandsch-Oost Indië* (Two backward labour systems for natives in the Netherlands East Indies), Haarlem, 1928.

water works under a system of free contract. In principle, therefore, though still allowing payment in labour for those not able to pay the tax, the government legally abolished the compulsory services and replaced them by a road tax system, which, however, had not been put into practice before the Japanese invasion.

Bruno Lasker seems to consider all these removals of what little institutional bondage still had remained, as important steps towards more freedom.[1] According to him, the increasing interest of government agencies and international organisations for the plight of the worker, coupled with more humane convictions among the employers, are warrants for a rapid improvement of labour conditions in Southeast Asia.[2] It seems to me that this optimistic view is not borne out by Lasker's own analysis of the very causes of human bondage. 'One of the main causes of both poverty and lack of freedom in Southeast Asia is insufficient productivity', the author states.[3] This factor was anything but remedied during the depression years – quite the reverse was true.

As we have already observed, replacement of institutional bondage by a formal freedom of contract does not necessarily mean an improvement of the worker's position. Whether abolition of the penal sanction was unqualified 'good fortune' for the workers, is a moot point. It is true that the elimination of coercion from labour conditions had a mitigating effect upon human relations. But the harshest aspects of the penal sanction system were, to some extent, neutralised by a regular, though not always effective control by the Labour Inspectorate. Moreover, the shortage of labour had induced the entrepreneurs to provide, if only for considerations of self-interest, for the material livelihood and the

[1] B. Lasker, *op. cit.*, p. 265 ff., 272 ff.

[2] See, for instance, B. Lasker, *op. cit.*, p. 13: '...further advances in welfare policy, while democratic labor organization is yet in its infancy, depend on the courage and unimpeded effectiveness of the forces which before the war had produced in Southeast Asia the beginnings of an industrial democracy. It would be unjust not to acknowledge the large efforts which legislators, public officials, industrial managers, labor leaders, research workers, missionaries and publicists have contributed to this end.'

[3] B. Lasker, *op. cit.*, p. 267.

bodily health of the workers. With an enlarged supply of labour, partly emanating from peasants settled on their own small plots of land in search of supplementary employment only, the danger arose that the gains achieved in human relations would be lost again by a deterioration in the economic sphere.

For the rest, the detrimental effects of the depression were mitigated, for Sumatra's Eastcoast Residency, by the possibility of sending the surplus labour back to Java, thus 'exporting' the threatening unemployment. To see the effects of crisis in their full weight, we thus have to direct our eyes to Java, where, generally speaking, institutional bondage had already ended and formal freedom of the worker seemed to be more or less assured.

Unemployment in Java assumed alarming proportions. Though those thrown out of work, either in the towns or in the plantations, were said to be absorbed by the *desa* in an admirable fashion, this meant in practice only that the disguised unemployment which already in normal times prevented the peasant from working at full capacity throughout the year, was considerably aggravated during the crisis. The sharp drop in employment especially in the sugar industry, owing to the drastic restriction of the cultivated area, led to unprecedented wage cuts, particularly for the *tanis* who worked for a supplementary income. The same phenomenon occurred in the upland estates in those regions where plenty of labour from the surrounding *desas* was available. In the years 1935 and 1936 daily wages amounted for the latter category to 4–9 guilder cents.[1]

Even for upland plantations where the workers were settled in estate *kampongs* especially built for them daily wages for plantation coolies fluctuated from 7 to 15 cents.[2] Even when, about 1937, business had improved and the plantations could make higher profits again, wages remained at an extremely low level.

The gravity of the labour situation can best be seen in the find-

[1] At a rate of one guilder equalling approximately 55 U.S. dollar cents.

[2] J. H. Boeke, *Economics and economic policy of dual societies as exemplified by Indonesia*, Haarlem, 1953, p. 300.

ings of the so-called Coolie Budget Commission which, shortly before the Japanese occupation, completed a report on 'Living conditions of plantation workers and peasants on Java in 1939–1940.'[1]

In cooperation with associations of estate owners a number of plantations had been selected from various more or less representative regions of Java. Each local investigation had been restricted to a sample of workers' families selected in cooperation with the estate manager again, with a view to observe for some time their manner of living relative to income, cash expenditures, nutrition and other consumption habits. In addition, a few local peasant families not connected with the estate were generally included in order to provide a basis for comparison with workers on the plantation.

A few of the more interesting findings of the Commission are the following.

Among the largest groups of workers, including plantation coolies and factory coolies, food accounted for 70 to 75 per cent of all expenditures, and reached 80 per cent on some estates. Foremen (*mandurs*) and technicians (*tukangs*) were the only groups presenting a somewhat different picture, outlays on food in this group being on the average appreciably lower.

A large part of the expenditures not spent on food – for some groups nearly a quarter – was spent on so-called 'religious and charitable purposes'. If account is taken of the fact that 90 per cent of these expenditures were for religious feasts (*slamatans*), on occasion of births, deaths, marriages or circumcision, which constituted the only occasions on which animal fats and proteins were consumed in appreciable quantities and thus provided an essential part of the workers' diets, it is easy to conclude that those expend-

[1] *Living conditions of plantation workers and peasants on Java in 1939–1940*, a translation of Vol. I of the *Eindrapport van de Koeliebudgetcommissie* (Final report of the Coolie Budget Commission), Translation Series, Modern Indonesia Project, Cornell University, Ithaca, 1956, referred to in the following as: *Living conditions*. See also W. F. Wertheim, 'The coolie budget report', in *Pacific Affairs*, Vol. XXVI, 1953, p. 158 ff.

itures might with equal propriety have been listed in the food category. The same observation applies to 'social obligations' which in fact involved contributions to *slamatans* given by others.

Expenses for medical and hygienic care (including bathing and hairdressing), education, sport and recreation etc. were negligible except in the case of foremen and technicians. Outlays on non-essentials, *i.e.* smoking and betel-chewing supplies, were also very low, but they rose sharply with increased income. Except in the case of foremen and technicians, expenditures on house maintenance (including those for household utensils) were also negligible.

Categories of expenditures [1]

Per family per day in guilder cents[2]

Division of the expenditures into 6 groups mentioned below	Resident workers[3]			Non-resident workers[4]			Local peasants
	plantation coolies	factory coolies	foremen and technicians	plantation coolies	factory coolies	foremen and technicians	
Food	5.9	6.2	7.4	2.9	3.6	5.6	3.0
Fuel, light & water	0.6	0.5	0.9	0.3	0.5	0.7	0.4
Clothing	0.4	0.6	1.0	0.1	0.2	0.7	0.1
House upkeep & rent	0.1	0.1	0.3	0.0	0.0	0.3	0.1
Non-essentials	0.7	0.7	1.0	0.2	0.4	0.6	0.2
Other	0.4	0.4	1.9	0.3	0.4	1.6	0.4
Total	8.0	8.5	12.5	3.8	5.1	9.5	4.3

As percentages of total expenditures

Food	73	73	59	75	72	58	71
Fuel, light & water	7	6	8	8	9	8	9
Clothing	5	7	8	3	3	8	3
House upkeep & rent	1	1	2	1	1	4	2
Non-essentials	8	9	8	6	7	7	5
Other	5	5	15	8	8	16	10
Total	100	100	100	100	100	100	100

[1] *Living conditions*, p. 77/78.

[2] At a rate of one guilder = approximately 55 pre-war U.S. dollar cents.

[3] Those living on the estate in special *kampongs*.

[4] Those living outside the estate.

Specified other expenditures [1]

Per family per day in guilder cents

Division of the group 'other exp.' into 11 items	Resident workers			Non-resident workers			Local peasants
	plantation coolies	factory coolies	foremen and technicians	plantation coolies	factory coolies	foremen and technicians	
Medical and hygienic care	0.02	0.04	0.19	0.01	0.02	0.10	0.01
Education	0.01	0.01	0.22	0.01	0.01	0.11	0.01
Transportation	0.02	0.01	0.35	0.02	0.00	0.19	0.03
Correspondence	0.00	0.00	0.01	0.00	0.00	0.01	0.00
Religious & charitable purposes	0.19	0.20	0.36	0.22	0.25	0.75	0.29
Social obligations	0.07	0.07	0.28	0.02	0.13	0.26	0.06
Support of relatives	0.07	0.05	0.29	0.01	0.00	0.09	0.01
Sport and recreation	0.00	0.00	0.06	0.00	0.00	0.01	0.00
Purchase and care of plants & animals	0.00	–	0.01	–	0.00	0.01	0.00
Servants' wages	0.02	0.01	0.04	0.00	0.00	0.02	0.00
Further	0.00	0.01	0.04	0.00	0.00	0.02	0.00
Total	0.40	0.41	1.86	0.29	0.42	1.56	0.42

[1] *Living conditions*, p. 95.

As far as indebtedness was concerned a large part of the workers investigated were worse off at the end of the investigation period than at its outset, the only group which had improved its position appreciably being the foremen and technicians.

Social services were most highly developed in areas where labour was scarce, but even then they were modest indeed. For workers living on the estates they might comprise, to quote the Report, 'high wages, good housing conditions, recreation and amusement facilities, opportunities for performing religious duties, proper medical and hygienic care, a supply of cheap commodities, bonuses on occasions of marriages, births and deaths', while furthermore 'on several plantations a beginning has been made towards providing pensions for a number of aged workers'. It

Specified other expenditures [1]

As percentages of total 'other expenditures'

Division of the group 'other exp.' into 11 items	Resident workers			Non-resident workers			Local peasants
	plantation coolies	factory coolies	foremen and technicians	plantation coolies	factory coolies	foremen and technicians	
Medical and hygienic care	6	11	10	4	4	7	4
Education	2	1	12	2	1	7	2
Transportation	4	3	19	7	1	12	7
Correspondence	0	0	0	0	0	0	0
Religious & charitable purposes	47	49	19	74	60	48	68
Social obligations	19	17	15	7	31	16	15
Support of relatives	17	11	16	4	1	6	2
Sport and recreation	0	0	3	1	1	1	0
Purchase and care of plants & animals	0	–	0	–	0	1	0
Servants' wages	5	3	2	0	0	1	1
Further	0	4	2	2	0	1	1
Total	100	100	100	100	100	100	100

[1] *Living conditions*, p. 96.

may be observed that 'good housing conditions' and 'high wages' were only relative, as appears from the detailed data given. The living area allotted per family averaged five by five meters, including kitchen space, while great local differences prevailed. Most living quarters on estates were constructed of wattled bamboo and half of them had earthen floors. The average income for resident male workers, who were wholly dependent on money wages, was 2.3 guilder cents per hour for plantation coolies and 3 guilder cents for factory workers. Yet, their situation was far better than that of non-residents, for whom money wages represented only a supplementary source of income. In Central Java even for such exhausting work as ditch-digging in sugar cane fields, the average hourly wage for non-resident male plan-

Caloric intake (including slamatans i.e. religious feasts) per person per day

	Resident workers			Non-resident workers			Local peasants
	plantation coolies	factory coolies	foremen and technicians	plantation coolies	factory coolies	foremen and technicians	
Tea 1 W.J. . . .	2465	2480	2196	2477	–	–	–
,, 2 ,, . . .	1947	2025	2033	1706	–	–	1504
,, 3 ,, . . .	2040	1794	2438	1742	–	–	1728
Rubber 1a ,, . . .	2195	–	–	2238	–	–	1888
,, 2b ,, . . .	2208	–	–	1974	–	–	2267
West Java	2164	2057	2252	2042	–	–	1906
Rubber 1 C.J. . .	2060	2028	2137	1594	–	–	2053
,, 2 ,, . .	–	–	–	1530	–	–	1229
,, 3 ,, . .	–	–	–	1081	1348	1861	957
Tobacco 1 ,, . .	–	–	–	1297	1878	2257	1329
Sugar 1a ,, . .	–	–	–	652	893	2143	894
,, 1b ,, . .	–	–	–	900	1482	1928	1090
,, 2a ,, . .	–	–	–	798	965	1758	1313
,, 2b ,, . .	–	–	–	850	1207	1492	1049
Central Java	2060	2028	2137	1065	1371	1853	1222
Coffee 1 E.J. . .	2535	2207	2145	–	–	–	–
,, 2 ,, . .	1827	2324	2037	–	–	–	–
,, 3 ,, . .	1647	2027	2732	–	–	–	1439
Rubber 1 ,, . .	2338	2337	–	–	–	–	1736
,, 2 ,, . .	1661	1674	2150	1027	–	–	1264
Tobacco 1a ,, . .	1506	–	2084	1522	–	–	1526
,, 1b ,, . .	1321	–	1914	1560	–	–	1414
Sugar 1a ,, . .	–	–	–	1028	989	1546	1167
,, 1b ,, . .	–	–	–	1097	1325	1865	1319
,, 2 ,, . .	–	–	–	1506	1398	2023	1164
Teak 1 ,, . .	–	–	–	1185	1768	2659	1336
,, 2 ,, . .	1717	–	1978	1414	–	1769	1270
East Java	1870	1995	2103	1217	1427	2059	1356
Java	1964	2017	2132	1282	1399	1983	1391
Tea	2132	2057	2252	2003	–	–	1615
Coffee	1942	2164	2292	–	–	–	1439
Rubber	2059	1842	2346	1449	1438	1861	1544
Tobacco	1421	–	1988	1376	1878	2257	1450
Sugar	–	–	–	959	1261	1755	1159
Teak	1717	–	1978	1294	1768	2420	1309

Consumption of animal proteins (including slamatans) in grams per person per day

	Resident workers			Non-resident workers			Local peasants
	plantation coolies	factory coolies	foremen and technicians	plantation coolies	factory coolies	foremen and technicians	
West Java	11	13	15	8	–	–	6
Central Java	8	13	11	2	2	6	3
East Java	7	6	11	3	5	10	3
Java	8	9	12	3	4	8	3
Tea	13	13	15	12	–	–	8
Coffee	6	5	10	–	–	–	2
Rubber	9	9	9	3	3	5	3
Tobacco	4	–	13	3	3	8	3
Sugar	–	–	–	2	4	8	4
Teak	4	–	9	2	6	10	2

tation workers was about 1.2 guilder cents. Besides, for non-resident workers social services were limited in the main to a free issue, upon application, of small quantities of the most common patent medicines.

It is interesting to note that educational facilities as element of the social services provided are never mentioned in the Report. Furnivall's statement, that 'the percentage of expenditure on native education is lowest where Western enterprise is most conspicuous,'[1] therefore seems quite justified.

As in all societies with a high percentage of expenditures spent on food, nutritional standards for plantation workers were low, both in quantitative and in qualitative respects, as is shown in the above tables.[2]

Average daily consumption by members of families of non-resident plantation coolies, including that at *slamatans*, was 1,282 calories; by non-resident factory coolies, 1,399; and by local

[1] J. S. Furnivall, *Colonial policy and practice. A comparative study of Burma and Netherlands India*, Cambridge, 1948, p. 412.

[2] *Eindrapport van de Koeliebudgetcommissie* (Final report of the Coolie Budget Commission), Vol. III (statistical materials, unpublished), tables 239 and 241.

peasants, 1,391. Although the intake of resident workers entirely dependent on wages and of foremen and technicians was considerably higher (as was to have been expected in view of the interest of the plantation management in maintaining their health), yet it barely exceeded 2,000 calories. Moreover, there were important regional differences, Western Java being distinctly above the average for the island and Central Java below. On sugar estates, all of whose labour force was non-resident, the plantation workers' average caloric consumption, including that at *slamatans*, amounted to 959 as against an average of 1,159 for peasants in the area. On one sugar plantation in Central Java, these averages were found to be 652 and 894 respectively.

Average daily consumption of proteins totalled 50 to 60 grams (approximately 1¾ to 2 ounces) for members of families of foremen and technicians and of resident coolies. Non-resident coolies and peasants averaged between 30 and 40 grams daily. Animal proteins were almost totally lacking in the diet of most families. Including their consumption at *slamatans*, the most privileged groups averaged about 10 grams daily. Outside Western Java, peasants and part-time workers consumed some three or four grams a day. The legendary piece of fish in the daily bowl of rice was apparently a luxury beyond the means of many plantation workers.[1]

The general picture of pre-war conditions, conveyed by those findings, may be completed with a few data on workers in other

[1] These are the findings which in a recent book by a Dutch expert are glossed over, without any corroborating figures, in the following way: 'Though deficiencies in the budget did exist, insufficient satisfaction of needs was certainly not observed. It could be ascertained that the general condition of plantation workers was better than that of the local peasantry, not working on the estate. The diet of the workers was rather poor in fats, but did not show a caloric intake too remote from the requirements established by the People's Food Institute'. Cf. E. A. van de Graaff, *De statistiek in Indonesië* (Statistics in Indonesia), The Hague/Bandung, 1955, p. 78. Needless to say that the disquieting innuendo as if the People's Food Institute in Jakarta would approve a diet not too far remote from the above statistics is unwarranted.

jobs. Just as replacement of forced cultivation or penal sanction by free contract had not proved an unqualified boon for plantation workers, so replacement of compulsory services by salaried labour on public works was no unequivocal gain for the workers concerned. In 1937 a budgetary investigation of living conditions among the municipal coolies in Batavia[1] showed that the situation of urban workers in municipal agencies was nothing to be proud of.

Out of a total of 1,871 workers investigated almost 75 per cent were unskilled, about 25 per cent were semi-skilled (technicians having acquired their skill on the job) and only 2 per cent were skilled labourers. Over half of the workers earned no more than 30 guilder cents a day. As housing required a far greater portion of the budget than was the case with plantation workers, the percentage of the income spent on food was appreciably lower.[2]

Categories of expenditures as percentages of total expenditures

Division of the expenditures into 7 groups	Wage-group in guilders:				
	0.30	0.35	0.40–0.50	0.50–0.75	1.00 and over
1 Food	60.5	56.5	58.5	56.5	52.–
2 Fuel, light, water	8.–	8.–	8.–	9.5	7.5
3 House-rent . .	15.–	20.5	13.5	14.5	14.–
4 Furniture . . .	–	0.5	0.5	1.5	0.5
5 Clothing . . .	6.–	3.5	8.–	4.5	9.–
6 Other expend. .	7.–	7.5	8.–	9.5	13.–
7 Taxes	3.5	3.5	3.5	4.–	4.–
Total expenditures	100	100	100	100	100

This did not signify, however, an improved food situation, as is shown by the following table.[3]

[1] The report has been included in *The Indonesian town. Studies in urban sociology*, Selected studies on Indonesia by Dutch scholars, Vol. IV, The Hague/Bandung, 1958, p. 87 ff.

[2] *Op. cit.*, p. 125.

[3] *Op. cit.*, p. 137.

Food consumption per person per day

	Wage-group in guilders:				
	0.30	0.35	0.40–0.50	0.50–0.75	1.00 and more
Total caloric intake	1581	1433	1389	1588	1677
Consumption of proteins in grams .	38	34	33	37	40
Consumption of fats in grams . . .	11	12	15	16	23
Consumption of carbohydrates in grams	331	298	279	323	328

The somewhat surprising decline of quantities consumed in the lower groups, as income rises, may, perhaps, be accounted for by an increase of the number of children as incomes rise. The average family lived on credit, and spent on the average 65 per cent of the wage received on the discharge of debts.

As on the plantation, expenses on furniture were all but negligible.[1]

Wage-group in guilders:	Expenditure on furniture in guilders per month:
0.30	0.03
0.35	0.08
0.40–0.50	0.07
0.50–0.75	0.12
1.00 and over	0.21

Accordingly, housing accomodation usually appeared to be very poor. A very large percentage of the houses had earthen floors. Nearly 25 per cent consisted of one room only. Half of the families had a separate kitchen. Only in 25 out of the 202 houses investigated there was a latrine, and even these were pits rather than Western-style privies. These conditions were the more serious, in view of the importance of hygiene and housing in urban areas.

[1] *Op. cit.*, p. 139.

The situation of industrial labour was little better. Especially in native small-size enterprises, such as *batik* manufactures, peanut shelling mills, copra kilns, etc., daily wages were abnormally low around 1933. According to Boeke[1] a labourer's wage for an eight hour day was sometimes no more than 2½ guilder cents. In the hat industry of Western Java in the same year seldom over 2½ to 3 guilder cents a day could be earned.

Wages in the new weaving industry in Western Java, which rapidly expanded after 1935, were at the outset considerably higher. Again, the misfortunes created by the crisis proved to be qualified. During the depression a number of peasants had lost their land and were driven to look for new sources of income. In this way the new weaving industry came into being. Though the industry as such was the product of dire need, it created relatively favourable labour conditions, as is generally the case with a nascent industry. The skill required was still rather scarce, and for a time the demand for labour exceeded the supply to such a degree that wages in the new trade were appreciably better than in the older manufactures. But after a few years a decline of wages started in the new industry as well.[2]

This development confirmed the general rule, that labour conditions do not primarily depend upon a formal freedom or bondage, but rather upon the relation between demand and supply.

Towards the end of the pre-war period, however, a new paradox appeared. Institutional bondage had been gradually abolished, not only out of humanitarian principles, but also on account of a more abundant labour supply. About 1941 the last legal remnants – penal sanctions and compulsory services in the Outer Islands – were officially abolished. But at the same time a new possibility for coercion arose. Under circumstances where the

[1] J. H. Boeke, *op. cit.*, p. 300.

[2] *De ontwikkeling van de kleine handweefnijverheid in het Madjalaja rayon* (The development of the small handweaving industry in the Majalaya district), Batavia, 1938, p. 60; G. Schwencke, 'De weefindustrie in het Regentschap Bandoeng' (The weaving industry in the Bandung Regency), in *Koloniaal Tijdschrift* (Colonal Journal), Vol. XXVIII, 1939, p. 159.

need for labour rose rapidly, there was still a readiness to sacrifice the principle of institutional freedom, if necessary.

The war situation called forth expectations about a quick development of a demand for labour, especially for objects of military importance. Therefore, a Civilian Service Ordinance was adopted to enable the authorities to get the required labour if necessary by compulsion. In practice this power was hardly used under Dutch rule, the only occasion, to my knowledge, being in the Sabang harbour when, after the first bombings, the dockworkers were running away.[1]

The equivocal honour of carrying the enforcement of compulsory labour for military purposes to extremes fell to the Japanese. Especially after military developments had taken an unfavourable turn for the Japanese, they began to exploit Java's manpower in a most ruthless manner. Not only Allied prisoners of war were dispatched hither and thither – mainly abroad (for instance to Siam, Burma and Malaya) for the construction of roads, railways and other works of strategic importance. The Javanese peasantry was also compelled to supply ever larger numbers of workers, both for Java and for overseas (from Burma to the Solomon Islands). That such a high toll was levied from Java in particular, was partly due to the presence in rural Java of large numbers of people, economically superfluous after the rigorous restriction of the cultivation of commercial crops formerly destined for export. But the army of occupation did not limit recruitment to such 'superfluous' people.

As long as possible the Japanese tried to keep up an appearance of recruitment on a voluntary basis. The social prestige of the workers recruited would equal the standing of those taking actively part in the fight. In official Indonesian terminology they were called '*prajurit ekonomi*' (economic soldiers), the term 'coolie' being avoided. But in practice all kinds of forcible means were

[1] A. J. Piekaar, *Atjeh en de oorlog met Japan* (Acheh and the war against Japan), The Hague/Bandung, 1949, p. 121.

used, varying from summoning workers on a mass scale by using false promises, via withholding rations from those unwilling to enlist, to random seizure of peasants working on their *sawahs* along the roads. There was a great diversity as to working conditions and the duration of this kind of work. For large groups of workers set at work not far from their homes the employment lasted for a few months only. But even if the duration was short, the summons could amount to a catastrophe for those taken.

Labour conditions in practice, including earnings, food, transport, hygiene, lack of medical care, beggar description. This human wastage may be accounted for by the abundance of labour in Java, combined with military corruption, mismanagement and a complete disregard for human life on the part of the Japanese military. Mortality among these workers was terrible. Still more unbelievable were conditions in transport overseas and on the so-called 'railroad of death' through Burma and the Kra-Isthmus. Statistics with regard to the coolies (so-called *romusha*) sent outside Java are not very reliable and the number of victims is not easy to assess, but there are reports about nearly 300.000 *romusha* being sent overseas. At the end of the war the number of those still alive seems to have been no more than 70.000, most of them in a pitiable physical condition.[1]

The political system prevailing in Japan may partly account for the use made by the Japanese of their full military and political power to exploit the available labour supply to the utmost for their war effort. But one wonders at the short-sighted way they completely forfeited their unmistakable goodwill with the Asian peoples within a few years.

A still more striking phenomenon however is, that Indonesian society proved all but powerless to resist the return to these extreme forms of compulsory labour.

Neither the fact that Indonesian officials were attached to the

[1] According to Virginia Thompson, *Labor problems in Southeast Asia*, New Haven, 1947, p. 163, the fate of about 90 per cent of those shipped was still unknown.

military administration in high positions, nor the establishment of Indonesian Advisory Councils and special committees on the fate of the *romusha* and their relatives, helped in practice to mitigate the lot of these unfortunates. Installing Indonesian committees and attracting Indonesian officials was, for the Japanese, rather a means to gain confidence with the Indonesian masses and to make recruitment go more smoothly. The practical administration was too much in the hands of local authorities who were continuously afraid of serious censure by their superiors if they failed to provide the labour quota required at a minimum cost.

Only when Indonesian officials on this lower level aimed (on the basis of a national solidarity in cooperation with the *romusha*, and with serious risks for their own life) at betterment of conditions for the workers, could some mitigation of their plight be realised, and some of the worst abuses checked. An interesting example of this appears in the autobiography of the internationally well-known revolutionary Tan Malaka, where he describes conditions prevailing among the *romusha* in the coal mines of South Bantam.[1]

Apart from the great harm done by the Japanese labour policy, it had very important consequences for the Indonesian social structure. The Indonesian peasantry were set adrift. Any person not indispensable for agriculture disappeared from the villages. In practice in several *desas* the Japanese went still farther and took nearly all able-bodied men away, leaving only women, children, invalids and old men. The general dislocation proved, at the end of the Japanese occupation, to have serious effects on the stability of the Indonesian social structure. Among the *romusha* in various parts of the archipelago were often to be found the most turbulent elements, who played an important role at the revolutionary developments in 1945 and after.

For the rest, it should not be concluded that all the workers in Japanese service were equally underpaid. The treatment depended to a large degree upon the interest the Japanese took in a

[1] Tan Malaka, *Dari pendjara ke pendjara* (From prison to prison), Jogjakarta, Vol. II, w.y., p. 147 ff.

particular kind of work in the framework of the total war effort, in connection with special skills and the possibility of substitution. On the one hand, the Japanese attempted to order the labour force about at will. Besides depriving the mass of labourers of what little freedom of organisation had existed under Dutch rule, they even largely robbed the individual worker of his freedom of choice of employment. During the first years of occupation they lowered wages and lengthened working days. In later years they tried to use the distribution system to direct labour primarily to the objects of importance for their war effort. In this way even Chinese craftsmen, such as carpenters, were forced to change their independent craft for employment with an enterprise under Japanese control.

On the other hand the group of more or less skilled labourers in vital enterprises were comparatively well cared for. The distribution system aimed at supplying urban industrial centres with food and other necessities. Qualified workers in the vital enterprises belonged, together with various groups of Indonesian public functionaries, to the groups with the highest allocations. Accordingly, rations for those working in enterprises the Japanese were not much interested in, were extremely poor, as was also the case with the unskilled *romusha* who could, as a rule, be easily replaced. Insofar as plantation workers were allowed to remain on the estates, they were obliged to provide for their subsistence by the cultivation of food crops in addition to the work they had to perform on the plantation. Urban groups whose work was considered by the Japanese of little economic importance were also forced to leave the overcrowded cities and to settle in the outskirts in order to cultivate vegetables and sweet potatoes for the city population.[1]

After the Japanese occupation labour conditions became as unstable and confused as the political situation. During the post-

[1] See *inter alia* A. J. Piekaar, *op. cit.*, p. 299; and J. D. N. Versluys, 'Maatschappelijke vernieuwing op Timor?' (Social change on Timor?), in *Indonesië*, Vol. III, 1949/50, p. 201 ff.

war years the British and Dutch administrations competed with the Republic attempting to obtain the labour force needed. Those working for the whites were abused by the Republicans as traitors. But despite the enormous shortage of labour due to the ruthless Japanese policy, the need for workers at first remained limited owing to the confused political conditions. Many parts of the economic mechanism had come to a standstill, and for the time being Japanese prisoners of war could largely provide for the needs of the landing forces. Thus, the temptation for the British and the Dutch to make use of compulsory labour was restricted to a few local objects.

In Republican areas a kind of civilian service was introduced. However, the labour policy of the Republican Government had nothing in common with the Japanese policy of coercion. For the first time in history Indonesian labourers had the opportunity to organise themselves on a large scale. It was part of the general policy during the revolutionary period to attempt to mould the labour movement into a spearhead of social revolution. In the areas occupied by the landing forces the labour movement also attempted to acquire influence and to use it in behalf of the Republican cause.

Both elements, the increased self-confidence of the labourers and the continuous interaction between the labour movement and politics, were bound to dominate further developments during the post-war period. Increasing confidence led to rapid growth of a trade union movement, and frequent use of strikes. But these were not used solely for direct economic ends. In a world where the entrepreneurs had never hesitated to exert their influence upon politics, all admonitions to the young labour movement to refrain from politics proved vain. The great political importance of the movement is clearly witnessed by the strong representation of the largest trade union federation, the SOBSI[1], in Parliament[2] and in several cabinets.

[1] Sentral Organisasi Buruh Seluruh Indonesia (Central Organisation of Workers in Whole Indonesia) formed in 1946.

[2] By Presidential decree of December 29, 1946, the membership of the K.N.

Strikes also became part of the political struggle. This did not apply only to areas occupied by the Dutch. Inside the Republic the well-known strike of agricultural labourers in the important Delanggu cotton growing region broke out in 1948, after the left wing had lost its direct influence upon the Republican Government. This action should undoubtedly be seen in the light of the prevalent left wing political agitation against the government, an action which culminated in the ill-famed communist led Madiun uprising in 1948.

Thus, within the Republic, an antithesis also arose between the government and the trade union movement – a cleavage which widened after the transfer of sovereignty. On the one hand, a labour legislation had been introduced during the Jogjakarta period, which went much farther than the pre-war protection. A seven hour working day and a forty hour working week were introduced, prohibition of child work and restrictions on female labour were enacted, provisions for paid holidays were made, indemnity regulations were introduced for the victims of occupational accidents.[1] Moreover, after independence a government agency was created to mediate conflicts between employers and workers. In contrast with the pre-war period the government took an active and official part in May Day-celebrations.

On the other hand the influence of SOBSI and affiliated trade unions became increasingly a cause of concern for businessmen and politicians.

It is not surprising, therefore, that several attempts were made to start trade unions and federations not associated with SOBSI and

I.P. (the Central Indonesian National Committee) was extended to 514, forty seats being assigned to labour representatives (see George Mc T. Kahin, *Nationalism and revolution in Indonesia*, Ithaca, 1952, p. 201). According to Ch. Wolf, *The Indonesian Story. The birth, growth, and structure of the Indonesian Republic*, New York, 1948, p. 70, SOBSI was represented by about 35 members.

[1] See *Undang-undang dan rentjana undang-undang dari Kementerian Perburuhan Republik Indonesia* (Regulations and legislative proposals of the Labour Ministry of the Indonesian Republic), w. p., w. y.

not sympathising with the W.F.T.U. These counter-movements found ready support among government circles. In particular since many Western enterprises resumed their activities on a large scale after the transfer of sovereignty, the recurring strike waves were anything but appreciated by the government. The strikes and prevailing labour unrest seriously hampered the drive led by the President for increased production, especially on the large estates working for export. The governement has, therefore, repeatedly made use of its special powers to prevent strikes and to take measures against those responsible.

Yet, the labour movement has gained such strength as to force the government to comply to a large degree with the demands of the workers. The decisions taken by the various mediation committees are as often unwelcome to the employers as they are to the workers. And the policy of supporting unions not associated with the SOBSI has in several cases strengthened the mediators' inclination to decide in favour of labour.

Yet, up to this time, the policy of inducing the labourers to associate themselves with organisations other than SOBSI has met with only modest success. Many workers suspect influences within those other organisations inimical to their basic interests. At the May Day-celebrations SOBSI and the associated unions show every year that they command a far larger following than all the other organisations taken together.

It is difficult to make accurate estimates of membership of the various unions and federations,[1] but one can gain an impression of the growth and the power of the labour movement by recalling that in August 1950 several hundreds thousand plantation workers went on strike to achieve certain improvements of labour conditions. The same phenomenon occurred in September 1953.

[1] Interesting figures are being provided by H. J. Wijnmalen, 'Aantekeningen betreffende het ontstaan, de ontwikkeling en het optreden van de vakbeweging in Indonesië na de onafhankelijkheidsverklaring van 17 Augustus 1945' (Notes on the origin, the development and the activities of the trade union movement in Indonesia since the declaration of independence of August 17th, 1945), in *Indonesië*, Vol. V, 1951/52, see in particular p. 550 ff.

This is evidence of the growing solidarity among a group as loosely knit before the war as the agricultural workers, and of the mass support unions have been able to achieve.

It should not be assumed, however, that this development has already brought into existence a stable, strong labour movement. The young organisations suffer from many of the infant diseases well-known to nineteenth century Europe. The organisation is often rather loosely built. Control is more often than not in the hands of persons who do not come from the labour movement itself, but belong to the urban class of intellectuals and near-intellectuals. Many ties are still of a personal character and the war chests are extremely small.

The most serious deficiency is that the labour movement seems to have been unable, as yet, to produce a lasting improvement in working conditions. Wage increases, bonuses and enforced issues of food in kind are repeatedly being outdone by the increasing costs of living.

Moreover, many of the demands made tend to restrict production or to decrease the willingness of capital owners to invest, and thus hamper increased production or even unwittingly foster unemployment. It is not easy to gain a clear insight into the level of consumption among different categories of labourers, since there have been almost no investigations making a comparison with pre-war conditions possible.[1]

Morally, the position of labour has definitely improved. The

[1] A recent publication, 'Penjelidikan biaja hidup di Djakarta' (Investigation of the cost of living in Jakarta), in *Ekonomi dan Keuangan Indonesia* (Economics and Finance in Indonesia), Vol. X, 1957, p. 738 ff., may provide a basis for comparison in particular with the investigation held in pre-war Batavia in 1937 (*The Indonesian town*, p. 87 ff.). Such a comparison would seem to indicate some improvement in food consumption among lower income groups, as compared with 1937, especially with respect to the intake of meat and fish; but on the other hand the investigated groups might be not quite comparable, the sample of 1953–1954 (the years in which the investigation was conducted) seeming on the average to be somewhat better off than the 1937 sample.

workers are no longer unprotected isolated individuals facing well-organised employers.

Materially, conditions for a few groups may also have improved. It may be that workers in vital enterprises, such as dockworkers and miners, fare better than before. For workers in large-scale industry and on plantations under European management an improvement has perhaps been achieved by trade unions action combined with the managements' interest to prevent labour unrest, insofar as the workers are receiving foodstuffs in kind. This is, no doubt, a very important factor in view of the preponderant place of food, as we have seen, in the Indonesian workers' budget. On the other hand, the real purchasing power of the money wages (nominally increased at a fantastic rate) is decidedly less than before the war. It is to be doubted, therefore, whether the overall position of the workers has really improved, especially as a widespread abuse seems to have developed in that foodstuffs (issued by the management) with the greatest nutritional value are often sold by workers in order to pay off debts.

Moreover, in a country with acute food shortages rationing of rice to certain groups of workers may tend to aggravate the dearth of food for others. Workers in small-scale industry and medium sized industry and agricultural labourers on native lands may bear the brunt of the decrease in real wages.[1] Many other factors (among them the high management costs involved in the purchase of foodstuffs for the workers and insufficient incentives for a native industry) are contributing to a serious unemployment problem as a result of which real wages tend to decline again and the plight of those out of work, both in the cities and in the country, is aggravated.

Though institutional bondage is definitely on the decrease, some remnants of feudalism, such as compulsory services on the private estates mainly in Western Java and on the so-called 'conversion lands' in the Principalities of Central Java being

[1] See for instance A. Aten, 'Some remarks on rural industry in Indonesia', in *Indonesië*, Vol. VI, 1952/53, p. 545 ff., especially p. 548. See also the cited report by H. ten Dam on Tjibodas.

largely abolished or in process of abolition, a few relics still persist. It is, for instance, reported that on account of the difficulty, in some remote regions, of getting the labour required for construction and upkeep of roads on a basis of free contract, compulsory services are illegally maintained, despite the provision of the Road Tax Ordinance.[1] In other regions the traditional concept of *gotong royong* (collective help) is not seldom used in a way which makes the tasks to be performed practically amount to something little short of compulsory services. It is quite understandable, that human bondage still persists in Indonesia in many forms. Of both factors which have led, in Western Europe, to rising prosperity among the mass of workers – namely, the organised struggle of labour and increased production *per capita* – only the former has hitherto been realised in Indonesia. The common fight of labourers for betterment of their position is, no doubt, required to achieve improvement, but it does not produce this improvement automatically. The workers are increasingly able to assure themselves of a reasonable share of the wealth produced, but the total product remains far too small. And where there is nothing, as goes the saying in Dutch, even the emperor loses his right.

Lasker's contention, that poverty and lack of freedom are primarily the products of insufficient productivity, is still valid for Indonesia. And as long as the worker is economically unfree, the danger of a return to other forms of bondage still persists.

A short bibliography

J. van den Brand, *De millioenen uit Deli* (The millions from Deli), Amsterdam, 1902.

R. Broersma, *Oostkust van Sumatra* (Sumatra's Eastcoast), Deventer, 1919–1922.

[1] See for instance for Flores: H. ten Dam, *Nita dan sekitarnja. Meninggikan kemakmuran dan masjarakat feodal* (Nita and surroundings. Feudal society and the advancement of welfare), a report of the Lembaga Penjelidikan Masjarakat Desa dan UsahaTani (Institute for rural sociological and farm-management research), Bogor, 1950, p. 29, 48 (Dutch edition); for Timor: J. D. N.Versluys, 'Maatschappelijke vernieuwing op Timor?', *loc. cit.*, p. 207.

E. J. A. Cosijn, *Beitrag zur Kenntnis der Arbeitszustände und der sozialen Massnahmen in Industrie und Gewerbe in Niederländisch-Ostindien*, Borna-Leipzig, 1934.

P. Endt, *Arbeiterverhältnisse in Niederländisch-Ost-Indien (mit besonderer Berücksichtigung von der Ostküste von Sumatra)*, Amsterdam, 1918.

The Indonesian town. Studies in urban sociology, Selected studies on Indonesia by Dutch scholars, Vol. IV, The Hague/Bandung, 1958.

P. de Kat Angelino, *Batikrapport. Rapport betreffende eene gehouden enquête naar de arbeidstoestanden in de batikkerijen op Java en Madoera* (Batik report. Report on an inquiry into the labour relations in the *batik* enterprises in Java and Madura), Weltevreden, 1930-1931.

G. H. van der Kolff, *The historical development of the labour relationships in a remote corner of Java as they apply to the cultivation of rice*, Batavia, 1937.

Bruno Lasker, *Human bondage in Southeast Asia*, Chapel Hill, 1950.

Living conditions of plantation workers and peasants of Java in 1939–1940, Translation Series, Modern Indonesia Project, Cornell University, Ithaca, 1956.

P. Levert, *Inheemsche arbeid in de Java suikerindustrie* (Native labour in the Java sugar industry), Wageningen, 1934.

W. Middendorp, *Twee achterlijke arbeidssystemen voor inboorlingen in Nederlandsch-Oost Indië* (Two backward labour systems for natives in the Netherlands East Indies), Haarlem, 1928.

Multatuli (E. Douwes Dekker), *Max Havelaar*, new edition, Amsterdam, 1949.

Multatuli, *Over vrije arbeid in Nederlandsch Oost Indië en de tegenwoordige koloniale agitatie* (About free labour in the Netherlands Indies and the present colonial agitation), Amsterdam, 1862.

Multatuli, *Nog eens: vrije arbeid in Nederlandsch-Indië* (Again: free labour in the Netherlands Indies), Delft, 1870.

'Penjelidikan biaja hidup di Djakarta' (Investigation of the cost of living in Jakarta), in *Ekonomi dan Keuangan Indonesia* (Economics and Finance in Indonesia), Vol. X, 1957, p. 738 ff.

A. H. Ruibing, *Ethnologische studie betreffende de Indonesische slavernij als maatschappelijk verschijnsel* (Ethnological study concerning the Indonesian slavery as a social phenomenon), Zutphen, 1937.

Virginia Thompson, *Labor problems in Southeast Asia*, New Haven, 1947.

J. D. N. Versluys, *Vormen en soorten van loon in den Indischen landbouw* (Forms and kinds of wages in the agriculture of the Indies), Leiden, 1938.

H. J. Wijnmalen, 'Aantekeningen betreffende het ontstaan, de ontwikkeling en het optreden van de vakbeweging in Indonesië na de onafhankelijkheidsverklaring van 17 Augustus 1945' (Notes on the origin, the development and the activities of the trade union movement in Indonesia since the declaration of independence of August 17th, 1945), in *Indonesië*, Vol. V, 1951/52, p. 434 ff., 539 ff.

Chapter Ten

Cultural Dynamics in Indonesia

1 Early Indonesian cultural patterns

Indonesia had already experienced a good deal of cultural development before the arrival of the first Dutch seafarers. Spiritual life in the archipelago had been intensely affected by some of the most elevated world-wide currents of thought, such as Buddhism, Hinduism and Islam. It was important that in these cultural contacts Indonesians had always played an active role.

It is a common delusion that foreigners have been the chief bearers of those currents of thought, culture and religion. A colonial prejudice designated Indians living in Indonesia as bearers of the Hindu and Buddhist cultures, while Arabs were considered as the foremost bearers of Moslem culture. The former prejudice in particular, which ascribed the great cultural achievements from the Hindu period, including the famous temple works of Borobudur, to Indians, appears to be very pertinacious. Even a present day scholar of the stature of Coedès seems to have difficulty in disengaging himself from the Greater India conception. Only a few years ago he wrote: 'Outer India did not enter history except in as far as it had been civilised by India'. Furthermore, he contends that the countries of Outer India (including, in his conception, Indo-China and Indonesia), owe all their patents of nobility to India. According to Coedès, the part played by Outer India with respect to Hindu culture, has been a 'purely receptive' one.[1]

Recent research has, however, demonstrated that Javanese

[1] G. Coedès, *Les états hindouisés d'Indochine et d'Indonésie*, Paris, 1948, p. 419.

played a very important and independent part in the acculturation process. The so-called 'Hindu-colonisation'[1] process is reduced, in the modern conception, to the presence at the Javanese courts of a comparatively small number of very influential Indian Brahmins, lending political support to Javanese rulers by providing them with a kind of investiture and with a genealogic confirmation of membership of a high caste, and acting at the same time as advisers in affairs of government and things sacral.[2]

Perhaps more influential still was the cultural impact of those rather numerous Indonesian pilgrims who came to the monasteries of the Asian mainland to study the mysteries and the scholastic sciences and, thus equipped with wisdom, were called to the courts of Java in order to fill prominent posts.[3]

One is, therefore, fully justified in considering the famous monuments of Indonesia as products mainly of an Indonesian civilisation. Beyond question, Indonesian civilisation, like that of Further India,[4] has throughout the centuries kept its peculiar

1 A concept, still accepted by Coedès (see *op. cit.* p. 45 ff.), in the wake of Krom and many others.

2 This conception is one of the most interesting ideas expounded on sociologic grounds in J. C. van Leur's *Indonesian trade and society. Essays in Asian social and economic history*, Selected studies on Indonesia by Dutch scholars, Vol. I, The Hague/Bandung, 1955, p. 103 ff., 167 ff., 250 ff. See further F. D. K. Bosch, *Het vraagstuk van de Hindoe-kolonisatie van den Archipel* (The problem of the Hindu colonisation of the archipelago), Leiden, 1946, p. 23/24.

3 Cf. F. D. K. Bosch, ''Local genius' en oud-Javaanse kunst' ('Local genius' and early Javanese art), in *Mededelingen der Koninklijke Nederlandse Akademie van Wetenschappen, Afdeling Letterkunde, Nieuwe reeks* (Communications of the Royal Netherlands Academy of Sciences, Literary Branch, New series), Vol. XV, 1952, Nr 1, p. 12 ff., which essay gives a critical review of the theories of H. G. Quaritch Wales. If Bosch's theory is to be accepted, the 'hundreds of Brahmins' noticed by Ma Juan Lin in the country of Tch'e-t'ou on the Malay Peninsula (cf. G. Coedès, *op. cit.*, p. 135) should be considered as mainly consisting of natives having performed a pilgrimage to the mainland, like the 1,000 Buddhist priests in Çriwijaya mentioned by I-tsing (G. Coedès, *op. cit.*, p. 142).

4 See for instance H. Marchal, *l'Architecture compareé dans l'Inde et l'Extrême Orient*, Paris, 1944, on Java, p. 196 ff.

character, because of the 'local genius' of the population, despite the strong cultural impulses derived from Hindustan.[1]

Early Indonesian culture was far from being a unity, however, several patterns being discernible within it. To a large extent these patterns were connected with the material foundations of society. In areas where shifting cultivation provided a basis for a subsistence economy and Indonesian tribes were living, consequently, in social groupings on genealogic lines, civilisation as it expressed itself in the arts of weaving, wood-carving, plaiting, forging, dancing, poetry and music, was preponderantly a popular culture. It was a civilisation narrowly linked with popular beliefs, magic and mythology, with the kinship structure and with the cyclic activities of agriculture, such as land-reclamation, tilling, sowing and harvesting. Yet, within this framework cultural diversity could extend very far, as is illustrated by the large number of languages, all of them belonging to the Indonesian stock, to be found on the scattered islands.

Areas where rice cultivation on irrigated fields was prevalent showed a quite different picture. Especially in those regions where large *sawah* complexes were to be found, a surplus of agricultural crops could be supplied making possible the maintenance of a principality with a bureaucratic apparatus. Moreover, *sawah* cultivation is an intensive form of land utilisation entailing high densities of population per cultivated area. Such populous areas permitted the establishment of strong administrations with sizable armies. Services exacted from the agrarian population ensured the construction not only of roads and irrigation works, but also of enormous temple works. Conversely, irrigation works and greater security provided by better communications fostered a more intensive rice field cultivation.

Thus, in *sawah* areas the territorial village communities were more often than not bound together under a central royal author-

[1] The active part, played by Indonesians in the process of acculturation, was equally stressed by Schrieke as early as 1927. See his *Indonesian sociological studies. Selected writings*, Part 1. Selected studies on Indonesia by Dutch scholars, Vol. II, The Hague/Bandung, 1955, p. 232 ff.

ity, residing in a *kraton* (court) city. This authority was represented in the various regions by officers, sometimes linked to the ruling dynasty by familial ties and trying to imitate the royal style as faithfully as possible.

It is not surprising, then, that in *sawah* regions, beside a popular culture, a court civilisation was also to be found, which sometimes dominated to the extent of suggesting an identity between this civilisation and the civilisation of the whole people. In Java in particular, attention was for many years all but exclusively directed to this court civilisation. The princes were the patrons of music and dance, temple building and goldsmith's art, *batik* weaving and literature. To a certain extent this court civilisation had penetrated to the common people as well. The *wayang* performances, accompanied by *gamelan* music, could always count upon an intense interest from the Javanese villagers.

Yet, a large portion of the court civilisation stood practically aloof from the popular culture. The poet laureate had hardly any interest in the life of the common people. From the court literature one may learn a good deal about the life of the ancient Indonesian courts, but little about that of the ordinary people.[1]

Hindu culture has left its deepest traces in this court atmosphere. Hindu influences are clearly distinguishable on Java and Bali, the centres of *sawah* cultivation and also the regions where throughout history large bureaucratic 'inland-states' were to be found.[2] This Hindu influence was, however, largely restricted to the sacral sphere, the bearers of Hindu culture being preponderantly Brahmins who had acquired high social positions and great prestige at the Javanese and Balinese courts.

It would be erroneous on the other hand, to consider the Indonesian court civilisation as Hindu import. Rather Indonesian society had to create conditions under which Hindu influences could operate. Possibilities for Brahmins to perform a social

[1] See C. C. Berg in F. W. Stapel (ed.), *Geschiedenis van Nederlandsch-Indië* (History of the Netherlands Indies), Amsterdam 1938-1940, Vol. II, p. 146.

[2] See for the political structure of ancient Bali V. E. Korn, *Het adatrecht van Bali* (The adat law of Bali), The Hague, 1932, p. 4ff., 10ff., 20ff.

function by using their bureaucratic schooling, their political experience and their knowledge of irrigation systems were dependent upon the existence of a society based on *sawah* cultivation and subjected to a fairly extensive princely authority. According to modern theory[1] those achievements in Indonesia pre-dated introduction of Hindu religion. It is understandable, therefore, that autochthonous elements continued to play a significant part in the Hinduised regions of the archipelago as well.

Beside the court sphere, however, the village remained a living source of Indonesian culture. As in *ladang* (shifting cultivation) areas, this popular culture was largely tied to myths and popular beliefs, to agriculture and crafts, to age-old *adats* (customs), and kinship relations, though in these *sawah* areas a social structure on a territorial basis had generally replaced a societal order on genealogical lines.

Certainly a link between court civilisation and popular culture existed. There has been a constant interaction between the two, each absorbing elements from the other.[2] First, the *mandalas* (autonomous estates under ecclesiastical authority, somewhat comparable to the West European medieval monasteries) may be mentioned as corporations occupying an intermediate position between both spheres. They were religious centres with a culture of their own and quite often stood in opposition to the official Brahmin priesthood which had put its imprint upon the Hinduised court civilisation.[3] Moreover, van Naerssen reckons among the *mandalas* also communities of handicraftsmen such as smiths, dyers and potters, representing quite clearly an intermediary

[1] Developed successively by such scholars as Brandes, Krom, Schrieke, Stutterheim, Bosch and van Leur.

[2] Th. Pigeaud, *Javaanse volksvertoningen. Bijdrage tot de beschrijving van land en volk* (Javanese folk performances. Contribution to the description of land and people), Batavia, 1938, p. 32 ff.

[3] See F. H. van Naerssen, *Culture contacts and social conflicts in Indonesia*, New York, 1947, p. 8 ff. See further Th. G. T. Pigeaud, *De Tantu Panggelaran. Een oud Javaansch prozaschrift, uitgegeven, vertaald en toegelicht* (The Tantu Panggelaran. An ancient Javanese prose scripture, edited, translated and commented), The Hague, 1924, p. 28 ff.

layer between the court sphere and the popular sphere. An important characteristic of all those communities is, according to van Naerssen, their tendency to retain the ancient Indonesian religion and *adat* and keep away from Hindu culture, contrasting with the prevailing attitude among court circles.

Looking for such connecting links one also thinks of the culture of early Indonesian cities. They were the gates connecting *ladang* areas as well as *sawah* areas with the outer world. Traders from the remotest corners of Asia brought their wares there, along with their customs and cultural peculiarities. It seems as if these centres would provide the greatest chance for a new urban culture to arise, as an intermediate culture between court and agrarian civilisations.

Still, the significance of this urban culture as a sphere apart should not be over-estimated. A new culture requires a social layer invested with substantial prestige. Even in the early Indonesian harbour cities such a social layer was lacking. These cities were almost completely dominated by the harbour princes with their retinue of relatives and officials, trade and handicrafts being carried on under sway of the aristocracy, assisted by a restricted patrician class mostly of foreign origin, which followed as much as possible the ways of the gentry.[1] The *kratons* were the most important customers of the handicraftsmen around the courts and of the trade goods from abroad. It was the aristocracy which put its hall-mark upon the urban culture. Foreign traders and artisans living in separate wards to a large extent kept their own culture, but a deeper penetration of these cultural elements into the life of broader masses of Indonesians was subject to many obstacles, unless the prince with his following (or a significant part of the aristocracy) had adopted these elements, thus lending it a certain prestige. This was the way cultural change could occur in a society based preponderantly on tradition, in which new elements could penetrate only if sanctified by those considered as the guardians of tradition. This was also the way new

[1] Cf. J. C. van Leur, *op. cit.*, p. 92, 133 ff., 137 ff., 201 ff.

technical inventions penetrated Eastern societies. Very often foreign merchants of standing, members of the urban patrician class, introduced usages and commodities from their own country at the Indonesian court. This dependence upon the whims of the court did not conduce to the rise of an independent urban culture.

Yet, the life of the harbour principalities was always more cosmopolitan, more open to outside influences, more lively than that of the large inland-states. This difference was emphasised, when it became connected with the new Islamic faith, imported by foreign traders. It is important to observe that the religion as such had already spread to broad layers of urban dwellers before it had attained the princely courts. Gradually a large number of cultural influences from the international world of Moslem traders and sailors, embodied in customs and tales, penetrated along the trade routes and were integrated into what Dr. Pigeaud calls the *Pasisir* civilisation.[1] In the long run, however, this culture was to lose its character of a civilisation apart from the main Javanese body, many elements of it later being absorbed either into the court civilisation of Central Java or into the popular culture of the Javanese. In this sense, the cultural influence of Islam has been greater on Java than is commonly assumed.[2]

But these developments were largely taking place at a time, when new influences from Europe were already working upon the Indonesian cultural patterns.

2 *European cultural influences*

Colonial historiography has devoted so much attention to the experiences of the handful of Western adventurers since the sixteenth century that one might easily believe the overall situation in Indonesia had drastically changed from that time. But the

[1] *Pasisir* – strand; often used for Java's north coast.

[2] Very enlightening thoughts about this *Pasisir* civilisation are to be found in Th. Pigeaud, *Javaanse volksvertoningen*, *op. cit.*, p. 52, 347 ff., 395 ff., 470 ff., 477 ff., and *passim*

notion that Europeans (Portuguese, Spaniards, Dutch and British) left an indelible mark on Indonesian society since that century, would be quite erroneous. The merchants from abroad got a chance to participate in the traditional Eastern trade, but their settlements, dispersed over the islands and dissociated for many years from Indonesian society, could hardly be said to radiate Western culture. This was partly due to the comparatively low esteem in which the European adventurers were held. Even when the Portuguese aimed consciously at spreading their religion among the surrounding population, they had largely to adapt themselves to cultural peculiarities of the Indonesians in order to achieve a measure of success. Just as the Portuguese language used in the South Asian port cities was a blend of Portuguese and Asian elements, Portuguese civilisation in those spots became a mixed culture.[1]

The Dutch did not escape this 'creolising' process either. During the first years of the Company's rule they attempted to create in the city of Batavia a counterpart of the Dutch towns. But the canals silted up, the stuffy two-storey dwellings along the canals proved to be breeding grounds for pollution and disease. Dutch bourgeois simplicity and frugality gave way to Eastern luxury and pomp as conditions for gaining prestige in an Asian country. Within the Company's settlement also a mixed culture came into existence which closely corresponded with that prevailing in Portuguese settlements on the Asian mainland. Descendants of Christian slaves freed by the Portuguese, and even the Portuguese language, became essential elements in the social structure of ancient Batavia.

Outside the Company's dispersed settlements along the coasts the impact of Western culture remained extremely small at first. Only after the Westerners' prestige rose could their cultural patterns exert some influence upon the Indonesian population. This process could be accelerated (as was generally the case with the

[1] A very colourful description of social life in Macao is provided by C. R. Boxer, *Fidalgos in the Far East, 1550–1770. Fact and fancy in the history of Macao*, The Hague, 1948, especially Chapters XIII ff.

penetration of new elements in Asia) if the princely court acting as intermediary paved the way. When the *Sunan* of Mataram deigned to wear a Dutch jacket and a feathered hat, the courtiers followed suit. From symptoms like these the enhanced prestige of the queer beings from the West could be deduced. But it was largely technical innovations in the fields of gun-foundry, gun-service and naval warfare which, through the intervention of Indonesian princes, found their way into the archipelago.

Even in the fields where adoption of cultural elements occurred, acculturation was mostly limited at this stage to externals. In Holland, England and the Hanseatic towns a bourgeois culture was flourishing, marked by an intense interest in all that was new, by a mercantile spirit of adventurous enterprise, by individualism and a high value attached to frugality and stern devotion to duty.

In order to take root in other parts of the world, however, this young bourgeois culture needed a fertile soil. This was to be found only where (as in the northern states of North America) an urban class of free citizens was present. If such a class was lacking, as was the case in Indonesia, the cultural transplanting would involve externals only, not the inner essential characteristics of European culture. Even Protestantism, as adopted by Indonesians, mainly in the Moluccas, distinguished itself most widely from the Western European pattern of thought. In a society not based upon individualism, where this faith could not get rooted in an independent urban bourgeoisie, nothing else could be expected. It is hardly surprising, then, if there were continuous complaints on the part of the Dutch about the impossibility of distracting the Ambonese from their ancient 'Satan's service and idolatry'.

Indonesian culture developed during the seventeenth and eighteenth century largely unaffected by the presence of the Dutch tradesmen. It was not merely the court civilisation at the Javanese *kratons*, which continued to flourish and even, in the slow tempo of the ancient Asian world, underwent certain innovations.[1]

[1] See J. C. van Leur, *op. cit.*, p. 278 ff.

Islamisation, which at that time in many regions had spread to the agrarian society as well, was also accompanied with a measure of renovation. Though at this stage it would be premature to call the *Pasisir* culture of Java's north coast an urban bourgeois culture, it did show the first beginnings of such a development. Contacts with the Islamic homeland, Arabia, led to an acquaintance with a sterner, more frugal manner of life than that of the harbour cities dominated by an aristocratic class. This sterner religious attitude was to prove, in the nineteenth century, to be a source of cultural rejuvenation as well.

Did cultural rejuvenation really occur in nineteenth century Indonesia? Certainly it did not dominate the picture. European superiority made itself clearly felt after 1800 in the archipelago as in other parts of Asia. Developments in Europe, such as the bourgeois revolution in France and the industrial revolution in England, enabled the European powers to establish a real colonial authority. This authority brought many economic innovations into being, the most remarkable consisting of intensive exploitation of the Indonesian labour force, particularly under the 'culture system' in 1830 and following years. But the social structure was artificially preserved by colonial policy in its original state.[1] In so far as there were movements of a bourgeois democratic character opposing the feudal structure of society (as for instance the *Padri* movement in Central Sumatra, which will subsequently be dealt with more extensively) they were resisted by the colonial regime and suppressed on behalf of the more pliable *adat* chiefs.

It is understandable that this social ossification led, in the cultural field, to a certain petrifaction as well. The Javanese princely dynasties saw that their real power (increasingly dependent on Dutch arms) still leaned upon their traditional authority only. They took refuge more and more in the ancient traditions and

[1] R. Kennedy once characterised the Dutch method as an anti-acculturation policy. Cited after A. I. Hallowell, 'Sociopsychological aspects of acculturation', in R. Linton (ed.), *The science of man in the world crisis*, New York, 1945, p. 187.

made an idol of them. During the second half of the nineteenth century the Javanese court civilisation had, indeed, become well-nigh static, and the whole feudal structure had degenerated into a dead weight.[1]

However, among the masses very few signs of cultural renovation were discernible either. The general reaction of Indonesians towards the new things from the West was one of avoidance, of a flight into isolation and magic.

Not unnaturally this period of cultural stagnation or decline was also a period when Westerners held Indonesian culture in low esteem. The colonial spirit led to rating all things 'native' as inferior. Though the impressive temple works were visible testimony of a high cultural level in the remote past, the colonisers tended to ascribe them to strangers (Indians) in order to be able to maintain the colonial myth of the 'primitive' Javanese.[2]

Clear signs of this colonial underrating of Javanese culture are still to be found in the second edition of the Encyclopaedia of the Netherlands Indies, under the heading *Javanese*.[3] The famous refined and highly developed Javanese *gamelan* music is lightly dismissed in the following terms: 'The music stands on a rather low level of development and to a degree only deserves the title of musical art.'

Still, some cultural developments did take place during the nineteenth century, though mainly in the most dynamic social layer of Indonesia, among the European group and their mixed-blood descendants.

Even during the Company's period a new mestizo culture had already appeared in the urban settlements. In the course of the nineteenth century this culture achieved its definite form among the European settlers in the colony. It was accompanied by the

[1] However, van Leur does not consider the static character of Javanese court culture a sign of decline. See *op. cit.*, p. 279.

[2] F. D. K. Bosch, *Het vraagstuk van de Hindoe-kolonisatie van den Archipel* (*op. cit.*), p. 5 ff.

[3] *Encyclopaedie van Nederlandsch-Indië* (Encyclopaedia of the Netherlands Indies), The Hague/Leiden, 1917–1939, Vol. II, p. 219, *sub voce* „Javanen".

open, spacious building style which had come into existence at the beginning of the century. The peculiarities of this typically urban mestizo culture have already been described in Chapter VII on *Urban Development*, but it was not restricted to the Europeans, of pure and mixed ancestry, in the colony. It spread, gradually, to those Indonesians and Indonesian Chinese, who were also part of the urban upper and middle class. Moreover, it was not confined to the cities. When, with the admission of private capital into Indonesia after the 'agrarian legislation' of the eighteen seventies, an increasing number of European planters settled in the country, cultivating a mode of living, which aimed at attaining a prestige at least equal to that of the *pryayi* class, they became the bearers *par excellence* of this mestizo culture. The large, roomy mansions of the planters at the start of this century became the centres where 'Indian' hospitality, receptions and dances, and the usual gentlemanly pastimes such as hunting and horsemanship were most widely practised.

The reaction of Indonesian society to the cultural influences from the West was by no means entirely passive. Though the nineteenth century may generally be considered from an Indonesian point of view as one of cultural stagnancy and petrifaction, it is still possible in retrospect to detect several forerunners of dynamic twentieth century developments.

The gradual growth of an urban bourgeois culture rooted in Islamic religion has already been noted. *Wahhabite* and related currents opposing the luxury and prodigality among the ruling class, had penetrated into Indonesia. Notably the *Padri* movement in Central Sumatra represented a trend of thought aiming at a purification of Islam from several admixtures and superstitions which were deeply rooted in Indonesian society. To some extent this movement could be considered a reaction of the newly Islamised agrarian areas upon luxury and laxity in the coastal towns under aristocratic rule. But there were also some elements of a new, sober, urban mode of living, which could be considered as forerunners of a bourgeois Islam (already dealt with in Chapter VIII on *Religious Reform*). It is important to note, in this context, that Pigeaud also mentions in connection with the Arabising tendencies, the rise of an urban and semi-urban middle class along the north coast of Java.[1]

Direct adoption of Western cultural elements by Indonesians should not be under-estimated. Especially among Javanese *pryayis* Western civilisation had penetrated deeper than is commonly admitted, perhaps the outstanding example of this being the personality of the regent of Sumenep (Madura), Panembahan Noto Kusomo, who was subsequently granted the name and title of Paku Nataningrat, Sultan of Sumenep. This man, described with so much sympathy and colourful detail by van Hoëvell,[2] did not only read Dutch and English, but had also been nominated as a member of the Batavian Society of Arts and Sciences on account of his services to Western science. Both Thomas Stamford Raffles and Wilhelm von Humboldt owed much of their knowledge of Javanese language, history and people, to the personal information supplied by this Indonesian *pryayi*.

The nineteenth century witnessed a steady growth of the number of Indonesian *pryayis*, especially among the younger ones, who had enjoyed a Western education and gave proof of being able adequately to absorb Western culture. Well-to-do Javanese were influenced not only in their external mode of living by the mestizo culture; their spiritual life was also affected by the Western impact. A phenomenon such as the young regent's daughter Raden Adjeng Kartini, who, at the end of the past century, wrote articles about Indonesian art and culture in fluent Dutch and kept up correspondence with prominent Dutchmen, was symptomatic of the trend. The artificial isolation of the colonial European upper layer of society from the life of the Indonesians concealed the degree to which Indonesians had been affected by the West, with the result that the publication,

[1] Th. Pigeaud, *op. cit.*, p. 141 ff.

[2] W. R. van Hoëvell, *Reis over Java, Madura en Bali in het midden van 1847* (Journey through Java, Madura and Bali in the middle of 1847), Amsterdam, 1849–1854, Vol. II, p. 50 ff.

in 1911, of the letters of the late Kartini,[1] came as a surprise. Upon closer scrutiny it appears, however, that in those years Western culture had already penetrated Indonesian society far more deeply than most people realised. The stormy developments of the early decades of this century thus appear as only an acceleration of a process already started during the previous century.

In this connection it is not quite correct in considering the cultural achievements of Indonesians, to think only of those with the legal status of '*Inlander*' (native). The incorporation of the so-called Indo-Europeans with the Europeans and of the Indonesian Chinese with the Foreign Orientals was quite arbitrary. In a country such as the Philippines, where no sharp division exists between mixed-bloods and Filipinos, the cultural achievements of Mestizos are ascribed without any reserve to the Filipino population. Since the Indo-Europeans in Indonesia were the first group to receive Western education on a large scale about the middle of the preceding century,[2] and since most of the Indonesian *pryayi* children and considerable numbers of Christian Indonesians were provided educational facilities only a few decades later, it naturally took some time before there could be any question of extensive adaptation to Western civilisation among Indonesians proper.

For the rest, it is most important that this adaptation was not confined to taking over cultural elements borrowed from the West, but that Indonesians sometimes reacted with creative cultural achievements as well. A striking example of this is to be found in the reaction in Java, about the middle of the century, to the inflow of Western industrial mass produced goods. The traditional Javanese *batik* industry was seriously threatened by this development, but at the right moment the invention was

[1] English translation: Raden Adjeng Kartini, *Letters of a Javanese princess*, London, 1921.

[2] See I. J. Brugmans, *Geschiedenis van het onderwijs in Nederlandsch-Indië* (History of education in the Netherlands Indies), Groningen/Batavia, 1938, p. 147 ff.

made, we do not know exactly by whom and when, of stencilling *batik* patterns in wax. Whether the invention was made by a Javanese, an Indonesian Chinese, an Indo-European, or an Indian, the important thing is that the new process spread very rapidly over the *batik* centres of Java and enabled the Javanese *batik* industry to restrict the Western mass import by countering it by a home production on a mass scale.[1]

More thorough scrutiny of nineteenth century history would probably reveal far more instances of a positive cultural adaptation in that period.

3 Cultural revival

The rapid changes which took place in Indonesian society since the beginning of this century were bound to reflect themselves in the cultural sphere. The great prestige the West had acquired throughout the East by its technical superiority meant that cultural activity of the young Indonesians was directed first to imitating as quickly as possible the Western cultural pattern, in the hope of making up the lag. Rapid Westernisation thus began among the upper stratum of the Indonesians. This process was fostered by the steady extension of Western or Westernised education, for the youth of the urban bourgeoisie in particular. The younger Indonesians borrowed much, both in their outward behaviour and in their spiritual life, from the Western mode of living. Rationalism, individualism, and even despite criticism by the Europeans and their own elders, freedom of speech, were assimilated by the Indonesian youth with an ease which was sometimes surprising. Imitation often went so far that mastery of the Dutch language, besides a knowledge of Western manners, was considered a sign of high social prestige, partly because this knowledge naturally opened the gates for all better salaried posts both in governments service and in private enterprise.

[1] See G. P. Rouffaer and H. H. Juynboll, *De batikkunst in Nederlandsch-Indië en haar geschiedenis* (The art of *batik* in the Netherlands Indies and its history), Utrecht, 1914, Text, p. 529 ff.

Attempts to imitate the Westerners was not confined to the upper layer of Indonesians. The extension of popular education was only one of the factors acquainting the Indonesian peasants and labourers to a certain degree with European habits, and perhaps not even the most typical ones. The increasing numbers of Europeans, who appeared also in the countryside, Western advertising pictures, and later the cinema, created models which proved attractive, especially to the youth. European dress, a fountain pen, horn-rimmed spectacles and gold teeth became symbols of distinction, as did sports, just as favourite a pastime of the youth in Indonesia as elsewhere. Nor did women and girls lag behind in their efforts at Westernisation. As education had carried Western culture within reach of many girls, Western habits of life and ideas of marriage and morality penetrated ever deeper into Indonesian society. The usual conflict between generations arose because the older people often preferred their traditional ways.

Nevertheless this process of borrowing was not pure Westernisation. For large sections of the population the external behaviour of Europeans living in Indonesia provided the only basis of knowledge of the West. As we have seen, the culture represented by the European group in nineteenth century Indonesia was not a pure Western civilisation, but rather a blend, a kind of mestizo culture. The pattern of behaviour adopted by the Indonesians from the Europeans thus also carried many pecularities of this mestizo culture. Precisely at a time when an increasing group of European new-comers was developing a new way of life, less 'Indian', more directed towards the creation of a counterpart of Dutch society in miniature, mestizo culture began to make headway among non-European groups.

This is easy to explain if one takes account of the fact that Western culture has come to development in a given social environment providing a fertile soil for it. In Indonesian society as it was developing in the first half of this century there was hardly room for several Western cultural elements, while others could take root only in a greatly modified form.

Even the Dutch, born in a European environment, succeeded only to a limited degree in carrying European civilisation to the Indies. It was possible, of course, to apply to Indonesia Western principles of science and technique, modern management, social and statistical research. Under the spur of imperial expansion these elements from Western civilisation flourished no less than in the home country and sometimes even more. The achievements of Western scientists in laboratories and institutes in Indonesia often equalled or surpassed scientific successes in the Western world.[1] But is was far more difficult to integrate such elements into a whole comparable with Western society. The social constellation which gave the immigrant Europeans in Indonesia the position of an upper layer in very easy circumstances, according to Western standards, influenced its cultural situation appreciably. The availability of a number of servants which was, despite its decline, still impressive, the habit of commanding and being obeyed, the desire to maintain the prestige of the whites, the susceptibility to fatigue in the tropical climate and the ensuing craving for cheap distraction, coupled with rather ample means, all these things together condemned the attempts of this group to build for themselves a second Europe to failure. At best they could imitate only a quite limited part of Europe: the prosperous villa parks in the environment of The Hague or Amsterdam, such as Wassenaar and Bussum.

It was even more difficult for the Indo-Europeans, Indonesian Chinese and the Indonesians, who had not experienced true European life in their youth, to appropriate Western culture in its pure form. Their life was still dominated by the feudal environment in Indonesia, where many among them still formed a kind of gentry elite towering above the masses and possessing a certain social ascendancy over the peasantry. For a long time feudal tradition remained a brake upon large scale Westernisation. This was not only true of the older *pryayis*, who strongly

[1] For a survey of scientific activities, see P. Honig and F. Verdoorn (ed.), *Science and scientists in the Netherlands Indies*, New York, 1945.

resisted the destruction of traditional ways and the introduction of modern ways of life (as Kartini and Achmad Djajadiningrat experienced in their youth with great sorrow). Even among those who were sympathetic towards Western influences the feudal tradition led to a contempt for manual labour and sometimes even for everything concerning tools and technology. Thus, the paradox arises that, while Western science was considered a means for catching up in the technical field, when it came to choosing a career, the Indonesian youth had a distinct preference for studies of a purely intellectual character, such as law. It was also noteworthy that among those who had chosen a technical education, for instance those who had attended an agricultural school, there were many who finally embarked upon a clerical career affording them a higher prestige than handling tools.[1]

In general there was often a stronger tendency to adopt in the easiest possible way the achievements of Western civilisation than to retrace laboriously the path Western society had followed to attain those results.

It is remarkable, however, that Western educated Indonesians were in some respects more Western minded than Indo-Europeans who stressed their European status. For the latter this status meant primarily being a part of an upper layer in the social hierarchy and thus enjoying a special prestige. Consequently their mental outlook was preponderantly conservative and those Western currents of thought which embodied some kind of social discontent thus remained a closed book to most of them. It was quite different with some of the younger educated Indonesians, their social grievances making them accessible to aspects of European culture which embodied a protest against the prevailing conditions. European literature on nationalism and socialism found a ready market among them.

Here we have a factor which has come to play an increasing role in the Indonesian cultural revival, namely a protest against

[1] Cf. J. S. Furnivall, *Colonial policy and practice. A comparative study of Burma and Netherlands India*, Cambridge, 1948, p. 381 ff.

influences from the West, which was sometimes coupled in a strange way with a tendency to imitate that very West. This protest could assume manifold shapes, and often presented itself in disguise. But it was always an attempt to maintain, in adopting the new cultural dynamics, some elements from the Indonesian culture, or at least to bypass, in borrowing Western cultural elements, the intermediary of the Netherlands, the colonial power.

To begin with the latter phenomenon, it was among the most gifted Indonesians that a tendency developed to turn directly to the sources of civilisation without making use of Dutch channels. Even Sjahrir, who was always considered by his co-nationalists a 'Hollando-phile',[1] writes that the American attitudes and feelings as expressed in art and literature are 'closer to us in Indonesia' than the questions occupying Dutch authors.[2] The novelist Mrs. Soewarsih Djojopoespito is much more outspoken, when she makes the chief character of her novel[3] say: 'To speak the truth, I think Dutch literature is dull, that is to say, at the moment I have no mind for it. There is so little movement in that country, all things are slow and heavy, solid and tedious... I am swearing now by foreign literature.'

But the protest against colonial rule often also took the shape of an attempt to keep elements of the indigenous cultural values intact in the face of the assault from the West. Soon after the turn of the century a movement started in Indonesia which had the character of a Moslem revival. In Chapter VIII on *Religious Reform* this current, which was mainly embodied in the *Muhammadyah* movement, has been discussed. Here it deserves mention that this movement was an attempt to modernise the way of thinking and the mode of living without at the same time abandoning the religious basis of Islamic faith. The urge for Westernisation had threatened to drive Islam into the back-

[1] Soetan Sjahrir, *Out of exile*, New York, 1949, p. 85.

[2] S. Sjahrir, *op. cit.*, p. 151 ff.

[3] Soewarsih Djojopoespito, *Buiten het gareel* (Out of harness), Utrecht, 1946, p. 169 ff.

ground. But for the urban *petite bourgeoisie* of Indonesia Islam had been one of the main forms in which they had been able to maintain something of their spiritual independence against the Westerners. It was understandable, therefore, that especially among the less prominent urban bourgeoisie, where Islam had always remained (in contrast with the *pryayi* world) a living spiritual asset, there began a tendency to accomplish the desired renovation within Islam rather than outside it. To that extent this reform movement may be considered a protest against Westernisation.

In the same way this antithetic form of acculturation which (though adopting Western cultural elements) was still directed against the main bearers of Western civilisation (the Dutch), made itself felt in the field of language. The tendency to stress knowledge of Dutch as a requirement to a rise in the social scale, was countered by a new tendency to develop the indigenous languages as a vehicle for modern thought. The great diversity of languages in Indonesia proved to be a problem in appearance only. The regional languages were never seriously pushed as competitors of Dutch. The most important of these regional languages (Javanese) was too much tainted with a feudal background to fulfil this function. The divergence within this language between ceremonial and common terms for the same objects had developed to such lengths that even Javanese often preferred to make use of a more modern and democratic vehicle.[1] No wonder, then, that Malay, which had already fulfilled so many different intermediary functions in the past, was now assigned the task of furnishing the main bulk of a modern Indonesian language

[1] It is often contended that Javanese consists of two or even more entirely different 'languages', one of them used in speech to superiors, the other one to inferiors (see for example Mrs. Hurustiati Subandrio, *Javanese peasant life. Villages in East Java.* Unpublished thesis, London University, 1951, p. 59; and W. I. Thomas, *Primitive behavior. An introduction to the social sciences,* New York, 1937, p. 84). This seems, however, to be quite an erroneous notion. See E. M. Uhlenbeck, *De tegenstelling Krama: Ngoko. Haar positie in het Javaanse taalsysteem* (The contrast Krama: Ngoko. Its place in the Javanese language system), Groningen/Jakarta, 1950.

which had to be created. At any rate, Malay had the advantage of being, through its affinity to the regional tongues, much easier to learn for Indonesians than any Western language. But at the same time the effort to develop a national language satisfied the ever-growing national feelings.

As pointed out in Chapter VII on *Urban Development*, the use of the Indonesian language remained, for the time being, largely confined to the urban areas. It became primarily a means of understanding, orally and in writing, between those city dwellers from different regions of the archipelago who had enjoyed a measure of Western education.

The newly-created language had to serve as an indigenous means of expression for thoughts of Western origin. But it was not bound to remain solely a medium for communicating concrete knowledge and abstract science. The Indonesian language had also to serve as an auxiliary for the creation of an Indonesian literature. This literature, however, confronted its creators with many problems. As a rule the theme was, of course, borrowed from the Indonesian scene, but in treating the subject Western models were followed. During the thirties several authors exerted themselves, in a somewhat strained way, to approximate standards of international literature as nearly as possible. This ambition stood, in particular, in the forefront among the group of Sumatran writers editing the magazine '*Poedjangga Baroe*' (The New Poet). Nearly all the novels had some modernist purpose. European conceptions on freedom of marriage, individualism and human value were set as ideals against the conservatism prevailing in Indonesian society.

It was, however, precisely the admiration, often uncritical, for the Western spirit and an overacted social purpose which formed the weakness of so many products of modern Indonesian literature. The language was being moulded into an instrument of intense expressive power, but as long as Indonesian authors had no message but a copy of the Western pattern, the most essential element of a cultural revival was lacking.

Moreover, paradoxical as it may sound, even this tendency to absorb Western culture completely has something of a protest against the West in it. It had been Western policy to keep the original Indonesian cultures intact as far as possible. Though the economic forces set in motion by Western rule had uprooted a good deal of old customs and traditions, and Western education had contributed to the crumbling of the ancient world, the professed aim of the government had been not to interfere with Indonesian culture if it could avoid it. In practice the Dutch policy of keeping the *adat* (customary law) intact had, despite the efforts of some scholars to confer upon the concept of *adat* law a more dynamic sense, a tendency towards conservatism.[1] This, combined with the traditional Dutch policy of maintaining the feudal order of society and propping up the traditional *adat* chiefs,[2] provoked among several Western educated Indonesians a reaction asking for a more complete Westernisation.[3] In their eyes the Dutch policy aimed at keeping the Indonesian population in a kind of antiquated preserve, hoping thus to prevent them from a full participation in the modern world's evolution, both economically and spiritually. Their craving for Western civilisation embodied a protest against both the feudal and the colonial order, which were seen as forces keeping the Indonesian population in backwardness.

Westernisation was thus accompanied by a loss of many cultural values from the past, more particularly those connected with the

[1] See for example B. ter Haar, *Adat Law in Indonesia*, New York, 1948, p. 228 ff. For a criticism of the official *adat* policy see Harry J. Benda, *The Crescent and the Rising Sun. Indonesian Islam under the Japanese occupation 1942–1945*, The Hague/Bandung, 1958, p. 68.

[2] See for example H. Bouman, *Enige beschouwingen over de ontwikkeling van het Indonesisch nationalisme op Sumatra's Westkust* (Some observations regarding the development of Indonesian nationalism on the Westcoast of Sumatra), Groningen/Jakarta, 1949, p. 33 ff.; J. M. Pluvier, *Overzicht van de ontwikkeling der nationalistische beweging in Indonesië in de jaren 1930 tot 1942* (Outline of the development of the nationalist movement in Indonesia 1930–1942), The Hague/Bandung, 1953, p. 15, 79 ff.

[3] The anti-traditional attitude among several young Indonesians found vivid expression in Sjahrir's pre-war letters (see *op. cit., passim*; see also A. D. A. de Kat Angelino, *Colonial policy*, Amsterdam/Chicago, 1931, Vol. I, p. 480).

aristocratic order of society. As we have seen, the urban lower middle class had for years already drifted away from the Javanese court civilisation. It was no longer Javanese *gamelan* nor Javanese *wayang* performances that interested them. The cultural sphere, in which they were living, had become an amalgam which later received many impulses from the West or, more correctly, from the mestizo culture typical of the urban upper class. This new urban culture *in statu nascendi* is decidedly less refined than the court civilisation, which it is replacing. Though it looks comparatively vulgar and unattractive, it is still an expanding culture, which, together with the Indonesian language, is quickly spreading to the urban lower classes and to parts of the agrarian population as well.[1] It seems almost certain, that a new, integrated Indonesian culture will originate largely from these clumsy but vital beginnings.

On the other hand, feudal culture, and, in particular, the age-old Javanese court civilisation is rapidly decaying. Before the war it was already fossilised, and was losing its attraction for large groups, especially the city people. But popular culture was also withering away in large areas. The importation of cheap Western mass products threatened completely to oust the skilled products of popular arts and crafts. In regions, where Christian missions were active, folk songs and dances, which in the eyes of the missionaries had a pagan bearing, were losing ground, as were traditional popular costumes too.[2] All those cultural assets were rapidly giving way to cheap imitations of what was taken for Western culture. It should be added, that the poorer part of the population very often adopted among the cultural elements derived from the West merely the most rubbishy and cheapest things in the craze for modernity. Among the intellectuals there were some, like Sjahrir, who followed the best Western examples,

[1] See Th. Pigeaud, *op. cit.*, p. 34 ff.

[2] See for example J. Kunst, *De inheemsche muziek en de zending* (The native music and the mission), Amsterdam, 1947; H. Th. Fischer, *Zending en volksleven in Nederlandsch-Indië* (Mission and folk life in the Netherlands Indies), Zwolle, 1932, p. 144 ff.

though a large (and since the war increasing) part of the educated youth decidedly prefers the 'penny-dreadfuls' edited in Sumatra's Eastcoast Residency.[1] The common people, however, were forced, either by lack of means or lack of judgment to content themselves with the most vulgar products of Western culture.

This development was also likely to bring a reaction. The uncritical admiration of many Indonesians for the West was resented by others. Political criticism of the Western world strongly stimulated by World War I, and in particular by objections against colonial rule, was bound to result in a criticism of Western culture as well, or at least some elements of it. Just as strict Moslems wished to accept new cultural values without losing their spiritual heritage, a tendency arose to preserve the valuable elements within the national culture. This tendency to warn that a too slavish imitation of the West will bring only unhappiness, is already discernible in the pre-war Indonesian literature.

A positive trend to build a national culture by preserving the valuable assets of the past and the adoption of new elements in a selective way only is to be found in the *Taman Siswa*[2] educational movement. This organisation owed its birth to the fascinating personality of Ki Hadjar Dewantoro, known in the initial period of Indonesian nationalism as Soewardi Soerjaningrat. The aim of this movement was to provide education on a national Indonesian foundation and thus make the youth grow up in a harmonious atmosphere. The aim was to give attention to a full development of all faculties of heart and mind and awaken among the Indonesian youth a consciousness of their place and task in the world they were living in. In contrast with the literary *Poedjangga Baroe* movement (which fought for a national language only,

[1] See the enlightening article of R. Roolvink, 'De Indonesiase 'dubbeltjesroman'' (The Indonesian penny novel), in *Bingkisan Budi* (The mental gift. Collection of articles presented to Dr. P. S. van Ronkel), Leiden, 1950, p. 255 ff.

[2] *Taman Siswa* – Garden of Pupils.

but aimed with respect to the cultural content at Westernisation) the *Taman Siswa* attempted to give education as such a more national character. The origin of the movement in Jogjakarta gave it an obvious Javanese flavour. During the first years stress was also laid upon the use of the Javanese language, the practice of Javanese dances, Javanese songs and Javanese arts. But this does not mean that the movement aimed at a Javanese regionalism. From its inception Malay played a part in the instruction as an inter-insular language, and in later years the unified Indonesian language was consciously adopted as a vehicle for the *Taman Siswa* instruction as well. Dewantoro opposed any local chauvinism, such as a tendency among some teachers to introduce Javanese dances at the *Taman Siswa* school in Macassar.[1]

The *Taman Siswa* movement was bound to render essential services as an expression of a desire for cultural independence parallel with the struggle for political independence. In the political arena of the thirties the struggle for national education had a very important function. The refusal of the *Taman Siswa* to accept any governmental subsidy which would imply that their schools would be equated with governmental schools and, on the other hand, the opposition, under Dewantoro's leadership, to the establishment of preventive governmental supervision was one of the most remarkable aspects of the national struggle in those years.[2]

Whatever complaints might be made about the intellectual level of the instruction given at the *Taman Siswa* schools, for which unqualified personnel was partly used, it has no doubt fulfilled an important function in personality building, if only by providing an alternative to the race for governmental jobs and the prestige of the knowledge of Dutch connected with it.

Yet the problem of building a national Indonesian culture has hardly been solved by the *Taman Siswa* movement. It was too much of a reaction against the over-admiration for the West on

[1] W. le Fèbre, *Taman Siswa, ialah kepertjajaan kepada kekuatan sendiri untuk tumbuh...* (*Taman Siswa*, representing the trust in one's own capacity for development...), Jakarta/Surabaya, 1952, p. 44.

[2] See J. M. Pluvier, *op. cit.*, p. 52 ff.

the part of others to be able to achieve such a synthesis. The search, among the relics of a glorious Javanese past, for cultural values to be preserved, was in practice often no less strained than the imitation of the West among the opponents centred around the *Poedjangga Baroe* club. It is true that the values elected from the past were mostly those adapted to the modern era. Moreover, the *Taman Siswa* was also open to influences from without, if only they did not originate in the West, but, for example, in India or Japan. On the other hand, if the past was too much stressed, the danger arose that a mental attitude of self-sufficiency would come into existence, of isolation from the dynamic developments outside the Indonesian cultural sphere.[1]

We may conclude, therefore, that the mixture of acceptance of Western civilisation with a struggle for the preservation of the own could assume manifold forms, and quite often forms different from those consciously aimed at. If anything in human history is difficult to mould within planned patterns, it is cultural dynamics.

4 The struggle for a cultural reintegration

Developments during the Japanese occupation were still more paradoxical. One of the aims of the Japanese was to tear the Indonesians loose from all ties with Western civilisation. But the consequence of their rule of over three years was that significant groups of Indonesians were more Westernised than ever before. First of all, there were a number among the younger people, from the circles of more or less Westernised intellectuals who, during the later years of occupation, rather than attending public manifestations staged by the Japanese, preferred to retire into isolation and to compensate for the lack of higher educational facilities through self-study and self-education. One of the most remarkable results is, that precisely during the years of Japanese occupation Western music and painting got a number of enthusiastic students

[1] See the interesting analysis by le Fèbre, *op. cit.*

among the younger Indonesians and Indonesian Chinese. Moreover, through their active cultural policy which embodied material support for several arts, the Japanese unwittingly fostered Westernisation, often because they did not realise how far they themselves had absorbed many Western cultural elements within their national way of life. Another reason was that through lack of capable personnel they were often unable to supervise Indonesian cultural activities sufficiently, with the result that the younger Indonesian artists moved in directions the Japanese could hardly have meant to foster. In addition, the crude manner in which the Japanese often pushed the ancient Indonesian *adat* aside to replace it by their own cultural manifestations could, under certain circumstances, make some Indonesians, even among the common people, more sympathetic to modern Western cultural factors.

Nor should the Japanese occupation be considered a purely negative period with respect to other cultural fields. In the linguistic field the Japanese, to a far greater degree than the Dutch had ever done, stimulated the use and the development of the Indonesian national language. Their attempt to arouse the rural population to their war effort resulted in the penetration of their propaganda, carried on in Indonesian, even into the villages. Neither is the balance of the Japanese occupation quite negative as to the spread of instruction. A serious decline in the level of higher instruction and of educational facilities in this field were counterbalanced by quantitative expansion of popular education. It would be naive, it is true, to take at face value the official extension of primary instruction (which under Dutch rule, as far as the mass of the population was concerned, had never exceeded a three year term) to a period of six years. Probably this regulation was brought into practice on an appreciable scale in the cities only. The official statistics as to the number of children attending school, in comparison with the pre-war situation, are rather contradictory. Yet, illiteracy, which at the 1930 census still had amounted to over 90 per cent of all Indonesians, was somewhat reduced during the Japanese occupation. An intensive wartime propaganda required a population able to read what is written. In the field of technical and agricultural education the Japanese also brought some positive achievements.[1]

On the other hand, a very unpleasant feature of Japanese policy was that *Taman Siswa* instruction was suspected on account of its nationalist character, and accordingly impeded. A good deal of Indonesian educational activity was carried on illegally in those years.

In the literary field, the most remarkable developments did not occur primarily in the official sphere of the *Pusat Kebudajaan* (Cultural Centre) but rather underground. It was the illegal literary activities of a number of young authors which developed into the prominent artistic school of thought of the revolutionary days, one of the foremost leaders being the poet Chairil Anwar. This group was afterwards called 'the generation of 1945'.[2]

In those years the foremost representatives of Indonesian culture underwent a feverish inner evolution. Revolutionary activity, the struggle against the British and the Dutch, participation in guerrilla fighting, not only provided subject-matter, but this bitter, strenuous life also contributed to an accelerated maturation process, to a more intense experience of life and a more direct expression of it. There was less talk about following of Western examples and about attempts to comply with international standards. But the technique of expression within the new vehicle, the Indonesian language, and the mastery of the new literary forms, such as novels, short stories and verses, was growing, with the result that these standards were more easily approximated by the most gifted authors among the 'young generation' than the somewhat stiff and constrained pre-war products had

[1] See A. A. Zorab, *De Japanese bezetting van Indonesië en haar volkenrechtelijke zijde* (The Japanese occupation of Indonesia and its international law aspect), Leiden, 1954, p. 102.

[2] See James S. Holmes, 'Angkatan Muda' (The young generation). A checklist of writings in Western language translation, in *Indonesië*, Vol. V, 1951/52, p. 462 ff.

ever been able to achieve. As is generally the case with the second generation, these young people mastered the best products of world literature with an ease, that seemed presumptuous to the older generation which had accomplished the conquest at so great pains.

But the balance of the revolution was not merely positive. The ambiguous character of a revolution, which achieved its national aims only, but failed in its social ends, put its hall-mark upon spiritual life as well. Precisely those who most intensely felt the failure of too high-pitched expectations to materialise were bound to experience a deeper revulsion. Indonesian literature of recent years reflects with an increasing obviousness the frustration among many Indonesian young men and women. This frustration expresses itself in despair, cynism or in a flight into an extreme individualism and subjectivism.

Products from world literature bearing witness to a spirit of *fin de siècle* or of a bourgeois culture in decay found an avid acceptance. It appears that the leading literary circles in Indonesia represent a restricted urban bourgeois group which has got stuck socially and sees no way out. Political and social impotence are reflected in the field of culture as well.

The formation of a national Indonesian culture would seem to be still in its beginnings. It is very far from a new crystallised way of life. However many cultural congresses may be held, with however much stress it may be declared officially that the *Pantja Sila* (the five fundamental principles)[1] will henceforth form the philosophical basis of Indonesian society, real cultural developments refuse to follow officially prescribed ways and keep moving in accordance with social developments. Those developments in the social field are not very conducive to the birth of a homogeneous culture rooted in the mass of the people. Even the remarkable evolution of painting and sculpture on Bali during the thirties,[2] which showed several traits of a true cultural renascence,

[1] The five principles are: 1 Belief in one God, 2 Respect for human values, 3 Democracy, 4 Social justice, 5 Nationalism.

[2] See Miguel Covarrubias, *Island of Bali*, New York, 1937, p. 186.

of a harmonious blend of old with new, did not develop, according to some observers, into an art of the Balinese people themselves. However, John Coast greatly exaggerates when he states that this art is now being produced exclusively for the tourist trade.[1] According to other experts, modern Balinese art is flourishing as ever, though, as was to be expected, much rubbish is being produced beside the real art created by Balinese artists.[2] But for other areas the situation is still less satisfying.

At the moment the picture conveyed by the state of Indonesian culture is largely one of disintegration. The crumbling of ancient forms of court civilisation and popular culture has, like the crumbling of early social institutions, proceeded much farther than before the war. This process cannot be much altered by an artificial attempt to make old cultural values revive under the slogan of 'national culture'.

The cultural disintegration is also closely connected with the disintegrated state of society, of urban society in particular. The various strata of urban society each possess their own way of life, more or less influenced by Westernisation, and particularly since the war by Americanisation, through such means of communication as the cinema and radio. Mestizo culture is no longer decisive for the whole society, but it still exerts a good deal of influence among large groups of urban dwellers. Indonesian small merchants, mostly observing Moslem rites in a rather strict manner, form a remarkable social layer with a way of life of their own. Their significance in the total frame of urban society is, however, not sufficient to speak of the birth of a typical bourgeois atmosphere in the Indonesian cities. One of the main reasons is that economic life in modern Asian cities is not dominated by small enterprise, but by large corporations, often of a monopolistic nature, and by a much expanded officialdom. Far more numerous than the Indonesian small traders are the members of a

[1] John Coast, 'The clash of cultures in Bali', in *Pacific Affairs*, Vol. XXIV, 1951, p. 403.

[2] See for example Jef Last, *Bali in de kentering* (Bali in transition), Amsterdam, 1955, p. 146 ff.

'dependent middle class', employed by government agencies or by business. And it appears that these people are still vainly trying to put old and new together, and to build from the bits of court civilisation, popular culture, mestizo culture and Western elements something of a new Indonesian culture.

Nor have the revolutionary processes produced a harmonious cultural interaction between the cities and the countryside. Though the term 'popular culture' is profusely used by many groups, the broad masses of the people, the agrarian masses in particular, have no active part in dynamic cultural growth. The extension of educational facilities is rather impressive as a sign of activating popular potentialities and of a generally awakened thirst for knowledge.[1] But it is especially the well-to-do urban class, forming at present the leading social group, which has profited most of all from this extension. A serious shortage of qualified teachers still weighs heavy upon educational extension and innovation in the agrarian sphere, except for a few regions, for

[1] According to an *Antara*-press communication of July 12, 1953, the following statistics on schools in Indonesia have been issued by the Ministry of Education:

Elementary Schools

	State-controlled		Subsidised schools		Other private schools		Total	
	39/40	51/52	39/40	51/52	39/40	51/52	39/40	51/52
Schools	18.091	24.254	3.364	2.058	–	1.421	21.455	27.733
Teachers	40.583	85.975	7.781	6.007	–	5.665	48.364	99.038
Pupils	2.021.990	5.597.658	337.502	236.103	–	318.725	2.359.492	6.152.513

The Statistical Pocketbook of Indonesia 1957, Jakarta, 1957, indicates for the school-year 54/55 again an increase in educational facilities, especially with respect to the number of teachers (p. 21–26). However, as the categories used are slightly different from those utilised in the above *Antara*-press communication, the more recent figures could not simply be substituted for those of 51/52.

For all types of secondary schools there is also an impressive increase of educational facilities as compared with pre-war years.

The above statistics do not include the Moslem schools under supervision of the Ministry of Religious Affairs, providing educational facilities for millions of pupils; see M. Hutasoit, *Compulsory education in Indonesia*, Unesco-publication, Paris, 1954, p. 74 ff.

example in East Indonesia where the political situation and missionary activities during the post-war years have fostered a rapid development.[1] The great stress, put upon an Indonesian national language, gives expression as a cultural phenomenon to the social ascendency of the same urban group. Though the national language is gradually spreading to the countryside as well, particularly among the younger people breaking loose from the traditional bounds of their *desa*, it still remains largely an urban language. As a means for expression of intimate thoughts among the peasantry the regional tongues offer, for the moment, decidedly better prospects; but they are so far largely neglected. Therefore, neither the new Indonesian literature, nor modern painting developing on Java, can yet grow into a popular art. If the latter attempts to make use of Indonesian motifs and symbols, it is still, owing to its technique borrowed from the West, too far remote from popular art to appeal to broader groups. Besides, both branches of modern art give too little expression to what is really felt among the common people. The artists take their inspiration largely from the thin urban layer to which they belong. Though many of the young artists were born in the country, their style of living has become purely urban, and they feel quite detached from agrarian life.[2] This estrangement is one of the main reasons for the general frustration among the young literary folk. They feel a need for composing works of art which have a positive meaning for broader masses, but they lack the means to do this.

Another sign of frustration is to be found in the tendency of a group of cultural leaders to flee into the past and to retire into a cultural isolation as a reaction upon the overvaluation of all things Western among many urban dwellers, in particular the

[1] Cf. R. Kennedy, *Field notes on Indonesia. South Celebes 1949–1950*, New Haven, 1953, p. 44.

[2] Asrul Sani, 'De maatschappelijke wortels van de Indonesische litteratuur' (The social roots of Indonesian literature), in *De Nieuwe Stem* (The New Voice), Vol. VIII, 1953, p. 390 ff. See further also S. Sjahrir, lecture given at the *Symposion tentang kesulitan-kesulitan zaman peralihan sekarang* (Symposion on the difficulties of the present period of transition), Jakarta, 1953, p. 13 ff.

younger people. The pre-war tendency, found among some Javanese circles, to see back to the past, especially to Javanese culture, has been temporarily reinforced by post-war developments. There was a sense of discouragement among those revolutionary fighters who felt that the transfer of the capital in 1950 from Jogjakarta to Jakarta had led to a change in atmosphere. Life in Jakarta was more extrovert, more open to influences from abroad. These influences along with the burdensome political and economic dependence of Indonesia since the achievement of formal sovereignty, naturally produced a longing for a return to the national fervour of the revolutionary years. But in so far as this cultural tendency was retrospective and introvert only, and directed its ideals toward a remote past of Javanese *grandeur*, it was but one more sign of the *impasse* Indonesian cultural life had got into. Neither an uncritical acceptance of all foreign innovations, nor a flight into a glorified past can solve the need for a new cultural integration. Both attitudes are in fact expressions of the present social situation, and reflect the schizoid condition of present Indonesian society.[1] As the Indonesian revolution seems to have been checked for the moment, Indonesian cultural dynamics also give the impression of having got temporarily stuck.

But the elements for a further dynamic outburst are still present. The creative potentialities are frustrated for the moment, but they are collecting strength and awaiting their opportunity. The artistic qualities of several modern products are very remarkable. Broader layers of society are beginning to master modern techniques, as a consequence of spreading education. In the fields of science and scholarship there is still a gap to bridge between the high level achieved by Europeans living in the colony and the accomplishments of the new Indonesian generation. But if one takes into consideration to which degree the sources of Western learning were withheld from most Indonesians by the pre-war

[1] J. Romein, 'De Garoeda broedt. Indonesische indrukken 1952' (The *Garuda* is brooding – the *Garuda* is an Indonesian mythical eagle, symbolising the people of Indonesia – Indonesian impressions 1952), in *De Nieuwe Stem* (The New Voice), Vol. VIII, 1953, especially p. 76 ff.

colonial policy, one may be astonished that the gulf is not much deeper.

The elements are waiting. In order to reintegrate them into a powerful whole, however, an inspiring social development is needed restoring a positive aim to the frustrated victims of an arrested revolution. One should not be surprised, if this revival will start, as in so many Asian regions, from the countryside and will harbour much more elements of regional civilisation than modern Indonesian culture in its present state has absorbed.

There are already signs that such a renascence, taking its origins in rural society, may emerge before long. There is an enormous urge for culture and knowledge among the Indonesian population. It would be a serious mistake to judge present conditions in Indonesia by the inefficiency, often obvious in the governments' offices in Jakarta. Life in the *daerah* (the 'regions') is often progressing quite independently from politics in the capital. It is there that we have to look for the sources of new vital forces that will bring cultural rejuvenation.

A short bibliography

F. D. K. Bosch, *Het vraagstuk van de Hindoe-kolonisatie van den Archipel* (The problem of the Hindu colonisation of the archipelago), Leiden, 1946.

F. D. K. Bosch, ',Local Genius' en oud-Javaanse kunst' ('Local Genius' and early Javanese art), *Mededelingen der Koninklijke Nederlandse Akademie van Wetenschappen, Afdeling Letterkunde, Nieuwe reeks* (Communications of the Royal Netherlands Academy of Sciences, Literary Branch, New series), Vol. XV, 1952, Nr 1.

I. J. Brugmans, *Geschiedenis van het onderwijs in Nederlandsch-Indië* (History of the education in the Netherlands Indies), Groningen/Batavia, 1938.

W. le Fèbre, 'Taman Siswa en de nationalisatie van het onderwijs in Indonesië' (Taman Siswa and the nationalisation of education in Indonesia), in *Orientatie* (Orientation), 1951, Nr 43, p. 348 ff.

W. le Fèbre, *Taman Siswa, ialah kepertjajaan kepada kekuatan sendiri untuk tumbuh...* (Taman Siswa, representing the trust in one's own capacity for development...), Jakarta/Surabaya, 1952.

J. S. Furnivall, *Educational progress in Southeast Asia*, New York, 1943.

M. Hutasoit, *Compulsory education in Indonesia*, Unesco-publication, Paris, 1954.

J. C. van Leur, *Indonesian trade and society. Essays in Asian social and economic history*, Selected studies on Indonesia by Dutch scholars, Vol. I, The Hague/Bandung, 1955.

K. Neys, *Westerse acculturisatie en Oosters volksonderwijs* (Western acculturation and Eastern popular education), Leiden, 1945.

Th. Pigeaud, *Javaanse volksvertoningen. Bijdrage tot de beschrijving van land en volk* (Javanese folk performances. Contribution to the description of land and people), Batavia, 1938.

Publicaties van de Hollandsch-Inlandsche Onderwijs-Commissie (Publications of the Commission for Dutch-Indonesian education), Buitenzorg/Weltevreden/Batavia, 1929-1931.

B. Schrieke, *Indonesian sociological studies. Selected writings*, Part 1. Selected studies on Indonesia by Dutch scholars, Vol. II, The Hague/Bandung, 1954.

Soetan Sjahrir, *Out of exile*, New York, 1949.

W. F. Stutterheim, *Iets over de cultuurbasis onzer leerlingen* (Remarks about the cultural background of our pupils), Publicatie van het Bureau van den Onderwijsraad (Publication of the Office of the Board for Education), Nr XII, Med. (Communications) VI, Batavia, 1931.

A. Teeuw, *Voltooid voorspel. Indonesische literatuur tussen twee wereld-oorlogen* (Accomplished prelude. Indonesian literature between two world wars), Jakarta, 1950.

D. de Vries, *Culturele aspecten van de verhouding Nederland-Indonesië* (Cultural aspects of the Dutch-Indonesian relationship), Amsterdam, 1947.

Chapter Eleven

NATIONALISM AND AFTER

In Chapter IV we have given a general outline of Indonesian political history, as a frame of reference for the following chapters. The rise and further development of Indonesian nationalism have already been dealt with in that chapter, in as far as they could be considered an integral part of political history. But the accent fell, in that context, upon the outward aspects of the movement rather than upon its internal dynamics. In order to understand the nationalist movement in its essential characteristics it is necessary to view the course of events against their social background. After the manifold aspects of social developments in Indonesia have been dealt with extensively in the previous chapters, we should now be able to achieve a better understanding of the realities and potentialities underlying the trends generally lumped together under the common denominator of 'nationalism'. Such an analysis may, at the same time, serve as a basis for a necessarily very sketchy and tentative look into the future.

1 Early Indonesian forms of association

To use the term 'nationalism' for movements in the remote past of Indonesian history would be an anachronism. The concept of a nation is so far removed from the sphere of human thoughts prevailing at that time, that it would contribute nothing to an understanding of developments during those early ages if either popular movements or the tactics of rulers were to be labelled nationalist.

In early Indonesian society the sense of community did not generally extend beyond the borders of the genealogical or territorial group. Despite similarities of origin, language and cultural background, there was no question of any general feeling of Indonesian unity. What wider forms of association did already exist were confined to the circles of the *adat* chiefs and princes. The innumerable small *adat* communities could be linked together by an alliance of chiefs or by a princely authority. And then the traditional bond uniting the people to their prince, or chiefs, could serve as a basis for political units of some size, such as Majapahit at the height of its power,[1] or Mataram in the seventeenth century. These units, however, depended on the will not of the people but of their rulers.

2 *The flight from the West*

When, in the days of the discovery of the Spice Islands, the West appeared on the Eastern scene, assuming commercial and political forms more or less familiar in the East,[2] the Indonesian chiefs and princes reacted at first in the traditional manner. That is to say, they formed alliances which could oppose the Western power but could also seek Western support in the event of internal conflict. Already at that time, however, a slight tendency to stress Asian characteristics – as opposed to Western ones – might be deduced from the large-scale conversion of Indonesian princes to the Islamic faith, a trend mentioned in the previous Chapter VIII on *Religious Reform*. Islam tied the believers together in the world-wide bond of a Moslem community, the *Ummat Islam*.[3]

[1] It has already been mentioned in Chapter IV, that the reality of a vast and mighty island empire of Majapahit has been seriously disputed recently. See C. C. Berg, 'De geschiedenis van pril Majapahit' (The history of early Majapahit), in *Indonesië*, Vol. IV, 1950/51, p. 481 ff., and Vol. V, 1951/52, p. 193 ff. See also the article by the same author 'De Sadeng-oorlog en de mythe van Groot Majapahit' (The Sadeng War and the myth of great Majapahit) in the same periodical, 1951/52, p. 385 ff.

[2] J. C. van Leur, *Indonesian trade and society. Essays in Asian social and economic history*, Selected studies on Indonesia by Dutch scholars, Vol. I, The Hague/Bandung, 1955, p. 221 ff.

[3] See Th. Pigeaud, *Javaanse volksvertoningen. Bijdrage tot de beschrijving van land en volk* (Javanese folk performances. Contribution to the description of nd and peop le), Batavia, 1938, p. 396.

But in actual fact, it was only in the nineteenth century, when the Western influx took on the form of a dynamic culture threatening the foundations of Indonesian society, that the West became a real problem for Indonesia. Disturbed, the Indonesian nobility and ruling class saw themselves confronted with a choice between joining forces under the banner of Islam with the peasant population, which had been converted to the Islamic faith and was under the guidance of the religious teachers, or allying themselves with Western power and entering the Western administrative system, under the guarantee that their traditional authority over the people would remain unimpaired as far as possible, or even be reinforced. The latter course proved seductive for many – probably, among other reasons, because an alliance with Islam was ultimately bound to undermine their traditional authority and that of the customary law, on which it was based. In this connection, the traditional alliances between the *adat* chiefs stood colonial authority in good stead, since regional chauvinism, encouraged by the *adat* chiefs, appeared to be a powerful weapon for combating the unifying effect of Islam.[1]

In the course of the nineteenth century, however, the reaction of Indonesian society to Western penetration often assumed an escapist character. A tendency developed among the Indonesian nobility which might be interpreted as an attempt to compensate their comparative loss of independence by a flight into the great legendary past. The old court culture of Java, in particular, provided a refuge for those who could not face the contemporary struggle. Dislike of the foreign invaders from the north was typified in conventional manner in the *wayang* play in which, despite initial reverses, the Javanese hero, more delicately built than his rough foreign opponent – but possessing magical powers, was always victorious in the end.[2] Javanese court culture of the period

[1] See for example H. Bouman, *Enige beschouwingen over de ontwikkeling van het Indonesisch nationalisme op Sumatra's Westkust* (Some observations regarding the development of Indonesian nationalism on the Westcoast of Sumatra), Groningen/Jakarta, 1949, p. 33ff.

[2] Though the social anthropologist's interpretation of this stereotyped pattern

was characterised by a certain ossification and by the exclusion of foreign influences.

This escapism did not, however, remain confined to the Indonesian ruling class. The great mass of peasants also tended at first to react to the disturbing dynamic influence of the West by a flight into their rustic past and to close their ranks against the new by strengthening old traditional bonds. In the nineteenth century, this dislike of intensified managerial activity and of the pressure exerted on village economy expressed itself in the form of a retreat into magic and mysticism and the expectation of a Saviour, a Messiah. An idealised picture of the past was cultivated and the hope was cherished that that past would return in the shape of the *ratu adil*, or Just Prince.

But this escapism found its clearest expression in the Samin Movement at the end of the nineteenth century and in the beginning of the twentieth. In several areas the *tanis* (peasants) reacted to highly intensified Western management by organised passive resistance. Samin, a farmer in Blora (Central Java), became the leader of a peasants' movement, which opposed economic capitalism and preached a return to the rustic simplicity of the pre-capitalistic society in which one might only procure food and clothes by one's own labour. Some supporters of this movement even went as far as to deny the legality of all authority, to regard access to arable land and woods as free from government restrictions and to refuse to pay taxes or render services.

The desire to be left in peace by the interfering West formed the background to this movement. It can to some extent be seen as an anti-acculturative movement although it is also possible to regard it, in another sense, as the precursor of a more dynamic nationalism.

3 *Indonesian nationalism*

All the factors already discussed in previous chapters – the eco-

is different (see *e.g.* Th. Pigeaud, *op. cit.*, p. 71, 79), the way most Javanese felt about the *wayang* play seems to have been nearer the interpretation furnished in the text.

nomic shifts, changes in the status system, urbanisation, Islam as a pre-nationalist unifying ideology, an incipient labour movement and an urge towards a cultural renascence – contributed to changing the passive reaction to Western influences into the active one of Indonesian nationalism. This was an idea borrowed from the West, but by its nature it caused those who adopted it to turn against the foremost exponents of Western civilisation.

This nationalism is an idea which comprehends a number of trends sometimes displaying great variety of nature and aim, according to the wishes of the particular group professing the national ideology. The nationalism professed by the younger, Westernised *pryayis* of the early years of this century was completely different in character from the nationalism of the strict Islamites among middle class traders. There is a whole world of difference between the nationalism of the dependent middle class employed in government functions and in the large Western businesses and that of the agrarian masses, or of the unskilled workers in the towns.

Yet all these various trends have two characteristics in common. They all contain an element of incipient solidarity on the basis of Indonesian unity which bridges over the various regional divisions; and they always comprise an element of conflict with – and opposition to – certain social groups, felt to be foreign and alien, or sometimes merely branded as such.

The various forms of regional chauvinism cannot, therefore, be included as one of these nationalist trends. This regional 'nationalism', which tried to draw strength from *adat* and tradition, was usually more in evidence among the feudal chiefs whose position was dependent upon the customary law than among the ordinary people. Besides this, regional chauvinism often received moral support from official quarters. And thus it is understandable why, in the eyes of more politically minded Indonesians, it was often identified with feudalism and the colonial policy of 'divide and rule'. There were, however, also several regional movements, such as for instance *Pasundan*, which could be best understood as ramifications of the main body of nationalism. In these movements nationalism received a more local accent, without losing its overall anti-colonial outlook.[1]

The trend among Netherlanders in Indonesia, especially the Indo-Europeans, who sought greater independence for Indonesia from the mother country, can, also, be regarded as part of the nationalist movement. The first political party in Indonesia was founded shortly before World War I by a number of Indo-Europeans in collaboration with a few Indonesian intellectuals. This *Indische Partij* put national independence on its program. Thus it looked as though mestizos would play a leading role in the struggle for national independence as they had done in the Philippines. But soon afterwards a more conservative trend among the Indo-Europeans proved to enjoy a far larger following. Their position in the Netherlands Indies machinery of government had become so strong that their main motive was fear of the rising class of Indonesian intellectuals. This more conservative trend found its principal expression in the *Indo-Europeesch Verbond* (Indo-European Union) founded in 1919. In this Union a social conservatism was dominant, a struggle on the part of the Indian Netherlanders to preserve their traditional privileges. Yet one could still trace an under-current in the movement which desired greater independence from the Netherlands, a desire motivated by ever-increasing interference by the mother country in Indian affairs and accompanied by a competitive struggle with the newcomers from Holland. To that extent, this movement could also be regarded as nationalist. But the nationalism of these Indo-Europeans was held in check by the realisation that a certain constitutional tie with the Netherlands was essential in order to preserve the privileged position of their own group in Indonesia, and also by the fear of joining forces with the Indonesian nationalist groups, since this might impair their own power position in the country.

[1] The difference between the two 'regionalist' trends has been very clearly analysed by J. M. Pluvier, *Overzicht van de ontwikkeling der nationalistische beweging in Indonesië in de jaren 1930 tot 1942* (Outline of the development of the nationalist movement in Indonesia 1930–1942), The Hague/Bandung, 1953, p. 79 ff.

The feudal nobility of Indonesia likewise found itself 'between the devil and the deep blue sea.' Its aspirations also conflicted with colonial rule, which, it is true, provided its members with certain positions of power yet accorded them, as '*Inlanders*', an inferior social status within the colonial 'caste' structure. On the other hand many of them were afraid of too powerful a nationalist movement among the people, which would inevitably bring its strength to bear not only against colonial domination but also against their own traditional authority. Hence the feudal nobility continually wavered between the desire to ally itself with the nationalist movement – in order to be able to assume the leadership and thereby maintain its traditional social authority even in the changed situation – and the need for moderation and loyalty with respect to the governing authorities. The nobility's nationalist ardour was also tempered by the fact that it had a position to lose.

The nationalism of the Indonesian middle class was more consistent, both among the numerically small group of traders and among the intellectual and near-intellectual class in the service of the government and Western business. They were a predominantly urban group competing in the social and economic fields with the upper class or with those groups which had already consolidated themselves in various functions. Their competitive struggle easily assumed a nationalist form since the groups against which they fought – the Europeans and Chinese – were partly of alien origin and even emphasised this characteristic in their social behaviour. Although the desire for freedom and patriotism naturally go deeper than the simple striving to better one's position in life, nevertheless, the wish to supersede the leading social strata of colonial days, played an important role with this group. And even though nationalist ideology caused it to appeal to mass feeling of dissatisfaction with social conditions, even though its expressed desire to improve the lot of the people may well have been perfectly sincere, a fundamental change in the existing social structure was not the primary aim of this group. Indeed, there were some who feared too radical reforms.

In so far as it was the aim of these Westernised Indonesians merely to secure for themselves leading posts in political and economic life, which had hitherto been occupied by aliens, they may be termed 'bourgeois nationalists.' Yet their nationalist aspirations also contained a certain social-revolutionary element beside an element of social and economic competition between adjacent groups. This bourgeois nationalist movement which, up to the communist rising of 1926, was mainly represented by the *Sarekat Islam* and, to a far lesser degree, by the *Budi Utomo*, also contained an element of resistance to the traditional feudal structure of society. This class struggle between the bourgeoisie and the feudal nobility was carried on in the form of the newly-rich Sumatran rubber planters' fight against the social position of the *adat* chiefs[1] as well as in the current criticism by the Javanese 'new style' *pryayis* (intellectual class) of those 'old style' *pryayis* (aristocracy) who clung to a career in the native Civil Service.[2]

The left wing revolutionary element in Indonesian nationalism became stronger when the aspirations of the Indonesian middle class met with increasing frustration after World War I. When it became clear that the economic situation offered sufficient opportunities neither for the rising Indonesian middle class traders nor the large group of intellectuals and near-intellectuals, the resistance to the existing social structure became more clearly pronounced, even quite apart from the colonial side of the question. More and more forces emerged from the middle class – especially out of its *dependent* section – which definitely sought no longer for better positions in society as it was, or for the substitution of colonial rulers by Indonesian leaders. What they now wanted was a better society.

Yet this left wing trend was obliged to seek its main support from the discontent of the masses with the existing social structure. The Indonesian peasants and city workers were becoming more and more susceptible to nationalist slogans. Nationalism

[1] B. Schrieke, *Indonesian sociological studies. Selected writings*, Part 1. Selected studies on Indonesia by Dutch scholars, Vol. II, The Hague/Bandung, 1955, p. 131.

[2] B. Schrieke, *op cit.*, p. 199.

for them, however, was chiefly a form of the class struggle. The foreign element their movement opposed was the Chinese middleman, or the European employer with whom they came into economic conflict. The resistance put up by the peasants to Western capitalism, in particular, was an extremely important social phenomenon and a source of great power for revolutionary trends. This resistance no longer took the form of escapism, as it had done in the days of the Samin movement. The peasants, too, now organised themselves in the *Sarekat Islam* on Western principles, fighting the West with its own weapons. The Java sugar plantations especially succeeded in transforming the Javanese *tani* 'who was once one of the most conservative types ever to be found in rural society' into a rebel.[1] Islam and, later, nationalism were for the rural and urban masses first and foremost symbols of class solidarity in the struggle for a better existence.

It is understandable from the foregoing that the pre-war nationalist movement could not achieve homogeneity. Ultimate aims were too divergent for this to be possible and, in particular, the gulf between the Westernised Indonesian middle class in the towns and the great mass of the peasants in the country was too great. The Indonesian intellectual, too, like the Indo-European and the Indonesian Chinese, was a 'marginal' man, standing on the frontier between two civilisations, a man who was often almost wholly unfamiliar with rural Indonesia.

The attempt made after the failure of the communist rising of 1926 to build one united nationalist movement centring around Sukarno's Nationalist Party (P.N.I.) won no lasting success either. In the thirties, when the economic situation also gave rise to increasing discontent among a section of the Indonesian middle class, the various currents within the nationalist movement merged once again into a decidedly rightist bourgeois nationalist branch (the *Parindra* of Dr. Sutomo, in which even various 'feudal' personalities felt themselves at home) and a more radical branch (Amir Sjarifuddin's *Gerindo*, which aimed at a social, as well as a

1 E. H. Jacoby, *Agrarian unrest in Southeast Asia*, New York, 1949, p. 61.

national revolution). This latter movement should have been, in principle, more consistently anti-colonial than the *Parindra* which was to some extent prepared to cooperate loyally with the colonial government. But tactical considerations reversed the position. As a bourgeois nationalist movement, the *Parindra* was less antagonistic in its attitude towards the Japanese. The aim of bourgeois nationalism was primarily to replace the old power groups in the political and economic fields. Temporary occupation by the Japanese could do something to help achieve this, while the latter could be expected to lend support in the attempt to preserve the old semi-feudal social structure, which, in the eyes of the Indonesian upper class, might prove of some use to keep the popular movement in check once they had achieved power. It was accordingly noticeable that shortly before World War II the left wing nationalists showed more readiness to cooperate with the colonial government than did the bourgeois groups.[1] They had, of course, more to fear from Japanese and German fascism than from the colonial regime of the Western democracies.

Despite these splits and internal conflicts, the unity achieved shortly before the war when the movement for a true Parliament was started was very impressive. The nationalist movement gave proof of a strength and a discipline which would stand the stormy vicissitudes of war and occupation.

As we have already seen, the Japanese, in contrast with the Dutch, attempted to make use of the nationalist movement. While one category of nationalists, mainly consisting of left radicals, went underground, another branch accepted the opportunity of building a monolithic movement under the cover of Japanese authority. In this process, however, the character of the movement underwent a change. One of the chief motives of Japanese policy was their fear of full-fledged popular movements. To prevent popular discontent from threatening their authority they initiated a policy of building up a dynamic mass movement under their own control. They even attempted to utilise the

[1] Cf., for example, Soetan Sjahrir, *Out of exile*, New York, 1949, p. 186 ff., 219 ff. See also J. M. Pluvier, *op. cit.*, *passim*.

Islamic religion to this end. By this expedient they hoped to achieve a double purpose: first, to weld the people together as an active force in support of their war effort, and second, to divert ill-feeling among the population against foreign enemies or other bogies. This method of activating popular movements in order to control them the better, is a typically fascist expedient to curb the masses. A disadvantage, from the standpoint of those in authority is, however, that movements thus organised become, in the long run, autonomous forces ever more difficult to handle for those in power and are liable eventually to become a threat to the initiators of the policy as well. Accordingly, the Indonesian nationalist movement, during the Japanese occupation, became a real mass movement, in the course of which feelings of national pride were greatly stimulated. In the later years of occupation, however, the policy of diverting discontent to foreign enemies proved no longer viable. Even before the Japanese surrender, contacts with the underground movement became ever more intensive, and anti-Japanese nationalist feelings came in undisguised form into the open. After the Japanese surrender both branches combined to form a revolutionary force strong enough to call the Republic of Indonesia into being.

The revolutionary years clearly showed how deeply national feelings had penetrated Indonesian society. People travelling through the countryside of Java in the first weeks after VJ Day reported already that red and white Republican flags were flown in remote villages. Simple male and female visitors of urban clinics, when asked by the physician for their nationality, called themselves Indonesians practically without exception, whereas they were certain before the war to have answered: Javanese, Sundanese or Batavian. Trade unions sprang up like mushrooms and proved a strong support to the nationalist cause. But the most obvious proof of the popular support the nationalist idea had been able to amass during the Japanese occupation was provided by the large-scale guerrilla activities in behalf of the Republican movement. Without a mass support among the peasantry the guerrilla movement could never have been carried on. And even if a large portion of the population was not actively engaged in guerrilla fighting, there was a large amount of sympathy and passive assistance, and but little inclination to give the young people engaged in fighting away. Kattenburg mentions that the people of Kalibening (near Salatiga, Central Java) designated the guerrilla fighters as '*anak kita*', our children.[1] Other strata of the population also showed increased organisational discipline and national consciousness. A very remarkable instance of this was the spontaneous strike of the entire Indonesian personnel, doctors included, of the Jakarta State Hospital, when the Dutch authorities took control of it in November 1948. Another instance, already mentioned, was the refusal of nearly the entire Sultanate's personnel in Jogjakarta to cooperate with the Dutch after the second military action.

The mass character of the nationalist movement does not imply, however, that distinctions as to mentality and purpose, or even internal conflicts, were lacking. The manifold shades of nationalism already apparent before the war became still more pronounced. For the peasantry *kemerdekaan* (freedom) had a quite different meaning[2] from what was expected by those bourgeois nationalists whose primary aim was to oust the Dutch. Nor were those aristocratic leaders supporting the Dutch Malino policy completely devoid of nationalist feelings. To a certain degree even their activities could assist the nationalist cause. But the interpretation they gave to this term was quite different again, their chief aim being to secure their traditional position in a free Indonesia, and to conserve the social structure as much as possible. The diversity of political parties and currents reflected the various shades of nationalism, and even led to a split between left and right, culminating in the communist-led Madiun uprising in 1948 and foreshadowing future developments. Nevertheless, up

[1] Paul M. Kattenburg, *A Central Javanese village in 1950*, Data paper Nr 2 of the Southeast Asia Program, Cornell University, Ithaca, 1951, p. 13.

[2] See for example H. ten Dam, *Desa Tjibodas*, a report of the Lembaga Penjelidikan Masjarakat Desa dan Usaha Tani (Institute for rural sociological and farm-management research), Bogor, 1951, p. 14.

to the achievement of sovereignty and even to the formation of a unitary state the movement kept its basic force and an amount of homogeneity and unity of purpose sufficient to carry the revolution to a successful conclusion.

4 *Problems of freedom*

But since this primary aim was achieved, the situation has basically changed. With the fall of the former rulers, the collapse of the old traditional scale of values and the development of a situation in which everything is fluid, the brakes which previously prevented the realisation of Indonesian group aspirations are now removed.

If one takes into account the diversity of movements, which nationalism in the past has included, it becomes clear that the achievement of political independence cannot end the social struggle fought so far under the banner of nationalism. The revolution has removed one of the social groups – the *Netherlanders* in their function as a power factor. Insofar as Indo-Europeans have opted for Indonesian citizenship, they are now experiencing the permanent loss of their privileged position.

The Indonesian nobility do not, however, regard their struggle to preserve a measure of their traditional prestige as definitely lost. The attempt of a section of them, in collaboration with the Dutch (witness van Mook's so-called Malino policy)[1] to make use of regional chauvinism in the guise of the federal idea – as a check on further social change, may now be regarded as a failure. Now, however, there are some who see their chance in an attempt to join forces with a group within the bourgeoisie in order to resist further revolutionary shifts. Since their aim (political sovereignty) has been achieved, a section of the bourgeois nationalists no longer see the revolutionary tendency of the masses as a support but as a danger. Among some groups of them there

[1] See George McT. Kahin, 'Indirect rule in East Indonesia', in *Pacific Affairs*, Vol. XXII, 1949, p. 227 ff.; also *Nationalism and revolution in Indonesia*, Ithaca, 1952, p. 351 ff.

is a tendency now to try to turn back the tide of revolution, or divert it, after the Japanese example, into the channel of aggression against others – Dutch or Chinese for instance.

Nationalist slogans may serve as a rallying cry to achieve group solidarity, and to divert popular discontent towards various scapegoats.

On the other hand, side by side with the social discontent of the numerically restricted groups of urban workers and underpaid lower middle class functionaries, 'agrarian unrest' is becoming a dominating force as it is elsewhere in Asia. The transfer of sovereignty has so far not realised the high expectations for a rapid improvement of the standard of living for the great mass of the population, urban and rural. The social revolution of 1946 in Northern Sumatra, a readiness to engage in gang activities in various parts of the archipelago, large-scale strikes on the Western plantations and in urban industries, the illegal occupation of plantation land by squatters – all these are expressions of the same class struggle which was originally canalised in the nationalist movement.

Thus we see that the two branches of the nationalist movement, the bourgeois branch and the left wing radical branch, now threaten to enter upon a struggle to the death. We have already seen in Chapter VIII on *Religious Reform* what role Islam plays in this situation. The distance separating the two branches is increasing by reason of the fact that the nobility and the middle class together form a group mainly urban in character, with little knowledge of the countryside and rural needs, while the great mass of the poor are still to be found in these rural areas.[1]

This state of affairs makes it all the easier for social-revolutionary elements to represent the fight against the new power groups – of aristocratic and bourgeois origin – as a struggle against alien elements, that is, as a continuation of the nationalist struggle. They are further helped in this by the tendency of the new

[1] See *e.g.* S. Sjahrir, lecture given at the *Symposion tentang kesulitan-kesulitan zaman peralihan sekarang* (Symposion on the difficulties of the present period of transition), Jakarta, 1953, p. 13 ff.

aristocratic and bourgeois ruling elite to ally themselves with foreign capitalists for support against the radical elements. Hence the struggle, waged by leftist groups against the maintenance of the Western plantation undertakings and against the power of the large urban business concerns can now be linked up with the fight against Indonesian townsmen – the absentee landlords in particular, who can be branded as 'tools of colonial capitalism.' Once political independence has been achieved, economic independence has become a major issue, especially to those groups for whom no new gates have been opened by the achievement of national sovereignty.

The present situation is naturally far more complicated than that delineated above. Class divisions and class solidarity are often cut across by considerations of ideology, tradition, economics, and by chance considerations having to do with the veneration in which certain personalities are held. But, at the moment, this only strengthens social-revolutionary forces, since an important section of the Indonesian middle class, too, threatens to come into serious conflict with the new ruling class. It is not only in the ranks of the intellectuals and near-intellectuals in government and business employ that many are to be found dissatisfied because freedom has brought them no economic improvement. The Indonesian middle class traders and small rubber growers also see their aspirations checked by the great power enjoyed by monopolist concerns. And again, they oppose not only foreign economic interests which have taken the place of the old-style colonialism, but also those Indonesian entrepreneurs, political leaders, feudal chiefs and large landowners who cooperate closely with these foreign interests. And they are also inclined to see this conflict once more as a continuation of the struggle for national freedom, a struggle aimed at those who, in their opinion, are frittering away national freedom for the sake of economic advantage.

On the other hand, after the attainment of freedom new counterforces, more or less hostile to the nationalist ideology, have come to the fore.

First, there is the desire in many areas for greater local autonomy. As long as the revolutionary fight for a national state prevailed, federalism was tainted with feudalism and colonialism and was kept in the background. But now things are different. Political freedom has largely failed to achieve its social aims, and a good deal of discontent in the remote areas is directed against the central government, which is spending in Java most of the foreign exchange earned by the Outer Provinces. Regional and local loyalties are regaining strength to the point of threatening national unity. Failure of the central government to effectuate an efficient decentralisation of powers and financial resources has fostered centrifugal tendencies which may, in the long run, become disruptive. Appointment of regional heads and members of councils is too often conditioned by party affiliations and runs counter to local preferences and therefore adds to the prevailing discontent outside the capital and to the urge for greater autonomy.

Another ideology which may, in the long run, prove a force opposed to nationalism, is the movement for an Islamic state. Inasmuch as some political parties in Indonesia are only striving after a transformation of the present Republic into an 'Islamic state' by legal means, this aim does not necessarily run counter to the national ideal. But if the fight is carried on by force, as is at present the case in Western and Central Java, South Celebes and Acheh, it becomes disruptive. Even in political discussions between the legal parties Islam and nationalism are sometimes considered mutually irreconcilable ideals. This a-national attitude of Indonesian Moslems has its roots in the past, from the time when *Sarekat Islam* had Pan-Islamic leanings. At any rate, the fight for an Islamic state may stimulate, even if the aim is being pursued by legal means, counter-movements by the other parties, as for example the Christians of East Indonesia, many of whom would be likely to attempt to break away from the unitary Republic if this should turn into an Islamic state.

But the greatest dangers for national unity arise from foreign sources. Indonesia is strongly affected by the Cold War, and as long as the central government is pursuing a more or less aloof and neutral policy as against the aims of the Western powers, the latter are likely to attempt anything in their power to strengthen their influence over Indonesian policy. If the central government opposes these infractions, the Western powers may be tempted to play upon regionalist sympathies or to support separatist movements such as the *Darul Islam* in order to call local governments into being, more sympathetic towards foreign capital.

If, on the other hand, the central government should align itself fully with the Western powers, leftist radical insurrections of a regional nature, supported by the outside communist world, would be within the range of possibilities.

On the whole, however, communism is, at present, rather to be found on the side of nationalist forces in Asia than on the opposite side, while capitalism is prone to play upon regionalism and provincialism, as it has done already for a century. This is understandable if one keeps in mind that the nationalist ideology is no longer restricted to urban groups of traders, who may be caught in clashing interests, but has spread to the peasantry as well. As an ideology, it receives its main impulse from the countryside. Nationalism has to a certain extent become an ideology for the fight of the impoverished peasants of Asia against all capitalists, foreigners and nationals alike, who are infringing upon their basic interests and rights. 'For the masses of the rural population, the movement for land has merged with the national movement.'[1]

From the foregoing it may be concluded that the nationalist struggle still continues for the time being to play a predominant role in Indonesian affairs, as an expression for various forms of social dissatisfaction. Even after the attainment of political freedom, nationalism remains a basic issue.

Moreover, nationalism is still an important source of the spiritual strength needed to build a new Indonesian society. Though the Indonesian people have already accomplished a revolution, their struggle was not a final but rather a first step in the process of the realisation of their full potentialities as individuals and as

[1] Erich H. Jacoby, *op. cit.*, p. 253.

a people. The Indonesians are only beginning to rediscover themselves and to regain their self-confidence. It is evident that they are digging in the past for the sources of their strength, and attempt to rewrite their history which has thus far mainly been written as a colonial history by historians for whom Indonesia was generally no more than a picturesque scene – a stage for Western adventure and Dutch national glory.[1] The way Indonesians are now glorifying their own national heroes, reasserting their own contribution to world history, and eliminating the Dutch language, Dutch names, Dutch books, may sometimes smell of chauvinism. Yet these phenomena are only too understandable reactions to a colonial past and at the same time conditions to free themselves from an inferiority feeling. It is to most Indonesians a great pride to show new things – modern schools, laboratories, experimental stations, monuments – they achieved by themselves, after having freed themselves from Dutch supervision.

There are, however, elements in this national revival which on the surface seem deleterious to Indonesian progress. Eliminating the Dutch language as a vehicle for university teaching before there are sufficient Indonesian professors available, and before Dutch textbooks and laws have been translated into Indonesian; ousting Dutch technicians before there is trained Indonesian personnel available to replace them on the same level; discouraging foreign capitalists though the supply of native capital is far from sufficient to accomplish the task of economic reconstruction, and though newly-established Indonesian trading companies are lacking in experience, foreign contacts and efficiency; diverting the people's energy from the task of patient reconstruction to the clamour for West Irian (Dutch New-Guinea) before Indonesia is able to administer this unwieldy area – all this seems rather negative and sterile chauvinism.

Yet there is more than mere xenophobia and a search for scape-

[1] See J. C. van Leur, who first of all realised the full theoretical implications of a rewriting of Indonesian history; *op. cit.*, p. 147 ff.

goats behind the consistent anti-Dutch policy of recent years. The power of Dutch capital was felt by many Indonesians as a brake on Indonesian economic development. Efficiency is not the only criterion of progress – the kind of economic activities and the overall structure of capital investment are at least as important. Though efficiency may temporarily suffer, the rapid formation of an Indonesian merchant class and of Indonesian manpower trained in business administration may in the long run be more important than a temporary slackening in economic activity. Many Indonesian experts were, not without justification, convinced that a real reconstruction policy could not be inaugurated unless the economic and financial paragraphs of the Round Table Conference (concluded in December 1949 between Indonesia and the Netherlands) had been completely abrogated in order to free Indonesian economy from its fetters. For the time being they contented themselves with bringing the maximum of pressure to bear upon Dutch capital and its representatives in Indonesia. Whether this policy was wise is another question.

Nor is the Indonesian New-Guinea claim mere demagogy. Apart from legal and historical arguments, Indonesian politicians consider the presence of a Dutch military force at its eastern confines as a real and continuous threat to its territorial integrity, the more so as support for the separatist movement in the South Moluccas has been rather freely expressed in the Netherlands, though never officially approved by the Dutch Government.

At the same time national slogans, such as the claim for West Irian, could serve as a rallying force and thus foster a positive attachment of the Indonesian people to the government and its ideals, as a precondition to economic reconstruction and to a drive to combat the rampant corruption.

The failure of many Dutch fully to realise both the psychological necessity and the deeper roots of these reactions, and their tenacious clinging to a legalistic position with respect to New-Guinea have caused relations between both countries to turn from bad to worse. The cleavage is made all the deeper by the fact that the majority of the Dutch people and of the newspapers in the Netherlands still persist in fretfully remembering past glory, and relish in exposing the numerous weaknesses of the young Indonesian state.

National susceptibility of the Indonesians, however, is not confined to their relations with the Dutch. The United States has also repeatedly learned, that the young Republic jealously watches its independence and is loath to accept help with strings attached to it (acceptance by the Foreign Minister Subardjo of American M.S.A. assistance caused the fall of the conservative Sukiman Government in February 1952). American capital investment meets restrictions, though less than Dutch interests. Attempts to make Indonesian foreign policy align, via SEATO (South East Asian Treaty Organization or Manila Pact), with that of the Western powers, have thus far completely failed. Indonesia is not willing to pay the price of its independent foreign policy even to secure American and Australian support for its West Irian claim.

But Indonesian foreign relations are not all negative. The very desire for self-expression and for a compensation of inferiority feeling inherited from the colonial past, which accounts for the Indonesians' impatience of Western interference, makes them gladly accept cooperation with the Asian countries. The Indonesian government took the lead in organising the epoch-making Bandung Conference (April 1955) of the Asian and African countries. Solidarity with the other coloured peoples, irrespective of their political affiliations, was not felt as an infringement upon national aspirations; on the contrary, the general rejection, at that conference, of all remnants of colonialism and racialism was felt as a further step toward the reasserting of national self-esteem, and toward breaking loose from age-old Western domination. At the same time the support of Asian and African countries for Indonesia's claim on West Irian, secured at that conference, was considered in Indonesia as a concrete achievement.

Thus apart from its economic implications nationalism remains a major spiritual force in free Indonesia.

Some prospects for the Future

It should be clear from the foregoing that the bond linking political problems with those economic and social questions dealt with in the preceding chapters is very close. The old economic structure, mainly based on agrarian production, can be maintained no longer. The large Western plantations, as foreign enterprises controlling vast tracts of land and large numbers of unskilled workers, are increasingly meeting with difficulties which, in the long run, may prove insurmountable.[1] That rural subjection – officially termed 'security' – on which they depend for their existence, at least if they are to function along the traditional lines, is gone for good; and the strikes – which can put an end to them in their present economic form – will by all appearances not decrease.

For the time being social unrest in rural areas and the conflict between town and country are likely to continue. And they will only serve to increase the burden of poverty already resulting from structural factors. As the foregoing description has shown, the situation in town and country is far from satisfying, while in Java the problem of over-population is severe.

Economically, Indonesia belongs to the 'underdeveloped countries'. This, however, is not a reason for sharing professor J. H. Boeke's pessimism with regard to Indonesia's economic prospects in the more remote future.[2] Just as Malthus' predictions were not fulfilled in Europe, the predictions of this new Malthus may in the long run be belied by the facts in Asia. We now know what means exist for solving the problem of over-population and for raising the standard of living. Harmonious planning, effective social organisation and a gradual increase in the productivity of labour, first by a full utilisation of the available man-power, and later on by agricultural and industrial mechanisation, are among the most important means at our disposal. What is required is a change in the total economic structure. In view of its enormous

[1] Pierre Gourou, *L'Asie*, Paris, 1953, p. 357.
[2] Cf. J. H. Boeke, *The interests of the voiceless Far East*, Leiden, 1948.

size and the scale distress has assumed in Indonesia, the problem there may well be of a different order from that which faced Western Europe at the beginning of the nineteenth century; but mankind is now equipped with the rich fruits of 150 years of experience and all the various means of modern technique and science enabling it to guide this problem, whatever its dimensions, towards a satisfactory solution. Moreover, vital forces have been awakened in the Indonesian people which seem likely to prove equal to the task of overcoming tremendous obstacles.

It does, however, seem pretty certain now that the building up of a new economic structure, in which industry will play an important role, cannot be left to the 'free play of economic forces.' Investment in primary products will still appear more attractive to foreign investors than investment in industry. As a consequence, the Indonesian Government will find itself obliged to proceed still further along the road of control and planning and to keep a tight rein on foreign capital. Social and political unrest will continue to increase and bring about the fall of one government after another, until a strong government is found, ready to aim in economic policy at a radical change in the social structure and, to this end, to impose a consistent control on foreign capital, whilst introducing agrarian reforms which will meet the desires of the farming population and put an end to rural unrest. Nationalist ideology will, no doubt, remain the chief incentive to this change of policy.

Only after such a policy has been initiated, will an integration between leaders and the mass of the people deeper than the 'charismatic' tie resulting from veneration of an individual, be possible – an integration which is the condition for a certain measure of social peace.

As the first reaction of Indonesians to contact with the West assumed the form of escape and was followed by a second phase in which Western models were faithfully copied in order to combat the West with its own weapons, so the process of acculturation will continue on a new basis in a third phase. Indonesia will discover that the only effective answer to the challenge from the West will be the assimilation of Western cultural factors in a manner adapted to the structure of Asian society.

In practice this will mean that much of Western economy on capitalist lines will prove unfit for Indonesia which will have to achieve industrialisation and economic development by means of a shortcut from pre-capitalist to post-capitalist forms. In this process of reform, factors of economic cooperation and collective action will play a far larger part than nineteenth century Western individualism.

At the same time, this implies that the consequent need for Asian countries to free themselves from the capitalist system and to restrict free enterprise before it has been able to develop fully will constitute a challenge to the Western world – a challenge still more serious than Indonesian nationalism in its political form was in recent years for the discountenanced Dutch rulers.

Whether the West will find the right response to this challenge is still highly questionable. Thus far much of the Western world failed to relinquish its traditional modes of thought and action, just as the majority of the Dutch failed to understand the deeper roots of the developments which compelled them to quit their Asian empire.

Not even the lofty idea of technical assistance to underdeveloped countries by Western countries is considered by all Asians a sign of a radical change of heart and a truly fresh approach to economic problems. Unless the Western world is ready to help Asia to inaugurate a process of rapid industrialisation Asians will see in this assistance a disguised continuation of traditional colonial policies. They will prefer to do the job alone, even though this may imply severe hardships, rather than accepting 'assistance' which will tie their economic structure down to the status of auxiliary producer of raw materials. Genuine assistance, on the other hand, would considerably relieve the task lying before new Asian countries like Indonesia. Such help, however, would not only imply a revolutionary change of mind in the West, but also little short of a revolution of its social and economic system.

It would be wise for Indonesians not to count upon such a miracle – but it would be equally wise for Westerners to try to bring such a miracle about.

A short bibliography

Alexandre von Arx, *L'évolution politique en Indonésie de 1900 à 1942*, Fribourg, 1949.

Robert C. Bone Jr., *The dynamics of the Western New Guinea (Irian Barat) problem*, Modern Indonesia Project, Cornell University, Ithaca, 1958.

H. Bouman, *Enige beschouwingen over de ontwikkeling van het Indonesisch nationalisme op Sumatra's Westkust* (Some observations regarding the development of Indonesian nationalism on the Westcoast of Sumatra), Groningen/Jakarta, 1948.

Willard H. Elsbree, *Japan's role in the Southeast Asian nationalist movements 1940–1945*, Cambridge (Mass.), 1953.

Rupert Emerson, Lennox A. Mills and Virginia Thompson, *Government and nationalism in Southeast Asia*, New York, 1942.

Herbert Feith, *The Indonesian elections of 1955*, Modern Indonesia Project, Cornell University, Ithaca, 1957.

Herbert Feith, *The Wilopo Cabinet. 1952–1953*, Modern Indonesia Project, Cornell University, Ithaca, 1958.

J. S. Furnivall, *Colonial policy and practice. A comparative study of Burma and Netherlands India*, Cambridge, 1948.

W. L. Holland (ed.), *Asian nationalism and the West*, New York, 1953.

E. H. Jacoby, *Agrarian unrest in Southeast Asia*, New York, 1949.

George McT. Kahin, *Nationalism and revolution in Indonesia*, Ithaca, 1952.

George Mc T. Kahin (ed.), *Major governments of Asia*, Ithaca, 1958.

D. M. G. Koch, *Om de vrijheid. De nationalistische beweging in Indonesië* (Towards freedom. The nationalist movement in Indonesia), Jakarta, 1950.

D. M. G. Koch, *Verantwoording. Een halve eeuw in Indonesië* (Justification. Half a century in Indonesia), The Hague/Bandung, 1956.

W. Macmahon Ball, *Nationalism and communism in East Asia*, Melbourne, 1952.

Tibor Mende, *Southeast Asia between two worlds*, London, 1955.

H. J. van Mook, *The stakes of democracy in South East Asia*, London, 1950.

J. Th. Petrus Blumberger, *De nationalistische beweging in Nederlandsch-Indië* (The nationalist movement in the Netherlands Indies), Haarlem, 1931.

J. Th. Petrus Blumberger, *Le communisme aux Indes Néerlandaises*, Paris, 1929.

J. M. Pluvier, *Overzicht van de ontwikkeling der nationalistische beweging in Indonesië in de jaren 1930 tot 1942* (Outline of the development of the nationalist movement in Indonesia 1930–1942), The Hague/Bandung, 1953.

S. J. Rutgers, *Indonesië. Het koloniale systeem in de periode tussen de eerste en de tweede wereldoorlog* (Indonesia. The colonial system during the period between World War I and World War II), Amsterdam, 1947.

Soetan Sjahrir, *Out of exile*, New York, 1949.
Virginia Thompson and Richard Adloff, *The left wing in Southeast Asia*, New York, 1950.
Verslag van de Commissie tot bestudeering van staatsrechtelijke hervormingen (Report of the Commission for the study of political reforms), New York, 1944.
Charles Wolf Jr., *The Indonesian story. The birth, growth and structure of the Indonesian Republic*, New York, 1948.
Dorothy Woodman, *The Republic of Indonesia*, New York, 1955.

Chapter Twelve

The Latest Phase

The Indonesian Revolution seemed to have come to an end in 1949. The transfer of sovereignty by the Dutch looked like an initial step towards a return to 'normalcy'. In spite of serious setbacks, and in spite of many disruptive tendencies which came to the fore and which constituted a challenge to the newly won independence and unity, the Republic seemed to be able to survive and to settle down to its task of economic and political reconstruction. But developments during the past few years have made clear that the revolution has not yet come to a stop. After protracted efforts to settle dissensions in 'an Asian way', that is to say by a procedure of compromises and half-way solutions intended to save all those concerned from 'losing face', had failed, Indonesia in 1958 was confronted with the tragedy of civil war. Though at the time of writing the Government in office seems to have won a victory, it would appear that Indonesia is to remain a trouble spot in the Asian world for several years to come, during which economic development will be seriously hampered by internal political strife aggravated by hidden or open interference from foreign sources. The near future of Indonesia is likely to be written in terms of revolution and counter-revolution rather than in terms of peaceful evolution.

After the formation of a unitary state in August 1950 – a more or less revolutionary process and a departure from the federal structure accepted at the Round Table Conference – there had at first been a general tendency to assume that, the revolution having attained its main end, political independence, the Indonesian people needed to set about peaceful reconstruction. For several years, the Indonesian Republic attempted the evolutionary way, revolutionary trends being largely restricted to a clamour for the incorporation of Western New-Guinea (West Irian) within the Republic and for the annulment of the burdensome economic stipulations of the Round Table Conference. However, under conditions of parliamentary democracy following a multi-party pattern borrowed mainly from the Netherlands, it proved not to be easy to get economic development going. It took some time before this was fully realised.

Kemerdekaan, freedom, had been expected to bring prosperity in its wake. When this expectation failed to materialise, the failures were first attributed to the colonial heritage left behind by the Dutch. After a few years it grew increasingly difficult to blame the Dutch for the many misfortunes. People became angered at the horse-trading and the incompetency characteristic of party politics as practised in Parliament. The shortcomings were attributed in the first instance to the 'incompleteness' of democracy – to the circumstance that the great majority of the membership of the Provisional Parliament were not elected, but appointed. This fact was considered the main source of the irresponsibility among the leading politicians resulting in short-lived cabinets following up one another at regular intervals. With the 17 October affair (of 1952) the misgivings prevalent in broad layers of Indonesian society, especially in army circles, came into the open.

The parliamentary elections were then looked forward to as a necessary step to cure Indonesian society. It was only when after the installation of an elected Parliament in 1956 things remained as they had been before, that it began to dawn that the source of the shortcomings might be looked for not in a lack of democracy but in an excess of it. To quote Herbert Feith, the multi-party system 'reflected the existence of a multiplicity of small power centers, each in a position to veto many types of government action'.[1] President Sukarno had already issued the warning 'not to think that the inauguration of the new Parliament opens the

[1] Herbert Feith, *The Wilopo Cabinet, 1952–1953. A turning point in post-revolutionary Indonesia*, Modern Indonesia Project, Cornell University, Ithaca, 1958, p. 206.

doors of paradise for us'. After returning from his tours of both the Western and the Eastern world in 1956 he developed his concept of a 'guided democracy' that would be more suited to Indonesian society than the Western types of democracy. In military circles a Nasserite type of ideology began to develop, which provoked para-legal actions by the military intended to eliminate the corruption and inefficiency prevalent among the ruling cliques of politicians. The local *coups d'état* which finally resulted in the armed rebellion of 1958 could be considered the first attempts to put this ideology in practice – with the result that not a few Indonesians are beginning to realise that military rule is not a guarantee against corruption and inefficiency either.

For a better understanding of what has happened we must first make a more detailed analysis of the election results of 1955 and the main determinants of the balance of power achieved at the polls.

In 1952 the unity between orthodox and modernist trends in Islam brought about during the Japanese occupation was disrupted. The *Masjumi*, which had originally been constituted as a federation of Moslem organisations, was converted in 1945 into a political party that was joined by both the modernist *Muhammadyah* and the orthodox *Nahdatul Ulama* as 'special members'. In 1952, however, the *Nahdatul Ulama* withdrew from *Masjumi*. Though the importance of this event was not generally realised at the time, it would prove to be a fact of major significance as a determinant of future political developments. Previously, the *Masjumi* had been earmarked as an easy winner at the coming elections. But its structure had always been rather loose, and it had, not without reason, been called by one of its adherents 'an elephant with beriberi'.

It is difficult to determine what were the real causes of the secession of N.U. On the surface the split was a result of discontent among the orthodox N.U. leaders provoked by the dominant position of reformists both in the *Masjumi* party organisation and in the successive Cabinets. But behind this jockeying for power and prominent positions there were, within Indonesian Islamic society, basic contrasts for which the usual distinction between 'orthodox' and 'reformist' was only a symbolic expression.

The reformists found their mainstay in the urban centres and in those regions outside Java where Indonesian farmers were actively engaged in production for a world market as cultivators of such crops as rubber or copra. They represented, in general, the more prosperous layers of Islamic society, both in the cities and in the countryside. On the other hand the orthodox found their main support in the countryside of Eastern and Central Java, where agriculture was generally practised in a traditional way, as a subsistence farming.

Before the split the *Masjumi* organisation was largely dominated by the reformists, who had an advantage over the orthodox as a result of their better training and their greater conversancy with economics and administration. Since the split foreign observers have tended to label *Masjumi* as more 'progressive' than *Nahdatul Ulama*. However, in so far as the orthodox were largely tradition-minded and inimical to Western or Westernising influences, this very conservatism has repeatedly led *Nahdatul Ulama* as a party to policies more radical than those advocated by *Masjumi*.[1]

In 1953, after the fall of the Wilopo Cabinet in which the two major parties, *Masjumi* and P.N.I. (National Party) had cooperated, the split within *Masjumi* had its first political repercussions. For the first time since the transfer of sovereignty *Masjumi* was excluded from the Government. The first Ali Sastroamidjojo Cabinet was based on a coalition in which the P.N.I. cooperated with a number of parties with a smaller representation in the Provisional Parliament, among them the *Nahdatul Ulama*. The P.K.I. (Communist Party), though not included in the Cabinet, in general supported its policies. The two main parties represented in the Government, the P.N.I. and the *Nahdatul Ulama*, succeeded, during the two years of the Cabinet's rule, in strengthening their position in the administrative apparatus in order to check the

[1] See the excellent analysis by Herbert Feith, *op. cit.*, p. 40 ff.

powerful position of the *Masjumi* party. The *Masjumi* party was not able to overcome this setback during the brief period of its political ascendancy as a major participant in the Burhanuddin Harahap Cabinet formed after the fall of Ali Sastroamidjojo's first Cabinet in July 1955.

On September 29, 1955, the first general elections were held for an Indonesian Parliament. Despite the incredible difficulties encountered in an archipelago where communications are poor, the majority of the population are illiterate, and insecurity prevails in several regions, the elections appear to have gone rather smoothly. As was to be expected, irregularities did occur, but they would not seem to have been widespread. Generally speaking, the organisation of the elections was an admirable achievement for the young Republic.

The great majority of the vote – a total of 37.8 million voters went to the polls – was rather evenly distributed among what appeared to be 'the big four': 8.4 million (57 out of a total of 257 elected seats) for P.N.I., 7.9 million (57 seats) for *Masjumi*, 7.0 million (45 seats) for N.U. and 6.2 million (39 seats) for P.K.I. The other parties, including the P.S.I. (Socialist Party) and the old P.S.I.I. (*Partai Sarekat Islam Indonesia*), achieved local successes only. The Christian parties were among the most important in this category of smaller parties. As was to be expected, they achieved considerable success in the Christianised regions of East Indonesia. Several parties that were rather influential in former Governments and in the Provisional Parliament were all but swept away.

At the second elections, held on December 15, 1955, for the Constituent Assembly, the balance of forces as evidenced at the first elections was largely confirmed. The position of P.N.I. was reinforced (over 9 million votes), mainly at the expense of the smaller parties and of *Masjumi*.

In Central and East Java the P.N.I., *Nahdatul Ulama* and P.K.I. were extremely successful. The successes of the P.K.I. were mainly in large coastal towns (such as Surabaya and Semarang), though its influence in several rural areas should not be under-estimated.

In Sumatra it achieved remarkable results in more or less industrialised areas like the oil centre of Palembang and the foreign estate area of Deli. In Borneo (Kalimantan) and East Indonesia its position proved to be very weak.

The *Nahdatul Ulama*'s successes at the expense of the *Masjumi* were the greatest surprise of the elections for Parliament. They indicate that the orthodox religious teachers still have a firm hold on the peasantry in various areas.

Like the *Nahdatul Ulama*, the P.N.I. profited greatly from its position as a Government party during the pre-election years. The two parties succeeded in preventing the *Masjumi* from winning a victory, and P.N.I. emerged as the largest single party. Its victory was considered a great personal success for President Sukarno, who was known to sympathise with this party.

The *Masjumi*'s great successes were in West Java and in parts of the Outer Islands. Its majority in several less populous districts favourably affected the total number of seats. Though still a very large party, *Masjumi* decidedly did not achieve the preponderant position it had expected to attain a few years earlier.

For a country without a parliamentary tradition like Indonesia it is dangerous to interpret the results of elections in terms of popular political preferences. Many votes are decided by local issues, or by irrational factors such as allegiance to personalities held in high esteem. Still, a few trends may be tentatively suggested.

First, as was to be expected, Islam appears still to hold a firm grip upon large numbers of Indonesians. Nearly half of the votes went to Moslem parties. However, the elections have also made clear that, even apart from East Indonesia where a large part of the population is Christian or (as in the case of Bali) Hindu, there would be a strong opposition from many quarters to the transformation of the present Republic into an Islamic state. The division of votes between Islamic parties (mainly N.U. and *Masjumi*) and non-Islamic parties (mainly P.N.I. and P.K.I.) probably coincided, as far as Central Java and the western part of East Java was concerned, with the distinction made by Clifford

Geertz between those participating in a *santri* culture and those living in a *pryayi* or *abangan* sphere.[1]

A second important conclusion to be drawn from the election results is that urban intellectual groups have scant influence in agrarian areas. The P.S.I., especially, made a poor showing at the elections, but another consequence has been that the position of the Westernised wing of *Masjumi* (headed at the time by Mohammad Natsir), which found strong support among the urban bourgeoisie and was more or less associated with the socialists, has also weakened. The rural population proved still to be largely under the influence of traditional leaders such as village chiefs, civil officers and religious teachers, whereas rural discontent seems mainly to have found expression in votes for the communists.[2]

As regards international implications one has to be extremely careful in interpreting the election results. International problems do not loom large in the minds of the majority of voters. Still, urban voters are, in general, more sophisticated than rural ones, and the strong communist sympathies among the former point towards an anti-Western attitude prevalent among many urban people. The large following of the parties previously represented in the Ali Sastroamidjojo Cabinet, and the moderate success of *Masjumi* and, still more, the failure of the P.S.I., which were the main participants in the Burhanuddin Harahap Cabinet and were known to be more pro-Western in their international orientation, point in the same direction.

Another important issue is the strength of communist sympathies in Indonesia. It is not easy to assess at all correctly the influence of communism on the evidence of the elections. Communist votes for Parliament turned out to amount to over sixteen per cent; but these votes are rather unevenly distributed, two large towns of Central Java even showing a communist majority.

[1] See p. 224 ff. above; see also Herbert Feith, *The Indonesian elections of 1955*, Modern Indonesia Project, Cornell University, Ithaca, 1957, p. 82 ff.

[2] See Soedjatmoko, 'The role of political parties in Indonesia', in Philip W. Thayer, *Nationalism and progress in Free Asia*, Baltimore, 1956, p. 128 ff.

Sympathy for the Soviet Union, and also for the Chinese People's Republic, is far greater in Southern Asia than in most countries of Western Europe. Though anti-communism is also rather outspoken among a good many Indonesians, more especially among Western-educated intellectuals, businessmen, religious leaders and politicians, the issue of communism, in general, does not evoke any of the frenzy and rancour attached to it in many of the Western countries.

Indonesia itself has had a good deal of unfavourable experience with Western colonialism. Its historical experience with communism is rather restricted. The ill-fated abortive Madiun insurrection of September 1948 aroused strong disapproval and opposition in many quarters. But the election results may be considered an indication that the P.K.I. has succeeded in overcoming the serious setback it had suffered as a consequence of that adventure.

Moreover, since 1953, the P.K.I. has followed a policy of active cooperation with other nationalist groupings and has toned down its revolutionary tendencies for the time being. On the other hand, to many Indonesians the experiments undertaken in the Soviet Union and in China represent successful or at least promising attempts at finding long-term solutions to the most serious and urgent problems affecting underdeveloped countries. The issue of political freedom for the individual does not loom large in the minds of many Indonesians, as in the past they knew little of political freedom or freedom of speech. Democratic institutions are very young in countries like Indonesia, and have still to prove their viability. 'Freedom from want' is, for the time being, of crucial importance, and the ways and means by which this freedom should be won are for them of secondary importance.

These are attitudes which have to be taken into account if one wants to assess the strength of communist sympathies in Indonesia. The number of convinced and theoretically trained Marxists may be very limited, but there is in many circles a general sympathy of a more diffuse nature for certain aspects of communism. This attitude is no less prevalent among various voters for other parties than among many of the voters for P.K.I.

After the ceremonial installation of the newly chosen Parliament (March 1956) a Cabinet was formed in which three of the four major parties cooperated, the communists being excluded from office. This Cabinet is known as the second Ali Sastroamidjojo Cabinet. It was only when people began to realise that none of the weaknesses of the governmental structure had been remedied by the formation of a genuine Parliament, and that corruption and inefficiency were flourishing as ever, that tensions that had been hidden behind a screen of legality revealed themselves. Things came to a head when Vice-President Hatta resigned, after the official inauguration of the Constituent Assembly in November 1956. There was, particularly after the fall of the Wilopo Cabinet (1953), in Indonesian politics a rather clear-cut split between, on the one hand, those who aimed primarily at economic reconstruction and were rather favourably disposed towards Western power and Western capital and, on the other, those distrustful towards Western capital, strongly nationalist and, if only for opportunistic reasons, not averse from cooperation with communists. To a certain degree, this distinction ran parallel with that between those advocating a 'return to normalcy' after independence had been achieved, and the proponents of a policy giving pride of place to completion of the hitherto unfinished revolution. Though the President and the Vice-President are formally supposed to be above the parties Mr. Hatta's views were more or less identified with the former group, while the President was deemed to side with the latter one. Whereas Hatta found his sympathisers mainly among *Masjumi* and P.S.I. circles, the President's views were generally identified with an influential faction of P.N.I. Whereas Hatta, himself from Menangkabau, found many adherents in the Outer Islands, Sukarno found his most fervent following in Central and East Java.

Hatta's resignation was interpreted by many of his followers as an act of disappointment at the relative impotence to which he had been reduced during the term of his office. They feared that Sukarno, no longer checked by Hatta's presence, would succeed in getting his own way. From these quarters a clamour arose for a restoration of the duumvirate Sukarno-Hatta under conditions acceptable to the latter. This movement found a strong support from the outlying regions, where complaints about neglect by the centre and unjust allocations of governmental funds and of the proceeds from foreign exchange had led to a growing discontent. It was also strongly applauded by those foreign observers who considered Hatta and his following a kind of bulwark against the advancing flood of communism. But in this movement for a restoration of Hatta in a responsible position a new factor came into play: the military cliques, which had been gaining increasing strength ever since the rise of the Republic.

As early as in the '17 October affair' of 1952 a group of officers had attempted a *coup d'état* in order to eliminate the inefficient Provisional Parliament. In actuality the friction had arisen around the problem whether the Indonesian Army, which still included several non-professional units formed during the Revolution, should be 'rationalised', that is to say transformed into a small but well-trained professional army. In practice this would have amounted to a disbanding of the units formed during the revolutionary struggle. Again, the conflict was one between those emphasising technical efficiency, persons such as Mohammad Hatta and the then Minister of Defence, Sultan Hamengku Buwono of Jogjakarta, who was known to sympathise with P.S.I. (Socialist Party), and those attaching more importance to a revolutionary fighting spirit. The 17 October affair was staged by the former group. Sukarno, however, foiled the *coup d'état*, and as a consequence a bizarre kind of poker play developed, with subcommanders or groups of officers in several military 'territories' deposing their commanders and expressing sympathy with one or the other of the parties. The final outcome of this bloodless struggle was that Sukarno won, and the Minister of Defence had to resign.[1]

[1] See Herbert Feith, *The Wilopo Cabinet*, *op. cit.*, p. 103 ff.

In the following years attempts were made to repair the rift within the officers' corps. In February 1955 a meeting of officers was held in Jogjakarta in order to restore the unity of the Army, and by July 1955 the military proved to have become a political force which had to be reckoned with: the Army, by opposing the appointment of a new Chief-of-Staff, toppled the first Ali Sastroamidjojo Cabinet. The success of this action, which resulted in an accession to power of those political groups commonly associated with Hatta, was to prove portentous for the future of Indonesia, though the unity achieved within the Army was soon lost. In December 1955 a group of officers again took independent action, aimed against an appointment signed by Hatta during the President's absence from the capital. But this time it was a group of officers sympathising with the President that had revolted, and again they succeeded in achieving their aim and in weakening the Cabinet in office, the *Masjumi*-led Burhanuddin Harahap Government, without incurring reprisals. The result was that in the second half of 1956 certain military leaders felt encouraged to attempt to influence political developments once more by taking arbitrary actions. In August Commander Kawilarang of West Java issued an order to arrest the Minister of Foreign Affairs, Roeslan Abdulgani, on the charge of corruption. It was the eve of the latter's departure to attend the London Conference on the Suez affair, and the Minister was released the same night after intervention by Prime Minister Ali Sastroamidjojo and Chief-of-Staff Harris Nasution. In November Colonel Zulkifli Lubis disappeared following an abortive attempt to stage a *coup* in Jakarta. After Hatta had resigned at the end of the same month, even more serious and consequential insubordinations began to occur. In Menangkabau a military *junta*, which had assumed the name of *Dewan Banteng* (Buffalo Council) and was headed by Lt.-Colonel Achmad Hussein, removed the Governor, who was Javanese, and proclaimed that it would henceforth have no relations with the Central Government. In Sumatra's Eastcoast Colonel Simbolon attempted to stage a similar *coup*, which was, however, thwarted. Consequently, Simbolon had to flee, but took some millions of rupiahs with him. He was suspended by Sukarno, acting in his capacity of Supreme Commander. In January 1957 the Commander of South Sumatra, Lieutenant-Colonel Barlian, formed a *junta* called *Dewan Garuda* (Garuda Council), and in March Lieutenant-Colonel Ventje Sumual took action in Macassar. His attempts to extend his power to the whole of East-Indonesia failed, but in Minahasa his organisation, the *Permesta*, succeeded in keeping in power throughout 1957.

Thus, a strange situation had arisen in which several regions, though not seceding from the unitary Republic, nevertheless refused to follow orders from the Central Government. The illegal action taken by the officers had far-reaching consequences, especially in the economic field. Before the dramatic actions there had already been a good deal of smuggling and barter of rubber and copra, conducted with the connivance of military commanders in outlying regions, in order to obtain the funds for the maintenance of the army units. The upshot of the regional actions was that henceforth the foreign exchange earned by those regions did not flow into the treasury of the Republic, but was directly used by the military leaders concerned. It is, however, difficult to decide in how far the proceeds were utilised for the benefit of the region, as any effective control was lacking. It is certain that within a short lapse of time corruption became as common as it had been under civilian rule.

In the political field the military *juntas* showed themselves strongly anti-communist, and they received some help and sympathy from foreign sources, especially from certain SEATO powers. Traders from neighbouring countries such as Singapore, Malaya, North Borneo and the Philippines profited a great deal from the barter conducted without interference from the Indonesian Government.

It strikes one as strange that the Central Government did not immediately take some sort of stern action against the insurgents. But behind this reluctance to use force there was a lack of experience which made it difficult for Indonesian political leaders to realise to the full the danger of the supreme power passing into the hands of the military. Both the unity of the Republic and the fundamental loyalty of the officers were wrongly taken for granted. The actions by the insurgent officers were seen as moves on the political chessboard which must be matched by counter-moves in order to establish the balance of power. The solutions had to be looked for in an 'Indonesian' way, by *musjawarah* (settling of dissensions by discussion) and compromise. In this vein conferences were organised, and the insurgent leaders invited. Some of them turned up, some others refused to come, but in either case this procedure encouraged them to go on, and to attempt to impose their conditions upon the Central Government.

Behind the reluctance of the Central Government to use force there was also a certain awareness of the fact that the complaints of the outer regions about a neglect of some of their urgent needs and their demand for a greater share in the governmental funds were justified. The legislation on the distribution of authority and the allocation of funds to regional units was still in preparation, and the construction and upkeep of roads, an elementary pre-condition for economic welfare, had to be postponed until the funds were available. Most of all, however, it was fear of civil war and fratricide, with ensuing foreign interference, that prevented the Central Government from taking stern action against the insurgents throughout 1957.

But the military rebellions also had serious repercussions in the political field. The *Masjumi* and some minor parties withdrew their ministers from Ali's second Cabinet, and finally, on March 13, 1957, after the *coup* staged by Sumual in Macassar, Ali had to submit his Cabinet's resignation. Immediately, President Sukarno declared martial law throughout the country and in this way again strengthened the position of the military leaders. Meanwhile, he had formulated his 'conception' for a guided democracy. A few months earlier, his speeches had made the impression that he was aiming at the abolition of political parties, but this idea met with such a resistance that he had to mitigate it. What he was advocating now was a so-called *Gotong Royong*

Cabinet, in which, in harmony with traditional Indonesian conceptions, party strife would have to be replaced by *gotong royong*, that is to say mutual cooperation. The attempt to fall back upon conceptions borrowed from traditional rural society for a solution of actual problems is in line with a way of thinking prevalent among many Indonesian leaders, most of all in P.N.I. circles. Such a cabinet would have to include at least the four major parties. Only in such a way would a real reconstruction be possible. And a National Council in which functional and regional groups should be represented had to be created to achieve coordination in the overall policy of the country.

Again, the conception as published by the President, while it was generally approved by the left wing, met with strong resistance in many circles. An attempt to form a government in accordance with the *gotong royong* idea failed, as the *Masjumi* refused to cooperate with the P.K.I. in a cabinet. It is probable that Sukarno had realised that if the communists were allowed to remain in the opposition they would be able to capitalise on the many failures of the ruling parties.

Finally President Sukarno followed a rather unorthodox course: he appointed citizen Sukarno to act as *formateur* and selected an extra-parliamentary cabinet of experts, the *Karya* (special task) Cabinet, with Djuanda Kartawidjaja, the former Director of the Planning Bureau, as Prime Minister. Besides Mr. Djuanda himself, there were several other non-party men in the Cabinet, among them the Minister of Foreign Affairs Subandrio (who, however, has since joined the P.N.I.). Of the major parties, P.N.I. and N.U. had rather strong representation. One *Masjumi* man who joined the Cabinet was removed from his party, whereas the communists as such were not represented, though they had one or two sympathisers within the Cabinet. In general, however, the P.K.I. supported the Cabinet within and outside the Parliament. As they were the only party which could not possibly be held responsible for the failures of the successive governments and for the rampant corruption, they were again able to achieve remarkable successes at the regional elections held between June 1957 and February 1958 in Java and somewhat later in certain other regions. Nearly everywhere the number of votes cast for the P.K.I. was appreciably higher than at the elections for Parliament and for the Constituent Assembly in 1955, in most cases at the expense of P.N.I., but not infrequently also at the expense of the large Moslem parties.

The successes of the communists in Central Java and East Java were such that they were able to achieve majorities in several municipal or regional councils, and to secure in this way the appointment of communist mayors or other high officials. For the first time in Indonesian history communists were faced with the situation of having to resist the temptation of being involved in corrupt practices, now that they were connected with power and confronted with a way of life out of gear with the salaries paid to them as officials. Until that time the communist leaders had been able to distinguish themselves from many others by a stern and sober conduct which without doubt added to their prestige among the rank and file.

The new communist victories at the polls heightened the uneasiness in certain political circles, inside and outside Indonesia, about the potential strength of communism in Java. Separatist tendencies in the Outer Islands were increasingly expressed in terms of anti-communism, with the danger of Javanese domination identified with the communist danger. However, such tendencies were largely neutralised by the awareness, among Indonesian and foreign politicians, that the communists were not likely to make a bid for power, considering their weak position in the Outer Islands, while any separatist adventure would provoke a communist counter-move in Java.

The decisive developments in the latter half of 1957 came in the economic field. The *Karya* Cabinet was expected to start a program of economic reconstruction. A National Council was formed, according to President Sukarno's conception, but as an advisory body only in order to respect the Provisional Constitution and the power of Parliament. As the existing Planning Bureau had not

Votes (1,000's) polled by major political parties in elections for Parliament (1955) and regional councils (1957–58)

Region	PNI		*Masjumi*		NU		PKI	
East Java								
September 26, 1955	2,251	(22.8%)	1,110	(11.2%)	3,371	(34.1%)	2,300	(23.3%)
July 29, 1957/February 25, 1958	1,900	(19.2%)	977	(9.9%)	3,000	(30.4%)	2,705	(27.4%)
Central Java								
September 26, 1955	3,020	(35.1%)	902	(9.6%)	1,772	(20.7%)	2,326	(25.9%)
July 17, 1957	2,236	(26.3%)	715	(8.4%)	1,772	(20.8%)	2,707	(31.8%)
Jogjakarta								
September 26, 1955	180	(19.9%)	127	(14.0%)	95	(10.5%)	229	(25.3%)
November 7, 1957	±164	(±16%)	±130	(±13%)	±92	(±9%)	±292	(±29%)
West Java								
September 26, 1955	1,542	(22.8%)	1,844	(25.3%)	674	(10.0%)	756	(11.9%)
August 10, 1957	1,056	(15.0%)	1,841	(26.1%)	597	(8.5%)	1,087	(15.4%)
Jakarta								
September 26, 1955	152	(19.8%)	200	(26.1%)	121	(15.7%)	96	(12.6%)
June 22, 1957	125	(17.6%)	154	(21.7%)	105	(14.8%)	137	(19.4%)
South Sumatra								
September 26, 1955	214	(14.7%)	628	(43.1%)	116	(8.0%)	177	(12.1%)
December 1, 1957	187	(12.9%)	553	(38.0%)	114	(7.8%)	229	(15.7%)

Compiled by Mr. A. van Marle on the basis of various published and unpublished data long before submitted a five years' plan, but lacked any power whatever to get the program under way, the creation of a new National Planning Board with sufficient authority to coordinate the activities of the different ministries was projected.[1]

The Cabinet also took some steps intended to stabilise the economic situation. An export and import regulation was introduced which amounted to a devaluation of the *rupiah* to its real value, in order to stimulate exports and to restrict imports of unessentials.

It had been the Government's intention to avoid an appreciable rise of the price level on the home market, but unfortunately the situation began to get out of hand, and in October 1957 even rice prices began to rise to alarming figures.

Many of the well-intended governmental measures were thwarted by the terrific shortage of foreign exchange, increased by illegal barter conducted especially in the regions where rebellious officers had severed all financial relations with the Central Government. The threatening economic catastrophe was probably one of the major factors inducing the Indonesian Government to start a widespread anti-Dutch action towards the end of 1957. At the same time, this action could be seen as a desperate attempt by President Sukarno to restore unity among the Indonesian people on an issue where the numerous disruptive tendencies could be bridged by action on a national scale.

The Dutch Government had refused for many years to reopen negotiations on the never-settled West Irian (Western New-Guinea) dispute. The problem was considered by Dutch politicians as shelved, and the periodical attempts of the Indonesian Government to submit it to United Nations in order to reopen negotiations were never taken very seriously by the Dutch, despite several warnings, including those emanating from Dutch people working in Indonesia.

In November 1957 Indonesia failed yet another time to secure in the General Assembly of the United Nations the required

1 This project, however, has not yet been implemented at the time of writing.

two-thirds majority for its proposal that the United Nations request both parties concerned to resume negotiations. This time, though, the Indonesian Government did not leave it at that, but opened a full-fledged campaign directed against the Dutch interests in Indonesia. As early as the first months of 1956 Indonesia had unilaterally annulled the provisions of the Round Table Conference of December 1949, with the argument that the Dutch had themselves violated the treaty by refusing further negotiations on West Irian and incorporating the area in the Constitution as Dutch territory. The action of 1957 was presented as an implementation of the decision taken in 1956. Officially the action was announced as a kind of pressure brought to bear upon the Dutch Government in order to compel it to resume discussions on West Irian. It is difficult to decide whether this was the true motive, or merely a justification for measures in the economic field. At any rate, in as far as they had hoped to change the Dutch attitude, the Indonesians failed. The Dutch were taken completely by surprise; they had never taken the threat of a firmer action seriously. But throughout 1958 their official stand was, if anything, more rigid than ever, with the argument that discussions could not be resumed 'under conditions of blackmail'. In the Netherlands an attitude prevailed that nothing could be done about the situation anyway, and that the interests in Indonesia should be considered a total loss. The relations between the two countries were allowed to go from bad to worse.

As far as is known, the action in Indonesia was conducted practically without violence. All the same, for those concerned it has become a great tragedy. It is difficult to decide in how far the tens of thousands of people of Dutch nationality leaving Indonesia were ousted or left of their own free will, but in any case there was a mass exodus of those who considered the situation unbearable. Many of those leaving were Indo-Europeans who had never been in Holland before and who were bound to become 'displaced persons' there. But the development was equally tragic for those numerous Dutchmen who had spent the best part of their life in Indonesia and were in full disagreement with the rigid Dutch policy they held responsible for the catastrophe.

At first the anti-Dutch action was led by a government-sponsored 'Central Action Committee for the Liberation of West Irian'. But in the first days of December 1957, in several enterprises members of the Indonesian personnel proceeded to independent action, taking over the direction of the enterprises from the Dutch. In several cases left-wing trade unions were said to have instigated such action. A few days later the Chief-of-Staff, General Nasution, issued a ban on all further actions to take over Dutch enterprises. Gradually all Dutch companies were placed under military control. The semi-official Central Action Committee was dissolved on December 21, 1957, and Prime Minister Djuanda announced that the National Security Council, under his chairmanship, would henceforth direct the campaign for the recuperation of West Irian. Little by little the actions were channelled into a National Front for the Liberation of West Irian, which increasingly came under military leadership, as a mass organisation ultimately led by General Nasution.[1]

The actions in the economic field resulted in nearly complete elimination of the Dutch from the economic life of Indonesia. At first, the enterprises were put under military administration, and the taking over was said to be only formal, without affecting the Dutch rights of ownership. But towards the end of 1958 a law was promulgated to nationalise all Dutch enterprises. Only after the Dutch had agreed to transfer West Irian would the Indonesians be ready to discuss indemnities.

The actions had very serious repercussions in the field of Indonesian economy as well. Certainly they had never been planned and prepared in advance. Especially the taking over of the buildings of the K.P.M. (the Royal Packet Navigation Company), which had previously occupied a near-monopolistic position in interinsular trade, had grave and lasting consequences. The directors in the Netherlands, afraid of confiscation, ordered the ships to sail to harbours outside Indonesia. The Indonesian

[1] Guy Pauker, 'The role of political organizations in Indonesia', in *Far Eastern Survey*, Vol. XXVII, 1958, p. 129 ff.

Government retorted by a seizure of K.P.M. vessels in Indonesian harbours. But finally, on March 26, 1958, the government was compelled to allow the ships to leave Indonesia, as otherwise it would have been confronted with a disastrous claim by the insurance companies concerned.

The upshot of all those complications was that interinsular shipping and interinsular trade were all but paralysed by December 1957. It is superfluous to dwell upon the consequences of such a situation for an archipelago to which inter-island shipping is of a vital interest. In particular for the outlying regions the disruption of overseas communications could cause serious hardships and even shortages of food and other necessities of life.

If the West Irian action had been intended as an expedient to restore the endangered unity of the Indonesian people, its consequence was rather the contrary. The opposition against the Cabinet in office, mainly consisting of *Masjumi* and P.S.I., criticised not so much the anti-Dutch action as such as the fact that its implementation was so ill-devised that it had wrought havoc to the Indonesian economy. Among the critics were such prominent personalities as Sjafruddin Prawiranegara, Governor of the Bank of Indonesia and one of the leaders of *Masjumi*, and Mr. Hatta, who despite several attempts to restore the duumvirate Sukarno-Hatta had persisted in his aloofness. The opposition became directed more openly against the President as such. On November 30, 1957, an attempt had been made on his life, and although it failed, it caused over one hundred casualties, around a dozen of them fatal. To recover from the mental shock, the President went abroad for a visit to different friendly countries, among them India, Egypt, and Yugoslavia. During his absence his opponents attempted to collect their forces, both inside and outside Indonesia, in order to provoke a change of government in Jakarta. The rebellious colonels in West Sumatra and the Minahasa formed a coalition and reinforced their relations with the neighbouring SEATO countries. Several *Masjumi* leaders such as Sjafruddin, Mohammad Natsir and Burhanuddin Harahap joined the rebels in Menangkabau. There they met Professor

Sumitro Djojohadikusumo, earlier a prominent P.S.I. member, who had been accused of irregular practices and had fled from Java to Sumatra's Westcoast. On February 11, 1958, Lieutenant-Colonel Achmad Hussein issued an ultimatum to President Sukarno and Prime Minister Djuanda to dissolve the *Karya* Cabinet within five days, in order to replace it by a new Cabinet under Hatta and Sultan Hamengku Buwono of Jogjakarta. On the fifteenth, two days before Sukarno's return from abroad, a Revolutionary Government of the Republic of Indonesia was proclaimed, with Sjafruddin Prawiranegara as Prime Minister.

The patience of the Central Government had come to an end. The 'Indonesian way' of handling the dispute was relinquished, and on February 23, 1958 the Indonesian airforce bombed the broadcasting stations of Padang and Bukittinggi. The Central Government's military force acted with remarkable efficiency. Landing troops were dispatched to the new oil harbour of Dumai on the Eastcoast of Sumatra, while paratroops were landed at the oil centre of Pakan Baru, in order to prevent the proceeds from the oil industry from falling into the hands of the rebels and at the same time to secure control of the overseas communications with Singapore and the coast of Malaya. At first, the rebels found a good deal of sympathy and more or less outspoken support from many circles in the Western world. But their inability to make a stand, their lack of fighting spirit and the amateurishness of their preparations for a military struggle, much in contrast with the impressive efficiency of the Central Government's forces, made the Western sympathisers more cautious. On April 18 landings from the sea and from the air were effectuated in Padang, and on May 5 Bukittinggi was occupied by the Government's troops. The rebels' forces were forced to repair to hiding places in the mountains, and the civil war in West Sumatra continued as a guerrilla struggle. In other parts of Sumatra where clashes had occurred the main centres were also gradually recovered by the Central forces. The Commander of South Sumatra, Barlian, who had tried to remain 'neutral', was sent on sick leave and replaced. The centre of the rebellion meanwhile shifted to North Celebes, where the rebel government had some harbours, and air communications with neighbouring countries such as the Philippines and North Borneo. The civil war had reached a dangerous phase, the rebels, who had secured some aircraft, bombing the adjoining harbours and airfields still in the hands of the Central Government in order to prevent an attack from the sea or from the air. The conflict threatened to expand into an international clash with an unmistakable cold-war aspect, the rebels using airfields outside Indonesia as a base, and employing foreign nationals to fly planes bought abroad, the Central Government on the other hand purchasing ships and aircraft from the Soviet Union and other East European countries.

A number of the Indonesian diplomatic representatives and lower personnel abroad had defected from the official Government and turned into advocates of the rebel cause. The situation became still more critical when a rebel aircraft was shot down on May 27, 1958 near Ambon and the captured pilot was identified as an American national. Quick action was taken by the Government forces resulting in the capture of Menado on June 26, 1958 and preventing the rebellion from developing into an armed international clash.

The aftermath of the rebellion, however, was to last throughout the second half of 1958. The rebels were no longer able to put up organised resistance, but they continued to harrass the Government's forces as guerrilla bands in large parts of Sumatra and Celebes. In Sumatra's Westcoast a situation seems to have developed comparable to that after the second military action by the Dutch of December 1948. Just as the Dutch had held the cities and the main arteries of communications, but the mountainous countryside had been largely dominated by guerrillas, at present the Central Government's control seems to be largely restricted to the urban centres. The result of the rebellion has been that the 'security problem', which in the years before had been mainly involved by *Darul Islam* activities in a few areas, now extends to much larger parts of the Outer Islands. It would be a serious mistake to assume that the rebellion has been finally suppressed. The wish for greater autonomy, which induced a good many Sumatrans and Minahasans to participate in the rebellion, is still far from satisfied, and the armed clash has embittered many people who had been true Indonesian nationalists before.

In the economic field the Government has been exerting every effort to overcome the dislocation resulting from the anti-Dutch measures and the rebellion. Recovery of the harbours from which illegal barter had been conducted has restored the Government's control over the sources of foreign exchange. But the difficulty in interinsular shipping caused by the departure of the K.P.M. fleet is only gradually being overcome by purchases of ships in other countries. Meanwhile, as stocks of copra are being piled up in Celebes, there rises a serious problem for the Government in view of the advantages which accrued to the coconut growers and traders from the illegal barter conducted until the rebellion was quelled. At the time of writing the foreign exchange position of Indonesia was still alarming, and though foreign trade was gradually increasing once more, the Indonesian economy was still hampered by regular attacks of guerrilla bands on the estates in Sumatra's Eastcoast. The lack of skilled personnel created by the departure of many Dutchmen could also be only gradually overcome.

Another problem was caused by the need to find new markets or transit centres for Indonesian export articles in order to replace the Dutch market. The Indonesians are trying hard to shift their export to other countries such as West Germany, Belgium, Britain and Yugoslavia. But as far as West Germany and Belgium are concerned the European Common Market planned for 1959 may become a serious hindrance in view of the discrimination against countries not belonging to this group. Still, Indonesia succeeded, in the course of 1958, in stepping up its trade relations with several countries, among them Japan, with which country Indonesia, after long and laborious negotiations, has finally been able to conclude a treaty on reparations to be paid for the damages suffered during the Japanese occupation. Trade with

East European countries and China increased as well, and those countries extended their help to Indonesia. There is also an increasing tendency to by-pass Singapore and to establish direct relations with foreign countries.

The United States and other Western countries, too, resumed their friendly relations with the Indonesian Government after the rebellion had been suppressed, even extending some military help by selling aircraft and ships – notwithstanding protests from the Dutch, who were afraid that they might be used for an attack on West Irian. The landings from the sea and from the air performed during the civil war had made the Dutch aware that the military proficiency of the Indonesians should not be underestimated. But the Americans have apparently shifted their sympathy from the rebel colonels to General Nasution, whom they consider sufficiently strong to be able to keep the communists of Java in check. The promulgation of a law regulating foreign investments has helped to assuage the fear of further interference with Western enterprise.

If the relations of Indonesia with the outer world have now been more or less normalised, with Indonesia keeping to its neutral policy as evidenced in recent visits by President Rajendra Prasad of India and President Tito of Yugoslavia, an exception should be made for relations not only with the Netherlands, but also with the Kuomintang. The Taiwan regime, which is not recognised by Indonesia, is held to have been responsible for a good deal of support to the rebels. Consequently, all kinds of organisations held to be affiliated with Kuomintang have been prohibited, foreign schools have been closed, papers with non-Latin characters have been banned, and enterprises owned by Kuomintang Chinese have been nationalised by law, along with those in Dutch hands. There is a general awareness among the Chinese in Indonesia that this anti-Kuomintang action has been largely used to give vent to the anti-Chinese sentiments prevalent in certain Indonesian circles. Therefore, among the great majority of Chinese who have not been affected by these measures there is a certain uneasiness that they might become the next target of frustrated ambitions if the Indonesian economy does not expand at a sufficient rate to provide opportunities for all. There are already some indications, as for instance a severe restriction of the number of Chinese admitted to higher education, casting doubt on the readiness of Indonesian society in its present constellation to allow those Chinese who ultimately opt for Indonesian citizenship to assimilate.

Another problem, one that has become increasingly pressing, is the growing power of the military leaders. The danger of war-lordism may have been eliminated for the time being. But the rising star of General Nasution and his associates has greatly reinforced the actual power of the Indonesian officers' corps. The martial law promulgated by President Sukarno in March 1957 was confirmed on a new legal basis in December 1957 for one year, and was again extended for the same term in December 1958. The creation of a Ministry for Economic Stabilisation in June 1958, under a Colonel as a Minister, has strengthened the grip of the military on economic life, already great since Dutch business was put under military administration. A ban on strikes in vital industries, enacted after the enforcement of martial law, has likewise enhanced the power of military leaders, at the same time detracting from the force of organised labour. Developments in neighbouring countries such as Burma and Pakistan may increase the tendency to replace democracy after the Western model by a military dictatorship, but for the moment the leading officers in Indonesia seem to be content with the present form of cooperation between themselves and the civil authorities. But the existing balance of power remains very unstable, and there are only a few people left in Indonesia who rely upon the Constituent Assembly still at work to play a decisive role in formulating the future structure of the Indonesian Government. This much is certain that the elections have created more problems than they have solved. Democratic institutions are not yet deeply-rooted in Indonesia, and even the unity and integrity of the territory of the Indonesian Republic would not appear to be firmly established. The near future of Indonesia seems to be one big question mark.

It is still more risky to try to prophesy the developments in a more remote future. There is a good deal of speculation, whether 'Indonesia will turn communist', whether 'Islam will prove a dam against communism' or whether 'Western New-Guinea will eventually be incorporated within the Republic of Indonesia'. It would be presumptuous to try to predict the shape of things to come.

But it should be possible for a sociologist to discern a few general trends, which are most likely to manifest themselves in the future (granted that humanity will not annihilate itself in a world-wide catastrophe), quite apart from the specific aspect which these trends may assume.

Thus, whether Indonesia will 'turn communist' or not, it seems pretty certain that several developments generally associated with communism will manifest themselves. Increasing state interference in economic affairs cannot be avoided. Growing discontent among the poor peasantry will eventually force some kind of land-redistribution. A cumulative industrial development will somehow be brought about. The economic power and influence of foreign companies will certainly be curtailed, and an increasing number of Indonesians will receive the necessary intellectual and technical training to replace foreign personnel. The dynamic forces awakened in Indonesia (as in any Asian country) cannot be prevented from budding forth, and if the Government does not fill popular needs, they may well find an outlet in a revolutionary form. Whether such a revolution could be called 'communist' depends, however, on many circumstances which cannot be predicted. On the other hand, if a 'communist' movement should come to power in Indonesia, it would have to adapt itself to the Indonesian scene in order to keep its ground, as it has been forced to in China.

In the same way, the question whether Islam will prove 'a dam against communism' cannot be answered in a simple formula. If it is to do so, Islam will have to adapt its social philosophy to the requirements and dynamics of contemporary Indonesian society. If Islam clings to its conservative economic tenets, it will soon lose its grasp upon a large part of the Indonesian population. Without advocating land-redistribution, without attacking poverty in an energetic way and wagering its spiritual strength on the side of the under-privileged, Islam will never be able to hold its own.

It is impossible to predict whether Western New-Guinea will eventually be embodied within the Indonesian Republic. It is even uncertain whether the Indonesian Republic will be able to retain its present form and territory as a unitary state. For the moment, the forces making for unity still seem definitely to exceed the disruptive tendencies. But Tibor Mende was right in characterising Indonesia's main problem as: *Man against geography*.

But it is certain that social developments in one corner of the world cannot possibly lag too far behind those in neighbouring corners. In this respect modern technology and growing economic interdependence are moulding an area like Southeast Asia into 'one world'. Even if New-Guinea remains separate from the main body of Indonesia, developments similar to those that have occurred there will make themselves felt before long. The colonial pattern will eventually lead to similar movements and phenomena, and Dutch colonial rule will probably come to an early end at the hands of Papuans, whether they join Indonesia or create a state on a narrower ethnic basis.

It is equally impossible to answer the specific question whether Western capital will continue to find an outlet and opportunity for investment in Indonesia. Even if a political party coalition not too unfavourably disposed towards foreign capital should serve as a base for a future government, it will be prevented from following an obvious pro-Western course by strong nationalist tendencies within each of the parties participating. The official political orientation of Indonesia is likely to remain, for the time being, one of non-commitment similar to the foreign policy pursued by India and Burma. It remains a moot point whether capital from Western countries will, under such circumstances, be easily available.

But it seems probable that if Western capitalists or Western governments desire to retain Indonesia as a field for investment and economic activity, they will have to adapt themselves to the requirements of Indonesian society. Only if foreign capital allows itself to be geared in with national economic planning, will it be able to keep its ground. If it does not, it will be forced to make way for national capital, whatever the sacrifices for the Indonesians themselves, or for capital equipment from countries under communist regimes more willing to adapt themselves to the needs of the new Southeast Asian countries.

Though the general trends of future developments may, thus, be forecast largely independently from 'the shape of things to come', it would be erroneous to conclude that the outward appearance is unimportant. The actual struggle between states, organisations, ideologies and personalities is usually fought without insight into their intrinsic likenesses and relationships. Moreover, even though the general trend of developments is established, the way those developments are brought about and the pace at which they occur make a good deal of difference. Though, from a sociologist's point of view, different ideologies may present common features, from the point of view of the people concerned it is the differences that matter. It depends on these differences and historical details who will starve and who will live, who will be the sufferers and who will benefit from the developments.

With respect to the precise shape of things to come the sociologist must keep silence. Forecasting the future in all its details should be left to prophets and soothsayers. Decisive though such details may prove to be, the scholar can only treat them in retrospect.

Considering Indonesia's future, then, the sociologist must content himself with the following quotation from an expert's unpublished report: 'The storm-and-stress period, which Indonesia is passing through, is leading to social progress, notwithstanding political and economic tensions. No force on earth can repel the trend of social development'.

Appendix

Registered Eligible Voters for the 1955 Elections

INDONESIA[1]

Region	Citizens	Number of eligible voters	Percentage of citizens eligible to vote
East Java	18,023,121	10,938,488	60.69
Central Java	17,692,821	10,077,068	56.95
West Java	14,884,941	7,861,722	52.81
Greater Jakarta	1,642,500	994,848	60.56
Total Java	*52,243,383*	*29,872,126*	*57.18*
North Sumatra	4,844,806	2,458,729	50.75
Central Sumatra	3,352,713	1,795,955	53.57
South Sumatra	3,156,635	1,739,332	55.10
Total Sumatra	11,354,154	5,994,016	52.79
East Kalimantan	350,976	208,832	59.50
West Kalimantan	1,095,655	563,274	53.36
South Kalimantan	1,627,914	903,517	55.50
Total Kalimantan	3,074,545	1,675,623	54.50
Southeast/South Sulawesi	3,682,669	1,677,599	45.55
North/Central Sulawesi	1,657,841	838,216	55.05
Total Sulawesi	5,340,510	2,515,815	47.11
Moluccas	692,882	364,160	52.55
East NusaTenggara	2,140,785	1,199,647	56.03
West NusaTenggara	2,627,009	1,427,012	54.32
Total Nusa Tenggara	4,767,794	2,626,659	55.09
Total Outer Islands	*25,229,885*	*13,176,273*	*52.22*
TOTAL INDONESIA	77,473,268	43,048,399	55.57

[1] The basic data for these tables were kindly made available to Mr. A. van Marle by Mr. Soelaeman Soemardi of the University of Indonesia, Institute for Social Research at Jakarta.

East Java

No.	Regency or City	Citizens	Number of eligible voters	Percentage of citizens eligible to vote
1	Surabaya	543,433	337,545	62.11
2	Sidoarjo	420,513	258,513	61.48
3	Mojokerto	454,282	271,997	59.87
4	Jombang	578,513	351,950	60.84
5	Tuban	533,877	339,588	63.61
6	Bojonegoro	591,489	367,087	62.06
7	Lamongan	658,403	421,400	64.00
8	Madiun	423,429	271,978	64.23
9	Magetan	441,911	262,975	59.51
10	Ngawi	488,096	296,225	60.69
11	Ponorogo	637,549	353,829	55.50
12	Patjitan	379,249	212,078	55.92
13	Kediri	793,756	462,454	58.26
14	Nganjuk	567,795	335,807	59.16
15	Blitar	707,457	437,964	61.91
16	Tulungagung	590,354	338,474	57.33
17	Trenggalek	370,236	204,676	55.28
18	Malang	1,226,754	744,271	60.66
19	Pasuruan	635,838	400,499	62.99
20	Probolinggo	605,270	380,532	62.87
21	Lumajang	539,829	328,270	60.81
22	Bondowoso	423,645	282,253	66.62
23	Panarukan	376,667	242,291	64.32
24	Jember	1,298,985	796,375	61.31
25	Banyuwangi	893,254	522,059	58.44
26	Pamekasan	319,669	194,794	60.94
27	Sumenep	635,640	367,062	57.75
28	Sampang	399,280	229,834	57.56
29	Bangkalan	486,581	291,475	59.90
30	Surabaya City	552,434	367,799	66.58
31	Madiun City	77,481	45,052	58.15
32	Malang City	238,425	149,032	62.51
33	Kediri City	133,027	72,350	54.39
	TOTAL	18,023,121	10,938,488	60.69

CENTRAL JAVA

No.	Regency or City	Citizens	Number of eligible voters	Percentage of citizens eligible to vote
1	Semarang	514,600	302,447	58.77
2	Demak	372,133	263,267	70.74
3	Kendal	435,721	226,076	51.88
4	Grobogan	564,806	322,560	57.10
5	Pekalongan	746,597	444,806	59.57
6	Pemalang	626,311	355,308	56.73
7	Tegal	666,829	368,907	55.32
8	Brebes	788,645	428,717	54.36
9	Pati	580,743	337,563	58.12
10	Kudus	300,479	177,578	59.09
11	Jepara	400,228	233,647	58.37
12	Rembang	246.909	155,183	62.85
13	Blora	421,713	252,961	59.98
14	Banyumas	820,245	456,129	55.60
15	Purbolinggo	481,324	280,113	58.19
16	Tjilatjap	764,145	430,929	56.39
17	Banjarnegara	453,750	261,122	57.54
18	Magelang	695,290	410,230	59.00
19	Temanggung	312,900	183,298	58.58
20	Wonosobo	339,035	205,404	60.58
21	Purworejo	501,455	279,797	55.79
22	Kebumen	720,252	414,258	57.51
23	Sukoharjo	345,083	191,027	55.35
24	Klaten	732,267	414,843	56.65
25	Sragen	440,355	242,945	55.17
26	Boyolali	512,999	295,045	57.51
27	Karanganyar	357,170	201,747	56.48
28	Wonogiri	740,335	408,797	55.21
29	Bantul	430,560	249,815	58.02
30	Sleman	485,895	245,313	50.48
31	Gunungkidul	477,708	251,298	52.60
32	Kulonprogo	307,903	166,613	54.11
33	Pekalongan City	80,163	49,615	61.89
34	Surakarta City	298,778	173,274	57.99
35	Semarang City	352,228	215,287	61.12
36	Jogjakarta City	243,276	137,830	57.47
37	Tegal City	77,991	43,319	55.55
	TOTAL	17,692,821	10,077,068	56.95

West Java

No.	Regency or City	Citizens	Number of eligible voters	Percentage of citizens eligible to vote
1	Serang	603,578	345,059	57.16
2	Pandeglang	362,871	187,915	51.78
3	Lebak	337,980	178,826	52.91
4	Tanggerang	673,977	344,895	51.17
5	Bekasi	563,099	289,181	51.35
6	Krawang	1,074,989	380,777	35.42
7	Purwakarta	887,700	545,456	61.44
8	Bogor City	104,189	58,307	51.16
9	Bogor	1,077,809	538,352	49.94
10	Sukabumi	824,425	440,564	53.43
11	Tjianjur	690,103	379,978	55.06
12	Bandung City	631,257	336,947	53.37
13	Bandung	1,289,478	713,055	55.29
14	Sumedang	469,948	246,531	52.45
15	Garut	798,945	421,224	52.72
16	Tasikmalaya	872,170	448,807	51.45
17	Tjiamis	870,212	470,047	54.01
18	Cheribon City	100,867	59,490	58.97
19	Cheribon	794,604	458,818	57.74
20	Kuningan	520,501	267,292	51.35
21	Indramayu	765,573	423,959	55.37
22	Majalengka	570,666	326,242	57.17
	Total	14,884,941	7,861,722	52.81

Greater Jakarta

No.	Regency or City	Citizens	Number of eligible voters	Percentage of citizens eligible to vote
1	North Jakarta	471,131	348,601	73.99
2	West Jakarta	474,755	266,579	56.15
3	East and South Jakarta	696,614	379,668	54.50
	Total	1,642,500	994,848	60.56

North Sumatra

No.	Regency or City	Citizens	Number of eligible voters	Percentage of citizens eligible to vote
1	Medan City	217,202	109,677	50.50
2	Deli/Serdang	612,357	327,273	53.44
3	Langkat	248,868	135,755	54.55
4	Asahan	260,897	142,961	54.80
5	Karo	120,013	61,418	51.18
6	Simelungun	474,751	245,053	51.62
7	Labuhan Batu	180,234	98,818	54.83
8	North Tapanuli	666,629	303,546	45.53
9	Central Tapanuli	107,275	55,936	52.14
10	South Tapanuli	406,301	200,800	49.67
11	Nias	261,469	134,927	51.60
12	Great Acheh	147,183	53,555	36.39[1]
13	Acheh Pidie	199,869	89,730	44.89[1]
14	North Acheh	293,434	159,942	54.51
15	East Acheh	176,092	99,357	56.42
16	Central Acheh	151,399	72,631	47.97
17	West Acheh	161,218	83,390	51.72
18	South Acheh	159,615	83,960	52.60
	Total	4,844,806	2,458,729	50.75

[1] That the proportion of citizens eligible to vote is so low is probably owing to the unsettled situation in the regency: a number of potentially eligible voters would seem not to have been registered by the authorities.

Central Sumatra

No.	Regency or City	Citizens	Number of eligible voters	Percentage of citizens eligible to vote
1	Bukittinggi City	40,915	20,528	50.17
2	Padang City	101,141	51,062	50.49
3	Tanah Datar	278,702	139,254	49.97
4	Agam	329,275	165,660	50.32
5	Pasaman	170,466	93,378	54.78
6	Limapuluh Kota	237,930	132,342	55.62
7	Solok	223,354	135,384	60.61
8	Padang/Pariaman	405,282	207,403	51.17
9	South Pesisir/Kerintji	316,299	172,269	54.46
10	Sawahlunto	131,673	70,066	53.21
11	Kampar	165,885	88,298	53.23
12	Bengkalis	182,522	92,272	50.55
13	Batanghari	204,309	109,504	53.60
14	Merangin	165,631	91,910	55.49
15	Indragiri	274,329	147,455	53.75
16	Riau	125,000	79,170	63.36
	Total	3,352,713	1,795,955	53.57

South Sumatra

No.	Regency or City	Citizens	Number of eligible voters	Percentage of citizens eligible to vote
1	Palembang City . . .	258,818	142,595	55·09
2	Pal./Banyuasin	224,523	123,344	54·94
3	Musi Rawas	118,725	68,415	57·71
4	Ogan/Komering Ulu .	283,153	153,136	54·09
5	Ogan/Komering Ilir .	287,628	151,436	52.65
6	Lahat	239,588	131,058	54·70
7	Muara Enim	284,152	141,317	49·73
8	South Lampong . . .	457,621	264,177	57·73
9	North Lampong . . .	210,773	127,942	60.70
10	Central Lampong . . .	209,112	119,531	57·16
11	North Bengkulen . . .	89,578	58,244	65.02
12	South Bengkulen . . .	110,996	60,287	54·31
13	Rejang Lebong	118,740	65,638	55·28
14	Bangka	191,486	95,883	50.07
15	Billiton	71,742	36,329	50.64
	Total	3,156,635	1,739,332	55·10

East Kalimantan

No.	Regency	Citizens	Number of eligible voters	Percentage of citizens eligible to vote
1	Special Region of Kutai	256,239	152,704	59·59
2	Special Region of Berau	21,289	11,894	55·87
3	Special Region of Bulongan	73,448	44,234	60.22
	Total	350,976	208,832	59·50

West Kalimantan

No.	Regency or City	Citizens	Number of eligible voters	Percentage of citizens eligible to vote
1	Pontianak City	68,676	34,412	50.11
2	Pontianak	266,495	133,638	50.15
3	Sambas	243,826	127,016	52.09
4	Sanggau	175,089	89,926	51.36
5	Sintang	147,244	77,058	52.33
6	Kapuas Hulu	71,661	37,875	52.85
7	Ketapang	122,664	63,349	51.64
	Total	1,095,655	563,274	53.36

South Kalimantan

No.	Regency or City	Citizens	Number of eligible voters	Percentage of citizens eligible to vote
1	Banjermasin City . . .	153,340	86,881	56.66
2	Banjar	323,939	169,721	52.39
3	South Hulu Sungei . .	356,145	210,214	59.02
4	North Hulu Sungei . .	275,298	164,259	59.67
5	Kapuas	112,398	56,069	49.88
6	Barito	119,892	66,050	55.17
7	Kotawaringin	145,596	77,765	53.41
8	Kota Baru	141,306	72,558	51.35
	Total	1,627,914	903,517	55.50

Southeast/South Sulawesi

No.	Regency or City	Citizens	Number of eligible voters	Percentage of citizens eligible to vote
1	Macassar City	225,536	121,505	53.87
2	Macassar	755,005	347,904	46.07
3	Bonthain	322,571	171,422	53.14
4	Bone	630,980	297,644	47.17
5	Pare-Pare	569,847	177,287	31.10[1]
6	Mandar	326,593	131,419	40.23[1]
7	Luwu	391,661	190,346	48.59
8	Southeast Sulawesi . .	460,476	240,072	52.13
	Total	3,682,669	1,677,599	45.55

[1] See note on p. 374.

North/Central Sulawesi

No.	Regency or City	Citizens	Number of eligible voters	Percentage of citizens eligible to vote
1	North Sulawesi	340,063	166,653	49.00
2	Menado City	56,729	32,326	56.98
3	Minahasa	419,882	214,155	51.00
4	Bolang Mongondow . .	129,311	65,254	50.46
5	Sangihe/Talaud . . .	150,849	79,003	52.37
6	Donggala	305,631	146,549	47.94
7	Poso	255,376	134,276	52.18
	Total	1,657,841	838,216	55.05

Moluccas

No.	Regency or City	Citizens	Number of eligible voters	Percentage of citizens eligible to vote
1	Ambon City	30,959	17,610	56.88
2	Central Moluccas . . .	245,680	133,152	54.19
3	North Moluccas . . .	252,145	126,588	50.20
4	Southeast Moluccas . .	164,098	86,810	52.90
	Total	692,882	364,160	52.55

EAST NUSA TENGGARA

No.	Regency	Citizens	Number of eligible voters	Percentage of citizens eligible to vote
1	Kupang	120,296	71,766	59.74
2	Central/South Timor .	172,672	92,593	53.62
3	Central/North Timor .	88,523	49,331	55.72
4	Belu	119,140	70,916	59.52
5	Alor	98,139	54,125	55.15
6	Roti/Sawu	111,074	61,051	54.97
7	Maumere	146,216	84,982	58.12
8	Manggarai	211,278	105,350	49.86
9	Ngada	101,164	59,995	59.30
10	Endeh/Lio	145,804	79,023	54.12
11	East Flores/Selor Island	179,044	101,253	56.55
12	West Sumba	140,905	82,189	58.32
13	East Sumba	85,895	55,645	64.78
14	Sumbawa	156,647	87,653	55.95
15	Bima	211,202	116,974	55.38
16	Dompu	52,786	26,801	50.77
	TOTAL	2,140,785	1,199,647	56.03

WEST NUSA TENGGARA

No.	Regency	Citizens	Number of eligible voters	Percentage of citizens eligible to vote
1	Buleleng	258,726	144,838	55.98
2	Jembrana	98,197	51,920	52.87
3	Tabanan	239,181	138,125	57.74
4	Badung	255,422	147,737	57.84
5	Gianyar	211,762	123,559	57.87
6	Bangli	107,216	64,539	54.96
7	Klungkung	117,122	59,259	50.59
8	Karangasem	231,531	131,348	56.73
9	West Lombok	335,690	191,565	57.06
10	Central Lombok . . .	361,159	160,824	44.52
11	East Lombok	411,003	213,298	51.89
	TOTAL	2,627,009	1,427,012	54.32

Index

abangan, 224, 225, 230, 231, 346
ABDUH, M., 210, 215
ABDULGANI, R., 350
Acheh, 4, 16, 24, 25, 29, 30, 54, 56, 76, 81, 85, 119, 122, 160, 165, 232, 269, 330; – War, 65, 66, 67, 68, 70, 203
adat, 5, 12, 30, 133, 140, 142, 143, 204, 236, 284, 285, 301, 306, 316, 353; – chiefs, 63, 66, 140, 142, 143, 147, 156, 203, 204, 205, 289, 316, 322
ADLOFF, R., 339
ADRIAANSE, C., 234
ADRIANI, N., 206, 233
Agama Djawa, 10, 208
agrarian legislation, 62, 93, 244, 291
agrarian reform, 50, 232, 233, 336, 365, 366
agricultural advisory service, 96, 115
agricultural education, 145, 297, 307
agriculture, 5, 12, 13, 18, 19, 20, 29, 32, 33, 40, 90, 95, 96, 102, 103, 105, 115, 120, 121, 133, 134, 135, 143, 205, 240, 243, 271, 282, 284, 335; – by Chinese, 64. See also *ladang; sawah*
AGUNG, Sultan, 54, 55, 237
Ahmadyah, 213
ALLEN, G. C., 131
AMANGKURAT I, 202
Ambon, 10, 25, 34, 54, 77, 148, 205, 288, 361. See also Moluccas, 'Republic of the South Moluccas'
Ambonese soldiers, 80, 84, 159
America: see United States
Annam, 45, 47
ani-ani, 13, 102
animism, 10, 205, 208, 224
ANWAR, Ch., 307
Arabia, 196, 202, 204, 289, 292. See also Mecca
Arabic language, 210
Arabs in Indonesia, 24, 28, 52, 95, 140, 141, 175, 254, 280
ARCHER, R. L., 207, 212, 233
aristocracy, 2, 3, 4, 5, 7, 37, 57, 60, 61, 63, 66, 67, 68, 69, 81, 82, 91 114, *134ff.*, *171ff.*, 203, 205, 208, 212, 215, 216, 226, 228, 230, 243, 245, 255, 285, 289, 291, 292, 293, 296, 301, *315ff.*, 346; – in Southern Asia, 40, 41, 42, 46, 47, 49, 195
artisans, 2, 7, 135, 136, 170, 171, 195, 220, 285; – in villages, 6, 41, 112, 113; non-indigenous –, 43, 141. See also industry
ARX, A. VON, 88, 338
Asian-African Conference, 28, 88, 163, 334
ATEN, A., 277
Australia, 20, 27, 80, 84, 334
AZIZ, M. A., 88

Bali, 2, 10, 20, 25, 33, 37, 63, 68, 81, 239, 283, 345
Balinese art, 308, 309
Banda, 56, 240
Bandung, 182, 187, 188, 191; – Regency, 111, 268. See also Asian-African Conference
Bangka, 17, 31, 64

Banjarese, 24, 25, 32
Banjermasin, 56, 62, 64, 203
Banjumas, 154
Bantam, 4, 31, 32, 54, 55, 56, 62, 171, 238, 271; communist revolt in –, 72, 222
bapakism, 167
Barito, 18
Barlian, 351, 360
Bastin, J., 239
Batak, 2, 25, 30, 32, 252; – mission, 10, 65, 74, 205, 216, 217. See also Christians
Batavia: see Jakarta
Batavian Republic, 59
Bateson, G., 37
batik, 13, 114, 152, 283, 293, 294; labour in – industry, 238, 254, 268
Bauer, P. T., 116
bauxite, 19, 97
Becker, C. H., 233
Beecher Stowe, H., 251
Belgium, 60, 61, 102, 362
Benda, H. J., 156, 157, 224, 225, 226, 233, 301
Bengal, 197
Bengkalis, 31
Bengkulen, 57
Berg, C. C., 52, 53, 211, 283, 316
Besuki, 112
Bhinneka Tunggal Ika, 1ff.
Billiton, 17, 31, 64
Bird's Head, 68
birth rate, 22, 23, 121, 191
Blitar, 79
Blora, 318
Boeke, J. H., 96, 97, 99, 101, 106, 107, 109, 110, 114, 115, 116, 131, 149, 187, 258, 268, 335
Boetzelaer van Asperen en Dubbeldam, C. W. Th., Baron van, 201, 233
Bone, R. C., Jr., 338
Borneo, 2, 3, 4, 9, 10, 17, 18, 19, 21, 25, 32, 56, 62, 64, 68, 77, 80, 97, 125, 143, 231, 345; British North–, 17, 63, 351, 361; East –, 25; South –, 25, 121; Southeast –, 32, 64, 68, 142; West –, 17, 18, 24, 32, 64, 119, 120, 155
Borobudur, 280
Bosch, F. D. K., 281, 284, 290, 313
Bosch, J. van den, 61, 92, 203, 243
Bouman, H., 219, 221, 233, 301, 317, 338
bourgeoisie, 111, 114, 115, 128, *141ff.*, 157, *165ff.*, 170, 175, 180, 183, 184, 185, *207ff.*, 289, 291, 294, 299 301, 309, *319ff.*, 346; Chinese – in Indonesia, 94, 100, 141; – in Asia, *44ff.*; – in Europe, 40, 61, 174, 288
Bousquet, G. H., 208, 233
Boven Digul, 72
Boxer, C. R., 287
Brahmins, 281, 283, 284
Brand, W., 188, 190, 191, 193
Brand, J. van den, 251, 278
Brandes, J. L. A., 284
Brantas, 19
Britain, 17, 54, 56, 57, 58, 59, 60, 63, 65, 68, 75, 98, 100, 102, 137, 180, 287, 288, 292, 362
British industry, 40, 41, 45, 59, 94
British interregnum, 59, 60, 76, 241
British occupation army, 80, 82, 273, 307
Brito, R. de, 197
Broek, J. O. M., 38
Broersma, R., 97, 152, 278
Brooke, Raja, 63
Brugmans, I. J., 147, 149, 293, 313
Brunei, 197
Burger, D. H., 92, 115, 131, 138, 140, 146, 147, 164, 168
Buddhism, 8, 10, 33, 91, 200, 280, 281

Budi Utomo, 69, 209, 322
Buginese, 24, 25, 34, 134, 168
Bukittinggi, 360
Burma, 35, 41, 43, 44, 47, 78, 269, 270, 364, 366
business class: see bourgeoisie
Buton, 21

Caliphate, 222
Calvinism, 200, 214, 215
capitalism, 9, *40ff.*, 66, 67, 68, *93ff.*, 175, 176, 216, 218, 219, 225, 245, 318, 323, 329, 334, 337, 366, 367
cassava, 13, 19
caste, 33, 134, 198, 207, 281; colour –, 42, 45, *137ff.*, 154, 175, 184, 207, 215, 321
Catholicism, 10, 34, 35, 200, 205
CATOR, W. J., 152
Celebes, 2, 20, 25, 34, 63, 80, 81, 84, 351, 361, 362; Central –, 20; North –, 10, 63, 65, 359, 361, 362; South –, 68, 85, 121, 231, 237, 311, 330; Southeast –, 20; Southwest –, 81
census, *21ff.*, 144, 306, *370ff.*
Ceylon, 11
CHABOT, H. Th., 168, 237
charismatic, 166, 336
Cheribon, 32, 242
China, 3, 6, 7, 28, 31, 68, 69, 85, 86, 97, 187, 255, 256, 347, 363, 365
Chinese, 24, 28, 29, 32, 33, 52, 58, 69, 85, 86, 94, 95, 98, 100, 111, 112, 120, 121, 124, 125, 136, 141, *143ff.*, *172ff.*, 213, 221, 240, 254, 272, 291, 293, 294, 296, 321, 323, 328, 363, 364; – in Southern Asia, 43, 49, 51; – in Sumatra, 31, 68, 97, 250, 251, 252; – in West Borneo, 32, 64, 119, 120
Christian Reformation, 210, 214
Christians, 10, 34, 35, 74, 114, 136, 158, 172, *198ff.*, 228, 239, 287, 293, 302, 330, 344, 345; Batak –, 30, 216; Dayak –, 32; – in Europe, 196, 211, 212, 213; Menadonese and Ambonese –, 34, 35, 148, 159, 205
CHRISTISON, Ph., 80
cinchona, 19, 93, 94
cities, 9, 11, 13, 17, 18, 19, 20, 32, 33, 37, 72, 80, 82, 83, 91, 98, 105, 110, 115, 119, 120, 123, 128, 143, *170ff.*, 212, 213, 224, 225, 226, 230, 232, 254, 266, 267, 272, 276, 277, *283ff.*, 319, 322, 323, 325, 328, 329, 335, 343, 344, 346, 361; – in early Indonesia, 3, 4, 6, 7, 91, 135, *170ff.*, 195, 196, 197, 199, 204, 237, 238, 239, 240, *283ff.*; – in Southern Asia, 44, 50
Civil Service, 115; Indonesian –, 156, 157, 322, 346. See also aristocracy
closed economy, 2, 13, 41, 90, 93, 94, 105, 107, 282
clove, 56
coal, 16, 18, 64, 97, 271
COAST, J., 309
coastal principalities: see harbour principalities
Cochin-China, 43, 47
coconut, 18, 20, 32, 97, 118, 124, 125, 238, 268, 351, 362
COEDÈS, G., 52, 280, 281
COEN, J. P., 172, 201, 237, 240
coffee, 13, 19, 57, 63, 92, 93, 97, 116, 118, 240, 263, 264
COLENBRANDER, H. T., 88
colonisation: see migration
colour line, 42, 44, *137ff.*, 161, 162, 163, 164, 179, 251, 334. See also caste
commerce: see trade
Committee of Good Offices, 82

communalism, 90, 236; – in India, 49, 221
communism, 72, 86, 166, 218, 222, 229, 231, 233, 274, 275, 331, *343ff.*, 365. See also *Partai Komunis Indonesia*
communist revolts, 72, 83, 142, 222, 232, 274, 322, 323, 326, 347
Company: see Dutch East India Company
compulsory services: see services
Congress Party, 47, 49, 72
Coolie Budget Commission, 109, *259ff.*
cooperatives, 73, 104, 111, 119, 131, 152
copra: see coconut
corruption, 86, 87, 192, 270, 333, 342, 350, 351, 353, 354
CORTESÃO, A., 53, 197
COSIJN, E. J. A., 279
cotton, 13, 41, 45, 94, 116, 120. See also *batik*
COVARRUBIAS, M., 308
Çriwijaya: see Sri Vijaya
crop delivery: see tribute
culture system, 61, 62, 92, 93, 100, 136, 139, 140, 203, 243, 244, 245, 247, 289
custom: see *adat*

DAENDELS, H. W., 59, 60, 92, 173, 242, 243
DAM, H. TEN, 114, 115, 124, 253, 278, 326
Damascus 196
Danes, 56
Darul Islam, 33, 85, 228, 229, 330, 331, 361
DAUD BEUREUH, 165
Dayaks, 2, 24, 25, 32
death rate, 22, 23, 93, *188ff.*, 253
Delanggu, 274
Deli, 17, 65, 93, 94, 97, 98, 105, 250, 251, 252, 253, 345
desa, 11, 12, 13, 105, 107, 108, 123, 128, 157, 167, 224, 225, 228, 230, 245, 250, 253, 254, 258, 271, 306, 307, 325, 326; – chief, 93, 94, 108, 246, 247, 346; Chinese in –, 161, 163; class divisions in –, 112, 113, 114, 115, 133, 134, 140, 253; – in early Java, 2, 5, 6, 93, 94, 95, 133, 134, 140, 200, 236, 240, 282, 283, 284, 318; – school, 12, 104, 145, 310
DESAI, A. R., 7, 39, 41, 51
DEVENTER, C. Th. VAN, 70
Dewan Banteng, 350
DEWANTORO, KI HADJAR, 73, 303, 304
DIPONEGORO, Prince, 60, 203
DJAJADININGRAT, P. A. A., 147, 215, 234, 297
Djakenan, 131
DJUANDA KARTAWIDJAJA, 353, 358, 360
DONNITHORNE, A. G., 131
DOUWES DEKKER, E., 62, 69, 244, 255, 279
DOUWES DEKKER, E. F. E., 69
DREWES, G. W. J., 10
DU BOIS, C., 51, 168
Dumai, 360
Dutch, *passim*
Dutch East India Company, 12, 36, *54ff.*, 136, 139, 172, 173, 200, 201, 202, 239, 240, 242, 287, 290
Dutch Indonesian Union, 15, 16, 88
DUYVENDAK, J. J. L., 187
DUYVENDAK, J. P., 38

East Indonesia, 77, 80, 81, 84, 311, 327, 330, 344, 345
education, 9, 34, 37, 73, 74, 87, 96, 98, 103, 104, *143ff.*, 174, 183, 184,

207, 209, 215, 226, 227, 255, 260, 261, 262, 264, *292ff.*; – in Southern Asia, 11, 44, 45, 46, 48; religious –, 200, 201, 205, 210, 211, 216, 223, 227, 310; – under Japanese, *305ff.* See also *desa*, – school
Egypt, 210, 259
ELSBREE, W. H., 76, 78, 88, 338
EMERSON, R., 338
emigration, 23, 28, 29, 94, 103, 162, 332, 357, 362
ENDT, P., 279
England: see Britain
estate: see plantation; *latifundia*
ethical policy, 66, 70, 96, 99, 102, 103, 104, 107
Eurasians: see Indo-Europeans

faith: see religion
Far East, 16, 39
farmer: see peasant
fascism, 75, 324, 325
FÈBRE, W. LE, 304, 305, 313
FEITH, H., 166, 224, 230, 231, 338, 341, 343, 346, 349
feudal chiefs: see aristocracy
FISCHER, H. TH., 234, 302
Flores, 10, 25, 34, 205, 278; – Sea, 20
forced labour: see services
Foreign Orientals, 24, 141, 142, 149, 152, 179, 293. See also Chinese; Arabs in Indonesia
foreman: see *mandur*
French, 58, 59, 60, 102, 174; – revolution, 58, 289
FRIEDERICY, H. J., 134, 168
FRUIN, Th. A., 132
FURNIVALL, J. S., 41, 51, 88, 99, 109, 132, 145, 242, 264, 297, 313, 338

GANDASUBRATA, S. M., 154, 155, 157, 168
GANDHI, M. K., 47, 107
GEERTZ, C., 224, 230, 345, 346
GELDEREN, J. VAN, 22, 101, 116, 132, 145
Gerindo, 75, 323, 324
Germans, 68, 75, 102, 216, 324, 362
GERTH, H. M., 166
GIBB, H. A. R., 234
GOBEE, E., 234
GOENS, R. VAN, 237, 238
gold, 3, 16, 18, 109, 295
GONGGRIJP, G., 92, 107, 132
GOPALAKRISHNAN, P. K., 41
Gorontalese, 25
gotong royong, 13, 236, 278, 352, 353
GOUROU, P., 335
GOUW GIOK SIONG, 138, 151
Governor-General, 57, 59, 61, 67, 70, 71, 73, 74, 97, 172, 237; Lieutenant –, 81
GRAAF, H. J. DE, 89, 199
GRAAFF, E. A. VAN DE, 265
Great Britain: see Britain
Greater East Asia, 77, 118, 155
Gujerat, 197
GUTKIND, E. A., 193

HAAN, DE, Dr., 237, 238
HAAN, F. DE, 136, 168, 173, 193
HAAR, B. TER, 133, 301
HAAS, J. H. DE, 190, 191, 192, 193
haji, 95, 140, 203. See also Mecca
HALLOWELL, A. I., 289
haamdjuon, 216
HAMENGKU BUWONO, Sultan, 83, 160, 162, 349, 360
HARAHAP, B., 344, 346, 350, 359
harbour principalities, 3, 4, 7, 9, *53ff.*, 63, 64, 134, 136, 170, 171, 172, 197, 199, 200, 238, 285, 286. See also cities; princes
Hatopan Kristen Batak, 216
HATTA, M., 73, 79, 82, 229, 348, 349, 350, 359, 360

HELBIG, K., 38, 194
HEUTSZ, J. B. VAN, 67, 97
HIGGINS, B., 132
Hinduism, 2, 8, 53, 54, 91, 134, *198ff.*, *280ff.*, 290; – in Bali, 33, 345; – in India, 49, 221
Hindustan: see India
HOËVELL, W. R. VAN, 241, 292
HOFSTRA, S., 39
HOGENDORP, D. VAN, 239
HOLLAND, W. L., 51, 338
HOLMES, J. S., 307
HONIG, P., 296
HOOYKAAS, C., 146
HOUTMAN, C. DE, 171
HUBER, A., 89, 238
HUENDER, W., 99, 112
Hulu Sungei, 18, 32, 64, 142, 152
HUMBOLDT, W. VON, 292
HUSSEIN, A., 350, 360
HUTASOIT, M., 227, 310, 313

I-TSING, 281
immigration: see migration; Chinese; Arabs in Indonesia
indentured labour: see services
India, 47, 49, 72, 85, 207, 211, 213, 221, 305, 359, 363, 366; ancient –, 3, 7, 11, 29, *39ff.*, 172, 195, 197, 199, 241, 280, 281, 282; census in –, 22
Indian Mutiny, 42
Indians in Indonesia, 24, 80, 281, 290, 294
Indisch, *173ff.*, 291, 295
Indische Partij, 69, 320
individualism, 100, 115, 142, 145, 146, 153, 158, 162, 165, 174, 176, 196, 288, 294, 300, 308, 337; – in modern Islam, *207ff.*; – in Protestantism, 200, 205; – in Southern Asia, *44ff.*
Indo-China, 11, 44, 45, 47, 280
Indo-Europeans, 24, 29, 35, 69, 80, 126, *136ff.*, 173, 174, 175, 179, 180, 181, 182, 183, 184, 239, 248, 254, *290ff.*, 320, 323, 327, 357
Indo-Europeesch Verbond, 150, 320
Indonesian language, 9, 73, 151, 154, 162, 185, 299, 300, 304, 306, 307, 311, 332
Indos: see Indo-Europeans
industrial program, 50, 131, 193, 335, 336, 337, 365, 367
industry, 19, 32, 103, *109ff.*, 144, 152, 162, 176, 177, 187, 238, 249, 254, *257ff.*, 293, 294, 328, 345; home –, 5, 12, 41, 94, 236; – in Southern Asia, 41, 44, 49, 50; – in the West, 40, 41, 44, 59, 66, 67, 94, 97, 102, 289
inland-states, 4, 7, 53, 54, 57, 134, 170, 199, 238, 283, 286, 316
Irian: see New-Guinea
iron, 20, 187
irrigated rice areas: see *sawahs*
irrigation works, 3, 6, 96, 103, 119, 237, 245, 257, 282, 284
Islam, 7, 8, 10, 30, 31, 32, 33, 34, 35, 54, 56, 63, 69, 71, 72, 79, 83, 85, 135, 140, 147, 160, 184, *195ff.*, 224, 225, 230, 231, 233, 280, 286, 289, 291, 298, 299, 303, *316ff.*, 342, 343, 345, 365; – in Southern Asia, 42, 49; modernism in –, *207ff.*
ius connubii, 142, 147

JACOBY, E. H., 51, 105, 323, 331, 338
Jakarta, 4, 19, 21, 22, 24, 33, 54, 55, 58, 60, 72, 76, 136, 154, 155, *173ff.*, 201, 239, 241, 242, 245, 265, 266, 267, 276, 287, 311, 312, 313, 325, 326, 350, 355, 359
Jambi, 16, 68, 69
Japan, 3, 15, 16, 19, 22, 23, 69, 75,

76, *77ff.*, 101, 102, *116ff.*, *152ff.*, 187, 192, 226, 257, 259, *269ff.*, 305, 306, 307, 324, 325, 328, 342, 362
Jatinegara, 186
Java, *passim*; Central –, 2, 8, 10, 33, 85, 96, 123, 128, 208, 224, 230, 231, 245, 246, 249, 262, 263, 264, 265, 277, 286, 318, 326, 330, 343, 344, 345, 346, 348, 354, 355, 360; East –, 2, 33, 52, 79, 112, 152, 223, 224, 230, 231, 249, 263, 264, 268, 299, 343, 344, 345, 348, 354, 355; West –, 19, 33, 54, 57, 79, 84, 85, 112, 114, 115, 123, 128, 190, 228, 231, 263, 264, 265, 277, 330, 345, 350, 355; – Sea, 18, 19; – War, 60, 139, 203
Javanism: see *Agama Djawa*
Jogjakarta, 57, 60, 80, 83, 84, 141, 152, 159, 161, 203, 208, 274, 304, 311, 326, 349, 350, 355, 360
JONGE, B. C. DE, 73
JONGE, J. K. J. DE, 237, 238
JOSSELIN DE JONG, P. E. DE, 30
JOUSTRA, M., 152
JUYNBOLL, H. H., 238, 294

Ka'ba, 220
kafirs, 140, 197
KAHIN, G. McT., 81, 83, 89, 122, 123, 124, 125, 143, 144, 152, 159, 160, 161, 163, 274, 327, 338
Kalibening, 326
Kalimantan: see Borneo
kampong, 151, *173ff.*, 248, 258, 260, 266, 267
KAMPTO UTOMO, 38
Kapuas, 17
Karens, 35
Karimata, Strait of –, 17
KARSTEN, TH., 176
KARTINI, R. A., 208, 234, 292, 293, 297
KAT ANGELINO, A. D. A. DE, 38, 301
KAT ANGELINO, P. DE, 254, 279
KAWILARANG, A., 350
KATTENBURG, P. M., 123, 168, 326
Kempeitai, 78
KENNEDY, R., 25, 38, 42, 46, 137, 147, 159, 168, 289, 311
KEYFITZ, N., 24, 38
KLERCK, E. S. DE, 89
K.N.I.L., 35, 84, 159
KOCH, D. M. G., 89, 149, 214, 338
KOLFF, G. H. VAN DER, 96, 106, 109, 132, 253, 254, 279
KOOREMAN, P. J., 237
Korean War, 127
KORN, V. E., 30, 283
Kra-Isthmus, 270
KRAEMER, H., 49, 234
KRAMERS, J. H., 234
kratons, 2, 90, 161, 170, 208, 237, 238, 239, 283, 286, 288
KROEF, J. M. VAN DER, 168
KROM, N. J., 281, 284
KRUYT, A. C., 134, 140
KUNST, J., 302
Kuomintang, 363
Kupang, 63
KUPERUS, G., 132
Kuta Gedé, 141, 179, 220
Kutawinangun, 109, 132
kyahi, 147, 215, 216, *224ff.* See also *ulama*

labour, 31, 32, 93, 94, 96, *102ff.*, 162, 173, 187, 192, 214 236ff, 289, 295, 316, 335, 364; – in Southern Asia, 41, 50; – inspectorate, 251, 252, 257; – requisitions: see services
ladang, *4ff.*, 11, 16, 18, 20, 29, 31, 90, 91, 97, 98, 102, 133, 143, 283, 284, 285
Lahore, 213

Lampongs, 17, 31, 38, 62, 63, 110
land redistribution: see agrarian reform
land rent, 59, 61, 92, 94, 107, 108, 123, 124, 128, 129, 241, 243
LANDON, K. P., 207, 212, 213, 234
LASKER, B., 244, 250, 255, 257, 279
LAST, J., 309
latifundia, 60, 177, 240, 243, 245, 246, 277
League of Nations, 105
LEEDEN, C. B. VAN DER, 132
LEHMANN, H., 171, 182, 194
LENIN, W. I., 208
Lesser Sunda Islands, 20, 25, 34, 63, 80
LEUR, J. C. VAN, 4, 7, 40, 51, 53, 54, 55, 57, 90, 91, 135, 171, 194, 198, 234, 238, 239, 281, 284, 285, 288, 290, 314, 316, 332
LEVERT, P., 249, 279
LEVY, R., 234
LIEM TJAY TIE, 190, 194
LIEM TWAN DJIE, 152, 168
LIMBURG STIRUM, J. P. VAN, 71
Lingga archipelago, 17, 31
LINTON, R., 42, 137, 168, 289
LOGEMANN, J. H. A., 194
Lombok, 33, 34, 63, 68
London, 75, 350; – Treaty, 65
LUBIS, Z., 350
Lutheranism, 214, 215
luxuries, 1, 3, 109, 128, 129, 130, 173, 174, 175, 197, 214, 265, 287, 291

MA JUAN LIN, 281
Macao, 287
Macassar, 20, 25, 34, 56, 63, 77, 81, 134, 168, 192, 194, 304, 351, 352; Strait of –, 20
MACMAHON BALL, W., 51, 338
Madagascar, 8
Madiun revolt, 83, 229, 274, 326, 347
Madura, 18, 19, 21, 25, 33, 52, 143, 144, 231, 241, 292
maize, 13, 19, 20
Majalaya, 111, 114, 268
Majapahit, 52, 53, 316
Malacca, 54, 55, 197; Strait of –, 16, 65
Malang, 187
Malay language, 9, 10, 33, 73, 151, 153, 299, 300, 304
Malaya, 3, 8, 9, 10, 11, 16, 17, 47, 49, 60, 199, 269, 281, 360
Malays, 1, 2, 10, *24ff.*, 97, 98, 110, 252
Malino, 81, 82, 83, 84, 159, 164, 326, 327
MALLINCKRODT, J., 143
MALTHUS, T. R., 12, 95, 335
mandala, 200, 284
mandur, 247, 248, 251, *259ff.*
Mangkunagaran, 57
MANOEL, King, 197
MARCHAL, H., 281
Mardijkers, 136, 172, 287
MARLE, A. VAN, 28, 29, 151, 355, 371
MARRISON, G. E., 197
MARSDEN, W., 202
MARX, K., 39, 208, 347
Masing, 254
Masjumi, 83, 86, 166, *226ff.*, *342ff.*, 359
Mataram, 54, 55, 56, 202, 237, 238, 240, 288, 316
Max Havelaar, 62, 244, 279
MEAD, M., 37
Mecca, 95, 140, 196, 202, 219, 220, 225
Medan, 17, 31, 251
MEEL, H. DE, 23, 24, 38
Melanesia, 35
Menado, 20, 25, 34, 63, 148, 159, 361
Menangkabau, 24, 25, 30, 56, 72, 81, 147, 152, 222, 231, 232, 348, 350, 359, 360, 361

MENCIUS, 187
MENDE, T., 51, 338, 366
merchant: see trader; Dutch East India Company
mestizo: see Indo-Europeans; – culture, 174, 175, 184, 287, 290, 291, 292, 295, 302, 309, 310
MEIJER RANNEFT, J. W., 99, 112
MIDDENDORP, W., 253, 256, 279
middle class: see bourgeoisie; Indonesian –, 73, 111, 112, 113, 114, 121, 125, *143ff.*, 180, 183, 209, 213, 215, 217, 329, 333; 'new –', 161, 166, 183, 232
Middle East, 16
migration, 1, 8, 31, 280, 281; – by Europeans, 28, 136, 138, 162, 172, 286, 287, 295, 296, 320; inter-island –, 8, 17, 30, 31, 34, 105, 110, 143, *250ff.*, 256, 258. See also emigration; *romusha*; Chinese; Arabs in Indonesia
MILLS, L. A., 338
Minahasa, 10, 20, 34, 35, 63, 65, 205, 351, 359, 361, 362
mines, 17, 18, 19, 20, 21, 31, 64, 101, 102, 103, 124, 129, 254, 277
Mogul, 199
Moluccas, 21, 25, 34, 35, 53, 54, 56, 57, 62, 63, 80, 84, 200, 205, 288, 316; 'Republic of South –', 35, 85, 333
money lender, 41, 95, 108, 124, 161
MOOK, H. J. VAN, 81, 89, 141, 179, 220, 327, 338
mortality: see death rate
Moslem: see Islam
Muhammadyah, *207ff.*, 342
mullah, 199. See also *ulama*
MULTATULI: see DOUWES DEKKER, E.
MUS, P., 45, 51
Muslim League, 49
NAERSSEN, F. H. VAN, 134, 135, 284, 285
Nahdatul Ulama, 86, 223, 229, 230, 232, 342, 343, 344, 345
Nagarakertagama, 52
NAPOLEON, 59, 60
NASSER, G. A., 342
NASUTION, H., 350, 358, 363, 364
natality: see birth-rate
NATANINGRAT, P., 241, 292
nationalism, 15, 30, *69ff.*, 114, 142, 151, 156, 159, 164, 165, 217, 222, 227, 297, 298, 303, 304, 307, *315ff.*, 347, 348, 362, 366; – in Southern Asia, *46ff.*; pre –, 204, 208, 215, 216
NATSIR, M., 234, 346, 359
NEDERBURGH, S. C., 36, 239
Netherlands: see Dutch
New-Guinea, 21, 25, 35, 68, 72, 80; – dispute, 15, 84, 332, 333, 334, 341, 356, 357, 358, 359, 363, 365, 366
NEYS, K., 314
N.I.C.A., 166
NIEUWENHUIJZE, C. A. O. VAN, 156, 223, 229, 234
NIEUWENHUIJS, R., 175, 194
NILAKANTA SASTRI, 53
NIX, C. TH., 194
Nji Pohatji Sanghjang Srie, 254
nobility: see aristocracy
NOTO KUSUMO, P.: see NATANINGRAT, P.
Nusa Tenggara: see Lesser Sunda Islands
nutmeg, 56, 240

October 17 affair, 86, 166, 341, 349
OEI TJONG BO, 132
oil, 9, 16, 18, 19, 21, 68, 97, 102, 107, 124, 360
ONG ENG DIE, 168

Ormeling, J., 38
Os, E. V. Ch. van, 22
Osmeña, S., 47
Outer islands, 8, 11, 18, 23, 32, 37, 38, 56, 59, 62, 67, 68, 97, 98, 102, 105, 110, 111, 112, 118, 125, 129, *141ff.*, 152, 158, 159, 205, 239, 242, *243ff.*, 268, 330, 345, 348, 349, 354, 361

Paauw, D. S., 129
Pacific War, 76
Padang, 360
Padri, 63, 203, 289, 291; – War, 63, 68
Pajang, 199
Pakan Baru, 360
Pakistan, 364
Palembang, 4, 16, 31, 62, 152, 345
Palmier, L. H., 168
Pan-Islamic movement, 222, 330
Pantja Sila, 228, 308
Papuans, 25, 35, 366
Parindra, 75, 114, 323, 324
Partai Komunis Indonesia, 71, 222, 230, *343ff.*, 353, 354, 355
Partai Nasional Indonesia, 72, 86, 222, 229, 230, 343, 344, 345, 348, 353, 354, 355
Partai Sarekat Islam Indonesia, 222, 232, 344
Partai Sosialis Indonesia, 166, 344, 346, 348, 349, 359, 360
particuliere landerijen: see *latifundia*
Partido Nacionalista, 47, 49
Pasei, 197
Pasisir civilisation, 286, 289
Pasundan, 319
Pati, 131
patricians, 7, 91, 135, 285, 286
Pauker, G., 358
pawnshops, 107, 109
Pearl Harbour, 76
peasant, *passim*; – unions, 166, 167
pedlar, see trader
Pekalongan, 152, 238
Peking, 28
pelopor, 28
penal sanction, 68, 250, 252, 253, 256, 257, 266, 268
People's Credit Bank, 108, 115
pepper, 4, 17, 31, 32
Pergerakan Tarbyah Islamyah (*Perti*), 232
Persatoean Moeslimin Indonesia, 231
pesantren, 200, 210. See also *santri*
petroleum: see oil
Petrus Blumberger, J. Th., 89, 338
Philippines, 8, 11, 27, 35, 43, 44, 45, 47, 49, 78, 293, 320, 351, 361
Piekaar, A. J., 81, 89, 119, 156, 157, 160, 269, 272
Pigeaud, Th., 184, 284, 286, 292, 302, 314, 316, 318
piracy, 4, 57, 58, 65, 91, 201, 236, 238
Pires, Tomé, 53, 197, 199
plantation, *93ff.*, *246ff.*, 328, 329, 335; – in Java, 13, 32, 82, 323; – in Moluccas, 240; – in Southern Asia, 11, 41; – in Sumatra, 16, 17, 31, 68, 81, 82, 142, 160, 362
Plas, Ch. O. van der, 159
Ploegsma, N. D., 112, 114
Pluvier, J., 74, 89, 301, 304, 320, 324, 338
Poedjangga Baroe, 300, 303, 305
Pontianak, 18, 32, 62
Portuguese, 39, 53, 54, 55, 56, 198, 199, 200, 287; – in Moluccas, 21, 34, 53, 205; – language, 287; – Timor, 20
Poso, 134
Pramoedya Ananta Toer, 158
Prapança, 52
Prasad, R., 363
Preanger, 4, 57, 112, 152, 243

Prince Priest of Giri, 202
princes, 63, 64, 67, 68, 187, 245, 246; – in early Indonesia, *2ff.*, *52ff.*, 90, 133, 134, 135, 141, 170, 171, *195ff.*, 237, 238, 240, *281ff.*, 316; – in Southern Asia, 7, 40, 43, 47. See also aristocracy; harbour principalities; inland-states
Principalities, 67; – of Central Java, 33, 57, 60, 141, 160, 245, 246, 277
PRINS, J., 223, 234
Protestantism, 10, 30, 32, 34, 35, 218, 288. See also Calvinism; Christian Reformation; Christians; Lutheranism
Protestant mission, 65, 200, 201, 205, 206, 216, 217
pryayi: see aristocracy; 'new –', 147, 322
PIJPER, G. F., 211, 213, 224, 234

QUARITCH WALES, H. G., 281
QUEZON, M., 47

RAFFLES, T. S., 12, 58, 59, 60, 61, 76, 92, 241, 243, 292
railroads, 19, 41, 103, 124, 177, 178, 254, 269
raja: see princes
rampokkers, 167
rationalism, 207, 212, 217
regent, 57, 61, 139, 156, 157, 159, 160, 208, 240, 241, 243, 247, 253, 292
religion, 6, 7, 8, 10, 11, 30, 31, 32, 33, 34, 49, 50, 136, 137, 142, *195ff.*, 261, 262, 284, 285, 287, 288, 289, 291, 298, 316, 317, 324, 325, 328, *342ff.*, 365, 366. See also *Agama Djawa*; animism; Buddhism; Catholicism; Christians; education; Hinduism; Islam; Protestantism; *ulama*
religious leaders, 47, 66, 68, 112, 113, 135, 146, 147, 156, 160, 165, 167, *195ff.*, 345, 346, 347
Rembang, 131
RESINK, G. J., 89
Riau archipelago, 17, 31
rice, 2, 3, 4, 13, 17, 18, 19, 20, 55, 59, 77, 90, 93, 109, 116, 118, 122, 126, 128, 237, 238, 247, 265, 277, 356; '– Christians', 201. See also *ladang*; *sawah*
rice cultivation on irrigated fields: see *sawah*
RODRIGUES, F., 53, 197
ROMEIN, J. M., 312
romusha, 23, 77, 119, 121, 158, 270, 271, 272
ROOLVINK, R., 303
ROSS, E. A., 164
ROUFFAER, G. P., 171, 238, 294
Round Table Conference, 15, 75, 84, 125, 126, 333, 340, 341, 357
rubber, 68, 97, 116, 124, 127, 142, 343, 351; – smallholdings, 8, 16, 18, 32, 97, 98, 110, 118, 125, 143, 146, 322, 329; – estates, 16, 17, 19, 102, 250, 253, 263, 264
RUIBING, A. H., 279
rupiah, 123, 126, 128, 356
Russian revolution, 69, 71, 217
RUTGERS, S. J., 89, 111, 112, 132, 238, 338

Sabang, 16, 269
Sadeng War, 52, 316
sago, 21
Salatiga, 326
SALIM, A., Haji, 73, 218, 234
salt, 19, 107
Samin movement, 215, 229, 318, 323
Sangirese, 25
SANI, A., 311
SANSOM, G. B., 40

santri, 224, 225, 226, 230, 231, 346
Sarekat Islam, 69, 71, 72, 104, 147, 213, 214, 215, 217, 218, 220, 221, 222, 224, 225, 226, 322, 323
SAROSO WIRODIHARDJO, 116, 132
Sasaks, 25
SASTROAMIDJOJO, ALI, 166, 343, 344, 346, 348, 350
sawah, 2, 4, 5, 6, 7, 8, 11, 17, 19, 20, 32, 34, 90, 91, 93, 96, 98, 102, 105, 133, 246, 247, 270, 282, 283, 285
Sayyids, 140, 195
SCHACHT, J., 233
SCHILLER, A. A., 89
schools: see education; *desa*
SCHRIEKE, B., 5, 13, 14, 54, 61, 96, 113, 134, 139, 140, 142, 143, 168, 169, 197, 198, 199, 207, 234, 235, 237, 238, 243, 282, 284, 314, 322
SCHWENCKE, G., 111, 114, 268
Security Council, 82, 83
segregation, 150, 162, 170, 171, 182
Semarang, 57, 194, 238, 241, 344
serfs, 91, 238, 240, 243, 245, 246
servants, 174, 183, 239, 254, 255, 261, 262
services, 61, 62, 65, 92, 137, 140, *242ff.*, 256, 257, *266ff.*; – in early Indonesia, 3, 6, 7, 53, 91, *236ff.*, 282; – in Southern Asia, 46; – under Japanese, 23, 77, 78, 119, 120, 121, 158, 187, 188, *269ff.* See also culture system; *romusha*
Sharifs, 195
Shiah, 211
shifting cultivation: see *ladang*
shipping, 19, 33, 40, 65, 100, 101, 117, 270, 358, 359, 361, 362
Shonan: see Singapore
short declaration, 67
Siam, 44, 47, 269
Silungkang, 142
SIMBOLON, M., 350, 351
Singapore, 16, 17, 32, 60, 75, 77, 122, 125, 351, 360, 363
Singkehs, 153
SITSEN, P. H. W., 109, 111, 132, 152
SJAHRIR, S., 73, 81, 185, 298, 301, 302, 311, 314, 324, 328, 339
SJAFRUDDIN PRAWIRANEGARA, 359, 360
SJARIFOEDDIN, A., 323
SKINNER, G. W., 51
slamatan, 13, 225, 259, 260, 264, 265
slaves, 91, 134, 135, 136, 140, 172, 174, 196, 199, *236ff.*, 287; house –, 3, 236, 239, 241
SMIT, C., 89
SMITH, W. C., 42, 48, 51, 207, 211, 221, 235
SMITS, M. B., 5
SNOUCK HURGRONJE, C., 66, 198, 203, 204, 206, 207, 233, 235
S.O.B.S.I., 85, 273, 274, 275
social distance, 4, 134, 135, 137, 138, 139, 156, 157. See also caste; status
social hierarchy: see status
socialism, 71, 72, 81, 166, 217, 218, 219, 221, 229, 232, 233, 297, 346; – in Holland, 96. See also *Partai Sosialis Indonesia*
social prestige, 43, 50, *133ff.*, 197, 201, 206, 216, 223, 236, 241, 285, 287, 288, 294, 296, 297
social strata: see status
SOEDJATMOKO, 346
SOEJITNO MANGOENKOESOEMO, 254
SOEKASNO, 108
SOELAEMAN SOEMARDI, 371
SOEMITRO, R., 192, 194
SOENARIO, 108, 132, 147, 149
SOEWARSIH DJOJOPOESPITO, 185, 298
Solo, 19, 57, 141, 152, 160, 187, 208
Solomon Islands, 269
Solo River, 19

Southeast Asia, 1, 8, 11, *39ff.*, 57, 60, 257, 366, 367
South East Asian Treaty Organization, 334, 351, 359
Southern Asia, *39ff.*, 195, 287, 347
Soviet Union, 85, 347, 361. See also Russian revolution
Spain, 200, 205, 287
Spice Islands: see Moluccas
spices, 1, 3, 56. See also clove; nutmeg; pepper
spinning, 5, 117, 120
Sri Vijaya, 53, 281
STAPEL, F. W., 89, 283
static expansion, 96
status, 6, 7, 36, *41ff.*, *133ff.*, 201, 248, 297, 319, 321
stereotypes, 36, 138
STEVENSON Scheme, 98
STRAUB, M., 253
STUTTERHEIM, W. F., 37, 284, 314
SUBANDRIO, 353
SUBANDRIO, H., 168, 299
SUBARDJO, A., 334
SUCHTELEN, B. C. C. M. M. VAN, 116
Suez canal, 65, 350
sugar, 19, 93, 97, 103, 106, 115, 116, 117, 118, 120, 323; labour on – estates, 72, 105, 106, 243, 246, 247, 249, 258, 262, 263, 264, 265
SUKARNO, 72, 73, 79, 222, 228, 230, 323, 341, 345, 348, 349, 350, 351, 352, 353, 354, 356, 359, 360, 364
Sulawesi: see Celebes
Sumatra, *passim*; Central –, 16, 30, 64, 68, 203, 289, 291; – Eastcoast Residency, 16, 31, 68, 81, 82, 97, 128, 160, 250, 253, 256, 258, 278, 303, 350, 360, 362. See also Deli; North –, 30, 56, 65, 197, 328; South –, 8, 16, 351, 355, 360; West –, 24; – Westcoast Residency, 13, 16, 113, 142, 207, 219, 222, 301, 317, 359, 360, 361. See also Menangkabau; – social revolution, 160, 328; – Treaty, 65
Sumba, 20
Sumbawa, 20, 34
Sumenep, 241, 292
SUMITRO DJOJOHADIKUSUMO, 108, 132, 360
SUMUAL, V., 351, 352
Sunan, 57, 160, 202, 240, 288
Sunda, Strait of –, 65
Sundanese, 24, 25, 33, 325
Surabaya, 19, 57, 80, 186, 242, 344
Surakarta: see Solo
Surinam, 94
SUTARDJO, 75
SUTOMO, 73, 323
Sweden, 102
SZEKELY, L., 253
SZEKELY-LULOFS, M., 253

Tajoe, 131
TAKDIR ALISJAHBANA, S., 146
Taiwan, 363
Talaud, 25
Taman Siswa, 303, 304, 305, 307, 314
TAN MALAKA, 271
Tarakan, 77
Tasikmalaya, 79, 190
TAWNEY, R. H., 214
taxes, 4, 46, 59, 61, 65, 90, 91, 92, 94, 99, 107, *122ff.*, 240, 241, 243, 245, 318; head –, 245; road –, 257, 278. See also land rent; tribute
T'che T'ou, 281
tea, 19, 93, 94, 97, 116, 118, 120, 263, 264
technician: see *tukang*
TEEUW, A., 314
Ternate, 54, 56
TESCH, J. W., 190, 194
Thailand: see Siam
THAMRIN, M. H., 73

THOMAS, W. I., 299
THOMPSON, V., 270, 279, 339
timber, 16, 18, 31, 124
Timor, 10, 20, 25, 34, 38, 63, 123, 239, 272, 278
tin, 17, 31, 64, 97, 116, 124, 127
TITO, 363
Tjibodas, 113, 114, 115, 253, 326
TJIPTO MANGUNKUSUMO, 73
TJOKROAMINOTO, R. U. S., 218
tobacco, 17, 19, 68, 93, 97, 118, 144, 250, 256, 263, 264
Torajas, 2, 20, 25, 34
Torquay, 127
towns: see cities
trade, *passim*
trade unions, 50, 71, 85, 104, 105, 131, 149, 166, 167, 192, 249, 250, 252, 254, 273, 274, 275, 276, 279, 325
trader, *passim*
tradition, *5ff.*, 32, *41ff.*, 90, 91, 110, 141, 144, 145, 146, 157, 158, 160, 171, 176, 178, 182, 184, 205, 212, 225, 226, 227, 236, 249, 287, 289, 290, 295, 296, 297, 301, 302, 311, 316, 317, 318, 319, 327, 329, 343; historical –, 199; Japanese –, 155; parliamentary –, 345; religious –, 32, 195, 197, 201, 209, 210, 212, 213, 215, 217, *223ff.* See also *adat*
traditional authority, 55, 61, 67, 71, 135, 142, 157, 158, 159, 164, 167, 215, 216, 225, 240, 242, 248, 255, 289, 317, 319, 321, 326, 327, 346
traditional bondage, 246, 247, 253, 254
traditional colonial policies, 103, 127, 128, 335, 337
traditional privileges, 320
tramways, 177, 178
transmigration: see migration
tribute, 59, 61, 63, 92, 93, 243, 244, 245; – in early Indonesia, 3, 4, 5, 6, 53, 55, 90, 91, 187, 237, 238; – in Southern Asia, 7, 46; – under Dutch East India Company, 55, 57, 92, 240, 241; – under Japanese, 77, 118, 119, 157. See also culture system
Trunk Road, 242
tukang, 143, 248, 259
Twente, 66, 116, 117

UHLENBECK, E. M., 299
ulama, 140, 147, 156, 160, *195ff.* See also education; *kyahi*; *santri*; *Nahdatul Ulama*
uleëbalangs, 160, 165
Ummat Islam, 196, 316
United East India Company: see Dutch East India Company
United Nations Organization, 82, 88, 356, 357
United States, 1, 15, 45, 65, 70, 77, 82, 84, 86, 101, 102, 162, 256, 290, 298, 309, 334, 361, 363
urbanisation: see cities

VANDENBOSCH, A., 38
VASCO DA GAMA, 201
VERDOORN, F., 296
VERSLUYS, J. D. N., 123, 272, 278, 279
VEUR, P. W. VAN DER, 148, 169
Vietnam: see Annam, Indo-China
village: see *desa*; – in Southern Asia, 40, 41, 43
village economy: see closed economy
VLEKKE, B. M. H., 89
Volksraad, 71, 75, 78
VOLLENHOVEN, C. VAN, 8, 38, 204
VOS, J., 237
VRIES, D. DE, 314
VRIES, E. DE, 100, 121

WAAL, E. DE, 62
Wahhabi, 42, 204, 214, 215, 291; new- –, 215
wali, 199
WARMELO, W. VAN, 111, 114
waterworks: see irrigation works
wayang, 13, 37, 283, 302, 317
WEBER, M., 166, 214
wedono, 61, 156, 160, 246, 247
WEERD, K. A. DE, 78, 89, 153, 154
W.F.T.U., 275
WEITZEL, A. P. W., 175, 194
Weltevreden, 173
WERTHEIM, W. F., 169, 191, 259
WESTERLING, R. P. P., 81
WIDJOJO NITISASTRO, 38
WILHELMINA, Queen, 96
WILLIAM, I, King, 61
WILLINCK, G. D., 30
WILOPO, 343, 348
WIRANATA KOESOEMAH, Al-Hadj R. A. A., 219, 235
Wirtschaftsgeist, 198
WOLF, CH., 274, 339
WOODMAN, D., 339
WRIGHT MILLS, C., 166
WIJNMALEN, H. J., 275, 279

xenophobia, 46, 88, 334

Yugoslavia, 359, 362, 363
IJZERMAN, J. W., 171

zaibatsu, 76
ZANEN, A. J. VAN, 74, 205, 206, 216, 235
ZINKIN, M., 7, 40, 41, 51
zoning, 177
ZORAB, A. A., 89, 307